MARGINALISED VOICES IN CRIMINOLOGY

This book is about people who are marginalised in criminology; it is an attempt to make space and amplify voices that are too often overlooked, spoken about, or for. In recognising the deep-seated structural inequalities that exist within criminal justice, higher education, and the field of criminology, we offer this text as a critical pause to the reader and invite you to reflect and consider within your studies and learning experience, your teaching, and your research: *whose* voices dominate, and whose are marginalised or excluded within criminology and *why*?

This edited collection offers chapters from international criminology scholars, activists, and practitioners to bring together a range of perspectives that have been marginalised or excluded from criminological discourse. It considers both obscured and marginalised criminological theorists and schools of thought, presents alternative viewpoints on 'traditional' criminal justice themes, and considers how marginalisation is perpetuated through criminological research and criminological teaching. Engaging with debates on power, colonialism, identity, hegemony and privilege, and bringing together perspectives on gender, race and ethnicity, indigenous knowledge(s), queer and LGBTQ+ issues, disabilities, and class, this concise collection brings together key thinkers and ideas around concerns about epistemological supremacy.

Marginalised Voices in Criminology is crucial reading for courses on criminological theory and concerns, diversity, gender, race, and identity.

Kelly J. Stockdale is a Senior Lecturer in Criminology at Northumbria University. Her main research relates to criminal justice, restorative justice, and people's lived experiences when in contact with criminal justice agencies. She also researches the criminology curriculum focusing on whose voices are marginalised and whose are prioritised in criminology, why it matters, and what we can do about it.

Michelle Addison is an Associate Professor at Durham University. Her research is concerned with a key long-term vision of social justice for those facing the greatest social and health disadvantages in society. She is interested in stigma as social harm arising out of and linked to criminalisation, marginalisation and minoritisation, and how this reproduces multiple complex axes of inequality and oppression.

This is a wonderful book! Emerging from the editors' critiques of tokenistic meanings and applications of Equality, Diversity, and Inclusion in academia, it outlines a criminological landscape constituted by structures of privilege, the attendant issues of epistemic injustice and develops an 'alternative' to the criminological canon! The result is a book that challenges us all to think differently, against the grain, to work with and from the 'marginalised' voices in criminology and create more affective listening, understanding and knowledge production, that at one and the same time unsettles the colonial logic, power relations and ways of thinking, experiencing and doing criminology. It also reflects upon how marginalisation is perpetuated through criminological research and criminological teaching whilst challenging us to pay attention to creating more effective ways of working together, collectively across an international terrain. This collection brings together authors from across the globe including those working with Dis/ableist criminology; Indigenous criminology and ethical protocols; and key marginalised voices, such as young women in rural Australia, Irish traveller men, incarcerated men, women's desistance journeys.

Professor Maggie O'Neill (MRIA, FAcSS, FRSA), *Director, Institute for Social Sciences in the 21st Century; Director, UCC Futures: Collective Social Futures, Department of Sociology & Criminology, University College Cork*

It has been a long time since I read something cover-to-cover that was so new, vibrant and interesting. A book that constantly insisted on making me think outside the box, and unapologetically reflect on my own positioning as a scholar. Stockdale and Addison accomplish a true tour de force with this new contribution to criminological literature, by gathering a team of authors who challenge and destabilise our current state of disciplinary knowledge. What each chapter achieves is a loud call for us to critically reflect on the (sometimes unforgivable) reasons why some vulnerable people have been woefully marginalised, pathologised or downright forgotten in criminological research and scholarship. What is particularly admirable, and refreshing too, is the relentless exercise each author goes through in establishing their own identity as researchers and academics within their own discourse. This book should be an inspiration to us all. A definite must-read.

Isabelle Bartkowiak-Théron, *Associate Professor, Head of Discipline, Policing and Emergency Management, School of Social Science, University of Tasmania*

MARGINALISED VOICES IN CRIMINOLOGY

Edited by
Kelly J. Stockdale and Michelle Addison

Taylor & Francis Group
LONDON AND NEW YORK

Designed cover image: © Getty Images / Afry Harvy
First published 2024
by Routledge
4 Park Square, Milton Park, Abingdon, Oxon OX14 4RN

and by Routledge
605 Third Avenue, New York, NY 10158

Routledge is an imprint of the Taylor & Francis Group, an informa business

© 2024 selection and editorial matter, Kelly J. Stockdale and Michelle Addison; individual chapters, the contributors

The right of Kelly J. Stockdale and Michelle Addison to be identified as the authors of the editorial material, and of the authors for their individual chapters, has been asserted in accordance with sections 77 and 78 of the Copyright, Designs and Patents Act 1988.

All rights reserved. No part of this book may be reprinted or reproduced or utilised in any form or by any electronic, mechanical, or other means, now known or hereafter invented, including photocopying and recording, or in any information storage or retrieval system, without permission in writing from the publishers.

Trademark notice: Product or corporate names may be trademarks or registered trademarks, and are used only for identification and explanation without intent to infringe.

British Library Cataloguing-in-Publication Data
A catalogue record for this book is available from the British Library

ISBN: 978-1-032-19810-1 (hbk)
ISBN: 978-1-032-19809-5 (pbk)
ISBN: 978-1-003-26096-7 (ebk)

DOI: 10.4324/9781003260967

Typeset in Sabon
by Taylor & Francis Books

The subaltern have always been able to speak. Being heard in a cacophony of voices (some very loud!) is exhausting – listening better is my work. And you, what is your work to be done?

CONTENTS

List of illustrations   xi
Foreword by Rona Epstein and Professor Steve Tombs, writing
  on behalf of the 'Is It a Crime to Be Poor?' Alliance   xiii
List of contributors   xvii

1 Marginalised Voices in Criminology   1
  Michelle Addison and Kelly J. Stockdale

PART I
Criminological Theory and Marginalisation   11

2 Dis/ableist Criminology: Applying Disability Theory Within
  a Criminological Context   13
  Stephen J. Macdonald and Donna Peacock

3 Engaging Indigenous Australian Voices: Bringing Epistemic
  Justice to Criminology?   32
  Stephen D. Ashe and Debbie Bargallie

4 Racialised Young Women Amid the Everyday Stigmatisation
  of the 'Anglo-Negroid' Family in Interwar Britain: A
  Decolonial Perspective   54
  Esmorie Miller

PART II
Marginalised Voices in Criminology 73

5 The Intersection of Age, Gender, and Rurality: Recentring Young Women's Experiences in Family Violence Discourse, Policy, and Practice 75
Bianca Johnston, Faith Gordon, and Catherine Flynn

6 Irish Traveller Men: Structural and Cultural Barriers, and Reoffending 92
Megan Coghlan

7 Russian Criminology: A Silenced Voice? 110
Yulia Chistyakova

PART III
Perpetuating Marginalisation 129

8 The Power of Listening: An Ethical Responsibility to Understand, Participate, and Collaborate 131
Natalie Rutter

9 Female Researcher Identities in Male Spaces and Places 148
Claudia Smith Cox, Kerry Ellis Devitt, and Lisa Sugiura

10 Who is 'The Public' When We Talk About Crime? Interpreting and Framing Public Voices in Criminology 166
Anna Matczak

11 Whose Criminology? Marginalised Perspectives and Populations Within Student Production at the Montreal School of Criminology 182
Alexis Marcoux Rouleau, Ismehen Melouka, and Maude Pérusse-Roy

12 Bringing Prison Abolition from the Margins to the Centre: Utilising Storywork to Decentre Carceral Logic in Supervision and Beyond 201
Latoya Aroha Rule and Michele Jarldorn

13 Final Reflections 220
Kelly J. Stockdale and Michelle Addison

Subject Index 228
Index of names 231

ILLUSTRATIONS

Figures

6.1 Understanding Reoffending: Global and Organising Themes   98
12.1 First Nations families and allies stop traffic on a busy city street, holding placards featuring Aboriginal People who have died in custody. Wurundjeri Land, Melbourne, Australia.   206
12.2 Latoya lays native flowers and a 30,000-strong petition on the steps of the Parliament of South Australia, calling for the legislated ban on spit hoods. Kaurna Land, Adelaide, South Australia.   213
12.3 Staged uniformed prison officers donning spit hoods, protesting outside the coronial court during the inquest into Wayne Fella Morrison's death. Kaurna Land, Adelaide, South Australia.   214
13.1 'Marginalised Voices in Criminology', by Kelly J. Stockdale and Michelle Addison   226

Tables

11.1 Summary of criminological perspectives   186
11.2 Variables and their dimensions per the coding guide   190
11.3 Descriptive statistics ($\mu=408$)   191
11.4 Binary logistic regression predicting non-conventional perspectives within student production at the Montreal School based on design, population, and domain ($\mu=408$)   193

FOREWORD

The fire at Grenfell Tower, London, on 14 June 2017, killed 72 people and irrevocably and detrimentally affected the lives of thousands. Almost immediately, talk of 'crime' and 'justice' proliferated, and within three months of the fire, the Metropolitan Police were gathering evidence of both corporate and individual gross negligence manslaughter on the part of the corporate bodies and senior individuals involved in the fatal refurbishment and management of the tower. No charges have yet been laid, while past experience of similar atrocities only reveals the inabilities of criminal law to deal effectively with such powerful offenders.

Yet it is not the case that all parts of the criminal justice system have been slow to shift decisively into punitive action. There have been 28 convictions of 27 separate defendants related to the fire and the tower. Almost all convictions were related to forms of fraud – effectively, people accessing emergency accommodation and/or financial assistance on the basis of falsely claiming that they had been directly affected by the fire. All have received custodial sentences, ranging from 18 months to six years – sentences which, taken together, total in excess of 80 years' jail time. Almost all of those convicted fit a pattern: they are poor, marginalised individuals, unemployed, mostly of no fixed abode, overwhelmingly non-white, many of whom were born outside the UK.

There is a gruesome irony here. If the convicted after Grenfell are overwhelmingly marginalised, Grenfell happened *because* the voices of the residents were marginalised: ignored, dismissed, indeed actively silenced, largely not because of what was being said but because of *who* was saying it. The Grenfell Action Group – formed by residents of the tower - had set out a long list of concerns during the tower's fatal refurbishment, between 2014–2016, at the top of which was the '(l)ack of meaningful consultation with residents and feeling of total disregard for tenant and leaseholders' well-being'. Concerns relating to the lack of fire safety instructions, power surges, single staircase egress in the event of a fire, and the exposure of gas pipes within the flats as a result of the refurbishment were commonly expressed. As the Group posted at 5 am on 14 June, as the Tower was still in flames:

> 'Regular readers of this blog will know that we have posted numerous warnings in recent years about the very poor fire safety standards at Grenfell Tower and elsewhere in the Royal Borough of Kensington and Chelsea. ALL OUR WARNINGS FELL ON DEAF EARS and we predicted that a catastrophe like this was inevitable and just a matter of time'.

The starkest of these warnings had been published in November 2016, seven months *before* the fire, under the eerily prescient headline 'KCTMO – Playing with Fire!', where the Group called out the 'ineptitude and incompetence of our landlord', the Kensington and Chelsea Tenant Management Organisation (KCTMO), which had 'ignored their responsibility to ensure the health and safety of their tenants and leaseholders. They can't say that they haven't been warned!' Little surprise that one teenaged resident stated outside the Tower as it continued to burn on 14 June, 'We're dying in there because we don't count'. Such views were widely articulated by the bereaved, survivors, and residents in the aftermath of the atrocity.

The speed and intensity with which the criminal justice system has moved against the relatively powerless compared to the powerful in the wake of the Grenfell Tower fire is unsurprising to students of critical criminology, yet still instructive. In 1979 Jeffrey Reiman published *The Rich Get Richer and the Poor Get Prison: Ideology, Class and Criminal Justice*, regularly revised and re-issued ever since. As he wrote: 'The poor feel the full clenched fist of the criminal justice system, while the well-off are rarely touched by the system at all, and when they are touched it is oh so gently.'

Those in and around Grenfell were the marginalised – and ripe for criminal *in*justice. Both the aetiology and then state responses to Grenfell are paradigmatic of the issues covered in this book, perfectly highlighted in the title *Marginalised Voices in Criminology*. This collection of studies is an important and hopefully landmark contribution to criminology. Covering a variety of countries with very different judicial systems, with contributions from researchers in Australia, the Netherlands, Ireland, Russia, Canada as well as the UK, this collection, addressing class, age, race and ethnicity, gender, rurality, disability, and the incarcerated and student populations – and their intersections – is a rich and thought-provoking source of empirical, epistemological, methodological, and theoretical insight. It is also, quite rightly, anger-provoking.

Marginalised Voices provides a heterogenous demand that criminology must reflect upon, and then take practical measures to be genuinely inclusive of those voices excluded *within* and *by* the discipline – in the words of the editors, the 'under-heard and under-served in criminology'. As they go on to say, if 'talk about equality, diversity, and inclusion within and of the Academy is just that – all talk', then this collection is based on the praxis of 'unpacking deeply rooted axes of power and oppression'. Representing a searing critique of criminology, of neoliberalised higher education and academia, and of power and inequality, *Marginalised Voices in Criminology* is not just a must-read text – it is a manifesto for change.

Rona Epstein and Steve Tombs, writing on behalf of 'Is It a Crime to Be Poor?' Alliance

CONTRIBUTORS

Michelle Addison is an Associate Professor at Durham University. Her research is concerned with a key long-term vision of social justice for those facing the greatest social and health disadvantages in society. She is interested in stigma as social harm arising out of and linked to criminalisation, marginalisation and minoritisation, and how this reproduces multiple complex axes of inequality and oppression.

Stephen D. Ashe is a researcher working on racism, class, the far right, anti-racism and antfascism, institutional whiteness and racial inequality in higher education, and workplace racism. His recent publications include 'Reframing the "Left Behind": Race and Class in Post-Brexit Oldham' (co-authored with James Rhodes and Sivamohan Valluvan), 'Racism Ruins Lives: An Analysis of the 2016–2017 Trade Union Congress Racism at Work Survey' (co-authored with Magda Borkowska and James Nazroo), and Researching the Far Right: Theory, Method and Practice (co-edited with Joel Busher, Graham Macklin, and Aaron Winter). Stephen is currently working towards completing his monograph, The Rise and Fall of the British National Party: A Sociological Perspective, for the Routledge Studies in Fascism and the Far Right Series. He has published articles in Ethnic and Racial Studies, Race & Class, and Discover Society.

Debbie Bargallie is a descendent of the Kamilaroi and Wonnarua peoples of New South Wales, Australia. She is Principal Research Fellow with the Griffith Centre for Social and Cultural Research, Griffith Criminology Institute, and Griffith Institute for Educational Research. Debbie is a critical race scholar. Her book Unmasking the Racial Contract: Indigenous Voices in Racism in the Australian Public Service (2020) is published by AIATSIS Aboriginal Studies Press.

Yulia Chistyakova is a Lecturer/Senior Lecturer in Criminology at the School of Justice Studies, Liverpool John Moores University. Her research interests focus on crime, criminology and policing in post-Soviet societies, transnational policing and policy transfer, and BAME groups and inequalities in the criminal justice system.

Megan Coghlan is an Assistant Professor in Criminology at the School of Law and Criminology at Maynooth University. Having worked as a Lecturer in Criminology at the University of Portsmouth (UoP) for four years, Megan was awarded her PhD that examined people's reasons for returning to or persisting with crime.

Claudia Smith Cox is Head of Curriculum, Centre for Initial Recruit Learning for the Metropolitan Police. Her research interests centre around diversity and inclusion within policing, particularly police culture, police education, and the policing of minoritised communities.

Kerry Ellis-Devitt is the Head of Research for Interventions Alliance. She has 24 years' experience as a researcher, and has worked in the public, private, academic, and charity sectors. Kerry's research interests include young adults in the CJS, women in the CJS, probation practice, families of people on probation, practitioner wellbeing, mental health in probation, and most recently, the life-stories of domestic abuse perpetrators.

Catherine Flynn is an Associate Professor of Social Work at Monash University. Her research focuses on the intersection of criminal justice and social work, and teaching and learning in social work.

Faith Gordon is an interdisciplinary scholar and an Associate Professor and Deputy Associate Dean of Research at the ANU College of Law, Australian National University. Faith has extensive experience of research and teaching in areas including youth justice, children's rights, criminal law, media and digital technologies, and youth climate action. Along with Dr Dan Newman she has edited collections in the areas of global perspectives to access to justice in rural communities, and law and social justice. Faith's research has been cited by the United Nations, the Northern Ireland High Court, the UK Court of Appeal, the Youth Court in Aotearoa, New Zealand, and referred to by the UK Joint Committee on Draft Online Safety Bill, House of Lords.

Michele Jarldorn is a Lecturer at the University of South Australia. Michele lives on the unceded lands of the Kaurna people in South Australia. Her research uses an intersectional lens to connect structural violence with social problems. She is committed to privileging the perspectives and voices of research participants through the use of participatory, inclusive research methods.

Bianca Johnston is a current PhD candidate at Monash University researching young women's experiences of intimate partner violence. Having spent her childhood and adolescence on a rural property in the Australian subtropics, she holds 15+ years' direct practice experience working in areas such as youth, family violence and crime prevention.

Stephen J. Macdonald is Professor of Social Work at Durham University. Stephen's work applies theoretical perspectives that emerge from within disability studies to the study of criminology and adult social work.

Anna Matczak is a criminologist and is currently appointed as a Lecturer-Researcher in Comparative Criminology at The Hague University of Applied Sciences. She holds a PhD from the Department of Sociology, LSE.

Ismehen Melouka is a PhD candidate in Criminology at the Université de Montréal, Canada. Her doctoral studies allow her to explore the recognition of victimisation surrounding the process of reconciliation with Indigenous peoples in Canada.

Esmorie Miller is a Lecturer in Criminology at Lancaster University. Dr Miller's research historicises the role of race and racialisation in contemporary youth justice. Her research explores beyond crime and punishment, investigating the racialisation of punitiveness in contemporary youth justice as continuities of the historic exclusion of racialised peoples from the benefits of modern, universal rights.

Donna Peacock is Head of Division of Social Sciences at the University of the West of Scotland. Donna's current research focuses on interactions between suspects who have been defined as 'vulnerable' and the police, particularly within the police custody setting.

Maude Pérusse-Roy is a PhD candidate in Criminology at Université de Montréal in Québec (Canada). Her dissertation research focuses on women activists' relationship to violence in their protest activities through a feminist perspective.

Alexis Marcoux Rouleau is a non binary trans and queer, disabled and autistic white settler based in Nitaskinan, on stolen Atikamekw Nehirowisiw land. They are a PhD candidate in Criminology at the Université de Montréal in Québec, Canada, where they research leisure in women's prisons. They are also Research Director at JusticeTrans.

Latoya Aroha Rule is an Aboriginal and Māori, Takatāpui abolitionist residing on stolen Gadigal Land, Sydney. They are a Research Associate at Jumbunna Institute at UTS and are undertaking their PhD on Aboriginal Australian Women's experiences in the coronial inquest system. They also lead the National Ban Spit Hoods Coalition.

Natalie Rutter is a Senior Lecturer in Criminology at Leeds Trinity University. Her research interests fall within the areas of desistance, gender, and probation delivery, with a focus on narrative and visual methodologies, publishing in these areas. Natalie's current research examines the role of shame and stigma on criminalised women and how this is experienced through online spaces and social media platforms.

Kelly J. Stockdale is a Senior Lecturer in Criminology at Northumbria University. Her main research relates to criminal justice, restorative justice, and people's lived experiences when in contact with criminal justice agencies. She also researches the criminology curriculum, focusing on whose voices are marginalised and whose are prioritised in criminology, why it matters, and what we can do about it.

Lisa Sugiura is a Reader in Cybercrime and Gender in the School of Criminology and Criminal Justice at the University of Portsmouth. She has previously conducted research into misogynistic language on social media, victims of computer misuse, and technology-facilitated domestic abuse. Lisa's current research is focused on online gender-based violence, in particular the harms arising from ideological online subcultural misogynistic groups.

1
MARGINALISED VOICES IN CRIMINOLOGY

Michelle Addison and Kelly J. Stockdale

Introduction

This book is about people who are under-heard and under-served in criminology; it is an attempt to make space and amplify voices that are too often omitted or overlooked, spoken about, or for. In essence, it is a project about *listening*, and not only that, paying attention, being engaged, and showing humility about what we do not know, instead of eagerly filling up that knowledge space with loud noise, chatter, and colonial practices. This book offers the reader a critical pause; we invite you to stay with us in the discomfort and reflect on how we come to know what we know (Le Bourdon, 2022), question what else there is to know (Trouillot, 1988), reflect on what pains and privileges this has afforded us, and consider who gets to speak about issues within and across the criminological landscape.

We start this edited collection from the standpoint that there are deep structural inequalities across higher education and we build from the knowledge laid out by others who have raised specific concerns that the marginalisation of certain voices (female, disabled, racialised, colonised, non-western, and LGBTQ+) has influenced and distorted the production of knowledge in relation to key criminological topics and issues (Agozino, 2003; Cunneen and Rowe, 2015; Connell, 2007; Bacevic, 2021; Boliver, 2017). As two white, working-class, female academics with permanent lecturership contracts we want to stand alongside our academic colleagues and push for change in the discipline, within criminological research, and the teaching we deliver to academics and practitioners of the future. We seek to inspire and encourage others to reflect on their practices too. In this edited collection, we offer a range of chapters from international criminology scholars, activists, and practitioners to bring together a range of perspectives that have been marginalised or excluded from criminological discourse.

DOI: 10.4324/9781003260967-1

This project arose out of a contemporary focus on equality, diversity, and inclusion (EDI) work in HE more broadly. Amidst progressive legislation, there is a retraction and a tangible lack of real, sustainable change in practice. For instance, whilst there is much talk about 'levelling up' and widening inclusion in education, what does this look like in practice? Is EDI work more of a theoretical project (co-opted as part of a shiny veneer of 'virtue signalling' and mobilised by marketing and brand management as capital)? Real change is difficult, complex, and oftentimes painful; this work too often becomes the labour of already minoritised people, and ends up detached from a political activism focused on tangible structural change (Addison et al., 2022; Breeze, 2018). This project arose out of this tension.

We know that 'the academy' – in terms of who takes up space within academic institutions, and whose work is published and used in academic thinking – is biased. Statistics show that senior academic positions in universities are still dominated by older, white men (HESA, 2023). According to higher education staff statistics (HESA UK, 2020/2021) only 28.5% of all professors are women, and only 11% of professors identify as Black, Minority Ethnic (BME), with almost half of all professors aged 56 and over. The ramifications of this should not be underestimated; these professorial leadership positions translate in practice to knowledge brokers and arbiters, with powers to steer degree programmes, staff recruitment, what gets taught in classrooms, to editors on leading flagship journals determining ultimately who and what gets published, as well as governing what research gets funded via overly long, restrictive, and punishing review processes. This has a profound impact on what topics get taught in the classroom and what subjects are researched. Further, this has a limiting effect on knowledge construction because of whose voices and experiences are present and absent in the criminology oeuvre (Stockdale and Sweeney, 2022). What is more, we know that there are more women taking social science courses now than ever (such as criminology, law, and sociology) – with 840,250 women graduating with a first degree in 2018 (OfS, 2023) compared to men (641,050). These women continue to learn about 'founding fathers' (Lombroso, Durkheim, Marx, and Weber), missing out on a broader and richer inclusion of voices cutting across identity, space, and time.

To counter this, there is a proliferation of activity focused on diversity, widening participation, and decolonising fields of study as an attempt to destabilise and diffuse long histories of power, colonialism, and oppression, and it is long overdue. However, the pressures that come with a neoliberalised higher education sector (Addison, 2016), and deeply entrenched structures of privilege and prejudice, mean that attention to epistemic injustice in the academy can be tokenistic, superficial, and glossed over. For instance, we know that there are deep structural inequalities in academic reading lists and pressures for academic staff to develop course material quickly and in the context of higher workloads and increased stress (Laccos-Barrett et al., 2022). This has led to an over-familiarisation and acceptance of dominant narratives with detrimental impacts on student learning, critical engagement, and knowledge production; this is particularly evident in criminology (Stockdale and Sweeney, 2019, 2022). Disciplinary 'knowledge' is reproduced by the continuation of entrenched epistemological paradigms (positivism), and reinforced through published work and classroom curricula design (Ahmed, 2012; Bacevic, 2021). Often, the difficulty for students and staff when attempting to rethink and 'decolonialise' the criminology curriculum, for instance, is where to start (Jones and Kunkle, 2022).

Our concerns are that talk about EDI within and of the academy is just that – all talk. As Bhopal (2020) notes, under-investment in EDI initiatives – particularly by white staff members – continues to preserve the interests of those benefiting from unequal systems. What is more, these practices further the neoliberal frontier in higher education and expand the 'entrepreneurial identity' of certain academics (Taylor, 2014), whilst painting over the ugly and painful parts of how power and prejudice function as part of an 'invisible reality' in academia. Added to this, expectations of an 'always upward' career trajectory that only ever champions the archetype 'winner' (more grants, more citations, more publications) in HE is at odds with an EDI framework that promotes fairness and inclusion (Breeze and Taylor, 2020). Instead, Breeze and Taylor (2020) reflect on the value of feminist conversation and collaboration to disrupt these competitive neoliberal narratives that seem to work in the interests of some in HE who already know how to 'play the game' and get ahead (Addison, 2012; Addison, 2016), whilst excluding and harming others (Arday, 2021).

Whilst some work is being done to decolonise academic reading lists, this can often be superficial and an attempt to shortcut the 'problem' without actually doing the hard work of unpacking deeply rooted axes of power and oppression, and structures of feeling. Paying attention to presences and absences within and across criminology is important. For example, Lamble et al. (2020: 505) note how queer theory and criminology have 'little contemporary crossover' and it remains a distinctly 'heteronormative, Anglocentric project' despite attempts to diversify its 'restricted geopolitical and conservative focus'. Indeed, they acknowledge that whilst more is known about LGBTQ+ people as victims or perpetrators, less is known about power and the social conditions structuring these encounters and subjectivities. Elsewhere, Roger (2008) discusses the continued criminalisation of marginalised people and communities via social policy; issues about social inequality and survival are submerged in individualisation rhetoric that acts as a conduit for political votes and hardened public attitudes towards those who commit low level/volume crime. This kind of knowledge production pulls the focus away from structural inequality and swamps any voice of lived experience that may give insight into the harms arising out of our current 'cost of living crisis' and causes of crime (Pemberton, 2015; Pemberton et al., 2017). We see many factions of the criminology discipline, like administrative criminology, crime prevention, and police science dominating knowledge production which is used to inform policy and practice at the expense of other ways of knowing. This is a problem *because* it is constructed through a white, Anglocentric lens and in the context of a positivist paradigm to the exclusion of any other kind of knowledge-as-value; in attempts to 'solve' the problem of crime this can lead to an over focus on methods of social control, increased securitisation, and surveillance measures which limit and constrain lives of already marginalised and minoritised individuals and communities. We also see, as a consequence to this approach to knowledge production, that interdisciplinary boundaries are purposefully blurred with public health and social work focusing on behaviour change interventions that serve to criminalise people for being poor (Pemberton et al., 2017; Roger, 2008).

Paying attention to presences and absences within and across criminology is important. Bhopal adds caution here, noting how discussions about representation, presence and absence in curricula can often lapse into competitive 'hierarchies of oppression' in which certain aspects of identity are foregrounded and prioritised over others (such as gender instead of race), whilst other intersections that are beneficial (such as whiteness) are ignored or downplayed (Bhopal, 2020). In order to truly challenge the status quo, Bhopal asks us to consider our own positions of privilege and how this has benefited us in HE. Le Bourdon calls this 'confronting the discomfort' (Le Bourdon, 2022). As we turn our attention to criminology, throughout this edited collection, we invite you to stay with us in the discomfort and reflect on how we come to know what we know – whose voices have been centred, whose marginalised? And, at points in the book we can think about how you or I may have been complicit in this production of 'knowledge' and power in criminology more broadly.

As such, in taking a step back so others can step forward, we try to address the imbalance of voices in criminology, to foreground those that might otherwise be under-heard through processes of marginalisation in knowledge production. This is important because it attempts to undo some of the epistemological harms that arise out of being known by the colonial other and makes space for other ways of knowing the world around us (Stockdale and Sweeney, 2022). We seek to encourage readers to rethink how criminological ideas have been shaped and presented, and to shine a spotlight on those whose voices have been left out of the criminological canon (Stockdale and Sweeney, 2022). By destabilising the 'centring' of dominant voices, this collection brings together interdisciplinary analyses of voices across criminology.

That said, the book serves as a *starting point* for readers, not a comprehensive address of all the epistemic problems afflicting criminology – that would be a lot for you to read. Nor is this framed as a simplistic, consciousness-raising exercise. We invite you to consider which voices are not widely recognised and embedded in our criminology curriculum and how this impacts knowledge production. We want to encourage you to rethink how criminological ideas have been shaped, normalised, and presented over time – facilitated by epistemological supremacy, and the social and political context in which some voices are accepted and adopted into the mainstream whilst others are marginalised. A cross-cutting aim of the book is to present new and emerging research that is aimed at decolonialising and de-contextualising criminology and which addresses the overarching power structures and dominant narratives of the discipline.

Overarching book structure

This collection presents an alternative canon of criminological thought. In this text, leading criminologists share alternative viewpoints, theories, and research that has been obscured from mainstream criminology.

The book is structured around the following three themes:

1. Criminological theory
2. Marginalised voices in criminology
3. Perpetuating marginalisation

The first theme considers both obscured and marginalised criminological theorists and schools of thought. In Chapter 2 Stephen J. Macdonald and Donna Peacock present a call to criminologists to re-engage with the voices of disabled people who have been pathologised, whose lived experiences have been excluded, and whose voices have been silenced from the field. Their chapter traces the history of criminological theories, demonstrating the parallel developments in disability theory, and explores where these schools of thought have failed to intersect. The authors highlight how this failure to learn from and acknowledge developments within disability studies has led criminology to only consider disabled people in ways that perpetuate marginalisation, i.e., as inherently vulnerable to being a victim of a crime, or as an offending risk. They call for a dis/ableist criminology to develop a multidisciplinary understanding of the relationship between disability, crime and victimisation, and to encourage the reader to re-engage with the marginalised voices of disabled people. Turning to the marginalisation of Indigenous populations in the field in Chapter 3, Debbie Bargallie and Stephen D. Ashe bring epistemic justice to criminology, highlighting the distinctive contribution Indigenous Australian scholars have made to the discipline and why their work deserves to be read. Their chapter reminds the reader of the ways in which Indigenous scholars have been marginalised by the academy - and specifically by criminology - and draws attention to the role of Indigenous ethics protocols to encourage academics to reflect on the impact of theirs and others' research on and with Indigenous populations. Continuing in the exploration of who has been marginalised within criminology theory, in Chapter 4 Esmorie Miller considers the intersectional issues of race and gender, taking us to Liverpool, England during the interwar years. Miller's detailed case study draws on historical documents, with a focus on the Fletcher report and its characterisation of a 'race problem', specifically on 'Anglo-Negroid girls', i.e., young girls born to white mothers and Black fathers. Miller's work highlights the individual experiences and the macro policy interventions these young women faced, making a significant contribution to decolonised understandings of racial stigmatisation and gendered penalty in youth penal reform.

The second section of the book presents alternative viewpoints on 'traditional' criminal justice themes. In Chapter 5, Bianca Johnston, Faith Gordon, and Catherine Flynn investigate an underexplored area of family violence considering the intersection of age, gender, and geographic location. Their research unpacks the gendered and racial myths of Australian rurality, which traditionally centres white masculinity, and focuses on the risks to women, particularly First Nations and Women of colour. This case study of young girls' experiences in rural and remote Australia highlights the distinct narratives and needs of this cohort who have previously been absent from many studies which focus on the older or urban populations. Providing the reader with another lens through which to consider broader criminological issues, in Chapter 6 Megan Coghlan explores the structural and cultural barriers faced by Irish Traveller men on their road to desistance. She argues that reoffending needs to be considered as a series of intertwining factors linked to Irish Traveller identity, masculine identity, and wider social, cultural, political, and economic marginalisation. Closing this section, in Chapter 7 Yulia Chistyakova invites us to explore how the discipline of criminology developed in Soviet and post-Soviet Russia and the historical legacies and political and ideological factors that led to the self-isolation and wider global marginalisation of scholars' voices from this country. Chistyakova's chapter also raises questions in relationship to the current war in Ukraine and how Russian criminology fits with postcolonial and decolonial dichotomies.

The third and final section of the book considers how marginalisation is perpetuated through criminological research and criminological teaching. In Chapter 8, Natalie Rutter explores the relatively nascent area of desistance and how ingrained criminology is to exploring and situating young, white, male experiences. She questions where the voices of women are in desistance narratives and challenges the process by which much academic research is undertaken with and on people who have offended. Her chapter presents an ethics of care that academics could, and should, use when consulting and listening to vulnerable and marginalised people. In Chapter 9, Claudia Smith Cox, Kerry Ellis-Devitt, and Lisa Sugiura reflect on their experiences as women researching policing, 'incels', and young adult men with prison experience. Their chapter discusses the gendered dynamics of interactions between the researcher and the research participants and ways in which they may have felt vulnerable or unsafe in the research process. They encourage the reader to engage with and understand the complexities of social research and to reflect on how women and other marginalised groups can often be left feeling unsafe, isolated, and under supported when undertaking it. Moving on, in Chapter 10 Anna Matczak turns our attention to thinking about how research on 'the public' and how they view and think of issues related to crime and criminology is influenced by narratives of a 'malevolent' uninformed and punitive public, or a 'benevolent' romanticised vision of citizens, both of which often fail to include the variety of narratives lay people from a full range of different communities may hold. Matczak further argues 'the public', as were considered known and presented decades ago, has changed both in online and offline public spheres, and the impact of this has yet to be captured in criminology. In Chapter 11, Alexis Marcoux Rouleau, Ismehen Melouka, and Maude Pérusse-Roy undertake an empirical investigation into the type of student research conducted within the Montreal School of Criminology. Their research explores two decades' worth of published theses and dissertations to highlight the overall prevalence of 'conventional criminology' and the marginalisation of work that explicitly explores issues relating to race, social class, Indigenous populations, sexuality, and gender, or which critiques or explores alternatives to current systems. Research such as this highlights the systemic issues with the way certain criminological ideas, theories, and research methods are presented when criminology is taught and is an important way to consider how the discipline perpetuates research into crime and criminal justice which often neglects the populations who are criminalised, victimised, and present within the systems and institutions that are studied.

The final chapter in the section, Chapter 12, by Latoya Aroha Rule and Michele Jarldorn reflects on the supervisor/student relationship and what happens when people who are members of marginalised communities enter university. Reflecting on their own positionality, they provide a detailed look at their research to abolish prisons and the role of yarning or storytelling as a decolonising methodology. Their chapter shares their story with the reader, taking us on a journey through their lives before entering the academy, their allyship, their activism, and their research; their voices and lived experiences presenting the nuance and context of these important issues. It encourages us to consider how, as criminologists, we must reflect on our own practices and be more empowered to ensure we are not always producing more of the same research and to use our voices and our platforms to speak out and campaign for transformation.

Key questions to reflect on as you read this collection

You may decide to jump straight to the chapter that you are drawn to, or you may decide to read front to back. It's up to you how you use this resource. Before you do, we invite you to consider these questions as part of your reflective journey as you read, and we will return to these at different points in the book:

- What do you notice about the centring of certain voices in criminology?
- From your perception, whose voices are marginalised? Who is under-heard?
- Who is benefiting from having their voice heard in criminology? How do you know this?
- Who are disadvantaged from not having their voices heard in criminology?
- What do you notice about how knowledge is constructed in criminology?
- What impact does this have on your own learning and understanding of critical issues in criminology?
- What mechanisms are in place to reproduce the status quo in this discipline?
- Do you think the status quo needs to change? What needs to stop and what needs to start?

- What are the barriers to a more inclusive criminology?
- What do you notice about confronting your own discomfort around these issues?
- Being aware of our own privileges in the discipline is hard and requires consciousness raising – would you agree?
- Undoing and unpicking privilege can be painful – what three things might you do to help with this?
- What could you do in your own teaching and learning practice that could make you an ally to marginalised and minoritised voices?
- If your voice is marginalised in criminology, what can we do to amplify your knowledge?

References

Addison, M. (2012). Knowing your way within and across classed spaces: The (re)making and (un)doing of identities of value within higher education in the UK. In Y. Taylor (ed.), *Educational Diversity: The Subject of Difference and Different Subjects*, (pp. 236–256). Palgrave Macmillan.

Addison, M. (2016). *Social Games and Identity in the Higher Education Workplace: Playing with Gender, Class and Emotion*. Palgrave Macmillan.

Addison, M. (2023). Framing stigma as an avoidable social harm that widens inequality. *Sociological Review*, 71(2), 296–314. doi:10.1177/00380261221150080.

Addison, M., Breeze, M., and Taylor, Y. (2022). *The Palgrave Handbook of Imposter Syndrome in Higher Education*. Palgrave Macmillan.

Agozino, B. (2003). *Counter-Colonial Criminology: A Critique of Imperialist Reason*. Pluto Press.

Ahmed, S. (2012). *On Being Included: Racism and Diversity in Institutional Life*. Duke University Press.

Ahmed, S. (2018). Doing diversity work in higher education in Australia. In L. Jackson and M. A. Peters (eds.), *Feminist Theory in Diverse Productive Practices: An Educational Philosophy and Theory Gender and Sexualities Reader* (Vol. 6, pp. 136–161). Routledge.

Ahmed, S. (2022). Women of colour as diversity workers. In L. Back and J. Solomos, *Theories of Race and Racism: A Reader*, third edition (pp. 639–648).

Arday, J. (2021). Race, education and social mobility: We all need to dream the same dream and want the same thing. *Educational Philosophy and Theory*, 53(3), 227–232. doi:10.1080/00131857.2020.1777642.

Arday, J., Branchu, C., and Boliver, V. (2022). What do we know about Black and Minority Ethnic (BAME) participation in UK higher education? *Social Policy and Society*, 21(1), 12–25. doi:10.1017/S1474746421000579.

Arday, J., Belluigi, D. Z., and Thomas, D. (2021). Attempting to break the chain: Reimaging inclusive pedagogy and decolonising the curriculum within the academy. *Educational Philosophy and Theory*, 53(3), 298–313. doi:10.1080/00131857.2020.1773257.

Bacevic, J. (2019). Knowing neoliberalism. *Social Epistemology*, 33(4), 380–392. doi:10.1080/02691728.2019.1638990.

Bacevic, J. (2021). Epistemic injustice and epistemic positioning: Towards an intersectional political economy. *Current Sociology*, 71(6), 1122–1140. doi:10.1177/00113921211057609.

Bhopal, K. (2020). Confronting white privilege: The importance of intersectionality in the sociology of education. *British Journal of Sociology of Education*, 41(6), 807–816. doi:10.1080/01425692.2020.1755224.

Bhopal, K. (2023). 'We can talk the talk, but we're not allowed to walk the walk': The role of equality and diversity staff in higher education institutions in England. *Higher Education*, 85(2), 325–339. doi:10.1007/s10734-022-00835-7.

Bhopal, K., and Myers, M. (2023). *Elite Universities and the Making of Privilege: Exploring Race and Class in Global Educational Economies*. Routledge.

Bhopal, K., and Pitkin, C. (2020). 'Same old story, just a different policy': Race and policy making in higher education in the UK. *Race Ethnicity and Education*, 23(4), 530–547. doi:10.1080/13613324.2020.1718082.

Boliver, V. (2017). Misplaced optimism: How higher education reproduces rather than reduces social inequality. *British Journal of Sociology of Education*, 38(3), 423–432. doi:10.1080/01425692.2017.1281648.

Boliver, V., Gorard, S., and Siddiqui, N. (2021). Using contextual data to widen access to higher education. *Perspectives: Policy and Practice in Higher Education*, 25(1), 7–13. doi:10.1080/13603108.2019.1678076.

Boliver, V., and Powell, M. (2023). Competing conceptions of fair admission and their implications for supporting students to fulfil their potential at university. *Perspectives: Policy and Practice in Higher Education*, 27(1), 8–15. doi:10.1080/13603108.2022.2063429.

Boliver, V., and Sullivan, A. (2018). Getting up and staying up: Understanding social mobility over three generations in Britain. In S. Lawler and G. Payne, *Social Mobility for the 21st Century: Everyone a Winner?* (pp. 54–66). Routledge.

Bourdieu, P. (1990). *The Logic of Practice*. Polity Press.

Bourdieu, P., and Wacquant, W. L. (1992). *An Invitation to a Reflexive Sociology*. Polity Press.

Breeze, M. (2018). Imposter syndrome as a public feeling. In Y. Taylor and K. Lahad (eds.), *Feeling Academic in the Neoliberal University*. Palgrave Studies in Gender and Education (pp. 191–219). Palgrave Macmillan.

Breeze, M., Johnson, K., and Uytman, C. (2020). What (and who) works in widening participation? Supporting direct entrant student transitions to higher education. *Teaching in Higher Education*, 25(1), 18–35. doi:10.1080/13562517.2018.1536042.

Breeze, M., and Taylor, Y. (2020). Feminist collaborations in higher education: stretched across career stages. *Gender and Education*, 32(3), 412–428. doi:10.1080/09540253.2018.1471197.

Connell, R. (2007). *Southern Theory: The Global Dynamics of Knowledge in the Social Science*. Allen & Unwin.

Cunneen, C., and Rowe, S. (2015). Decolonising Indigenous victimisation. In D. Wilson and S. Ross (eds.), *Crime, Victims and Policy: International Contexts, Local Experiences* (pp. 10–32). Palgrave Macmillan.

Doharty, N. (2020). The 'angry Black woman' as intellectual bondage: being strategically emotional on the academic plantation. *Race Ethnicity and Education*, 23(4), 548–562. doi:10.1080/13613324.2019.1679751.

Doharty, N., Madriaga, M., and Joseph-Salisbury, R. (2021). The university went to 'decolonise' and all they brought back was lousy diversity double-speak! Critical race counter-stories from faculty of colour in 'decolonial' times. *Educational Philosophy and Theory*, 53(3), 233–244. doi:10.1080/00131857.2020.1769601.

Fox, J., and Sangha, J. (2023). White, Brown, mad, fat, male and female academics: a duoethnography challenging our experiences of deficit identities. *Journal of Organizational Ethnography*, 12(1), 46–60. doi:10.1108/JOE-07-2022-0024.

Higher Education Statistics Agency (HESA) (2020/2021). Higher education staff statistics: UK, 2020/21. https://www.hesa.ac.uk/news/01-02-2022/sb261-higher-education-staff-statistics#working (last accessed 30 June 2023).

Higher Education Statistics Agency (HESA) (2023). Higher education student statistics: UK, 2021/22 – Subjects studied. https://www.hesa.ac.uk/news/19-01-2023/sb265-higher-education-student-statistics/subjects (last accessed 20 June 2023).

Jones, V. A., and Kunkle, K. (2022). Unmarked privilege and marked oppression: analyzing predominantly white and minority serving institutions as racialized organizations. *Innovative Higher Education*, 47(5), 755–774. doi:10.1007/s10755-022-09610-z.

Laccos-Barrett, K., Brown, A. E., West, R., and Baldock, K. L. (2022). Are Australian universities perpetuating the teaching of racism in their undergraduate nurses in discrete Aboriginal and Torres Strait Islander courses? A critical race document analysis protocol. *International Journal of Environmental Research and Public Health*, 19(13), Article 7703. doi:10.3390/ijerph19137703.

Lamble, S., Serisier, T., Dymock, A., Carr, N., Downes, J., and Boukli, A. (2020). Guest editorial: Queer theory and criminology. *Criminology and Criminal Justice*, 20(5), 504–509.

Le Bourdon, M. (2022). Confronting the discomfort: a critical analysis of privilege and positionality in development. *International Journal of Qualitative Methods*, 21. doi:10.1177/16094069221081362.

Lee-Johnson, Y. L. (2023). Whitewashedness in teacher education: intertextuality between colorblindness and the Ferguson event. *Urban Education*, 58(3), 518–546. doi:10.1177/0042085919857803.

Office for Students (OfS)(2023). Access and participation data dashboard. https://www.officeforstudents.org.uk/data-and-analysis/access-and-participation-data-dashboard/data-dashboard/(last accessed30 June 2023).

Pemberton, S. (2015). *Harmful Societies: Understanding Social Harm*. Policy Press.

Pemberton, S., Pantazis, C., and Hillyard, P. (2017). Poverty and social harm: challenging discourses of risk, resilience and choice. In G. Bramley and N. Bailey (eds.), *Poverty and Social Exclusion in the UK: Volume 2 – The Dimensions of Disadvantage* (pp. 245–266). Policy Press.

Roger, J. J. (2008). The criminalisation of social policy. *Criminal Justice Matters*, 74(1), 18–19. doi:10.1080/09627250802478755.

Shimomura, F. (2023). The voice of the Other in a 'liberal' ivory tower: Exploring the counterstory of an Asian international student on structural racism in US academia. *Whiteness and Education*. doi:10.1080/23793406.2023.2198536.

Stockdale, K. and Sweeney, R. (2019). Exploring the criminology curriculum. In *Papers from the British Criminology Conference*, 19, 84.

Stockdale, K. J., and Sweeney, R. (2022). Whose voices are prioritised in criminology, and why does it matter? *Race and Justice*, 12(3), 481–504. doi:10.1177/21533687221102633.

Stockdale, K. J., Sweeney, R., McCluskey-Dean, C., Brown, J., and Azam, I. (2022). Exploring the criminology curriculum—Reflections on developing and embedding critical information literacy. In In S. Young and K. Strudwick (eds.), *Teaching Criminology and Criminal Justice: Challenges for Higher Education* (pp. 13–34). Palgrave Macmillan.

Taylor, Y. (2014). *The Entrepreneurial University: Engaging Publics, Intersecting Impacts*. Palgrave Macmillan.

Taylor, Y., and Addison, M. (2013). *Queer Presences and Absences*. Palgrave Macmillan.

Trouillot, M. R. (1988). *Peasants and Capital: Dominica in the World Economy*. Johns Hopkins University Press.

Wacquant, L. (2008). *Urban Outcasts: A Comparative Sociology of Advanced Marginality* Polity Press.

PART I
Criminological Theory and Marginalisation

2

DIS/ABLEIST CRIMINOLOGY

Applying Disability Theory Within a Criminological Context

Stephen J. Macdonald and Donna Peacock

Introduction

Until recently the concept of disability has been marginalised within criminological studies of crime and victims (Shaw et al., 2012; Thorneycroft and Asquith, 2021). Disability is typically (mis)understood as exclusively a health issue that impacts on offenders' or victims' experiences within the criminal justice system (Soothill, 2008; Eastman et al., 2012). In criminology, when links have been made between disability, victims and criminality, particularly within studies of mental health or neurodiversity, these have emerged from research in forensic psychiatry and psychology (Soothill, 2008; Eastman et al., 2012). Explanations presented by these medico-psychological disciplines are grounded in a biomedical 'deficit' model of disability (Roulstone and Sadique, 2013; Macdonald, 2015). Mental or neurological 'disorders' are linked to an increased pathological risk of offending behaviours, or victims are considered to be inherently vulnerable to criminal exploitation, resulting in some disabled groups being in contact with the criminal justice system (Soothill, 2008; Thorneycroft, 2017; Roulstone and Sadique, 2013; Macdonald, 2012, 2015).

To challenge this biomedical perspective, the chapter will apply a disability studies approach to critique the pathological explanation of disability and vulnerability that is emerging from within contemporary criminology. Within disability studies, disabled people are conceptualised as an oppressed minority population, who are structurally vulnerable to criminality and victimisation (Sherry, 2016; Macdonald, 2012, 2015, 2020; Thorneycroft, 2017). We present the parallel histories of criminology and disability studies to illustrate the points at which these could have intersected to develop a criminology that fully incorporates the structural experiences of disabled people both as offenders and as victims within its analyses. The chapter will conclude by arguing for a dis/

DOI: 10.4324/9781003260967-3

ableist criminology to fully conceptualise the theoretical intersections between disability, crime and victimisation and to outline the need for a criminology which is opposed to ableism and disablism.

Criminology and biological positivism

At the turn of the 20th century there was a significant focus on the pathologisation of criminal behaviour, particularly seen in the work of Cesare Lombroso (1835–1909) and the Italian school of criminology. Central to biological positivism was the notion that physiology (including physiognomy and phrenology) directly correlated with criminality (Lombroso, 1879; Knepper, 2018). Lombroso's contribution was influenced by the writings of Francis Galton who had championed the concept of scientific Darwinism. For Galton, undesirable populations, such as the lower working classes, disabled people and ethnic minorities, presented an existential threat to 'civilised' society by passing their hereditary undesirable traits down from generation to generation (Gabbidon, 2020). Women were also seen to be biologically inferior and perpetrators of specific (emotional/sexual) types of criminality (Lombroso and Ferrero, 1893). Thus, early biological positivists constructed the notion of 'degenerative criminal populations' through an intersection of disability, gender, race and social class. Pathology and body types were seen in the early 20th century as predictors of criminality and deviance (Garofalo, 1914).

In the 1920s and 30s, significant critiques of biological positivism emerged in the UK, and this approach started to fall out of favour in criminology. By the 1930s and 40s, Nazi Germany had embraced the eugenics movement, resulting in the mass extermination of numerous ethnic minorities, and disabled and gay populations as part of their 'Final Solution' plan (Bengtsson, 2018). Because of the horrors of the Second World War, the eugenics movement was characterised as pseudoscience and abandoned by the sciences and social sciences (Bengtsson, 2018; Gabbidon, 2020). In criminology, the focus moved toward social and environmental analyses (Sutherland, 1924), yet in psychiatry, biological and psychological explanations still dominated early studies of crime and criminality (Burt, 1944).

Although the 1940s effectively brought an end to the eugenics movement, this did not result in the abandonment of biological positivism, rather it became more sophisticated and added a social dimension. The focus moved from biological traits to genetic markers and the environment. By the 1960s, Lombroso's eugenicist ideas had almost entirely disappeared from criminology, however since the late 20th century and the turn of the 21st century we have witnessed a re-emergence of biomedical theorising of crime and ideas of degeneracy and heritable criminality (e.g., Wilson and Herrnstein, 1985). Recent advances in the study of genetics also seek to understand pathways into criminality, with the aim of identifying and managing risky populations. These new biological deterministic approaches have engaged in debates concerning disability, particularly in the fields of mental health and neurodiversity. This new eugenics presents itself in the guise of public health concern rather than population control (Rose, 2000), with the implication that those individuals who are biologically or genetically predisposed can be identified by screening, and interventions then implemented or enforced.

The biomedical model of disability and crime

Steele and Thomas (2014) describe a paradoxical centrality and marginality characterised by the overrepresentation of disabled offenders and victims. Disabled groups often encounter criminal justice agencies, but this population has been excluded from theory and knowledge production. Contemporary criminology has moved away from biological theories of criminality towards analyses of structural causes of crime (Taylor et al., 1973/2013; Matthews, 2014). Criminal courts have also typically preferred ideas of agency and free will over predetermination (Rose, 2000). But despite this move away from the biomedical model, the treatment of offenders in practice has started to return to its biomedical roots. As disability has emerged as a significant issue within the prison system and in victim populations, the model is used to explain the impact of disability, i.e., a health and illness issue, on offender and victim populations.

The biomedical model emerged in the 19th century and was first applied within hospital settings to understand human physiology in the study of infectious diseases. In the 19th and 20th centuries, medicine applied a scientific methodology to observe, measure and quantify human pathology to discover how the body functions, or dysfunctions (Porter, 2003). Observations were used to explain how disease or injury affected a person's biological function. From this perspective, birth defects, injury, disease, illness, impairment and disability are all conceptualised through notions of pathology. The application of this model subsequently developed into numerous successful interventions that have helped to treat major diseases such as cholera, smallpox, syphilis and measles, as well as to treat minor and more serious injuries (Porter, 2003). The World Health Organization adopted the biomedical model definition of disability in its 1980s' 'International Classification of Disability', where disability and impairment are defined as:

Impairment: any loss or abnormality of a psychological, physiological or anatomical structure or function.

- A deviation from a statistical 'norm' in an individual's biomedical status
- Includes loss/defect of tissue-mechanism-system-function
- Temporary or permanent

Disability: any restriction or lack (resulting from an impairment) of the ability to perform an activity in the manner or within the range considered normal for a human being.

- Functional limitation expresses itself as a reality in everyday life
- Tasks, skills and behaviour
- Temporary or permanent

(Adapted from Semple and Smyth, 2019).

This definition can still be found in a number of medical and educational textbooks (e.g., *The Oxford Handbook of Psychiatry*) despite having been replaced by the *International Classification of Functioning, Disability and Health* (2001) which adopts a biopsychosocial approach (see next section in this chapter). From a biomedical perspective, impairment relates to biological function and dysfunction, where disability results from the functional limitation caused by impairment. From this perspective, medicine must develop treatments to cure the physiological aspect of impairment to overcome disability; thus, disability and impairment are understood entirely within pathological and medical terms.

Critiques of the biomedical model emerged from the 1960s onwards through various civil rights movements, including the disability movement, the anti-psychiatry movement and more recently the neurodiversity movement. These suggest that the biomedical model does not consider the impact of social and psychological factors on disabled people's lives (Thomas, 2017; Oliver, 2009). The adoption of the biomedical model within psychiatry is linked to a succession of failed and oppressive treatments; the concept of 'mental illness' is synonymous with 'mental distress', and there is very little evidence to suggest that many major conditions which affect people's mental wellbeing, such as schizophrenia, anorexia, bipolar or mood disorders, are caused by disease (LeFrancois et al., 2013). Recently, debates have surfaced around whether mental distress is determined by biological sex. While differences have been found in prevalence of PTSD and anxiety, these have been found to be largely determined by differential exposure to trauma type rather than any biological predeterminant (Wamser-Nanney and Cherry, 2018). Further, bipolar disorders are misdiagnosed more frequently in adult females than in males (Dell'Osso et al., 2021). The biomedical model applied to neurodivergent groups, which have no association with disease, can offer no effective treatments and so has resulted primarily in the institutionalisation of this community (Macdonald, 2020).

In criminology, a 'new' biomedical approach to risk and crime has emerged. Psychologist Adrian Raine and colleagues have recently updated the bio-positivist approach with the use of brain scan technologies such as fMRI. Raine coined the term 'neurocriminology' in his book *The Anatomy of Violence: The Biological Roots of Crime* (2013). He examines the neurological functions of offenders within the prison system who have committed specific offences, particularly crimes of violence or rape, and compares them against a control sample. As Coppola (2018: 104) states:

Over the past two decades, research in the neurosciences, and particularly neurocriminology, has started to explore neurobiological markers that appear to correlate to an individual's predisposition to engage in antisocial behaviour. Notably, research in neurocriminology has identified specific brain features – both structural and functional – that seem to be consistently associated with antisocial traits featuring specific categories of offenders, such as murderers and child abusers.

Offender samples usually consist of individuals with personality 'disorders' and intellectual impairments, ADHD, bipolar disorder or schizophrenia, which then come to be seen as pathological risk factors concerning the onset of violent or criminal behaviours (Raine, 2013). Within the studies, biological markers such as impairment type, right- or left-handedness, or sex, are central to the inclusion of offenders; sociological notions of socioeconomics, race and ethnicity are considered unimportant. In the tradition of Lombroso, physiological dysfunctions are seen as the primary cause of criminality within neurocriminology. This 'new' biomedical model differs from early biological positivism as there are no recognised identifiable physiological determinants of crime and victimisation based on racial, gender or other social determinants within the approach. Thus, neurocriminological research is solely interested in conceptualising the pathological nature of crime and criminality. The work of Raine (2013) is used as justification for use of medication within the prison system. In its proper context, medication can help with the treatment of conditions; however, in the context of crime this is problematic as it ignores the wider sociological factors which contribute to violence, disorder and antisocial behaviour.

The biopsychosocial model of disability and crime

By the mid-1970s several criticisms had emerged from scholars and activists concerned with mental health, from the anti-psychiatry movement, and the disability movement, suggesting that the biomedical model was overly simplistic. The biopsychosocial model was defined by George Engel in his 1977 paper 'The Need for a New Medical Model'. Engel suggested that the biomedical model was too deterministic and could not explain the complexities of experiencing illness or living with an impairment. From Engel's perspective, the biopsychosocial model was not an attempt to discard the biomedical model, but rather he aimed to elaborate on this model to include the psychological and sociological elements of illness and impairment (Engel, 1977).

When conceptualising the link between impairment and disability, social environments must be considered because certain situations present higher levels of risk. Manual labour, for example, presents a higher level of physical risk than professional or administrative employment, due to the physical demands of the role. Illness and impairments are not static or objective experiences; multiple subjective factors impact the individual which must be incorporated within a new medical model. Engel suggested that a person's life choices, stress levels or even leisure activities and employment choices affect risk factors associated with the onset of impairment. Issues such as masculinity, ethnicities and social class can also impact a person's outlook, particularly concerning long-term illness or impairment. Engel developed the model beyond the biological and social to include the psychological; for example, becoming a wheelchair user could detrimentally impact on mental health, manifesting itself as depression, anxiety or another mental illness. Psychological factors can significantly impact the healing process of illnesses and can be the difference between a person adjusting or becoming alienated and disillusioned.

Within criminology, there has been a recent movement calling for a biopsychosocial analysis of crime causation. Three key areas are examined in terms of their influence on perpetrator behaviours: biological factors, i.e., is there a neurological or other impairment that can be assessed or diagnosed?; psychological factors, i.e., does the individual manifest delusional, psychopathic or violent behaviours?; and social factors, i.e., has the person experienced trauma within their environment, such as within the family? An early example of this can be seen in the work of Lewis et al. (1985) who advocate for a biopsychosocial framework in their study of homicide by children. They identified key biopsychosocial factors in predicting homicidal behaviour. As they conclude:

> It seems that severe CNS [central nervous system] dysfunction, coupled with a vulnerability to paranoid psychotic thinking, created a tendency for the nine homicidal subjects to act quickly and brutally when they felt threatened. Living within psychotic households, they were frequently the victims of and witnesses to psychotic parental rages, experiences that undoubtedly further exacerbated their tendencies toward the physical expression of violence
>
> *(Lewis et al., 1985: 5).*

The biopsychosocial model has now become the dominant theoretical framework within forensic psychiatry and psychology (see, for example, *The Oxford Handbook of Forensic Psychiatry*) and now defines the treatment of mentally 'disordered' patients within the criminal justice system (Eastman et al., 2012). Because the approach is clinically central, theorising in criminology through this perspective has come to view mental illness, neurodivergent conditions and disability as the key causes of offending behaviour. As with neurocriminology, impairment is at the forefront of the analysis; however, this approach differs in its acknowledgement of environmental factors and traumas within its analysis. Thus, in biopsychosocial criminology, experiences of crime and victimisation are still pathologised but structural explanations, particularly regarding socio-economics, are secondary factors to this approach.

Critical criminology and the social model of disability

By the late 1960s/70s, a critique of biological positivism emerged from what is now referred to as critical criminology (Matthews, 2014; Lea, 2015; Madfis and Cohen, 2016). Critical criminology developed from a neo-Marxist perspective and focused on the criminogenic nature of capitalism. This developed alongside the separate neo-Marxist critique of the biomedical model by disability activists which led to the disability movement. At this time, there was a change of focus within the discipline of criminology away from individualised causes of criminal behaviour, and towards examining the social causes and consequences of offending behaviour (Madfis and Cohen, 2016). Critical criminology and the disability movement shared a similar structural critique of the outcomes of capitalism, which created the need to include and exclude certain types of bodies based upon perceived productivity (Dowse et al., 2009; Oliver, 2009; Madfis and Cohen, 2016).

Taylor et al. (1973/2013) illustrated that previous studies of crime and deviance had narrowly focused on issues of street crime and crimes of the powerless. The focus had either been on pathology or the labelling of working-class communities as criminal by nature. Although critical criminology set out a convincing critique of biological positivism and ideas around pathology and criminal behaviour, as Dowse et al. (2009) illustrate, this school of thought has completely overlooked the importance of the intersectional relationships of inequalities, particularly concerning issues of disability and exclusion. Within the study of disability, there was a parallel sociological turn that critiqued the pathological explanations concerning disabled people's experiences of inequality and deprivation. Within disability studies the critique of the biomedical model emerged from social activists and grassroots politics, whereas in criminology this developed from within academia; hence, disabled people were central to the emergence of what is now defined as disability studies. This neo-Marxist approach to disability was defined as the 'social model of disability' and it transformed professional practice, particularly in the field of social work (Oliver, 2009).

The social model of disability developed from the meeting of two political activists, Paul Hunt and Vic Finkelstein. Both were wheelchair users and met due to a letter Hunt had sent to the *Guardian* newspaper calling for the creation of a consumer group to represent disabled people's voices and experiences (Oliver, 2009). Hunt describes living within an institutional regime where every part of his life was controlled by medical staff. Medicine could offer no intervention or cure for his impairment, so this institution offered no medical treatment except for a system of confinement. From his perspective, this institutional space removed the rights of disabled people to be active members of a community or wider society. For disabled people, institutional care became an oppressive system that excluded disabled people from social life rather than improving their living standards.

Hunt and Finkelstein recognised that the medical profession and the charitable sector were run entirely by nondisabled people. Disabled people's voices seemed to be missing from the production of knowledge and practices. Hunt and Finkelstein established a political group named the Union of the Physically Impaired Against Segregation (UPIAS), which was the first organisation run by disabled people to represent the experiences and needs of disabled people. Inspired by the neo-Marxist politics of the time, this organisation suggested that medicine and the biomedical model were employed to medicalise the social problems experienced by disabled people (Shakespeare, 2013). Although they accepted that the biomedical model was effective in treating illness and disease, once the body had permanently changed or become impaired then this model offered no solutions to disabled people in the community. Hunt and Finkelstein rejected the notion that disability was a physiological dysfunction that resulted in the social exclusion of disabled people, but argued that disability is an outcome of inaccessible environments or the attitudes of others.

The phrase 'social model of disability' was coined by another activist and academic named Mike Oliver in his book *Social Work with Disabled People*. Oliver, a sociologist, describes being discouraged from undertaking work in the field of disability due to perceptions that his subjective experiences as a wheelchair user would limit his ability to be an objective researcher. Once Oliver became involved in activism, he soon moved into studying the sociology of disability. Like Finkelstein and Hunt, Oliver was significantly influenced by a Marxist perspective. He asserted that disability was created because of disabling barriers, fundamentally caused by capitalist relations looking for nondisabled cheap labour, which resulted in social inequalities and structural exclusion of disabled people. The disability movement initially aimed to represent the voices of physically impaired people, but soon extended to include all disabled groups, such as people with sensory impairments, neurodivergent conditions and mental health issues.

Early disability scholars suggested that the relationship between impairment and disability needed to be redefined; impairment should be viewed as a biological or neurological difference/variation, and disability as the result of environmental factors which lead to the segregation or exclusion of disabled people from social participation. A new definition was produced to redefine the concept of disability and move away from the biomedical model:

> Disability: a disadvantage or restriction of activity caused by a contemporary social organization which takes no or little account of people who have ... impairments and thus excludes them from the mainstream of social activities
>
> *(Oliver, 2009: 42).*

When applying the social model, the focus is on disability (i.e., disabling barriers), and the person's impairment type (e.g., spina bifida, ADHD, schizophrenia, etc.) is viewed as an unimportant factor. As explained by Oliver, people with the same impairment experience dissimilar disabling barriers, as they are affected by their social and structural circumstances in different ways. Therefore, impairment (i.e., the medical label attached to a diagnosis) is irrelevant compared to disability (i.e., the environmental effects that exclude people with impairments), which is the key focus of the social model.

Until recently, social model scholars paid little attention to the criminalisation or victimology of disabled people. Yet, in recent years a small movement of academics within disability studies has acknowledged links between disability and crime. Dowse et al. (2009) suggest that an increasing number of disabled people with mental health or neurodivergent conditions are incarcerated or criminalised by criminal justice systems across the world. Yet very little attention has been given to comprehending the overrepresentation of disabled people, particularly neurodivergent or mental health communities, within the criminal justice system. Dowse et al. (2009) advocate that disabled people within criminal justice must be understood as a minority group and their behaviours conceptualised in the same way as any other overrepresented minority population. From a social model perspective, neurodivergent or mental health communities are overrepresented within the criminal justice system, but this is not because of their pathological conditions. This is due to structural and economic disabling barriers which directly exclude and discriminate against disabled people, leading to them being criminalised (Dowse et al., 2009; Macdonald, 2012). From this standpoint, neurodivergent or mental health communities experience poverty, educational exclusion, long-term unemployment and social deprivation (Macdonald, 2012). In critical criminology, the links between poverty, capitalism and crime have been long established; thus, from a social model perspective, links between disabling barriers, poverty and crime are crucial in conceptualising the overrepresentation of disabled people within offender populations and represent a significant missed opportunity for the two disciplines to intersect.

Realist movements in criminology and disability studies

A significant critique of critical criminology came from the development of left realism (Lea and Young, 1984). Left realism developed as a reaction primarily against the emergence of neoliberal governments, which viewed crime through an individualistic notion of rationality or pathology. It was suggested that critical criminology had been overly idealistic and had ignored the harms experienced by victims of crime, particularly within working-class communities. Critical criminology had romanticised the offender as a victim of capitalist exploitation, and therefore justified redistributing the spoils of capitalism that should rightfully have been theirs. Critical criminology had advocated that crime was 'not a real problem for the working classes' but was in fact a form of class conflict (Lea and Young, 1984). The victim's movement and the associated production of victim data, such as the 'Islington Crime Survey' and the 'British

Crime Survey', meant that for the left realists it had to be acknowledged that crime was a real problem for the working class as crime was intra- rather than inter-class. Left realism, unlike critical criminology, did not call for the abolishment of capitalism but tried to develop realistic interventions for crime and victimisation (Matthews, 2014; Lea, 2015).

Although left realists were interested in listening to victims of crime and responding appropriately, they overlooked the intersectional relationships between social class, poverty and disability. Like critical criminology, left realism did not incorporate disability as an intersecting factor and there was no attempt to theorise the relationship between disability, criminality and victimisation. It was not until 2003 that disability was recognised as a protected characteristic within criminal justice policy (CJA, 2003), and it was only in 2009 that the British Crime Survey began to include questions relating to disability. Although disability emerged as a significant factor within both crime and victim statistics, realist criminology has not attempted to theorise this relationship; rather, it has been within disability studies that this study has taken place (Sherry, 2016; Quarmby, 2011; Macdonald, 2015).

By the end of the 20th century, the social model of disability had become a significant theoretical framework that redefined professional practice within social work and social care, and shaped social policy within the New Labour government of 1997 under Tony Blair. Within disability studies, the social model became the defining theoretical framework to conceptualise the lived experiences of disabled people, nationally and globally. Yet, criticisms of the social model started to emerge within disability studies, particularly concerning its neo-Marxist origins (Shakespeare, 2006). In parallel to the realist movement in criminology, within disability studies similar critiques emerged from realist disability studies scholars concerning the social model's idealistic construction of disability. This analysis predominantly focused on the relationship between people's bodies and social and economic factors that included or alienated those bodies within a capitalist society. Key criticisms emerged concerning the debate between the construction of disability, i.e., structural barriers, and that of impairment, i.e., biological/neurological variations/deficits. From a neo-Marxist perspective, impairment is a personal issue and cannot be the basis for a political movement (Oliver, 2009). From a realist perspective, if we are to conceptualise the real impact of disability, we must also theorise impairment and how it impacts on people's lives, through pain, restrictions and the shortening of life course (Shakespeare and Watson, 2001).

The origins of the realist movement in disability studies can be traced back to Liz Crow's 1996 paper on disability and impairment. Crow (1996), a disability activist, presented the first significant critique of the social model from a feminist standpoint. In her paper, entitled 'Including All of Our Lives: Renewing the Social Model of Disability', she outlines how the social model had been an empowering force within her life. She states that the 'social model of disability has enabled me to confront, survive and even surmount countless situations of exclusion and discrimination' (Crow, 1996: 55). She further describes the impact that physical pain has on her daily activities and suggests this must be acknowledged in conjunction with disabling barriers. As Crow (1996: 60) suggests:

> Impairment, at its most basic level, is a purely objective concept which carries no intrinsic meaning. Impairment simply means that aspects of a person's body do not function, or they function with difficulty. Frequently this has taken a stage further to imply that a person's body, and ultimately the person, is inferior. However, the first is fact; the second is an interpretation.

Crow (1996) advocates for the development of a theory that not only includes disability, i.e., structural disabling barriers, but also impairment, i.e., functional difficulties or variations. Disability studies can therefore develop realistic interpretations of living with a disability and impairment. This call to include impairment within disability studies was further developed by Tom Shakespeare and Nick Watson, who were central to the early development of disability studies and had initially been strong advocates for the social model of disability. In their paper, entitled 'The Social Model of Disability: An Outdated Ideology?' (2001), they argue that disability theory must include an accurate analysis of disability, impairment and impairment effect if it is to be able to fully explain the experiences of disabled people. They suggest that not only is the biomedical model over-simplistic, but so is the social model of disability. They argue that it is impossible to separate impairment and disability as both interact with one another. As Shakespeare and Watson (2001: 17) illustrate:

> People are disabled both by social barriers and by their bodies. This is straightforward and uncontroversial. The British social model approach, because it 'over-eggs the pudding', risks discrediting the entire dish.

Shakespeare (2006) suggested that disability research must acknowledge that while societies and cultures may interpret and define disability differently, impairment exists, and it has its own experiential and ontological reality. Shakespeare argues that to conceptualise the lived experience of disability, we must recognise the impact that pain has on a person's life, which is comparable to structural factors such as unemployment, stigmatisation and segregation. Shakespeare and Watson (2001) recognise how micro disabling barriers are often specific to a particular impairment type; for example, it is argued that a person with bipolar disorder or schizophrenia will experience different disabling barriers from someone with an intellectual or sensory impairment.

Similar to realist criminology, research that has emerged from realist disability studies on crime has predominantly focused on the experiences of disabled victims. In these studies, there is a particular focus on how disability and impairment intersect with other social variables such as social class, poverty, deprivation and exploitation (Mikton et al., 2014). Although disability studies predominantly applies a qualitative approach to the lived experience of disability, realist methodologies also incorporate a quantitative analysis of crime and victim trends (Sherry, 2016; Macdonald, 2015). Emerging from the scholarship is a focus on how different forms of victimisation and crime affect particular disabled groups within particular community settings. Thus, not only is the structural nature of disability acknowledged within this analysis but also how particular impairment groups, such as people with an intellectual impairment or autism, are more/less at risk of becoming the victim of crime (Macdonald, 2015; Forster and Pearson, 2019).

Macdonald (2015) found that almost two-thirds of disabled hate crimes, at 63%, were perpetrated against people with intellectual impairments. His findings suggest that although it is vital to consider the shared experiences of disability and victimisation across disabled groups, it is also important to conceptualise how particular impairment groups experience discrimination in different ways (Clement et al., 2011; Shakespeare, 2013). This is not to pathologise the experience of hate crime and ignore the structural nature of this form of victimisation, but rather to recognise the reality that certain disabled groups are more at risk of experiencing this form of victimisation than others. To develop a realist theory of disability and crime, researchers must acknowledge disability and impairment and how both can result in people becoming structurally vulnerable within their communities (Hall, 2019). This realist perspective has resulted in an updated version of the social model of disability, often referred to as the social relational model, which attempts to fully incorporate disability and impairment within the study of victimisation and crime.

Cultural criminology, cultural/critical disability studies, and the production of crime and victimisation

In the UK, cultural disability studies is often referred to as critical disability studies. Shakespeare (2013) states that to align critical disability studies with the global movement of disability studies we need to redefine this movement according to its cultural theoretical origins. In line with criminology, we refer to critical disability studies as cultural disability studies.

Cultural criminology emerged in the 1990s to explore crime as a cultural phenomenon and move away from a cause-and-effect approach to criminality and victimisation. By exploring 'crime as culture', cultural criminology seeks to conceptualise the relationship between criminal behaviour and the social and cultural contexts from which it emerges. From this perspective, cultural criminologists have expanded the study of crime beyond a society's legal system to understand how institutions such as the media, education, politics, and social and health services are also central to the criminalisation process. Dominant discourses that emerge from the media are central in the criminalisation process, which defines and reproduces cultural morality within neoliberal society. This has a significant role in reinforcing morality and shaping political and criminal justice agendas that demonise and criminalise subcultural communities and cultural activities.

Cultural criminology was significantly influenced by the work of Michel Foucault, whereby concepts of criminality and deviance become technologies of power which define the morally undesirable within society to develop an institutional, i.e., criminal justice, response. Thus, cultural criminology illustrates the symbolic importance of recognising deviance to advance a set of transformative practices, realigning the immoral behaviours of the 'deviant' with that of moral codes of late modern, i.e., neoliberal, cultural practices. Criminality and deviance are an array of cultural performances, which are socially produced, and are reproduced by individuals, communities, law enforcement agencies and the media (Ferrell, 1999; Presdee, 2000). Arising out of cultural criminology, we see the emergence of cultural perspectives that attempt to decolonise the field of criminology (Ilan, 2019); however, notions of disabled identity, community and culture are again overlooked and marginalised within a criminological context. Emerging alongside cultural criminology, cultural theory has also had a significant influence on disability studies. Cultural disability studies developed alongside the realist shift and emerged at the turn of the 21st century. Like cultural criminology, the development of this movement has been significantly influenced by prominent poststructuralist scholars such as Foucault, Derrida and Lacan (Goodley, 2014). This movement emerged as a cultural analysis of disability, drawing inspiration from linguistic perspectives focusing on the multiple constructions of disability and impairment.

Maria Corker was an early advocate of this cultural perspective and critiqued the social and medical models of disability. She argues that both models are binary linguistic constructs and that both define impairment as a biological deficit. Cultural disability studies scholars such as Davis (1995), Tremin (2006) and Goodley (2014) have championed this approach and propose that not only is disability a social and cultural product, but impairment is also a cultural phenomenon that is culturally and economically defined and not biologically determined. From a cultural disability studies perspective, diagnostic labels and categories emerge because of the sociocultural political landscape of medicine. For Dan Goodley (2014), disability is inherently devalued by medical discourse and is based on cultural assumptions of normalcy and what it is to be human. Medicine is conceptualised as an institution of power that manufactures discourses that categorise physical, behavioural and intellectual variations through the normative notion of pathology. For Cameron (2011), normalcy is constructed through the cultural performance of everyday life, which relates directly to a set of societal norms and emerges from neoliberal societies. At the heart of neoliberalism is a bourgeois culture where the construction of normality is celebrated and where dis/ability is devalued.

Like cultural criminology, cultural disability studies has engaged in an intersectional analysis of disability by employing cultural theory. Meekosha (2011) suggests that disability studies has been dominated by white western male theorists who have prioritised the voices of Eurocentric disabled cultures over that of the Global South (Kumari Campbell, 2007; Bell, 2010; Meekosha, 2011; Stienstra, 2020). Thus, cultural disability studies, similar to cultural criminology, has begun a decolonisation project that aims to produce new systems of knowledge from a global perspective, rather than its current western, Eurocentric constructions of disability (Kumari Campbell, 2007; Meekosha, 2011; Presley, 2019). Not only does cultural disability studies present an intersectional analysis of disability incorporating race, gender and sexuality within its analysis, but it also offers a radical interpretation of disability and impairment.

Within cultural disability studies there has been a recent critical analysis of the cultural construction of disability, crime and victim discourses (Thorneycroft, 2017; Matthews, 2018). Cultural disability studies scholars have illustrated dominant discourses of othering that categorise disabled victims and perpetrators as either pathologically 'vulnerable' or 'dangerous' (Thorneycroft, 2017; Mathews, 2018). As Mathews (2018) illustrates, disabled perpetrators are often represented as 'mad' or 'evil', which is linked to their biological differences. From this perspective, we see similar binary constructions in the media when defining disabled victims as 'vulnerable', where vulnerability becomes shorthand for notions of pathological dependence, and where the victim becomes a 'justified' object of exploitation. Within notions of 'vulnerability' or 'dangerousness', structural factors of deprivation, austerity and poverty are completely overshadowed by the cultural construction of impairment. Disabled people who engage in or are the victim of crime are distanced from nondisabled populations because their pathological differences position them outside of mainstream society. Thus, from a cultural disability studies perspective, disabled victims and offenders are removed from the 'normal codes of conduct' within contemporary culture (Mathews, 2018).

Towards a dis/ableist criminology

By constructing parallel timelines of the theoretical development of criminology and disability studies we can identify simultaneous ideological and conceptual trends. Until the 1950s, essentialist interpretations of criminality and impairment dominated the studies of both crime and disability. Within criminology, criminal behaviour is explained as biological and psychological deviance and the link between disability and criminality was constructed as a significant risk factor for offending. Within health and social welfare studies, disability was conceptualised entirely through a deficit approach, where problems experienced by disabled people were explained through individual biological dysfunction, i. e., impairment. Therefore, biology played a fundamental role in defining the physical body and also behaviour as a pathological problem or dysfunction. Within criminology, stigmatised assumptions concerning intellect and mental health were also used to conceptualise and explain criminality and criminal behaviour.

During the 1960s and 1970s, we saw the emergence of a neo-Marxist perspective that transformed the theoretical conceptualisations of offending behaviour and disability. Capitalism became the key focus of analysis, both within criminology and within the emergence of disability studies. From a criminological perspective, capitalism is a criminogenic system where the oppressed engage in criminality as a political act against structural inequalities. From within disability studies, capitalism requires cheap labour, and it therefore invests in bodies that are physically and neurologically productive, which then excludes and alienates bodies that cannot service the means of production. Populations are labelled as disabled and excluded from the workplace, resulting in these individuals becoming economically marginalised.

By the 1980s and 1990s, we saw critiques emerging within both disciplines from the broader neo-Marxist shift in sociology, which led to the formulation of realist theoretical perspectives. Critical criminology is critiqued as idealistic and romanticised, and therefore failing to respond to the day-to-day experiences of crime, victimisation and criminality. Within disability studies, we saw a similar critique of the neo-Marxist social model of disability which, it is argued, does not take into consideration the impact of impairment effects, pain and the shortening of lifespans on the lived experiences of disabled people. Within criminology, early realist approaches very much focused on the complexities of crime and victimisation, particularly within working-class communities. The aim was to offer real solutions to real problems, based on evidence of what worked; yet this analysis failed to include the experiences of disabled people. In realist disability studies the focus shifted to include the real lived experiences of disability *and* impairment; however, disability studies was late to include an analysis of violence, victimisation and offending behaviour. Further advances in criminology and disability studies moved to incorporate cultural theory within the analysis of criminality and disability so that crime and victimisation, and disability and impairment, would be seen as sociocultural constructs. From within cultural criminology, crime has no ontological reality and is culturally specific. From a cultural disability studies perspective, not only is disability a social construction, but impairment is culturally produced and is a product of ableist neoliberal society. These theoretical developments were parallel but unconnected, resulting in a cultural exploration of crime and criminality, and of disabled lives, but not of the relationship between the two.

Although these sociological approaches have transformed criminology and disability studies, both have seen a shift back to an essentialist theoretical approach. Over the past decade, George Engel's biopsychosocial model has re-emerged to replace the medical and social models within contemporary health and social welfare practices (Shakespeare et al., 2017). Within criminology, we have also seen the parallel re-emergence of the biomedical perspectives, with the newly evolving subdisciplines of neurocriminology and biopsychosocial criminology. In the 21st century we have seen a resurgence of explanations that are founded on pathology, identifying mental health and neurodiversity as risk factors for criminal behaviour. Like the historical biological positivist approach within criminology, genetic explanations and neurological function become central to a new criminology which individualises offending behaviour and plays down the importance of structural factors, such as class and deprivation, and lacks any critique of the criminogenic nature of neoliberalism.

Recognising the theoretical similarities between disability studies and criminology acknowledges commonalities between the disciplines. By developing these theoretical commonalities, we can develop a sociological understanding of the relationship between disability, crime and victimisation which gives us a toolkit that critiques the individualistic nature of essentialism and the emergence of new biomedical models of crime. We can engage in the epistemological analysis of crime, victimisation and disability alongside a recognition of the real ontological nature of experienced individual/social harm and impairment. The neo-Marxist, realist and cultural perspectives which have emerged in criminology and disability studies allow for the commonalities between the two disciplines to merge into a dis/ableist criminology which can apply a structural and cultural approach to conceptualising disability and victimisation. Disability studies and criminology can bring together the different sociocultural perspectives that have developed alongside each other in both disciplines as a space for a dis/ableist criminology to materialise.

A dis/ableist criminology enables a multidisciplinary analysis of the theorisation of disability, victimisation and crime to occur at the macro, meso and micro levels, which moves away from the essentialist interpretation of crime and disability. This may grant a level of flexibility to critique the harmful nature of capitalism at the macro level, the reproduction of culture and systems of power at the meso level, and the embodied experience of crime effects and harm, and disability and impairment effects, that impact on social interaction at the micro level. Thus, a dis/ableist criminology may create a space to develop a multi-dimensional theoretical approach to critique essentialism, and still give us space to develop a multidisciplinary critical theory of disability within a criminological context. By doing this, criminology can re-engage with the marginalised voices of disabled people who have been excluded, pathologised and silenced from this field of study.

References

Bell, Chris. 2010. 'Is Disability Studies Actually White Disability Studies?' *The Disability Studies Reader*. 5:402–410.
Bengtsson, Steffan. 2018. 'The Nation's Body: Disability and Deviance in the Writings of Adolf Hitler.' *Disability & Society*. 33, no. 3: 416–432.
Burt, Cyril. 1944. 'Psychoanalysis and Crime.' *The Canadian Bar Review*. 22, no. 1: 20–29.
Cameron, Colin. 2011. 'Not Our Problem: Impairment as Difference, Disability as Role.' *Journal of Inclusive Practice in Further and Higher Education*. 3 no. 2: 10–25.
Clement, Sarah, Elaine Brohan, Liz Sayce, James Pool and Graham Thornicroft. 2011. 'Disability Hate Crime and Targeted Violence and Hostility: A Mental Health and Discrimination Perspective.' *Journal of Mental Health*. 20, no. 3: 219–225.

Coppola, Federica. 2018. 'Mapping the Brain to Predict Antisocial Behaviour: New Frontiers in Neurocriminology, "New" Challenges For Criminal Justice.' *UCL Journal of Law and Jurisprudence*. Special Issue 1, no. 1: 103–126.
Corker, Mairian. 1999. 'Differences, Conflations and Foundations: The Limits to "Accurate" Theoretical Representation of Disabled People's Experience?' *Disability and Society*. 14, no. 5: 627–642.
Criminal Justice Act (CJA). 2003. London: The Stationery Office
Crow, Liz. 1996. 'Including All of Our Lives: Renewing the Social Model of Disability.' In *Exploring the Divide: Illness and Disability*, edited by Colin Barnes and Geof Mercer, 55–72. Leeds: Disability Press.
Davis, Lennard J. 1995. *Enforcing Normalcy: Disability, Deafness, and the Body*. London: Verso.
Dell'Osso, Bernardo, Rita Cafaro and Terence A. Ketter. 2021. 'Has Bipolar Disorder Become a Predominantly Female Gender Related Condition? Analysis of Recently Published Large Sample Studies.' *International Journal of Bipolar Disorders*. 9, no. 1: 1–7.
Dowse, Leanne, Elaine Baldry and Phillip Snoyman. 2009. 'Disabling Criminology: Conceptualising the Intersections of Critical Disability Studies and Critical Criminology for People with Mental Health and Cognitive Disabilities in the Criminal Justice System.' *Australian Journal of Human Rights*. 15, no. 1: 29–46.
Eastman, Nigel, Gwen Adshead, Simone Fox, Richard Latham and Sean Whyte. 2012. *Forensic Psychiatry*: Oxford. Oxford University Press.
Engel, George. L. 1977. 'The Need for a New Medical Model: A Challenge to Biomedicine.' *Science*. 196, no. 4286: 129–136.
Fallin, Mallory, Owen Whooley and Kristin Kay Barker. 2019. 'Criminalizing the Brain: NeuroCriminology and the Production of Strategic Ignorance.' *BioSocieties*. 14, no. 3: 438–462.
Ferrell, Jeff. 1999. 'Cultural Criminology.' *Annual Review of Sociology*. 25, no. 1: 395–418.
Forster, Samantha, and Amy Pearson. 2019. '"Bullies Tend To Be Obvious": Autistic Adults Perceptions of Friendship and the Concept of "Mate Crime".' *Disability & Society*. 35, no. 7: 1103–1123.
Gabbidon, Shaun. L. 2020. *Criminological Perspectives on Race and Crime*. 4th ed. Oxford: Routledge.
Garafolo, Raffaele. 1914. *Criminology*. Boston: Little, Brown.
Goodley, Dan. 2014. *Dis/ability Studies: Theorising Disablism and Ableism*. Oxford: Routledge.
Goring, Charles. 1913. *The English Convict: A Statistical Study*. London: HM Stationery Office, Darling and Son.
Hall, Edward. 2019. 'A Critical Geography of Disability Hate Crime.' *Area*. 5, no. 2: 249–256.
Ilan, Jonathan. 2019. 'Cultural Criminology: The Time Is Now.' *Critical Criminology*. 27: 5–20.
Knepper, Paul. 2018. 'Clocks and Crime: Conceptions of Time in the Writings of Cesare Lombroso.' *Crime Histoire & Sociétés/Crime, History & Societies*. 22, no. 2: 9–29.
Lea, John. 2015. 'Jock Young and the Development of Left Realist Criminology.' *Critical Criminology*. 23, no. 2: 165–177.
Lea, John, and Jock Young. 1984. *What Is To Be Done About Law and Order?* London: Penguin Books.
LeFrancois, Brenda A., Robert Menzies and Geoffrey Reaume. 2013. *Mad Matters: A Critical Reader in Canadian Mad Studies*. Toronto: Canadian Scholar's Press.

Lewis, Dorothy Otnow, Ernest Moy, Lori D. Jackson, Robert Aaronson, Nicolas Restifo, Susan Serra and Alexander Simos, 1985. 'Biopsychosocial Characteristics of Children Who Later Murder: A Prospective Study." *The American Journal of Psychiatry*. 142, no. 10: 1161.

Lombroso, Cesare. 1879. *Sull'incremento del delitto in Italia e sui mezzi per arrestarlo*. Torino: Fratelli Bocca Editori.

Lombroso, Cesare, and Ferrero Guglielmo. 1893. *The Female Criminal, the Prostitute and the Normal Female*. New York: Appleton.

Kumari Campbell, Fiona A. 2007. 'States of Exceptionality: Provisional Disability, Its Mitigation and Citizenship.' *Socio-Legal Review*. 3: 28.

Macdonald, Stephen. J. 2012. '"Journey's End": Statistical Pathways into Offending for Adults with Specific Learning Difficulties.' *Journal of Learning Disabilities and Offending Behaviour*. 3, no. 2: 85–97.

Macdonald, Stephen. J. 2015. '"Community Fear and Harassment": Learning Difficulties and Hate Crime Incidents in the North-East of England.' *Disability & Society*. 30, no. 3: 353–367.

Macdonald, Stephen. J. 2020. 'Therapeutic Institutions of Violence: Conceptualising the Biographical Narratives of Mental Health Service Users/Survivors Accessing Long Term "Treatment" in England.' *Journal of Criminological Research, Policy and Practice*. 7, no. 2: 179–194.

Madfis, Eric, and Jeffrey Cohen. 2016. 'Critical Criminologies of the Present and Future: Left Realism, Left Idealism, and What's Left In Between.' *Social Justice*. 43, no. 4:1–21.

Mathews, Ian. 2018. 'Representations of Vulnerability, Innocence and Evil in the Murder of a Disabled Person.' *Disability & Society*. 33, no. 10: 1620–1683.

Matthews, Roger. 2014. *Realist Criminology*. London: Springer.

Meekosha, Helen. 2011. 'Decolonising Disability: Thinking and Acting Globally.' *Disability & Society*. 26, no. 6: 667–682.

Mikton, Christopher, Holly Maguire and Tom Shakespeare. 2014. 'A Systematic Review of the Effectiveness of Interventions to Prevent and Respond to Violence Against Persons with Disabilities.' *Journal of Interpersonal Violence*. 29, no. 17: 3207–3226.

Muncie, John, and Eugene McLaughlin. 2019. *The Sage Dictionary of Criminology*. London: Sage.

Oliver, Mike. 2009. *Understanding Disability from Theory to Practice*. 2nd ed. Basingstoke: Palgrave Macmillan.

Porter, Roy. 2003. *Madness: A Brief History*. Oxford: Oxford University Press.

Presdee, Mike. 2000. *Cultural Criminology and the Carnival of Crime*. London: Routledge.

Presley, Rachel. 2019. 'Decolonizing the Body: Indigenizing Our Approach to Disability Studies.' *The Activist History Review*. 29.

Quarmby, Katharine. 2011. *Scapegoat: Why We Are Failing Disabled People*. London: Granta.

Raine, Adrian. 2013. *The Anatomy of Violence: The Biological Roots of Crime*. New York: Pantheon.

Rose, Nikolas. 2000. 'The Biology of Culpability: Pathological Identity and Crime Control in a Biological Culture.' *Theoretical Criminology*. 4, no. 1: 5–34.

Roulstone, Alan, and Kim Sadique. 2013. 'Vulnerable to Misinterpretation: Disabled People, "Vulnerability", Hate Crime and the Fight for Legal Representation.' In *Disability, Hate Crime and Violence*, edited by Alan Roulstone and Hannah Mason-Bish, 32–46. London: Routledge.

Semple, David, and Roger Smyth. 2019. *Oxford Handbook of Psychiatry*. 2nd ed. Oxford: Oxford University Press.
Shakespeare, Tom. 2006. *Disability Rights and Wrongs*. London: Routledge.
Shakespeare, Tom. 2013. *Disability Rights and Wrongs Revisited*. London: Routledge.
Shakespeare, Tom, and Nick Watson. 2001. 'The Social Model of Disability: An Outdated Ideology?' In *Exploring Theories and Expanding Methodologies: Where We Are and Where We Need to Go*, edited by Sharon. N. Barnartt and Barbara Altman, 9–28. London: Emerald.
Shakespeare, Tom, Nicholas Watson, and Ola Abu Alghaib. 2017. 'Blaming the Victim, All Over Again: Waddell and Aylward's Biopsychosocial (BPS) Model of Disability.' *Critical Social Policy*. 37, no. 1: 22–41.
Shaw, Linda R., Fong Chan and Brian. T. McMahon. 2012. 'Intersectionality and Disability Harassment: The Interactive Effects of Disability, Race, Age, and Gender.' *Rehabilitation Counseling Bulletin*. 55, no. 2: 82–91.
Sherry, Mark. 2016. *Disability Hate Crimes: Does Anyone Really Hate Disabled People?* London: Routledge.
Soothill, Keith. 2008. *Handbook of Forensic Mental Health*. London: Routledge.
Steele, Linda, and Stuart Thomas. 2014. 'Disability at the Periphery: Legal Theory, Disability and Criminal Law.' *Griffith Law Review*. 23, no. 3: 357–369.
Stienstra, Deborah. 2020. *About Canada: Disability Rights*. Nova Scotia: Fernwood Publishing.
Sutherland, Edwin H. 1924. *Criminology*. Philadelphia and London: J. B. Lippincott Company.
Taylor, Ian, Paul Walton and Jock Young. 1973/2013. *The New Criminology: For a Social Theory of Deviance*. London: Routledge.
Thomas, Carol. 2017. *Sociologies of Disability and Illness: Contested Ideas in Disability Studies and Medical Sociology*. London: Bloomsbury.
Thorneycroft, Ryan. 2017. 'Problematising and Reconceptualising Vulnerability in the Context of Disablist Violence.' In *Policing Encounters with Vulnerability* edited by Nicole L. Asquith, Isabel Bartkowiak-Theron, and Karl A. Roberts, 27–45. Switzerland: Palgrave Macmillan.
Thorneycroft, Ryan, and Nicola L. Asquith. 2021. 'Cripping Criminology.' *Theoretical Criminology*. 25, no. 2: 187–208.
Tremain, Shelley. 2006. 'On the Government of Disability: Foucault, Power, and the Subject of Impairment.' In *The Disability Studies Reader*, 2nd ed., edited by Lennard. J. Davis, 185–197. London: Routledge.
Wamser-Nanney, Rachel, and Kathryn E. Cherry. 2018. 'Children's Trauma-Related Symptoms Following Complex Trauma Exposure: Evidence of Gender Differences." *Child Abuse & Neglect*. 77, no. 1: 188–197.
Wilson, James Q., and Richard J. Herrnstein. 1985. *Crime and Human Nature*. New York: Simon & Schuster.

3
ENGAGING INDIGENOUS AUSTRALIAN VOICES
Bringing Epistemic Justice to Criminology?

Stephen D. Ashe and Debbie Bargallie

Introduction

As Amanda Porter, a scholar from the Brinja clan of the Yuin nation on the South Coast of New South Wales (NSW), Australia, has noted, the publication of *Indigenous Criminology* (Cunneen and Tauri, 2016) coincided with 'a series of scandals and mounting inquiries into Indigenous justice issues around the globe' (Porter, 2019: 122), including rising levels of Indigenous incarceration. What is more, in reviewing *Indigenous Criminology*, Porter called on criminologists to 'ask some unsettling questions', namely: '[H]as criminology as a discipline failed Indigenous peoples? And, if so, how can we do things differently? To what degree has criminology been complicit in the rising rates of Indigenous incarceration internationally? And what, if anything, does criminology have to offer the crises in criminal justice which have been the experience of Indigenous peoples around the globe?' (Porter, 2019: 122). These questions are particularly pertinent given that Indigenous communities around the world have endured a fraught history in terms of their relationship with academic researchers in western institutions – finding themselves essentialised, pathologised, marginalised and, until the late 20th century, explicitly excluded from tertiary institutions. In this exclusion, western research practices have tended to disempower Indigenous peoples, and problematise Indigenous beliefs and cultural practices. This has been evident throughout the development of criminology as a field of study, where Indigenous voices continue to be routinely sidelined. This has led criminologists Chris Cunneen, a non-Indigenous Australian scholar, and Juan Marcellos Tauri, a Māori scholar of the Ngāti Porou iwi of Aotearoa (New Zealand), to question whether American and European criminological traditions can provide an adequate starting point for understanding Indigenous peoples' contact with criminal justice systems in white settler-colonial societies

DOI: 10.4324/9781003260967-4

(Cunneen and Tauri, 2016). In this chapter, we argue that mainstream criminology has subjected Indigenous scholars, and peoples more generally, to forms of 'epistemic injustice' (Fricker, 2007) and 'epistemic positioning' (Bacevic, 2021). Not only this, when considered alongside the other marginalised voices explored in this collection, we suggest that the field of criminology has drifted into a state of 'disciplinary decadence' (Gordon, 2015). Despite this, Indigenous scholars have long made significant contributions to decolonising the academy, ways of approaching questions of justice, and pragmatic processes which look to embed Indigenous perspectives in research practices. Alas, they have been overlooked, if not 'willfully ignored' (Mills, 1997, 2007; Alcoff, 2007; Pohlhaus, 2012). Thus, this chapter will contribute to ongoing efforts to address these injustices by drawing attention to Indigenous Australian contributions to criminological theory, with particular emphasis placed on highlighting the scholarship of Indigenous women who have found themselves marginalised as a result of the intersection of Indigeneity and patriarchy. Moreover, by celebrating the work of Indigenous women and their allies, this chapter points towards ways in which the aforementioned forms of epistemic injustice and positioning might be repaired.

Linda Tuhiwai Smith, a Māori scholar of the Ngāti Awa and Ngāti Porou of Aotearoa (New Zealand) has remarked that the word 'research' is 'probably one of the dirtiest words in the Indigenous world's vocabulary' (Smith, 2012: xi). Indeed, there are strong grounds for such a claim as there have been too many occasions whereby non-Indigenous researchers have deployed unethical, individualistic, and extractive practices which have led to them being rewarded for 'telling half-truths and down-right lies' (Smith, 2012: xi). Since colonial invasion and conquest, Indigenous peoples have endured a long history of having their bodies, cultures, traditions, and beliefs objectified, essentialised, pathologised, and ultimately oppressed by settler-colonial institutions and Eurocentric knowledge systems. So much so, Indigenous knowledge systems have been deemed unscientific and lacking the 'objectivity' and 'rigour' commonly associated with the value-free, positivistic epistemologies of the Enlightenment era. Dehumanised and treated as passive objects of study, Indigenous peoples have become accustomed to being disregarded as 'agents themselves, as capable of or interested in research, or as having expert knowledge on themselves and their conditions' (Smith, 2012: xi).

Similarly, Indigenous voices have been routinely marginalised and subjected to epistemological oppression in westernised educational and research institutions situated on stolen lands. The role and function of criminal justice systems in settler-colonial societies have been such that the Indigenous and non-Indigenous experience of these systems are substantively different. More specifically, the conceptualisation of crime and the formation of criminal justice systems are a significant feature of the enduring settler-colonial state apparatuses. Thus, they are core components of what Walter Mignolo (2018) has referred to as the 'colonial matrix of power' in that they have been designed to maintain social order and control (everyday, not just in terms of 'offending' behaviour), perpetuate adverse life outcomes for Indigenous peoples, and to eradicate Indigenous populations (Tauri and Porou, 2014). Indeed, the longstanding neglect of settler-colonialism and Indigeneity in mainstream criminology has resulted in ahistorical and decontextualised accounts of how Indigenous peoples experience crime and criminal justice systems.

Stephen is a white sociologist based in Britain who teaches on both sociology and criminology programmes. Debbie is an Indigenous Australian interdisciplinary critical race scholar from the Kamilaroi and Wonnarua peoples of the north-west and Upper Hunter regions of NSW. Our interests converge through our shared research focus in antiracism, workplace racism, racism and equality in higher education, critical racial and decolonial literacies, and Indigenous research ethics and methodologies. We come together in this chapter to centre Indigenous Australian contributions to criminological knowledge. To do so, we begin with a discussion of the forms of 'epistemic injustice' (Fricker, 2007) and 'epistemic positioning' (Bacevic, 2021) endured by Indigenous scholars and peoples in mainstream criminology. In doing so, we contend that this is one of several avenues (as this edited collection laments) whereby mainstream criminology has sunken into 'disciplinary decadence' (Gordon, 2015). The discussion will then move on to celebrate where Indigenous scholars and their non-Indigenous collaborators have already made distinct contributions to a range of core criminological areas of study. In doing so, it is hoped that this chapter makes a contribution to realising epistemic justice and theoretical renewal in criminology. By centring the contributions of Indigenous scholars, especially women, and their allies, it is our hope that the enduring legacies of racism and colonialism, and their intersections with other modalities of oppression, are taken seriously.

Epistemic injustice, epistemic positioning, and the danger of disciplinary decadence

Indigenous knowledge systems have largely been marginalised because they are said to be deficient of the 'objectivity' and 'rigour' attributed to the value-free and positivistic epistemologies of the Enlightenment era. We contend that this constitutes a form of 'epistemological injustice' (Fricker, 2007) and 'willful ignorance' (Mills, 1997, 2007; Alcoff, 2007; Pohlhaus, 2012) which perpetuates the disparities that can be seen in terms of contact with the criminal justice system, including the overrepresentation of Aboriginal and Torres Strait Islander peoples throughout the criminal justice system, from higher contact with the police and deaths in custody to juvenile detention and victimisation rates. Larissa Behrendt, a writer, lawyer, and legal scholar of the Eualeyai and Kamillaroi peoples of north-western NSW, has challenged how we understand value-freedom and encourages us to consider the colonial legacies within ways of knowing:

As Aboriginal researchers, we do not assume to be objective. We know there is no such thing. If we thought our position in the world could be passive, we wouldn't introduce ourselves by our nations, our clans, our kinship networks. We place ourselves in the world as an act of sovereignty and it reinforces our worldview. In our research approaches, we take this on by not pretending that we are neutral. We are proud advocates and activists for our people. We march and protest. We publish and critique. We confront wilful blindness and we will not be silenced. We research to empower our community and build our communities. We research to honour the history and battles of our ancestors and we research to arm the next generation of warriors. Our most powerful tool in this is the assertion of our sovereignty, our unapologetic stance that our Aboriginal culture, our philosophies, our values are the things that define us as we work in the institutions of the colonizer – whether that is within the courts, within the bureaucracy, or within the academy

(Behrendt, 2019, n.p.).

At the same time, Porter (2019) has called into question the nature and extent to which the field of criminology has engaged with Indigenous criminological scholarship, particularly in relation to how the field conceptualises the democratisation and decolonisation of social scientific inquiry. Indigenous scholars have also criticised criminology in Australia (and New Zealand) as being 'a discipline made up largely of white, middle-class academics, many of whom appear woefully ignorant of the colonial underpinnings of the discipline' (Tauri, 2018: 2). As Tauri explains, many of these people 'are often regarded by the wider discipline and the policy sector, as *the* "experts" on Indigenous people and crime' (p.2). The exclusion of certain voices in the production of knowledge has significant effects, not only on the people who are marginalised, but also in terms of the overall quality of academic research. The exclusion of voices in educational institutions, such as criminology departments in westernised institutions, lead to them becoming sites of 'epistemic injustice'. As such, some Indigenous academics in the field of criminology have declined opportunities to work in this field or engage with the Australian and New Zealand Society of Criminology.

Miranda Fricker defines 'epistemic injustice' as a form injustice 'done to someone specifically in their capacity as a knower' (Fricker, 2007: 1). That is, epistemic injustice in practice strategically diminishes a person's ability to be a knower and be recognised as a knower in particular spaces. This is both an ethical issue and an epistemic issue whereby certain knowledge claims are substantially impacted, reduced, or denied by the virtue of others' perception of the knower's characteristics, such as 'skin colour, gender or age'. Too often, and for too long, Indigenous contributions to knowledge have found themselves subjected to what Jana Bacevic (2021) has referred to as 'epistemic bounding' and 'epistemic domaining'. In terms of the former, Indigenous knowledge is reduced due to aspects of personal identity (i.e., Indigeneity and its intersection with other modes of domination and oppression such as patriarchy). Whereas the latter, 'epistemic domaining', has seen Indigenous criminological knowledge shut out of different disciplines and fields of study and cordoned off into departments such as Indigenous Studies, and/or journals dedicated to the study of Indigeneity.

Alongside deep-seated inequalities and the underrepresentation of Indigenous scholars in educational institutions on stolen lands, interactions between Indigenous communities and educational institutions on these lands have been shaped by settler-colonialism. That is, 'a distinct type of colonialism that functions through the replacement of Indigenous populations with an invasive settler society that, over time, develops a distinctive identity and sovereignty' (Baker and Lowman, n.d.). In view of settler-colonial histories, Cunneen and Tauri (2016) question whether American and European criminological traditions can provide an adequate starting point for understanding Indigenous peoples' contact with the criminal justice systems in white settler-colonial societies. Echoing Smith (2012), Cunneen and Tauri (2016; see also Tauri, 2013) contend that positivistic and Eurocentric strands of authoritarian/administrative criminology (i.e., research supported by the state, including authoritarian governmental regimes) have shown a tendency to undertake *research on*, rather than *research with*, Indigenous peoples. As a result, Indigenous peoples' demands for their knowledges, customs, laws, and alterity to the West, as well as calls for the right to self-determination, have been marginalised. For Cunneen and Tauri, this stems, in part, from the use of conceptual and theoretical frameworks that essentialise, pathologise, and disempower (not to mention dehumanise) Indigenous peoples as 'uncivilised', 'backwards', and 'savage', while simultaneously problematising Indigenous beliefs, cultural practices, and knowledge systems. So much so, Indigenous peoples throughout the world have endured violent criminal justice policies and practices that maintain their oppression precisely because authoritarian and administrative criminological traditions have served as the intellectual foundations of, and justification for, the settler-colonial criminal justice systems and practices which are key components of a broader colonial power matrix (Mignolo, 2018) which includes privileges and delegitimises particular systems of knowledge. This is arguably most evident in mainstream criminological accounts of Indigenous criminality and victimisation. So, in addition to acknowledging its complicity in obfuscating Indigenous peoples' experiences of dispossession, genocide, and social control, it is imperative that mainstream criminology recognises both the value of using colonialism and Indigeneity as part of its theoretical and conceptual frameworks, especially when seeking to comprehend and explain contemporary crime and justice issues. What is more, such recognition must also acknowledge the epistemic use-value of engagement with the knowledge produced by Indigenous peoples and scholars.

By addressing epistemic traditions which have framed and positioned Indigenous peoples as 'problem populations' (Cunneen and Tauri, 2016), bringing Indigenous voices in from the criminological periphery must also entail attention being paid to Indigenous rights and claims to self-determination. As Cunneen and Tauri explain, rather than being a threat to existing state-based criminal justice systems, Indigenous approaches to the question of justice have the potential to lead to progressive reform. This is perhaps most evident in terms of how criminal justice systems, and criminologists, theorise 'harm', 'healing', 'restorative justice', and 'rehabilitation' in meaningful rather than tokenistic and symbolic ways. For example, the website of 'Why me?', 'a national charity delivering and promoting Restorative Justice for everyone affected by crime and conflict' in Britain, makes no mention of the fact that First Nations people of Canada and the United States and Māori peoples of New Zealand had developed localised forms of 'restorative justice' long before it became a fashionable and constituent component of the criminological canon (see https://why-me.org/, last accessed on 18th May 2023). For Cunneen and Tauri, addressing what Behrendt (2019) refers to as the 'wilful blindness' evident in much of the criminological knowledge produced by colonial settlers requires proper attention being paid to the 'historical, structural and biographical appreciation of the experiences of colonialism and settler colonialism' (2016: 20). Moreover, doing so will result in the field of criminology being better placed to map and theorise the similarities and differences between 'colonial strategies in settler-colonial societies and the enduring effects of colonialism on crime, criminal justice and Indigenous resistance' (Cunneen and Tauri, 2016: 20). In contrast to mainstream/'traditional' criminology, Cunneen and Tauri contend that this means engaging meaningfully with different Indigenous approaches to questions of 'law and order', 'social control', and 'policing', as well as bringing Indigenous conceptions of 'healing' into dialogue with western concepts of 'deterrence' and 'rehabilitation'.

Amidst the ongoing calls for the decolonisation of higher education, Irene Watson, a legal scholar of the Tanganekald, Meintangk Boandik peoples of the Coorong and the south east of South Australia, has referred to the 'the murder of knowledge' that occurs when different voices are routinely and perpetually marginalised and excluded by hegemonic epistemic systems. In relation to questions of 'justice' in Australia, Watson argues that:

> ... the law cannot be extinguished, the potential for a *juridicide* looms if Aboriginal laws continue to be ignored ... We might also add that there is the potential for a death of knowledge of First Nations' Peoples as the carriers of law, notwithstanding the fact that the law will go on as it has always done, in its relationship to the natural world
> *(Watson, 2022: 371–372, emphasis added).*

For this to be avoided, Watson contends that horizontal forms of dialogue are necessary if we are to go beyond the western-centric universalism and the alleged incommensurability that is said to exist between Indigenous and settler cultures. For Watson, such dialogue requires that we transcend colonial matrixes of power so that we can imagine equitable power relations, 'shared authority', and 'the possibility of First Nations' voices being registered, heard and understood from a centred First Nations space'. However, for this to happen, Watson contends that the following questions need to be addressed:

> How do the power relations between First Nations and states translate into Western law? What place or space is there to speak of coloniality; are there spaces that are free of colonialism? Can 'proper' dialogue only flourish where there is a commitment to decolonising power relations? Can we know and/or imagine other ways of being law-full than being within the colonial matrix?
> *(Watson, 2022: 372)*

Thus, Aboriginal ways of being must be foregrounded. Settler-colonial states are required to sincerely engage First Nations' perspectives on authority and power. As Watson argues, the non-Indigenous world has a long way to go in terms of developing an ability to listen deeply to the Indigenous world and knowing how to *reciprocate* and *share responsibility*, as opposed to doing so in merely symbolic and piecemeal ways.

Failure to address the forms of epistemic injustice, if not 'juridicide', identified by Watson, Porter (2019), Cunneen and Tauri (2016) can result in what Lewis Gordon (2015) has referred to as 'disciplinary decadence'. For Gordon, a discipline (or field of study) is susceptible to this when it seeks to maintain the status quo and epistemic, ethical, and practical orthodoxies to the point where it is resistant to new ideas, approaches, or critiques. So much so, disciplinary decadence limits the creation of knowledge by setting criteria which undervalues and delegitimises marginalised voices in ways that lead to epistemic stasis. This leads Gordon (2015) to argue that disciplinarity and hegemonic epistemological, theoretical, and methodological suppositions in different fields of study must be suspended. It is our view that the field of criminology, specifically, risks further consolidating epistemic injustice and 'disciplinary decadence' by positioning and compartmentalising Indigenous knowledge in ways that relegates such knowledge to spaces such as Indigenous Studies departments and research centres, and/or journals dedicated to the study of Indigeneity, such as the *Indigenous Law Bulletin*. Moreover, if epistemic injustice is to be circumvented, then criminology needs also to be attentive to the ways in which Indigenous knowledge is policed, whereby it is only able to transcend disciplinary borders and enter other fields of scholarship in 'small manageable chunks' (Chaka et al., 2022: 16) without unsettling hegemonic knowledge systems and orthodox praxis. If the current state of affairs were to endure, the field of criminology risks becoming stagnant in its approach to teaching and research. Perhaps, as we show in the later sections of this chapter, the first step towards realising epistemic justice might just be by broadening the research questions asked and by embracing interdisciplinarity.

As the discussion here has shown, both epistemic injustice and disciplinary decadence help us understand the enduring fraught relationship that exists between Indigenous peoples and criminology. Indigenous peoples and scholars have been subjected to epistemic injustice and violence. Even in recent times, amidst calls for the decolonisation of the academy and cries of #BlackLivesMatter, Indigenous scholars have reported fraught encounters with academic research governance structures which continue to demonstrate little, if indeed any, knowledge of Indigenous cultural traditions and protocols (see Australian Institute of Aboriginal and Torres Strait Islander Studies, 2020; George et al., 2020). We argue that this is epitomised in criminology work in Australia – a field of study exhibiting signs of disciplinary decadence. In the following section, we point towards further ways in which criminology might address disciplinary decadence through engagement with Indigenous scholarship and ways of knowing that can be found in other disciplines and fields of study.

Indigenous Australian contributions to criminological knowledge

In this section we aim to address the forms of epistemic injustice outlined above. In doing so, we celebrate knowledge produced by a range of Indigenous scholars, peoples, and their allies on core criminological research areas. As noted earlier, intersectionality must be recognised if we are to grasp the full extent of epistemic injustice and the specific ways in which different scholars and knowledges are positioned in the academy (see Bacevic, 2021). Alas, it is beyond this chapter's capacity to be able to cover all Indigenous scholars and knowledges. Therefore, in an effort to help address the epistemic injustice that stems from the intersection of Indigeneity and patriarchy, the discussion that follows is based around a selection of vital contributions Indigenous women have made to criminological knowledge. In bringing attention to these contributions, the discussion focuses on those scholars that have endeavoured to address the 'significant crises in Indigenous criminal justice' (Porter, 2019: 122) that stem from and perpetuate the harms brought about by racism, settler-colonialism, and western criminological epistemologies. These crises include, but are not limited to, the wholly derisory investigations into the sexual violence inflicted on, and murder of, Indigenous women and girls; Indigenous deaths in police custody; how Indigenous youth experience maltreatment in 'correctional facilities'; not to mention what appears to be never-ending inquiries into mass victimisation and hyper-incarceration of Indigenous peoples (Porter, 2019: 122). The aim of doing so is to draw further attention to the violence and injustice inflicted upon Aboriginal and Torres Strait Islander peoples as they come into contact with different arms of settler-colonial state apparatus. By drawing attention to this, the section recognises both the contributions Indigenous scholars have made to academic knowledge, but also the depth of commitment to social justice through critical public interventions.

On domestic, family, and sexual violence

Marlene Longbottom, a Yuin scholar of the South Coast of NSW, Crystal McKinnon, an Amangu Yamatji scholar of the mid-western region of Western Australia, and Amanda Porter have individually and collectively made several important interventions and contributions to knowledge on how Indigenous women experience domestic and family violence, as well as their experiences of police stations (see DesLandes et al., 2022; Longbottom and Porter, 2021). Longbottom's 2019 doctoral research examined the experiences of Aboriginal women from the south coast of NSW who had survived, but had been traumatised by, life-threatening violence. DesLandes et al. (2022) have also made vital contributions highlighting that knowledge produced *with*, *by*, and *for* Indigenous communities reveals a number of concrete alternatives for Indigenous women and families experiencing violence. More specifically, DesLandes et al. (2022) point towards different culturally safe, community-based legal support services, thus challenging white feminists to listen to and hear the voices of Indigenous women. Relatedly, Kyllie Cripps, a Palawa Tasmanian scholar and researcher on Indigenous family violence, child abuse, and sexual assault has worked on a variety of studies committed to defining violence on Indigenous terms (see Cripps, 2011, 2012; Cripps and McCreery, 2013; Cripps and Laurens, 2015; Cripps and Habibis, 2019). In doing so, Cripps and her allies have critically examined the different factors contributing to violence towards women, as well as the availability of culturally appropriate services for Aboriginal women who have experienced violence. What is more, Cripps' work has identified both opportunities for, as well as barriers to, Indigenous peoples playing a central role in developing sustainable policy and practice-based solutions to child abuse, and family and sexual violence. Hannah McGlade, a Bibbulmun Noongar human rights lawyer and scholar from Western Australia, has also published widely on justice for Aboriginal people, race discrimination law and practice, Aboriginal women and children, family violence, and sexual assault (see McGlade, 2019; McGlade and Tarrant, 2021).

On subjects of domestic and family violence, Indigenous Australian scholars Bronwyn Carlson and Madi Day, along with Terri Farrelly, a non-Indigenous collaborator, have undertaken work on behalf of Australia's National Research Organisation for Women's Safety (ANROWS) (see Carlson et al., 2021). For example, their first publication from this project considers the effectiveness of Aboriginal and Torres Strait Islander healing programmes for survivors of domestic, family and sexual violence. Rather than utilising criminal justice perspectives, Carlson et al. adopt an 'active approach' based on a preference for perspectives that understand, acknowledge, value, and respect local Indigenous cultures. In doing so, Carlson et al. also identified a number of gaps in existing literature, particularly in relation to the experiences and needs of disabled Aboriginal and Torres Strait Islander peoples, and LGBTQA+ and intersex Aboriginal and Torres Strait Islander peoples (Carlson, et al. 2021).

Marcia Langton, a renowned activist-scholar of the Yiman and Bidjara nations of Queensland, has also led research into the practical and legal support available to Aboriginal and Torres Strait Islander male perpetrators of family violence, as well as experiences of Aboriginal and Torres Strait Islander men working within the services (see Langton et al., 2020). Langton et al. also draw attention to the cultural appropriateness of mainstream behavioural change programmes for Aboriginal and Torres Strait Islander men who are perpetrators of family violence in the Victorian and New South Wales towns of Mildura and Albury–Wodonga. What is more, Langton et al. argue that the lack of culturally appropriate services which address issues such as mental health, neurological disability, or substance issues can contribute to the perpetration of violence. Langton et al. (2020: 47–53) also documented the Koori Court hearings as 'a specialised sentencing court for Aboriginal and Torres Strait Islander clients in Victoria' after it had shown promising alternatives to the mainstream legal system, calling for it to be extended to matters of family violence across Victoria.

On missing Aboriginal women

Amy McQuire, a Darumbal and South Sea Islander scholar and journalist from coastal Central Queensland, has drawn attention to issues of media silence and representations of violence against Aboriginal women (see McQuire, 2016, 2018, 2021a, 2021b; McQuire and McGrady, 2018; McQuire, et al., 2023). Despite considerable media attention being granted to issues of family violence, McQuire notes that, by contrast, there is an ongoing silence when it comes to violence inflicted upon Aboriginal women, which hinders Aboriginal agency and resistance by denying Aboriginal women a voice. McQuire et al. (2023) also note that the term 'missing' is typically used in ways which suggests that Aboriginal women have left their communities of their own accord rather than being endangered by violence. As McQuire explains, the colonial white-gaze of the media plays a key role in dehumanising Aboriginal women by framing them as 'disposable' and 'unworthy of justice'. Such representations oftentimes run parallel to racist stereotypes which depict Aboriginal men as inherently 'violent' and 'savage', and Aboriginal communities more broadly as 'infantile' and 'uncaring'. The essentialising logics of the colonial white-gaze also depicts violence towards Aboriginal women as an essentialised cultural practice *within* Aboriginal communities. All the while, white perpetrators of violence, particularly towards Aboriginal women, are overlooked as non-Indigenous Australians take up the self-appointed position of 'arbiters of morality'. McQuire's work also focuses on how violence and trauma intersect in the lived experiences of Aboriginal women. Rather than being 'a response to White feminism', McQuire explains that this work seeks to advance Indigenous feminism as a tool to advocate for Aboriginal women. By undertaking this work, McQuire challenges carceral conceptualisations of justice, noting that carceral systems were predicated on colonial logics of 'disappearance, and specifically Indigenous disappearance'. For McQuire, this is 'predicated on the idea of disconnection' which entails the connection Indigenous peoples have with the land being ruptured and a disconnecting of the ties Indigenous peoples have with both community and place. As McQuire explains, Aboriginal peoples resist attempts at rupturing and disconnection through acts of 'presencing'. Moreover, McQuire contends that Aboriginal peoples pursue 'Black justice' though culturally specific means of remembering, grieving, and mourning such as 'photos on display in the court room, or in the hands of the mother in the first row' and through 'chanting of spirit'. For McQuire, these can be forms of protest whereby Aboriginal families and communities demonstrate that these women 'do not "cease to exist" but are always present'.

On forced removal and murdered children

Adopting a self-determination framework that recognises Indigenous storytelling as a legitimate method of knowledge production, Larissa Behrendt has exposed the way in which Aboriginal and Torres Strait Islander children and their families have experienced child removal, noting how these stories are sharply juxtaposed to those that are told about them through care and protection law and related policy (Behrendt, 2019: 191). What is more, when Aboriginal and Torres Strait Islander stories are 'told in their own voices', and 'heard on their own terms', they reveal that 'the removal of Aboriginal and Torres Strait Islander children from their families [as being] a key pillar of a concerted and complex colonial project' and that 'people working in law come to see the power of storytelling within and outside legal institutions' (Behrendt, 2019: 191). Moreover, in everyday institutional contexts undergirded by colonisation and patriarchy, Behrendt notes that these stories can carry transformational energy, as demonstrated by the families in the small NSW town of Bowraville in their two-decade long struggle for social justice for their murdered children.

As noted earlier, a number of Indigenous knowledge producers have undertaken academic roles, as well as being at the forefront of Indigenous human rights campaigns and bringing the attention of international scholar-activists to the stories of missing and murdered Indigenous women and children in Australia through their journalistic and/or scholar-activist work beyond the academy. These include Amy McQuire (discussed in the previous section); Allan Clarke, a Muruwari man from far western NSW and an investigative journalist host of NITV's flagship news and current affairs program, *The Point*; and Martin Hodgson, a Yuin man, human rights activist, senior advocate with the Foreign Prisoners Support Service, and a freelance writer, who works with a variety of Indigenous rights groups to bring their issues to public attention. Hodgson edits the Indigenous website, 1 DEADLY NATION (https://1deadlynation.wordpress.com). In 2014, a documentary film titled, *Innocence Betrayed*, was released telling the story of the parents of three murdered Aboriginal children and their 23-year-long fight for justice (see also Behrendt, 2019). Written, directed, and narrated by Larissa Behrendt, *Innocence Betrayed* provides space for the parents of Colleen Walker, Evelyn Greenup, and Clinton Speedy to share their stories of loss, as well as the impact of the trial and acquittal of the single white suspect and the broader actions of the Australian legal system on the families' fight for justice.

On policing, counter-policing, Indigenous patrols, and community safety

The work of Amanda Porter has focused on the colonising trajectories that underpin how police powers have been constructed and actualised, as well as constructions of police accountability, violence, and genocide. Moreover, Porter produced knowledge on nature and the effectiveness of community safety and defence initiatives such as night patrols, custody notification services, and 'no jurisdiction' cases, as well as the history of the Australian police and police unions, and deaths in police custody. In addition to this, Porter has conducted research on premature deaths, near misses, missing and murdered Indigenous women and children, strategic litigation, and the politics of Indigenous refusal in the justice context.

Porter's work on Indigenous community safety questions the theoretical, conceptual, and analytical use-value of westernised/mainstream criminology in settler-colonial contexts. In posing these questions, Porter also challenges calls to decolonise the police, arguing that there is much need to engage with localised Indigenous histories and voices, noting that state policing in Australia cannot be disconnected from 'a long history of colonial oppression and racism' (2016: 548). In a study on 'Indigenous patrols, counter-policing and safety', Porter (2016: 562–563) adopted a localised Indigenous 'bottom-up' approach to explore how policing might be reformed through localised Indigenous knowledge and self-governance. For Porter, mainstream criminology is often susceptible to 'replicating the colonial gaze and colonial processes of knowledge control' (2016: 562). Thus, overlooking or wilfully disregarding Indigenous approaches to social order, such as Indigenous patrols, Porter also interrogates the terms 'policing' and 'counter-policing', noting that Indigenous community safety and defence initiatives have been referred to as 'counter-policing' precisely because such initiatives seek to limit unnecessary contact and confrontation between Indigenous youth and the state police as a result of over-policing. However, Porter is critical of the term 'counter-policing', arguing that while such initiatives sometimes seek to build bridges with the state police rather than serving as alternatives to state policing, Indigenous patrol workers and community members do not always see such initiatives as policing or as seeking to limit unnecessary contact with the state police. Instead, Indigenous actors undertaking this work consider their remit as having social work and welfare functions, thus serving as a form of crime prevention, with Indigenous patrol workers and community members seeing themselves as 'mentors' and 'youth care-takers' looking to promote wellbeing and ensuring 'safety', while also minimising Indigenous youth's exposure to 'risk' and 'harm'.

In short, Porter shows that the continued use of terms such as 'policing' and 'counter-policing' in mainstream criminological discourse obscures the reality of the activities undertaken by, and perspectives of, the mainly Indigenous peoples carrying out this work. Moreover, the use of these terms undermines Indigenous peoples and their role as knowledge producers, who have something worth contributing and which might even make disproportionate arrests rates and deaths in custody a thing of the past.

On deaths in custody

Alison Whittaker, a Gomeroi poet and legal researcher from NSW, has made numerous public interventions in response to disproportionate levels of First Nation deaths in police custody. In doing so, Whittaker (2018, 2020) has lamented on the lack of attention paid to the situation in Australia, particularly when there is greater public knowledge pertaining to racist policing and prison violence in the white settler-colony which we commonly refer to as the United States. Whittaker's work has also identified a complex 'system of complicity and perceived normality in Indigenous deaths at the hands of police and prisons' which are often interpreted as a 'co-morbidity' rather than as acts of violence (2020, n. p.). For Whittaker, the settler-colonial state apparatus is a system upheld by transparency issues which 'give a legal structure to silence about Indigenous deaths in custody' (2020, n.p.). This includes practices such as the non-publication of reports and suppression orders being sought by state parties in coroners' courts, coroners seldomly referring Aboriginal deaths in custody to prosecutors, and quashed indictments and/or acquittals. This has led Whittaker to argue that

> Prosecution or referral seems to come only from cases where First Nations families have strong public advocacy and community groundswells behind them and strategic litigation resources (not just inquest legal aid)
>
> *(2020, n.p.).*

In attending to Aboriginal deaths in custody, Whittaker has theorised Australia as having established a system of complicity predicated on colonisation and white supremacy, whereby the injustice of racial violence and the loss of Indigenous lives in police custody has been normalised and bolstered by 'media ignorance and racist editorial decisions', a 'lack of institutional support for Indigenous journalism', and 'plaintiff-friendly defamation laws'.

On hyper-incarceration and prisons

Hyper-incarceration, or 'mass imprisonment', emerged as a means of conceptualising the severely high rates at which African American men living in disadvantaged neighbourhoods were being imprisoned. Alongside slavery, Jim Crow laws, and notion of the 'the ghetto', Loïc Wacquant (2000) argued that mass imprisonment was one of four 'peculiar institutions' trusted with controlling and subjugating African American peoples to racial rule. Aboriginal and Torres Strait Islander scholars have also made significant contributions to knowledge in this area; thus, nuancing our understanding of the enduring nature of hyper-incarceration and social control on stolen lands.

Juanita Sherwood, a Wiradjuri scholar from NSW and Thalia Anthony, a non-Indigenous scholar with Cypriot heritage, posit a 'post-disciplinary framework' as an alternative to positivist criminology (Anthony and Sherwood, 2018). For Anthony and Sherwood, western positivist criminology gained ascendancy precisely because it spoke to the western epistemological notions of objectivity and rigour, which Indigenous epistemologies were deemed to be lacking. Moreover, such punitive and deficit logics have been used to normalise and legitimise the supposed inherent criminalisation and hyper-incarceration of Indigenous peoples since colonisation. Anthony and Sherwood have sought to counter such deficit narratives by drawing attention to the approach taken by Tangentyere Research Hub (TRB) in Alice Springs, Central Australia, which foregrounds Indigenous interests and leadership. As part of broader efforts to decolonise criminology, Anthony and Sherwood highlight the 'benefits of Tangentyere's reliance on local Indigenous knowledges and perspectives' in 'empowering, strengthening and supporting Indigenous communities and self-governance' (2018: 1). They also draw attention to the positive relationship between Indigenous wellbeing and Indigenous self-determination through their work on 'Indigenous crime and the punitive role of the state' (2018: 1). These findings are also echoed in other Indigenous-led studies discussed below.

Krystal Lockwood, a Gumbaynggirr and Dunghutti scholar from NSW, and Bhiamie Williamson, a Euahlayi scholar from north-west NSW, have contributed to carceral criminology through their work on Indigeneity and prison masculinities. As well as noting the nature of 'invader masculinities' and how settler-colonial perceptions of Indigenous masculinities criminalise Indigenous peoples, Lockwood and Williamson (2022) trace the ways in which Indigenous peoples have been subjected to an extensive and pervasive system of social control. They also challenge traditional assumptions about the nature of masculinity and violence, demonstrating that the performance of masculinity in prisons is shaped by a complex set of factors (i.e., race, class, sexuality, and institutional power dynamics) which shape the everyday lives of both incarcerated men and prison staff. Using the concept of the 'carceral archipelago', the racialising and gendering logics of white 'invader masculinities' sees western ideals of hegemonic masculinity underpin institutional forms of control and the regulation of Indigenous bodies, both inside and outside of prison. By examining the social and cultural dimensions of prison life, Lockwood and Williamson shed light on the often overlooked human costs of incarceration, and further challenge the assumption that imprisonment is either an effective form of punishment or an effective means of attending to the underlying causes of crime. This enables Lockwood and Williamson to make unique Indigenous-centred contributions to arguments in favour of decarceration and prison abolition by drawing attention to Indigenous identities and masculinities which empower Indigenous men within themselves, their families, and their communities, thus undermining the dehumanising and pathologising logics which undergird 'invader masculinities'.

Barbara Nicholson, a writer, poet, and Elder of the Wadi Wadi people of the Illawarra region in NSW has collaborated with Elena Marchetti, an Italian-Australian legal scholar, to examine the use of 'culturally-safe creative writing programmes to empower and heal Aboriginal and Torres Strait Islander men in prison' (see Marchetti and Nicholson, 2020). Working with 30 Indigenous male prisoners participating in the 'Dreaming Inside: Voices from the Junee Correctional Centre' writing programme, Marchetti and Nicholson explored how poetry and storytelling can be a mode of empowerment, as well as offering therapeutic benefits whereby Indigenous men can express their thoughts and feelings. Moreover, the writing programme offered a culturally appropriate way for the men to improve their social and emotional wellbeing by attending to deep-rooted emotional trauma and grief. In exploring this programme, Marchetti and Nicholson further challenge hegemonic understandings of punishment and imprisonment for Aboriginal and Torres Strait Islander peoples.

In reviewing the 'Dreaming Inside' programme, Marchetti and Bargallie (2020: 515) argue that creating such culturally safe learning spaces in prisons means the ability to locate the experiences of the men 'firmly within the world of Aboriginality', thus creating a collective sense of cultural belonging wherein incarcerated Aboriginal men can '(re)connect with or reinforce their cultural identity' in ways that inspire them to 'choose a different pathway, both while they are in prison and once they are released' (2020: 515). Indeed, the Dreaming Inside programme adds further weight to research discussed earlier which demonstrates the importance of culturally specific, rather than generic, services and programmes. In this instance, such an approach has shown that a relationship between cultural identity, cultural engagement, and non-recidivism can be forged by disrupting 'the harmful and disempowering relationship between Aboriginal and Torres Strait Islander people and settler-colonial structures, of which the prison is a part' (Marchetti and Bargallie 2020: 515; see also Shepherd et al., 2018; Gee et al., 2014).

On First Nation and settler-colonial law

Megan Davis, a Cobble Cobble woman of the Barunggam nation in south-west Queensland, has made significant contributions to Aboriginal struggles for civil rights, social justice, and the right to self-determination in her role as a constitutional lawyer and public law expert. While advocating for Aboriginal peoples, Davis contends that liberal democratic governance and participation are enhanced when they engage Indigenous peoples' right to self-determination. Drawing on the 2017 and 2019 reports of the United Nations' 'Expert Mechanism on the Rights of Indigenous Peoples', Davis highlights examples in which various settler-colonial 'liberal democracies' are wrestling with questions similar to those in Australia, most notably in terms of how Indigenous voices can be better integrated into public institutions and democratic decision-making in ways that *satisfy* Indigenous peoples on their terms (see Tingle, 2022). As a member of the Expert Panel on Constitutional Recognition of Aboriginal and Torres Strait Islander Peoples, Davis has played a role in trying to temper the 'majoritarian tendency' of the Australian parliament (Tingle, 2022).

Indigenous scholars have also made vital contributions to what is commonly referred to as 'green criminology'. Irene Watson, for example, provides an Indigenous analysis of the social and political relations of climate breakdown. In doing so, Watson contends that 'The West has reached the endpoint of its progress project and does not have the solutions' to the existential environmental catastrophe that is staring us in the face (2022: 372). Moreover, Watson argues that First Nation laws and 'other-named environmental laws' do not have 'the capacity to protect the environments that are vital to our survival' (2022: 373). If the current situation is to be arrested, Watson believes that we will need to transgress western-centric universalism and the 'incommensurability' that exists between Indigenous and settler cultures. In making this claim, Watson calls for 'horizontal dialogue' so that we can imagine equitable power relations, 'shared authority', and 'the possibility of First Nations' voices being 'registered, heard and understood from a centred First Nations space' (2022: 372). That is to say, settler-colonial states must engage First Nations' perspectives on authority and power. As Watson explains, this is a longstanding practice rather than a novel idea. However, at this conjuncture, Aboriginal ways of being must be given parity. For Watson, climate justice can only be realised if the non-Indigenous world develops an ability to listen deeply, rather than symbolically and tokenistically, to the Indigenous world, as well as learning to reciprocate and share the responsibility for the existential crisis that we now face. This will require halting the 'ongoing colonialist progress trajectory' which prioritises 'progress at any cost' and 'has us set upon a track to global environmental destruction' (Watson, 2022: 373).

Summary

Throughout this section, we have focused on where Indigenous scholars, communities, and their collaborators have made critical contributions to core areas of criminological research: namely, questions of power, jurisdiction, violence (ranging from sexual violence to state violence), victimisation, harm, crime and criminality (including crimes of the state), policing, law, social order and control, deviance, punishment, deference, rehabilitation, and non-recidivism. In doing so, it is argued that Indigenous scholarship ought to be recognised as having played a pivotal part in developing temporally and spatially contingent criminological knowledge that is attentive to the structuring role played by institutional racism and ongoing settler-colonialism.

What is more, this section has further emphasised the role that disappearance, erasure (from genocide to 'juridicide'), connection, disconnection, and reconnection have played in the construction, maintenance, as well as Aboriginal and Torres Strait Islander resistance to, the social, cultural, and political contours of ongoing settler-colonialism. In terms of Indigenous resistance, the discussion above has drawn further attention to the way in which the settler-colonial power matrix seeks to disable the cultural ties and identities that exist, and intimately connect, Indigenous people to family, kin, community, and land. Here we have seen how Indigenous knowledge provides a critical basis for truth-telling, calls for Aboriginal sovereignty, and demands for cultural autonomy precisely because of the cultural safety and protection that this provides against harmful and enduring intergenerational experiences of coerced assimilation which only serves to disempower Aboriginal and Torres Strait Islander peoples and communities, while reinforcing whiteness and the hegemony of settler-colonial liberal democratic governance.

Lastly, this section has provided a limited, but important, overview of the depth of insight that can be gained from sincerely listening to the unique voice of Indigenous women. Indeed, the insights provided by Indigenous women must be epistemically positioned as essential to any attempt at fully comprehending the violence, disproportionate sentencing, and overrepresentation of Indigenous peoples throughout the Australian criminal justice system. In stark contradiction to the positivism of authoritarian and administrative criminology, the discussion here, once more, makes the case for accepting the epistemic validity of Indigenous-feminist-activist scholarship. Indeed, Indigenous women represent but one of many marginalised voices that can no longer be wilfully ignored in any serious and sincere attempt to democratise and realise epistemic justice in the field of criminology. From now on, surely any and all claims that it is difficult to locate Indigenous knowledge on core areas of criminological research ought to be met with the following response: 'You haven't been looking in the right place or you simply haven't been looking'!

Conclusion

In this chapter we have attempted to address the epistemic injustice which has seen Indigenous criminological scholarship bounded and domained in ways wherein Indigenous knowledge and experience have been marginalised within mainstream criminology. In doing so, we have sought to contribute to ongoing discussions as to how to decolonise criminology. More specifically, we have endeavoured to draw further attention to the legacies and ongoing injustices of coloniality and its intersection with other modes of domination (especially patriarchy) through a specific focus on how Aboriginal and Torres Strait

Islander peoples experience and theorise crime and criminal justice. However, as we stated at the outset, the ground we have covered here is just a small sample of Aboriginal and Torres Strait Islander contributions to criminological knowledge, never mind Indigenous contributions to criminology on other continents.

By calling into question the deep-seated precepts of the criminality of the 'Other', the defence of penal institutions, and the righteousness of universalising western methods we can imagine a different world. Failure to acknowledge the history of Indigenous knowledge production would be an act of neo-coloniality. It would represent an act of epistemic erasure which not only means that disciplinary decadence in the field of criminology is a very real and present danger but would also undermine Indigenous struggles in pursuit of civil and human rights, social justice, and sovereignty. If all this is to be avoided, it is vital that mainstream criminology looks beyond that gates and fences which control and permit entry to the field and further embraces interdisciplinarity and scholarly-activist work beyond the academy.

Acknowledgments

The authors would like to thank Krystal Lockwood for her generous contributions and insights during early discussions relating to themes, topics, studies, and Indigenous Australian knowledge producers included in this chapter.

References

Alcoff, L. M. (2007). 'Epistemologies of ignorance: Three types'. In Sullivan, S. and Tuana, N. (eds.), *Race and Epistemologies of Ignorance*. Albany: SUNY Press.

Anthony, T. and Davis, V. N. (2023). 'Alcohol bans and law and order responses to crime in Alice Springs haven't worked in the past, and won't work now', *The Conversation*. Available at: https://theconversation.com/alcohol-bans-and-law-and-order-responses-to-crime-in-alice-springs-havent-worked-in-the-past-and-wont-work-now-198427 (Accessed 28th June 2023).

Anthony, T., and Sherwood, J. (2018). 'Post-disciplinary responses to positivism's punitiveness', *Journal of Global Indigeneity*, 3 (1), 1–33.

Australian Institute of Aboriginal and Torres Strait Islander Studies (2020). *AIATSIS Code of Ethics for Aboriginal and Torres Strait Islander Research*. Canberra, ACT: Australian Institute of Aboriginal and Torres Strait Islander Studies.

Bacevic, J. (2021). 'Epistemic injustice and epistemic positioning: Towards an intersectional political economy', *Current Sociology*, 71 (6), 1–19.

Baker, A. and Lowman, E. B. (n.d.). 'Settler colonialism', *Global Social Theory*. Available at: https://globalsocialtheory.org/concepts/settler-colonialism/ (Accessed 28th June 2023).

Behrendt, L. (1993). 'Aboriginal women and the white lies of the feminist movement: Implications for Aboriginal women in rights discourse', *Australian Feminist Law Journal*, 1 (1), 27–44.

Behrendt, L. (2014). Innocence betrayed [Documentary]. Written by Behrendt, L. Directed by Behrendt, L., De Santolo, J., and Longman, C. Produced by Lavarch Productions. Ronin Films: National Indigenous Television.

Behrendt, L. (2019). 'A personal reflection on self-determining documentary filmmaking practice', *Artlink*. Available at: https://www.artlink.com.au/articles/4757/a-personal-reflection-on-self-determining-document/ (Accessed 28th June 2023).

Carlson, B. (2021). 'Data silence in the settler archive: Indigenous femicide, deathscapes and social media'. In Perera, S. and Pugliese, J. (eds.), *Mapping Deathscapes: Digital Geographies of Racial and Border Violence*. Abingdon, Oxon: Routledge.

Carlson, B., Day, M., and Farrelly, T. (2021). *What Works? Exploring the Literature on Aboriginal and Torres Strait Islander Healing Programs that Respond to Family Violence*. Sydney, NSW: Australia's National Research Organisation for Women's Safety.

Chaka, C., Shange, T., Ndlangamandla, S. C., and Mkhize, D. (2022). 'Situating some aspects of the scholarship of teaching and learning (SoTL) in South African higher education within southern theories', *Journal of Contemporary Issues in Education*, 17 (2), 6–24.

Cripps, K. A. (2011). 'Speaking up to the silences: Victorian Koori courts and the complexities of Indigenous family violence', *Indigenous Law Bulletin*, 7 (26), 31–34.

Cripps, K. A. (2012). 'Indigenous children's 'best interests' at the crossroads: Citizenship rights, Indigenous mothers and child protection authorities', *International Journal of Critical Indigenous Studies*, 5 (2), 25–35.

Cripps, K. A. and Habibis, D. (2019). 'Another stolen generation looms unless Indigenous women fleeing violence can find safe housing', *The Conversation*. Available at: https://theconversation.com/another-stolen-generation-looms-unless-indigenous-women-fleeing-violence-can-find-safe-housing-123526 (Accessed 28th June 2023).

Cripps, K. A. and Laurens, J. (2015). 'Protecting Indigenous children's familial and cultural connections: reflections on recent amendments to the Care and Protection Act 2007 (NT)', *Indigenous Law Bulletin*, 8 (17), 12–15.

Cripps, K. A. and McCreery, R. (2013). 'Indigenous engagement with the Royal Commission into institutional responses to child sexual abuse', *Indigenous Law Bulletin*, 8 (5), 22–25.

Cunneen, C. and Tauri, J. (2016) *Indigenous Criminology*. Bristol: Policy Press.

Davis, M. J. (2006). 'A culture of disrespect: Indigenous peoples and Australian public institutions', *University of Technology Sydney Law Review*, 9, 135–152.

Davis, M. J. (2009). 'Restorative justice in South Australia: An Indigenous Bill of Rights'. In Berg, S., Rigney, D., and Hemming, S. (eds.), *The Legal Implications of Letters Patent and Founding Documents Upon Aboriginal Land in the Colonisation of South Australia*. Cavendish: Routledge.

Davis, M. J. (2011). 'A reflection on the Royal Commission into Aboriginal deaths in custody and its consideration of Aboriginal women's issues', *Australian Indigenous Law Review*, 15 (1), 25–33.

Davis, M. J. (2016a). 'Constitutional reform in Australia: Recognition of Indigenous Australians and Reconciliation'. In Macklem, P. and Sanderson, D. (eds.), *From Reconciliation to Recognition: Essays on the Constitutional Entrenchment of Aboriginal and Treaty Rights*. Toronto: University of Toronto Press.

Davis, M. J. (2016b). 'Putting meat on the bones of the United Nations Declaration on the Rights of Indigenous Peoples'. In Esmaeili, H., Worby, G., and Tur, S. (eds.), *Indigenous Australians, Social Justice and Legal Reform: Honouring Elliott Johnston*. Annandale, NSW: Federation Press.

Davis, M. J. (2016c). 'Political timetables trump workable timetables: Indigenous constitutional recognition and the temptation of symbolism over substance'. In Young, S., Nielsen, J. and Patric, J. (eds.), *Constitutional Recognition of Australia's First Peoples Theories and Comparative Perspectives*. Leichhardt, NSW: Federation Press.

Davis, M. J. (2017a). 'Indigenous women and constitutional recognition'. In Irving, H. (ed.), *Constitutions and Gender*. Cheltenham: Edward Elgar Publishing.

Davis, M. J. (2017b). 'Self-determination and the right to be heard'. In Pearson, N. and Morris, S. (eds.) *A Rightful Place: A Roadmap to Recognition*. Melbourne: Melbourne University Publishing.

Day, M. and Carlson, B. (2023). 'Predators and perpetrators: White settler violence online'. In Callander, D., Farvid, P., Baradaran, A., and Vance, T. (eds.), *(Un)Desiring Whiteness: (Un)Doing Sexual Racism*. Oxford: Oxford University Press.

DesLandes, A., Longbottom, M., McKinnon, C., and Porter, A. (2022). 'White feminism and carceral industries: Strange bedfellows or partners in crime and criminology?', *Decolonization of Criminology and Justice*, 4 (2), 5–34.

Fricker, M. (2007). *Epistemic Injustice*. Oxford: Oxford University Press.

Gee, G., Dudgeon, P., Schultz, C., Hart, A., and Kelly, K. (2014). 'Aboriginal and Torres Strait Islander social and emotional wellbeing'. In Dudgeon, P., Milroy, H., and Walker, R. (eds.), *Working Together: Aboriginal and Torres Strait Islander Mental Health And Wellbeing Principles And Practice*. Canberra: Australian Government Department of the Prime Minister and Cabinet. Available at: https://www.telethonkids.org.au/globalassets/media/documents/aboriginal-health/working-together-second-edition/working-together-aboriginal-and-wellbeing-2014.pdf (Accessed 28th June 2023).

George, L., Te Ata o Tu MacDonald, L., and Tauri, J. (2020). *Indigenous Research Ethics: Claiming Research Sovereignty Beyond Deficit and the Colonial Legacy*, Volume 6. Bingley: Emerald Publishing.

Gordon, L. R. (2015). *Disciplinary Decadence: Living Thought in Trying Times*. New York: Routledge.

Langton, M., Smith, K., Eastman, T., O'Neill, L., Cheesman, E., and Rose, M. (2020). 'Family violence policies, legislation and services: improving access and suitability for Aboriginal and Torres Strait Islander men (Research report, 26/2020)'. Canberra: Australia's National Research Organisation for Women's Safety.

Lockwood, K. and Williamson, B. (2022). 'The shackles of masculinity: Indigenous men, settler colonialism, and the carceral archipelago'. In Bartlett, T. and Rosemary, R. (eds.), *Prison Masculinities: International Perspectives and Interpretations*. Abingdon, Oxon: Routledge.

Longbottom, M. A. (2019). 'Balwalwanga bhulungs: We are strong women'. PhD Thesis: University of Newcastle.

Longbottom, M. (2021). 'Submission to the Commission inquiry into Queensland Police Service response to domestic and family violence'. State of Queensland: Parliament of Queensland. Available at: https://www.qpsdfvinquiry.qld.gov.au/public-hearings.aspx (Accessed 28th June 2023).

Longbottom, M. and Porter, A. (2021). 'Submission to the Women's Safety and Justice Taskforce: Discussion Paper 1 – Options for legislating against coercive control and the creation of a standalone domestic violence offence'. Queensland Government: Women's Safety and Justice Taskforce. Available at: https://www.womenstaskforce.qld.gov.au/__data/assets/pdf_file/0009/691218/wsjt-submission-dr-marlene-longbottom-and-dr-amanda-porter-university-of-wollongong-and-university-of-melbourne.pdf (Accessed 28th June 2023).

Marchetti, E. and Bargallie, D. (2020). 'Life as an Australian Aboriginal and Torres Strait Islander male prisoner: poems of grief, trauma, hope, and resistance', *Canadian Journal of Law and Society*, 35 (3), 499–519.

Marchetti, E. and Nicholson, B. (2020). 'Using a culturally safe creative writing programme to empower and heal Aboriginal and Torres Strait Islander men in prison', *The Howard Journal of Criminal Justice*, 59 (4), 423–441.

McGlade, H. (2019). 'Australia is turning a blind eye to violence against Indigenous women, but we will not stay silent – our lives matter', *ABCNews*. Available at: https://www.abc.net.au/news/2019-10-06/jodygore-release-domestic-violence-indigenous-aboriginal-women/11570042 (Accessed 28th June 2023).

McGlade, H. and Tarrant, S. (2021). 'Say her name: naming Aboriginal women in the justice system'. In Perera, S. and Pugliese, J. (eds.), *Mapping Deathscapes: Digital Geographies of Racial and Border Violence*. Abingdon, Oxon: Routledge.

McQuire, A. (2016). 'If you think Aboriginal women are silent about domestic violence, you're not listening', *The Guardian*. Available at: https://www.theguardian.com/commentisfree/2016/oct/05/if-you-think-aboriginal-women-are-silent-about-domestic-violence-youre-not-listening (Accessed 28th June 2023).

McQuire, A. (2018) 'We can't dismantle systems of violence unless we centre Aboriginal women', *Indigenous X*. Available at: https://indigenousx.com.au/we-cant-dismantle-systems-of-violence-unless-we-centre-aboriginal-women/unless we centre Aboriginal women – IndigenousX (Accessed 18th October 2023).

McQuire, A. (2021a). *Black Witness: The Power of Indigenous Media*. Queensland: University of Queensland Press.

McQuire, A. (2021b). 'Forty years in an unmarked grave: Family of murdered woman Queenie Hart fight to bring her home', *The Guardian*. Available at: https://www.theguardian.com/australia-news/2021/jul/03/forty-years-in-an-unmarked-grave-family-of-murdered-woman-queenie-hart-fight-to-bring-her-home (Accessed 28th June 2023).

McQuire, A. and McGrady, K. (2018). 'The families of the murdered Bowraville children have waited too long for justice', *The Guardian*. Available at: https://www.theguardian.com/commentisfree/2018/jul/07/the-families-of-the-murdered-bowraville-children-have-waited-too-long-for-justice (Accessed 28th June 2023).

McQuire, A., Watego, C., Singh, D., and Strakosch, E. (2023). 'What happened to the Senate inquiry into missing and murdered Indigenous women?', *The Conversation*. Available at: https://theconversation.com/what-happened-to-the-senate-inquiry-into-missing-and-murdered-indigenous-women-201755 (Accessed 28th June 2023).

Mignolo, W. D. (2018). 'The invention of the human and the three pillars of the colonial matrix of power: racism, sexism and nature'. In Mignolo, W. D. and Walsh, C. E. (eds.), *On Decoloniality: Concepts, Analytics, Praxis*. Durham: Duke University Press.

Mills, C. (1997). *The Racial Contract*. Ithaca, New York: Cornell University Press.

Mills, C. (2007). 'White ignorance'. In Sullivan, S. and Tuana, N. (eds.), *Race and Epistemologies of Ignorance*. Albany: SUNY Press.

Pohlhaus, G. (2012). 'Relational knowing and epistemic justice: Toward a theory of willful hermeneutical ignorance'. *Hypatia* 27 (4): 715–735.

Porter, A. (2016). 'Decolonizing policing: Indigenous patrols, counter-policing and safety', *Theoretical Criminology*, 20 (4), 548–565.

Porter, A. (2019). 'Aboriginal sovereignty, 'crime' and criminology', *Current Issues in Criminal Justice*, 31(1), 122–142.

Shepherd, S., Delgado, R. H., Sherwood, J., and Paradies, Y. (2018). 'The impact of Indigenous cultural identity and cultural engagement on violent offending', *BMC Public Health*, 18 (50), 1–7.

Smith, L. T. (2012). *Decolonizing Methodologies: Research and Indigenous Peoples*, second edition. London: Zed Books.

Tauri, J. M. (2013). 'Indigenous critique of authoritarian criminology'. In Carrington, K., Ball, M., O'Brien, E., and Tauri, J. M. (eds.), *Crime, Justice and Social Democracy: International Perspectives*. Basingstoke: Palgrave Macmillan.

Tauri, J. M. (2018). 'Editorial note for the special edition – decolonising criminal justice: Indigenous perspectives on social harm, journal of global Indigeneity', *Journal of Global Indigeneity*, 3 (1), 1–6.

Tauri, J. M. and Porou, N. (2014). 'Criminal justice as a colonial project in settler-colonialism', *African Journal of Criminology and Justice Studies*, 8 (1), 20–37.

Tingle, L. (2022). 'Why Megan Davis remains optimistic about a Voice to Parliament', *ABCNews*. Available at: https://www.abc.net.au/news/2022-12-21/why-megan-davis-remains-optimistic-about-a-voice/101799550 (Accessed 28th June 2023).

Wacquant, L. (2000). 'Class, race and hyperincarceration in revanchist America', *Daedalus*, 139 (3), 74–90.

Watson, I. (2014). *Aboriginal Peoples, Colonialism and International Law: Raw Law*. Abingdon, Oxon: Routledge.

Watson, I. (2022). 'Inter-nation relationships and the natural world as relation'. In Natarajan, U. and Dehm, J. (eds.), *Locating Nature: Making and Unmaking International Law*. Cambridge: Cambridge University Press.

Watson, N. (2021). *Aboriginal Women, Law and Critical Race Theory: Storytelling from The Margins*. Basingstoke: Palgrave Macmillan.

Watson, N. and Douglas, H. (eds.) (2021). *Indigenous Legal Judgments: Bringing Indigenous Voices into Judicial Decision Making*. Abingdon, Oxon: Routledge.

Whittaker, A. (2018). *Blakwork*. Broome: Magabala Books.

Whittaker, A. (2020). 'Dragged like a dead kangaroo': Why language matters for deaths in custody', *The Guardian*. Available at: https://www.theguardian.com/commentisfree/2018/sep/07/dragged-like-a-dead-kangaroo-why-language-matters-for-deaths-in-custody (Accessed 28th June 2023).

4
RACIALISED YOUNG WOMEN AMID THE EVERYDAY STIGMATISATION OF THE 'ANGLO-NEGROID' FAMILY IN INTERWAR BRITAIN

A Decolonial Perspective

Esmorie Miller

Young women and the racialised family in British interwar youth penal reform: a case study

> All the circumstances of their lives tend to give undue prominence to sex; owing to the nature of the houses in which they live their moral standards are extraordinarily low, and owing to the persistence of the men it is practically impossible for coloured girls to remain pure even should they desire to do so. The methods by which coloured girls are obliged to obtain clothing and finery were freely discussed in the neighbourhood, and those mothers of a better type regretted the fact that they had brought these children in the world handicapped by their colour
>
> *(Fletcher, 1930: 34).*

> From her mother the half-caste girl is liable to inherit a certain slackness, and from her father a happy go lucky attitude towards life. She has not therefore much incentive to work, and from an early age knows that she will have no difficulty in finding someone to keep her. Even if they find work therefore the majority of coloured girls have no hesitation in throwing it up on the slightest provocation
>
> *(Fletcher, 1930: 34).*

In 1930 social worker and ethnographer Muriel Fletcher published the report titled 'An Investigation into the Colour Problem in Liverpool and Other Ports' (hereafter the Fletcher Report or the Report). It forewarned interwar Britain of an emerging race problem (Christian, 2008, 1998). Against the backdrop of these histories, expanded presently, this chapter explores the relationship between racial stigmatisation and gendered penalty in interwar British youth penal reform.

DOI: 10.4324/9781003260967-5

This is a correlate of the epistemic inequality epitomised by what is explored in this chapter as the Report's concomitant colonial knowledge development process. To explore this link the chapter adapts the decolonial perspective of philosopher and poet wa Thiong'o (2018, 2005 [1986]) about colonialism's totalising harms on the mind, body, and wider community of the colonised. This is a logic asserting the centrality of penalty (and its cognate exclusion), underpinning modernity's purported spread of neutrality, proportionality, and rationality. This logic asserts an understanding of penalty beyond criminology's putative associations between racialised peoples, crime, criminality, and the carceral estate. The logic, instead, draws attention to the roots of racialised penalty as criminalisation and deviance invention, a correlate of everyday stigmatisation – and an outcome of entrenched colonial ideals and practice.

The Black, racialised young women referenced in the opening quotations as 'coloured girls' populate Fletcher's findings. The Report introduced the purported colour problem, starting with interest in the plight of the so-called coloured children held by anthropologist Rachel Fleming of the University College Wales, Aberystwyth. Fleming, who had become 'impressed by the unhappy conditions of their life and the dismal character of their prospects' had engaged with schools in the south end of the city (Liverpool) to measure the development of the so-called 'half-caste' children (Fletcher, 1930: 5). Fleming, having involved Fletcher, engaged numerous public officials she believed could support these youth's employment prospects, inaugurating the Liverpool Association for the Welfare of Half-Caste Children. A sub-committee was formed, and funds were raised to support its work, including employing Fletcher 'to make a full survey and to explore both the nature of the problem and the possible solutions for it' (Fletcher, 1930: 5). Historian Laura Tabili's (1994: 60) analysis on the construction of race in early 20th century Britain has relevance here. At various historic points, the term Black included 'Africans and West Indians, South Asians such as Burmese and Indians, Arabs, and people of mixed race'. However, my characterisation relies on Fletcher's use of the term. In the opening quotations, she is speaking of men of African heritage, the white women who married them, and their progeny. Fletcher placed this category of family at the bottom of racial hierarchies constructed during this time. (See Miller, 2022 for the origins of the analysis on which this chapter relies).

Trained in the Liverpool School of Social Science, Fletcher's research 'extended over two years' and was described as one with 'acumen, tact, and sympathy' despite what was correspondingly a 'depressing and insidious task' (Fletcher, 1930: 6). Evidently neither the Anglo-Chinese, the Anglo-Lascar, or the other mixed-Anglo youth, represented the purported 'colour problem' Fletcher associated with Anglo-African young people. Therefore, 'attention was concentrated on the Anglo-Negroid population' particularly the 'Anglo-Negroid girls' characterised as 'hopeless' in their prospects 'from the time they leave school' (Fletcher, 1930: 6). Specifying need for a 'special welfare worker' for 'Anglo-Negroid children' the Report decried uniquely 'deplorable environmental' and 'systemic' issues faced by these youth's families, including 'the total exclusion of negro labour on ships entering port' (Fletcher, 1930: 6).

The Report's first chapter, titled 'History of the Colour Problem in Liverpool', details the wider origins of the so-called race problem. Here, the origins are linked to the employment of 'coloured seamen' on ships sailing between Liverpool and the African West Coast. Fletcher reported this practice to be 60 years old, with the subsequent 25 years seeing West Africans exclusively replacing white workers (who commanded higher wagers). The end of the First World War, according to Fletcher, saw 'a large number of West Africans and West Indians' demobilised and populating port cities like Liverpool. It was said that 'antagonism' emerged, within the white population, due to 'post-war trade depression' and the 'unions … formed between white women and coloured men' (Fletcher, 1930: 7). This culminated in the 1919 riots, which saw crowds of 2,000 to 10,000 rampaging around Liverpool, between May and June. Influenced by these tensions, in 1925 the Coloured Alien Seamen Order was passed, an Act limiting 'coloured' men's entry into the UK, despite many having British passports. Concerned and unsure about the exact size and scale of the purported 'Negroid' colour problem, it was deemed 'necessary to collect information … from social agencies who have contact with the coloured man and his family' (Fletcher, 1930: 9). After a process eliminating mixed-race families of [Anglo] Italian and Spanish heritage, Fletcher tallied 450 Anglo-Negroid families in interwar Liverpool.

The case study of racialised young women in interwar Liverpool aligns with contemporary criminological appeals for greater epistemic equalisation (Blagg and Anthony, 2019). Characterised by efforts to understand the putative relationship between race and punishment, this includes the potential for minority (Phillips and Bowling, 2003) and decolonial (Seal, 2021; Choak, 2020) perspectives, to enable and prioritise the oft-overlooked gendered account of such concerns. The chapter uses decolonial concerns with the relationship between epistemic inequality and penalty to give a formative account at the intersection of race, gender, and youth.

Decolonial scholarship emphasises the correspondence between the dominance of knowledge development, public discourse, and peneality (Smith, 2021 [1999]; Posholi, 2020; wa Thiong'o, 2018, 2005 [1986]; Fanon, 1967). Following wa Thiong'o's characterisation of language as an instrument of colonial domination, the chapter posits that Fletcher's characterisation of racialised young women as sexually transgressive is far from benign. Both opening quotations allow consideration of how stigmatisation begins with labelling the racialised family unfit for purpose and, as is argued in the analysis, has the wider punitive effect of placing the progeny at a moral impasse (Valverde, 2006). Notions of a moral impasse speak to a categorisation rationalising the exclusion of so-called Anglo-Negroid young women from the considerations of care and welfare informing nascent interwar youth penal reform ethos (Miller, 2022). Extant scholarship of the interwar period following the deviance invention logic demonstrates a similar relationship, but through the lens of class and gender (Ward, 2012; Shore, 2011, 2003; Magarey, 1978; Platt, 1969a, 1969b). Black British racialised youth's plight during this period remains hidden in criminological scholarship, despite the rich histories of these youth and their families (Bland, 2005; Tabili, 1994). The chapter, therefore, does the important task of writing race into interwar criminological histories, responding to contemporary scholarship decrying British criminological 'amnesia' regarding Black British history (Phillips et al., 2019: 13; Choak, 2020; see also Miller, 2023 2022). The logic of the wider punitive effect reflects my original contribution, starting with writing race into British interwar youth penal reform history. Ultimately, the wider punitive logic does what decolonisation exhorts, seeking to expand the orthodox criminological understanding of penalty by offering a vocabulary for interpreting the relationship between epistemic (marginality) domination, the active process of racial stigmatisation, and penalty.

The chapter is structured in four parts. Section one comprises the methodology grounding the logic of the wider punitive contribution. Defined in accordance with the decolonial perspective, this logic structures the expanded notion of penalty the chapter endorses. According to this logic, (contemporary) concerns with the amplification and racialisation of punishment in Britain could benefit from an expanded understanding which centres hidden racial histories. This is a focus beyond concerns with the widespread extremes of punishment (disseminated in term of disproportionate incarceration) typically populating contemporary criminological scholarships. Located within British interwar youth penal reform histories, this expanded understanding of penalty is characterised as a development that is (a) more widespread than incarceration, and (b) synonymous with racialised youth's exclusion from those resources and opportunities identified by reformers as key for actualising youth's transformative potential. Section two features interwar British youth penal reform: funded as an academic piece of social inquiry, the Fletcher Report draws attention to the everyday colonial trajectories informing interwar British youth reform. Coloniality, thus, can be understood as a phenomenon coterminous with burgeoning modern institutions like youth justice. Emphasis is placed on the punitive role of stigma in everyday life; this is a crucial emphasis given reformers' repudiation of punishment and their prioritisation of everyday cross-institutional support.

While section two contextualises the colonial logics shaping Fletcher's study, section three demonstrates criminology's complicity, consistent with the epistemic domination and stigmatisation in which interwar reformers are implicated. Consistent with narratives encouraging minority and decolonial perspectives, conceptual approaches like the wider punitive logic offer an opportunity to expand how penalty is understood. Therefore, this focus on criminology's complicity is useful for reinforcing the proliferation of everyday penalties for the racialised. Here, the idea of criminology as a science (Agozino, 2004) also helps realise the legitimacy and power built into the efforts of Fletcher and her superbly influential associates.

Section four, the final part, details the logic of the wider punitive effect, the decolonial informed account offering a vocabulary for the more expanded understanding of punishment this chapter explores. The wider punitive logic develops from my previous work (Miller, 2022). The case study concretises efforts to expand this logic, using the representation of Fletcher's racialised young women to demonstrate the wider punitive relationship between a loss of control over one's narrative, everyday stigmatisation, and the punitive effect of what it means to be placed at a moral impasse.

Methodology: writing gendered, racial exclusion into interwar British penal reform

The chapter, in adopting the decolonial lens, relies on three main data sources. The analysis draws on historical documentary sources, enabling the exploration of race in interwar British youth penal reform. Documents comprise the Fletcher Report (1930), the Liverpool University Settlement records (1913–1937), and the digitised catalogue of the *Eugenics Review* (1909–1968), a journal discredited for the pseudoscience it disseminated. Historical documents enable the assessment of race in interwar youth penal reform, including the narratives labelling the racialised family unfit – a labelling with the wider punitive effect of stigmatising their progeny. According to Fletcher (1930: 38):

> The problem of the half-caste child is a serious one, and it appears to be growing in most of our towns. The coloured families have a low standard of life, morally and economically. It is practically impossible for half-caste children to be absorbed into our standard industrial life and this leads to grave moral results, particularly in the case of the girls. The white women themselves mostly regret their marriage with a coloured man and their general standard of life is usually permanently lowered.

Settlement records hold similar findings enabling us to demonstrate the epistemic routes by which racialised youth were represented as intractable, placed outside the redemptive scope identified by the interventionist reform regime as the salvation for the white, working-class youth (Miller, 2022). Settlements were a crucial part of the interventionist reform machinery, acting as both conceptual and physical spaces, for reform efforts nationwide. Conceptually, Settlements served as spaces of intellectual development, conveying the epistemological authority legitimising reform efforts. Participants like Fletcher, Fleming, and the cohort of reformers with whom they associated helped shape the understanding of Britain as progressive, reflecting the modern efforts to implement Enlightenment ideals, including universal equality. Physically, Settlements offered definitive opportunities for participation, enabling the deprived communities, youth, and families on whom they intervened to escape from their dire constraints of poverty.

The latter source, the *Eugenics Review*, is a historic journal steeped in biological determinism, whose contributors formed the power base informing modern institutional development (Christian, 2008, 1998). This is a crucial detail. It is these pseudoscientific logics which ground the rationalisation of powerful ideological categories steeped in racial, gendered, and class differentiations. Scholars of race, for instance, draw attention to the gendered derogation sustained despite the neutrality, coterminous with those powerful ideological binaries constituting the contemporary social arrangement: white/other; male/female; normal/deviant; insider/outsider; superior/inferior; good/bad (da Silva, 2007; Hills-Collins, 2000; Featherstone, 1994; Walby, 1990).

Aligning with a decolonial logic, the method of analysis adopts wa Thiong'o's critical linguistic insights on the role of colonial epistemologies in the contemporary struggles of post-colonial subjects. This approach identifies the historical origins of dominant meanings responsible for placing individuals and groups according to powerful ideological categories, as noted earlier in this chapter. These categories are sustained by embedded trajectories of knowledge development. Within this context, Black feminist critique reveals the intersecting racial, gendered character of such derogation, emphasising the oppositional placement of racialised women, by white, western-dominated mainstream feminism and male-dominated antiracist movements (Hills-Collins and Bilge, 2020; Hills-Collins, 2000; Crenshaw, 2013, 1991, 1989; Dube, 2000). From the perspective of those like wa Thiong'o, the compounding androcentrism and Eurocentrism sustaining derogations is a crucial signifier of epistemic inequality (Agozino, 2004, 2003; Cohen, 1986). Arguably, it is these differentiations contemporary scholars critique as colonial continuities of epistemic marginality.

British interwar youth penal reform politics: epistemic domination, racial stigmatisation, and penalty

The racialised young women in Fletcher's report offer an opportunity to interrogate the relationship between epistemic domination, everyday racial stigmatisation, and penalty. This perspective adheres to the decolonial logics on the brutality that control (or loss) of language can occasion. The outline of the report's socio-political backdrop is therefore presented here as a space steeped in an ethos scholars identify as colonial (Hobsbawm, 1989). Historian Eric Hobsbawm's (1989) characterisation of the *Age of Empire* signifies the synonymity between imperialism and modern development. In taking us up to the interwar period, Hobsbawm's characterisation allows insight into the coloniality in which this period is grounded. Scholars (Bruno-Jofré and Stafford, 2020) identify nascent institutional development like educational reform during this period as colonial projects. Driving burgeoning decolonial logics was 'Colonial instruction [which] relied on developments in Europe and the United States [and Japan] [the modern colonial powers] in terms of methods and various motivations behind the extension of schooling to large segments of the population' (Bruno-Jofré and Stafford, 2020: 7). Consistent with Smith (2021 [1999]), this implicates methodologies as part and parcel of coloniality. Like the deviance invention framework, decolonial logics foreground the centrality of penalty to the emerging modern institutional development. Decolonial thinking, however, allows room for understanding youth penal reform through the lens of race and gender. The deviance invention scholarship typically shaping our understanding of youth in the context of interwar penal reform has, after all, been race blind.

The deficit characterisation of racialised young women as sexually transgressive in Fletcher's report reflects British interwar youth penal reform politics. Indeed, this chapter's analysis builds on recent publications by this author emphasising the need to critically explore how interwar youth penal reform politics shaped an intersecting racial, gendered marginalisation (Miller, 2022, 2023). As a starting point, the interwar era marks an important period for defining Britain as a modern, socially progressive society (Bradley, 2008). The case study details the report's role as constitutive of that process. Central to interwar modernisation were the epistemological processes informing Fletcher's commission to investigate and map the plight of those in need of resources and opportunities. Settlements were key to this. Indeed, in 1913 the opening of the Liverpool University Settlement was overseen by the Archbishop of York. Historian Kate Bradley (2008) emphasises the national mandate of Settlements, established across Britain, as prototypes for modern child welfare. In leading the discourse about citizenship, they aimed to make deprived urban youth good citizens. Of the Liverpool University Settlement, one observer described Fletcher, Fleming, and their cohort as 'Men and women that care for their country, their city, or their fellow men of lower fortune' (Marquis, 1913: 1). Meanwhile, recipients of Settlement philanthropy were described as those 'herded in destitution, inarticulate and incomprehensible [who] pose a real danger to society' (Marquis, 1913: 1). The purported dangerousness of the inarticulate, destitute urban hordes was to be mitigated through an interventionist regime supporting both policy and practice towards good citizenship. That philanthropic activities were part and parcel of everyday life is important for comprehending the punitive implications of being excluded. To be excluded within this context is to be denied access to resources and opportunities – effectively denied access to one's transformative potential (Miller, 2022).

A critical interdisciplinary scholarship identifies poor working-class family structures as primary sites for intervention (Mahood, 1995; Hendrick, 1994; Bailey, 1987; Donzelot, 1979). Sociologist Jacques Donzelot's (1979) analysis on the policing of the working-class family broke ground for the critical lens it shone on wider philanthropic history to which Settlement efforts are indelibly linked (Miller, 2015). Donzelot, and others like Mahood (1995), reinforce the Foucauldian (Foucault, 1975, 1973) claim regarding the nefarious dispersal of power, occasioned through nascent modernising social institutions (Miller, 2015). The Fletcher Report shows this dispersal, as noted in the cross-section of officials engaged with Settlements, including the anthropologist, the social-worker-ethnographic-researcher, the archbishop, and others like police chiefs and school superintendents, all of whom comprise Bradley's (2008: 134) description of 'a constellation of reformers and child activists in child welfare'. Crucially, the deviance invention scholarship interrogates this intervention by this constellation as constitutive of how working-class families and their offspring were labelled in and out of respectability (Ward, 2012; Shore, 2011, 2003; Magarey, 1978 Platt, 1969a, 1969b).

Central to this chapter is the juxtapositioning of the interwar British racialised family and their progeny amongst the asserted slovenly, inarticulate, incomprehensible hordes. Scholars like Smith's (2021 [1999]) identification of the stigmatisation of racialised, Indigenous families in contexts like Australia and New Zealand speak to the universality of colonial ideals and practice. Recall Hobsbawm's characterisation of 'the Age of Empire'. Recall, also, the understanding that the Age of Empire speaks to the domination of the vast majority by a select few, including what wa Thiong'o terms the brutality of cultural and linguistic erasures. These modes of domination are key to Smith's analysis of the domination Indigenous families and their children experienced. Smith, indeed, proposes research itself as something historically grubby, identifying a nefarious process whereby the Indigenous families in colonised contexts like Australia and New Zealand were defined out of their humanity.

Smith (2021 [1999]) implicates the research processes of colonisers in historically defining Indigenous families unfit to raise children – unfit for purpose. Here Smith's take, in capturing the widespread character of research, also captures the widespread character of penalty. Indigenous peoples were, for instance, rendered powerless as their offspring were forcibly removed and adopted to white families, whose language and culture were upheld as standard, modern, and progressive. Similar policies were witnessed globally, as in the Canadian context, where religious institutions, including the Catholic and Anglican Churches, forcibly removed Indigenous youth from their families, housing them in Residential Schools with the aim to make them white (Macdonald, 2016). Here whiteness denotes one of those powerful ideological categories synonymous with a normal, modern, acceptable insider.

Smith's (2021 [1999]) exposition of these concerns sits alongside a critical interdisciplinary canon of logics exposing the link between colonialism, knowledge development, and exclusion (Anthony et al., 2020; Blagg and Anthony, 2019; Agozino, 2004, 2003). Smith's call for the recentring of Indigenous knowledges, to counter continuities of colonial methodologies in contexts like Australia and New Zealand, reverberates in related appeals in the British context. Fletcher's report demonstrates this wider socio-political reach. As Fletcher notes, 'The white women themselves mostly regret their marriage with a coloured man and their general standard of life is usually permanently lowered' (Fletcher, 1930: 38). Viewed through the post-colonial lens, it is argued here that the racialised youth, particularly the young women on whom the analysis is focused, were written out as the normal recipients of welfare and care. Consider what it means to be deemed permanently lowered, during a conversation emphasising the possibilities for redeeming youth itself – for enabling good citizens. Fletcher (1930: 38), indeed declared it 'practically impossible for half-caste children to be absorbed into our standard industrial life and this leads to grave moral results, particularly in the case of the girls'. I have previously defined this exclusion as something synonymous with penalty, emphasising how exclusion considered in concrete terms as denial of access to resources and opportunities for citizenship, including social acceptance, is necessarily experienced punitively (Miller, 2022). The next step is to outline criminology's complicit positioning as a science within this history of epistemic inequality.

Black, post-colonial feminist criminology: race, gender, and criminological complicity

Emphasising the role of epistemic inequality in shaping marginality is key to the decolonial logic informing this chapter's analysis. The case study of racialised young women in interwar Britain exposes the multi-layered character of epistemic inequality – layers made evident by the decolonial lens as will presently become clear. First, extant post-colonial scholarships calling for expanded minority perspectives, for instance, expose criminology's complicity in epistemic inequality. Biko Agozino's (2004: 346) argument that 'Europe discovered the new "science" of criminology as a tool to aid the control of the Other' places the discipline within this important wider trajectory of global social, political, and economic transformation. Criminology's role, consistent with Agozino's (2004) larger claim, was key to this, overseeing an 'advancement on classicist philosophies of justice'. Here, criminology's complicity in epistemic inequality oversaw the institutionalisation of universal ideals of progress, including those promulgating notions of a nascent Age of Reason – rationality, neutrality, and proportionality. Therefore, while those like Fletcher and Fleming deployed particular practices within poor communities, these practices can be traced back to ideals birthed in an age of reason for which criminology can be attributed scientific responsibility (Agozino, 2004).

Feminist scholarships expose a gendered element to criminology's complicity in epistemic inequality. Feminist critique, for instance, commenced with decentring presumptions of a neutral modern arrangement (Hills-Collins, 2000; Crenshaw, 2013, 1991, 1989; Featherstone, 1994; Smart, 2013, 1977). Here neutrality implies impartiality in law, signifying equal access to resources and opportunities, including the classicist agenda to support universal rationality and proportionality ahead of bias and brutality (Bell, 2018, 2004, 1980). The established canon capturing this research notes criminology to be biased, favouring a vocabulary such as andro-centrism and malestream. Indeed, feminist scholars like Freda Adler (1975) decry criminology's historic gendering of knowledge production, problematising criminology's formative prioritisation of men as the normal subjects of inquiry.

Latterly, scholarship assessing an ostensible gender crime gap exposes a key example of criminology's complicity in gendering epistemic inequality. Examples include feminist criminological explorations of how women's deviance was recorded as psychiatric while men's was deemed criminal (Gelsthorpe and Sharpe, 2015; Adler, 1975). Far from being an advantage, this oppositional positioning contributes to both the invisibility and distortion of women's concerns, including their victimisation and consequential denial of access to justice (Watson, 2021; Choak, 2020). Anita Gibbs and Fairleigh Gilmour's (2022) recent collections speak to the historic continuities of gendered violence among families in Australia and New Zealand. Among the key concerns is that despite prominent campaigns about the prevalence of violence against women and girls (VAWG), including #MeToo era shifts in discourses, 'There is limited evidence of progress' (Gibbs and Gilmour, 2022: 1). Concerns with criminology's complicity, particularly the romanticisation of men's role in crime as both natural and normal, can be understood against the backdrop of logics in feminist scholarship. To romanticise men's criminality, for instance, is to ignore victims (Gibbs and Gilmour, 2022). Similarly, to normalise the criminal as a male is to prioritise concern with individual behaviour and to ignore the role of structural inequality (Britton, 2000).

The decolonial lens invites racial specificity within these wider contemporary mainstream feminist concerns with epistemic inequality. Black feminists, for instance, draw attention to a distinct position of exclusion, understood as an intersection between race and gender (Crenshaw, 1991, 2013). This chapter thus explores the race and gender specificity subsumed within the initial exposé of criminology's formative epistemic inequality. This takes the discussion to the second layer of complicity implicated in epistemic inequality. Adler's perspective on African American women is a good example of this. In identifying criminology's tendency to favour men's issues over women's, Adler also admonishes criminology's male centric-ness as a romanticisation of male deviance, implicating this in ignoring victimhood. Interestingly, however, despite Adler's critical takedown of the orthodoxy, her efforts expose its own romanticisation of crime itself, as she links the high rates of punishment among African American women to what she categorises as their purportedly more liberated positioning. In taking African American women's exposure to punishment as a signifier of their liberation, Adler reveals the limits of mainstream feminism in explaining the link between race and punishment introduced earlier. For the white, western women at the centre of Adler's analysis, an increase in their rate of punishment would signify increased liberation, according to Adler. In this scenario, African American women are positioned as Robin Hood – praised for a presumed rebellion, as all the while Adler subsumes the structural concerns against which this purported rebellion is levelled. This is the seat of romanticisation the decolonial perspective exposes and seeks to move beyond. A key claim here is that while concerns with epistemic inequality are apparent in critical feminist concerns, the romanticisation of punishment distorts and subverts the role of inequality; this is to say, crime and punishment are disconnected from the broader processes of structural inequality decolonial scholars identify. Indeed, Crenshaw's warning of the hypervisibility paradox in which Black women find themselves has relevance here; for Crenshaw, hypervisibility speaks to the loss of control over the narratives representing oneself. The racialised women in both Fletcher's and Adler's accounts epitomise this loss, speaking to how representations of their stories distort their circumstances of inequality – leaving them vulnerable to stigma and exclusion.

Criminologist Lizzie Seal's (2021: 14) recent work on the intersection between gender, crime, and justice is one way to distinguish between knowledge development centred around equality and inclusion. Indeed, according to Seal, a key role for feminist criminology is to interrogate the 'ways colonialism continues to shape approaches to crime and punishment in the present'. Similar works emphasise the relationship between penalty and epistemic inequality with which this chapter is concerned (Britton, 2000). In this way, the ethos informing historic Settlement philanthropic efforts, including Fletcher's investigation, is attributed to clearer origins in this chapter. Notions about what it means to be modern and progressive in interwar Britain can thus be understood as an advancement of classical concerns with neutrality, rationality, and proportionality. In the absence or marginalisation of minority perspectives, however, notions of neutrality, rationality, and proportionality can be tailored, paradoxically, to rationalise exclusion instead of the universalisation of equality these ideas purport to support. Placing Fletcher's analysis of racialised young women within the context of this logic enables this expanded assessment. This concerns how ideas form meanings, which impacts the individuals' positioning within the broader social sphere once ideas disperse and take root.

Thus, the decolonial lens aims to, (a) contribute something consistent with deviance invention by, (b) unearthing and centring racialised young women in interwar British penal reform through a decolonial explanatory scope.

The wider punitive effect: writing gendered, racial penalty into interwar youth British penal reform

> Although the relations between white and half-caste children in the schools are quite friendly, the coloured children begin to feel outcast almost as soon as they leave school, and this feeling develops very rapidly. Conscious of their colour handicap they withdraw from organizations existing for white juveniles
>
> *(Fletcher, 1930: 31).*

> It is a peculiar sensation, this double consciousness, this sense of always looking at one's self through the eyes of others, of measuring one's soul by the tape of a world that looks on in amused contempt and pity
>
> *(Du Bois et al., 1903: 8).*

My recent book explores the relationship between race and punishment in England (and Wales) (Miller, 2022). The book's analysis introduced a concept called the wider punitive effect, specifying a vocabulary for defining a more expanded understanding of the relationship between race and punishment. The wider punitive logic considers penalty more widespread than incarceration, detailing it as something synonymous with exclusion from lenience, proportionality, and care. The book looks at this as an outcome of the contemporary association between race and deviance, amidst the acknowledged racialisation of punishment. In the contemporary, stigmatising 'ideas disseminated from the institutional level are adopted and adapted by the wider public who, having witnessed the customary normalization of punishment meted out to racialised peoples, take up the mantle to exact similar blame and recompense, but crucially, this is informal' (Miller, 2022: 129–130).

Historicisation is key to this chapter's adaptation. In the context of interwar youth justice reform history in England, penalty is noted as a process synonymous with one's relegation from those resources identified by reformers, like Fleming and Fletcher, as crucial to the redemption of the poor deprived and the poor delinquent. Regarded as a gateway to delinquency, deprivation was identified as a key rationale for intervention into the working-class family by reformers. Explained as penal welfarism, scholarship has long identified the elements of penalty constitutive of this relational link between deprivation and delinquency (Garland, 2001; Hendrick, 2003; Ignatieff, 1978). Such scholarship is consistent with the deviance invention paradigm – an established framework critically problematising the more orthodox characterisations of penal reform and the reform movements supporting it. To reiterate the central concern contributed by the wider punitive logic, the extant deviance invention paradigm suffers from race blindness. This is the absence this chapter joins in the effort to rectify.

My use of the racialised young women identified by Fletcher gives that gendered, racial specificity identified as absent from criminological histories. The opening quotations to this section capture an element of the logic underpinning these young women's positioning: Du Bois' double consciousness notion helps characterise Fletcher's depiction of not just the race problem, but the particular *negroid* orientation of the problem. This is the seat of racial stigmatisation with which the young women in Fletcher's case study were faced. Thus, the claim that they were excluded from resources and opportunities due to a wider punitive effect starts with their wider deviant depiction. They were portrayed as lazy, sexually transgressive, and born of an institution unfit for British society and, thereby, support. Unlike the Indigenous youth populating works such as Smith's, Fletcher's research subjects were described as ones beyond transformation. Importantly, and consistent with cautions from those like Platt (1969b), this chapter takes Smith's positioning that the presumed redemptive effort to which Indigenous youth were subjected did not prove redemptive at all. Here, Du Bois' characterisation is seen – the colonial lens necessarily lacks redemptive potential, and this is due in part to the punitiveness it occasions, steeped as it is in the contemptuous blameworthiness of stigma.

Smith's (2021: 1) argument that 'the term "research" is inextricably linked to European imperialism and colonialism' has relevance here. Methodology is key to this. Those who control the pen and write the words also control the power to, as Fanon (1967) notes, invent and reinvent. The case of racialised young women in interwar Britain, at the centre of this chapter's analysis, exemplifies this. For these women, powerful and authoritative representations casting them as a 'moral problem … handicapped by their colour' (Fletcher, 1930: 34) to British society, immeasurably undermined any subsequent efforts of care driving the youth penal reform machinery purportedly supporting them. A carefully constructed vocabulary stigmatised them out of the ostensibly progressive benefits rationalised for the modern subject. The case study method I rely upon is intended to raise these young women from the marginal space such epistemic imbalance relegated them to. As Smith (2021: 1) notes, this is part of a history of epistemic derogation 'that still offends the deepest sense of our humanity'.

wa Thiong'o (2005 [1986]: 9) speaks of the punitive role of language in colonialism, particularly the capacity to imprison the soul: 'The bullet was the means of physical subjugation. Language was the means of the spiritual subjugation.' Examples from his youth in his native Kenya demonstrate how penalty and reward were tied to the policing of language, underpinning the colonial process. Encouraged to report on each other for speaking in native languages, those reported would be labelled and punished with beatings by school officials. Ultimately, one's success became tied to the ability to successfully pass university exams in English. This prioritisation of the English language, however, was an arrangement correspondingly overseeing the elimination of native languages and accompanying cultural artefacts – like storytelling. wa Thiong'o emphasises the devastation of this loss to cultural continuity. For wa Thiong'o the immediacy of the bullet correlates with the longer intergenerational trauma occasioned by the enforced relegation from one's cultural logics and practices.

Such questions align with decolonial efforts, particularly this chapter's aim to emphasise the widespread, historically embedded normalisation of penalty in racialised people's existence. That this is beyond concerns with criminality and the penal estate is crucial to understand the wider punitive logic. Indeed, consistent with developing modes of Black feminist literature, the intersection between decolonial logics with gender and race draws attention to ways that the marginalisation of racialised young women from critical interrogation, in the contemporary, has a long history of exclusion. It is this exclusion which is defined here as having a wider punitive effect, signifying the wider implications of exclusion from key opportunities earmarked as progressive and essential to youth's transformation into adulthood.

Two final points adjourn this analysis. The first is the everyday element of punitiveness, starting with the stigmatisation of youth's families as institutions (a) unfit for purpose, and (b) beyond the redemptive scope of reform efforts. This is the antithesis of reform efforts. Indeed, the very decision to separate youth justice from the adult system during this period indicates belief in youth as a transformative period. Here, stigma takes and sutures exclusion into the minutia of racialised young women's everyday pursuits. Fletcher's characterisation of the young women as ones with no commitment to work can also be read by wider society as their lack of commitment to transformation. Fletcher alludes to this as something outside young women's control. Stigma, constituted according to Du Bois' double consciousness, can be read as something rife with pity for the intractable, doomed to their immutable fate. This takes us to the second of the two final points: the message Fletcher's report disseminated about the Anglo-Negroid family, specifically the particularised category in which the Black racialised young women were placed. This is a positioning consistent with what sociologist Mariana Valverde (1991, 2006) terms a moral impasse – placement beyond redemption. According to Fletcher's categorisation, the young women's social condition was constitutive of an unhappiness. This is not unlike other *slovenly* poor. However, unlike the non-racialised and other working-class poor, '*[racialised youth's] moral standards are extraordinarily low*' (Fletcher, 1930: 34; italics added). Their purported slovenliness, therefore, placed them beyond the redemptive scope for which reform was deployed. According to the wider punitive effect, colonial rationalities, including the authoritative control of language and discourse, remain historically key to the construction of colonial subjects as other. Imbued by the decolonisation perspective, the wider punitive effect thesis allows that the construction of colonial subjects as other reflects a deviant status enabled by epistemic inequality. As wa Thiong'o (2018, 1986) notes, the co-optation of language erodes epistemic autonomy by first denying the colonised 'the authority of naming self and the world, [and] to delegitimise the history and the knowledge they already possessed' (wa Thiong'o, 2018: 124).

Conclusion

The goal of this chapter has been to challenge British criminology's putative associations between racialised peoples, crime, criminality, and the carceral estate. The analysis draws attention to the roots of racialised penalty as criminalisation and deviance invention, a correlate of everyday stigmatisation – and an outcome of entrenched colonial ideals and practice. According to this, (contemporary) concerns with the amplification and racialisation of punishment in Britain could benefit from an expanded understanding which centres hidden racial histories. This is a focus expanding concerns with the widespread extremes of disproportionate punishment typically populating contemporary criminological scholarships. Located within British interwar youth penal reform histories, this expanded understanding of penalty is characterised as a development that is (a) more widespread than incarceration, and (b) synonymous with racialised youth's exclusion from those resources and opportunities identified by reformers as key for actualising youth's transformative potential. Funded as an academic piece of research, documents like the Fletcher Report draw attention to the everyday colonial trajectories informing interwar British youth reform. Coloniality can be understood as a phenomenon coterminous with burgeoning modern institutions like youth justice. Emphasis is placed on the punitive role of stigma in everyday life; this is a crucial emphasis given reformers' prioritisation of everyday cross-institutional support.

Consistent with narratives encouraging minority and decolonial perspectives, conceptual approaches like the wider punitive logic offer an opportunity to expand how penalty is understood. Therefore, a focus on criminology's complicity as (a) a colonial science, (b) responsible for the exclusion of women, is (c) expanded to reveal a further layered exclusion of racialised women's realities. Here, it is understood that despite mainstream feminism's attempts to engender and overcome criminology's formative gendered exclusions, racialised women still remain hidden within the margins. Therefore, while particular attention is placed on criminology's formative complicity in the colonial project, as a starting point for contextualising epistemic inequality, specific attention is paid to a gendered, racial derogation absent from this feminist history. Thus, British interwar youth penal reform, specifically the defaming of the so-called 'Anglo-Negroid' family and progeny, offers a specific example of how such inequality took shape, historically. The analysis is helmed by a case study, demonstrating the defaming of the racialised family's foundation, particularly stigmatised young female offspring. The analytical logic of a wider punitive effect offers a unique perspective on penalty as a colonial tool, demonstrating the disciplinary effect of stigma. The case study concretises efforts to expand this logic, using the representation of Fletcher's racialised young women to demonstrate the wider punitive relationship between a loss of control over one's narrative in the everyday, stigmatisation, and the punitive effect of what it means to be placed at a moral impasse.

References

Adler, F. (1975) *Sisters in Crime: The Rise of the New Female Criminal*. New York: McGraw-Hill.

Agozino, B. (2004) Imperialism, crime and criminology: Towards the decolonisation of criminology. *Crime, Law and Social Change*, 41(4), pp.343–358.

Agozino, B. (2003) *Counter-colonial Criminology: A Critique of Imperialist Reason*. London: Pluto Press.

Anthony, T., Sentence, G., and Bartels, L. (2020) Transcending colonial legacies: From criminal justice to Indigenous women's healing. In: George, L., Norris, A.N., Deckert, A., and Tauri, J. (eds.), *Neo-colonial Criminal Justice: The Mass Imprisonment of Indigenous Women*. Basingstoke: Palgrave Macmillan, pp.103–132.

Bailey, V. (1987) *Delinquency and Citizenship: Reclaiming the Young Offender 1914–1948*. New York: Clarendon Press.

Bell, D. (2018) *Faces at the Bottom of the Well: The Permanence of Racism*. London: Hachette.

Bell, D. (2004) *Silent Covenants: Brown v. Board of Education and the Unfulfilled Hopes for Racial Reform*. Oxford: Oxford University Press.

Bell Jr., D.A. (1980) Brown v. Board of Education and the interest-convergence dilemma. *Harvard Law Review*, 93(3), pp.518–533.

Blagg, H. and Anthony, T. (2019) *Decolonising Criminology: Imagining Justice in a Postcolonial World*. London: Palgrave Macmillan.

Bland, L. (2005) White women and men of colour: Miscegenation fears in Britain after the great war. *Gender & History*, 17(1), pp.29–61.

Bradley, K. (2008) Juvenile delinquency, the juvenile courts and the settlement movement, 1908–1950: Basil Henriques and Toynbee Hall. *Twentieth Century British History*, 19(2), pp. 133–155.

Britton, D.M. (2000) Feminism in criminology: Engendering the outlaw. *The Annals of the American Academy of Political and Social Science*, 571(1), pp.57–76.

Bruno-Jofré, R. and Stafford, J. (2020) Shaking teacher preparation/education: The postwar period and the 'long 1960s'. In: Bruno-Jofré, R. and Stafford, J. (eds.), *The Peripatetic Journey of Teacher Preparation in Canada*. Bingley: Emerald Publishing, pp.1–6.

Choak, C. (2020) British criminological amnesia: Making the case for a Black and postcolonial feminist criminology. *Decolonization of Criminology and Justice*, 2(1), pp.37–58.

Christian, M. (2008) The Fletcher Report 1930: A historical case study of contested Black mixed heritage Britishness. *Journal of Historical Sociology*, 21(2–3), pp.213–241.

Christian, M. (1998) An African-centered approach to the Black British experience: With special reference to Liverpool. *Journal of Black Studies*, 28(3), pp.291–308.

Cohen, S. (1986) Bandits, rebels or criminals: African history and western criminology. *Africa*, 56(4), pp.468–483.

Crenshaw, K.W. (2013) From private violence to mass incarceration: Thinking intersectionally about women, race, and social control. *University California Los Angeles Legal Review*, 59, pp.20–50.

Crenshaw, K.W. (1991) Mapping the margins: Intersectionality, identity politics, and violence against women of color. *Stanford Law Review*, 43(6), pp.1241–1299.

Crenshaw, K. (1989) Demarginalizing the intersection of race and sex. *Feminist Legal Theory*, pp.57–80.

da Silva, D.F. (2007) *Toward a Global Idea of Race* (vol. 27). Minneapolis: University of Minnesota Press.

Donzelot, J. (1979) *The Policing of Families*. New York: Random House.

Dube, M.W. (2000) *Postcolonial Feminist Interpretation of the Bible*. Missouri: Chalice Press.

Du Bois, W.E.B., Levitt, P., and Khagram, S. (1965 [1903]) Of our spiritual strivings. In Du Bois, W.E.B. (ed.), *The Souls of Black Folk*. London: Longmans, Green and Co. Ltd, pp.28–33.

Fanon, F. (1967) *Black Skin, White Mask*. New York: Grove Press.

Featherstone, E. (1994) *Skin Deep: Women Writing on Color, Culture and Identity*. Berkeley: Crossing Press.

Fleming, R.M. (1930) Human hybrids. *Eugenics Review*, 21(4), pp.257–263.

Fletcher, M.E. (1930) *Report on an Investigation into the Colour Problem in Liverpool and Other Ports*. Liverpool: Liverpool Association for the Welfare of Half-Caste Children.

Foucault, M. (1975) *Discipline and Punish: The Birth of the Prison*. London: Penguin Books.

Foucault, M. (1973) *The Birth of the Clinic: An Archaeology of Medical Perception*, transl. A.M. Sheridan Smith. New York: Pantheon.

Garland, D. (2001) *The Culture of Control: Crime and Social Order in Contemporary Society*. Chicago: University of Chicago Press.
Gelsthorpe, L. and Sharpe, G. (2015) Women and sentencing: Challenges and choices. In: Roberts, J.V. (ed.), *Exploring Sentencing Practice in England and Wales*. London: Palgrave Macmillan, pp.118–136.
Gibbs, A. and Gilmour, F. (eds.) (2022) *Women, Crime and Justice in Context: Contemporary Perspectives in Feminist Criminology from Australia and New Zealand*. London: Routledge.
Hendrick, H. (2003) *Child Welfare: Historical Dimensions, Contemporary Debate*. Bristol: Policy Press.
Hendrick, H. (1994) *Child Welfare: England 1872–1989*. London: Routledge.
Hills-Collins, P. (2000) *Black Feminist Thought*. New York: Routledge.
Hills-Collins, P. and Bilge, S. (2020) *Intersectionality*. Cambridge: Polity Press.
Hobsbawm, E. (1989) *The Age of Empire, 1875–1914*. London: Abacus.
Ignatieff, M. (1978) *A Just Measure of Pain, The Penitentiary in the Industrial Revolution, 1750–1850*. New York: Pantheon Books.
Macdonald, N. (2016) Canada's prisons are the 'new residential schools'. *Macleans*, 18 February 2016. https://realpeoples.media/canadas-prisons-new-residential-schools/ (18 March 2017).
Mahood, L. (1995) *Policing Gender, Class and Family*. London: University College London Press.
Magarey, S. (1978) The invention of juvenile delinquency in early nineteenth-century England. *Labour History*, 34, pp.11–27.
Marquis, F.J. (1913–1937) *The Settlement's Problems*. Liverpool University Settlement Publications, Volume 1, pp. 3–4.
Miller, E. (2023) The road from history: gender and race in early twentieth century English youth penal reform. In: Levell, J., Young, T., and Earle, R. (eds.), *Critical Questions of Youth, Gender and Race*. Bristol: Bristol University Press, pp.20–38.
Miller, E. (2022) *Race, Recognition and Retribution in Contemporary Youth Justice: The Intractability Malleability Thesis*. London: Routledge.
Miller, E. (2015) Recognition, retribution and restoration: Youth penal justice and the issue of youth gangs and crime in Canada and England (Unpublished PhD Thesis, Queen's University Belfast, Belfast).
Phillips, C. and Bowling, B. (2003) Racism, ethnicity and criminology: Developing minority perspectives. *British Journal of Criminology*, 43(2), pp.269–290.
Phillips, C., Earle, R., Parmar, A., and Smith, D. (2019) Dear British criminology: Where has all the race and racism gone? *Theoretical Criminology*, 24 (3), pp.427–446.
Platt, A. (1969a) The rise of the child-saving movement: A study in social policy and correctional reform. *The Annals of the American Academy of Political and Social Science*, 381 (1), pp.21–38.
Platt, A. (1969b) *The Child Savers: The Invention of Delinquency*. Chicago: The University of Chicago Press.
Posholi, L. (2020) Epistemic decolonization as overcoming the hermeneutical injustice of Eurocentrism, *Philosophical Papers*, 49(2), pp.279–304.
Seal, L. (2021) *Gender, Crime and Justice*. Cham: Springer Nature.
Shore, H. (2011) Inventing and reinventing the juvenile delinquent in British history. *Memoria Y Civilización*, 14, pp.105–132.
Shore, H. (2003) 'Inventing' the juvenile delinquent in nineteenth century Europe. In: Godfrey, B., Emsley, C., and Dunstall, G. (eds.), *Comparative Histories of Crime*. Devon: Willan Publishing, pp.110–124.

Smart, C. (2013) *Women, Crime and Criminology (Routledge Revivals): A Feminist Critique*. London: Routledge.
Smart, C. (1977) Criminological theory: Its ideology and implications concerning women. *British Journal of Sociology*, 28(1), pp.89–100.
Smith, L.T. (2021 [1999]) *Decolonizing Methodologies: Research and Indigenous Peoples*. London: Bloomsbury.
Tabili, L. (1994) *'We Ask for British Justice': Workers and Racial Difference in Late Imperial Britain*. Ithaca, New York: Cornell University Press.
Valverde, M. (2006) Introduction to the age of light, soap, and water: Moral reform in English Canada, 1885–1925. In: Glasbeek, A. (ed.), *Moral Regulation and Governance in Canada: History, Context and Critical Issues*. Toronto: Canadian Scholars' Press, pp.117–142.
Valverde, M. (1991) *The Age of Light, Soap, and Water: Moral Reform in English Canada, 1885–1925*. Toronto: McClelland & Stewart.
Walby, S. (1990) *Theorizing Patriarchy*. Oxford: Basil Blackwell.
Ward, G.K. (2012) *The Black Child-Savers: Racial Democracy and Juvenile Justice*. Chicago: University of Chicago Press.
wa Thiong'o, N. (2018) The politics of translation: Notes towards an African language policy. *Journal of African Cultural Studies*, 30(2), pp.124–132.
wa Thiong'o, N. (2005 [1986]) *Decolonizing the Mind: The Politics of Language in African Literature*. London: James Curry.
Watson, N. (2021) *Aboriginal Women, Law and Critical Race Theory*. London: Palgrave Macmillan.

PART II
Marginalised Voices in Criminology

5

THE INTERSECTION OF AGE, GENDER, AND RURALITY

Recentring Young Women's Experiences in Family Violence Discourse, Policy, and Practice

Bianca Johnston, Faith Gordon, and Catherine Flynn

Introduction: the hidden women in Australia's family violence dialogue

Family and intimate partner violence are forms of violence against women that are recognised globally as serious human rights issues, driven by gender inequality (World Health Organization, 2021). In the Australian context, a significant body of work has been undertaken over decades to centre family violence discourse as part of a broader national discussion. However, despite the progress made in recognising family violence as a core social and policy issue in Australia, there remain women who have been historically hidden in this dialogue. As Australian family violence discourses continue to evolve in ways that encompass further intersectional complexities, the needs of such hidden women, particularly those who hold multiple dimensions to their identities, are becoming increasingly evident. This awareness has occurred alongside the establishment of a deeper understanding of the structural marginalisation, vulnerabilities, risks, and difficulties they face in accessing justice and support. Historically, First Nations people, migrants and refugees, people who identify as LGBTQ+, those who are disabled, and rurally located and young women, are all examples of those whose experiences of family violence have not been historically recognised in the designing of family violence service provision, or the support landscape.

This chapter adopts intersectional, social constructionist, and feminist lenses to review existing knowledge of three intersecting identity dimensions – age, gender, and geographical location – with specific reference to young women residing in rural and regional areas in Australia. Through a review of scholarly literature, the chapter firstly applies an intersectional lens to explore how family violence, rurality, and remoteness are defined in Australia. Understandings of adolescent intimate partner violence are then explored, with emphasis given to

DOI: 10.4324/9781003260967-7

the marginalised positioning of young women in the Australian family violence discourses. The chapter discusses the cultural, social, and political features of Australia that contribute to enhancing the rural and remote family violence risks and implications for both adult women and young women. It concludes by exploring and raising awareness of young women's justice and support needs and presents key recommendations for reforms to policy and service provision.

Defining family violence

Historical analyses demonstrate that violence against women in Australia has a long history and is deeply rooted in the country's colonial past (Saunders, 1984). It was only with the second wave of feminism that Australia saw the establishment of many important social and policy actions to address such violence and gender inequality; these became early scaffolding for current Australian family violence discourses (Murray and Powell, 2009). This era saw many initiatives evolve including the establishment of women's refuges, increased access to contraception, and gendered critiques of Australian history (Summers, 1981). Harnessing the momentum of this movement, a deliberate social policy shift from the 1980s onwards sought to adopt 'family violence' rather than the previously used 'domestic violence' as the preferred term to describe the violence and abuse that occurs within intimate and family relationships (Murray and Powell, 2009: 538). This shift in language was a part of the broader push to shift the conceptualisation of family violence away from being perceived as a private issue hidden 'behind closed doors', to instead a broader public, social, political, and legal responsibility which needed to be addressed (Murray and Powell, 2009: 538).

The term 'family violence' is legally defined in all Australian states and territories, except for New South Wales where it is known as 'family and domestic violence', and is the preferred term in First Nations communities due to the term's ability to encompass violence occurring in kinship, clans, extended families, and descent groups (Langton, 2020: 20). Since their emergence onto the broader Australian social and policy landscapes, the family violence discourses in Australia have further evolved to adopt a strong survivor-focused paradigm (Ragusa, 2012: 687), with a primary prevention framework that centres gender equality and the adoption of an increasingly intersectional lens (Our Watch et al., 2015: 14). Notably, however, some groups such as young women, continue to remain largely marginalised in these discourses (Johnston et al., 2022; 11).

Despite contemporary work undertaken to centre family violence in the broader national political and social narratives, rates of reported family, domestic, and sexual violence in Australia have remained relatively stable over the preceding decade (AIHW, 2019: 10). National data published in 2019 indicates that 17% of Australian women (1.6 million women) have experienced physical or sexual violence from a current or former partner and 23% of Australian women (2.2 million women) have experienced emotional abuse by a current or former partner (AIHW, 2019: viii). In addition to the increasing body of existing empirical research (see Dillon et al., 2015: 19), police data from various Australian states indicate that family, domestic, and sexual violence occurs frequently in regional, remote, and rural areas, with 23% of women residing outside of major Australian cities reporting experiences of partner violence (AIHW, 2019: 101). Echoing findings from international research which identifies that family and intimate partner violence in rural contexts may be more chronic and severe (Edwards, 2015: 363–364), Australian women residing in very remote areas are at higher risk of experiencing family and intimate partner violence that requires hospitalisation at 24 times the rate of those who reside in major cities (AIHW, 2019: 101). The scope of these statistics raises important concerns in relation to how women in rural and remote areas experience family violence, vulnerability, and risk. The existing adult (Johnston et al., 2022) and urban normative gazes (Magnus and Donohue, 2022: 437) of family violence inquiry highlight the evident gaps in criminological knowledge regarding the need to engage with and hear a range of voices and experiences and develop responses that are reflective of diverse needs, including those experienced by young women in rural and remote areas.

Young women's experiences of violence

Young women aged between 10–20 years old who experience intimate partner violence have been largely overlooked within the dominant national family violence discourses (Johnston et al., 2022: 11). In Australia, young women have not been recognised as a distinct cohort, and their experiences of intimate partner violence are frequently submerged amongst those of adult women in the family violence data and existing literature (Johnston et al., 2022: 11). Intimate partner violence amongst young people involves concerning actions ranging from individual and/or co-occurring experiences of stalking, jealousy, possessiveness (Taylor and Sullivan, 2017: 3), through to threats of harm, physical violence, sexual assault, coercion, isolation, and other behaviours designed to instil fear (Chung, 2007: 1281–1283). Multi-dimensional impacts are described, including disordered eating (Gervais and Davidson, 2013: 28), bullying (Connolly and Josephson, 2007: 3), sexual victimisation, increased mental health concerns and fear (Burton et al., 2013: 807–810), as well as impacts on connections to social institutions such as education and the community (Banyard and Cross, 2008: 1005). Despite the severity of this problem, it lacks the 'power of a name' (Lombard, 2013: 1141), with young women in Australia having no common nomenclature to describe the unique discourses of power, control, and violence that occur in adolescent intimate partner relationships. A myriad of phrases are used to refer to violence in these relationships, including: 'teen dating violence', 'adolescent relationship abuse', 'dating aggression', 'courtship violence', and 'adolescent intimate partner violence' (Maurer, 2019: 58).

National statistics indicate that young women are more at risk of intimate partner violence and sexual violence than older women (AIHW, 2019). As the 2017 Population Health Survey in the state of Victoria identified, young women aged between 18–24 years experienced the highest prevalence of reported family violence compared to any other age group of their gender (Victorian Government, 2020: 25). Furthermore, recent national sexual assault statistics outline that young women aged 15–19 years old have the highest rate of reported sexual assault victimisation of their gender (AIHW, 2019: 5).

Of the limited Australian research into young women's experiences of intimate partner violence, much of the existing focus has been on young women residing in urban centres and capital cities (Hooker et al., 2019: 543). There are very few Australian studies that directly consider adolescent women's experiences of intimate partner violence in rural and remote locations (Hooker et al., 2019: 543) and whether these experiences echo that of rural adult women or contain unique complexities resulting from the intersections of gender and age. In this regard, much like young women generally (Johnston et al., 2022), rural young women remain hidden in the broader family violence literature in Australia. The impacts of androcentric cultural scripts of rural identity (Saunders and Easteal, 2013: 122), the architecture of rural life (Owen and Carrington, 2015: 230), and exposure to natural disasters (Parkinson, 2019: 2347) that have all been linked to family violence risks in adult rural contexts, are largely unknown in relation to rural young women's experiences of intimate partner violence.

Rurality, rural identities, and gender inequality

Australia is one of the most urbanised nations globally (Owen and Carrington, 2015: 230) and is home to hundreds of diverse First Nations language groups and cultures. Holding a total population of more than 25 million people (Australian Bureau of Statistics, 2023: para.1), around 28% of the Australian population (equating to 7 million people) are living outside of major cities in remote and rural areas (AIHW, 2019: 101). The Australian government utilises five classes to objectively define remoteness, which is based on road distance to the nearest population-defined urban areas and localities (Australian Bureau of Statistics, 2023: para 1). Under this definition, very remote areas are furthest from major urban areas and include the tropical islands of the Torres Straits as well as the arid deserts of the central Australian outback as examples (Australian Bureau of Statistics, 2016). Expanding out from the Major Cities of Australia, Inner Regional Australia straddles the Southern, South Eastern, and South Western seaboards, spanning outwards to Outer Regional Australia, Remote Australia, and Very Remote Australia (Australian Bureau of Statistics, 2016). Rurality and remoteness in Australia are spatially, geographically, and climatically diverse with many distinct differences in populations, economies, and local histories.

Yet despite the arbitrary geographical and population parameters used to identify rural and remote regions, the socially constructed definition of Australian 'rurality' is much more complex (Owen and Carrington, 2015: 230). The meaning of 'rural' in Australia has been considered both ideologically illusionary (Owen and Carrington, 2015: 230) and as much 'culturally imagined as physically located in rural landscapes and towns' (Murray et al., 2019: 94). The social constructions of 'rural' and 'rural identity' involve continuous reproducing, consolidating, performing, and habituating of meanings (Dymitrow and Brauer, 2017: 30). These socially constructed meanings are then applied to, and become lived experiences through, behaviours, places, identities, and interactions (Dymitrow and Brauer, 2017: 30). In Australia, despite a large diversity in rural and remote geography, industry, population, and climate, there exists a persistent Anglocentric (Murray et al., 2019: 93) and androcentric cultural myth of Australian rurality (Owen and Carrington, 2015: 230). The performance and habituating of this cultural myth significantly increase the family violence vulnerabilities, risks, and access to justice experienced by Australian women living in rural and remote locations.

Androcentric cultural narratives and family violence

The androcentricity of rural narratives can reinforce patriarchal norms and systems that position women as unequal, as evidenced in research on Australian (Murray et al., 2019: 94) and international rurality (Little, 2017: 474–476). Australia's geographical diversity results in rural and remote locations with distinct geographical and climate differences and diverse industries such as mining, agriculture, and fishing. However, despite a broad range of national geography, common cultural scripts upholding a romanticised ethos of masculinity permeate the Australian rural identity (Saunders and Easteal, 2013: 122), which in turn reinforce and sustain both normative and performative dominant heterosexual masculinity (Pini et al., 2013: 173). Such cultural scripts are particularly linked to notions of the Australian bush and are reinforced by Anglocentric folklore of stories about bushrangers, pioneers, stockmen, farmers, and conceptions of 'mateship' (Saunders and Easteal, 2013: 122).

'Mateship' is a revered characteristic of both Australian social relationships and the collective national psyche, involving a dis-concern about social status, relaxed friendliness, and easy egalitarianism (Horne, 1964: 26), despite being grounded in whiteness and masculinity (Dyrenfurth, 2007: 213). In qualitative studies, such as that undertaken by Saunders and Easteal (2013: 130), the presence of such heavily masculinised cultural scripts and 'mateship' codes within Australian rural male-dominated workplaces, such as mining and agriculture, position women as 'outsiders'. This positioning could create workplace risks for both individual and pack-on-one sexual harassment behaviours, impacting women's safety in these environments (Saunders and Easteal, 2013: 130) as has been evidenced recently in the Australian rural mining industry (Miolin, 2022).

Similar scripts of rural masculinity are reflected in qualitative and observational research undertaken by Pini et al. (2013: 168–176), who explored rural heterosexuality and the positioning of 'skimpies' (lingerie-clad barmaids) in a rural mining town in Western Australia. This study identified the presence of stereotypical narratives of local 'morally virtuous' women, young women skimpies as 'outsiders', and mining men as 'highly sexed' (Pini et al., 2013: 175). The androcentricity that permeates these narratives reinforces stereotypical hegemonic masculine images of rural men as rugged, dominant, iconic heroes taming the Australian bush, and women as sidekicks (Saunders and Easteal, 2013: 125), limited to binary identities of either 'damned whores' or 'God's police' (Summers, 2016: 108). Such gendered discourses devalue the social status and personal experiences of women, having serious implications for women's safety, justice, and support-seeking, both generally and specifically in rural and remote communities, by contributing to a system of 'rural patriarchy' which enables social stigma, shame, fear of retaliation (Magnus and Donohue, 2022), and very serious family violence risks for adult rural women (Websdale, 1995: 334; DeKeseredy, 2015: 182–183). International research into adolescent sexuality in non-rural contexts has identified the impact of such 'slut/angel' tropes and other hegemonic and heteronormative gender stereotypes, enabling and reinforcing problematic power discourses that exist (Hird and Jackson, 2001: 1279–1282). The presence of such patriarchal youth social narratives serve to naturalise and justify young men's entitlement to sex and reputation as being more valuable than young women's safety, autonomy and rights (Hird and Jackson, 2001). Such scripts have also been linked to the justification of violence, anger, and aggression by Australian rural young men (Edwards et al., 2019: 167) and to the high rate of suicide of men in rural locations (Alston, 2012: 516). Rural young women are at risk of experiencing the intersecting problematic social scripts and structural barriers of both patriarchal rurality and adolescence.

Within the architecture of rural life in Australia, there are historical and political cultures (Owen and Carrington, 2015: 230–231) which are conducive to reinforcing patriarchal systems, which in turn increase the risk of family violence and the need for service provision (Owen and Carrington, 2015: 233–237). Many rural communities elsewhere internationally have been described as holding characteristics of 'old boys' networks', which are thinly veiled under the guise of 'mateship' (DeKeseredy, 2015: 181). As DeKeseredy (2015: 181) asserts, these networks afford men the patriarchal peer male support that can impact social responses to family violence. The increased risks of family violence in rural Australian areas are shaped and exacerbated by historical patterns including patrilineal inheritance of rural property (Carrington and Scott, 2008: 654), financial dependence due to limited employment options, and vestiges of a culture of historical exclusion of women from important economic and decision-making spaces (Wendt and Hornosty, 2010: 53). Access to social spaces including pubs (public bars) was historically disallowed to women, First Nations people, and non-European immigrants (Kirkby, 2003: 47–248), reinforcing what has been described as a 'masculinist conception of national culture' by associating the activities of Australian rural social spaces with 'ockerism' (working-class identity), masculinity, and mateship (Kirkby, 2003: 246–247).

Small rural townships are characterised by socio-spatial relationships that hold high degrees of community-centrism, intimacy, recognition, and active 'gossip' networks that can impact visibility and privacy in accessing family violence supports and services (Owen and Carrington, 2015: 233–234). This can reinforce feelings of shame or embarrassment in seeking help for family violence, particularly in contexts where rural townships are occupied by generational families who have strong investment in the sociocultural construction of rural communities (Owen and Carrington, 2015: 234) as being idyllic hamlets characterised by notions of 'country hospitality' and locales of 'rural bliss' (Ragusa and Ward, 2017: 72).

Anglocentric cultural narratives and family violence

The Anglocentric narrative of the rural identity further maintains colonisation by creating and reinforcing distinctions between First Nations and non-First Nations people in Australia (Cowlishaw, 1998, cited in Owen and Carrington, 2015: 230). The intersections of residing in rural and remote communities are recognised as compounding the likelihood of family violence experienced by First Nations women, with location exacerbating the existing barriers to seeking support (Langton, 2020: 21). Many First Nations women may decline to report intimate partner and family violence due to a variety of complex and intersecting reasons, including concerns of systemic racism, of being misidentified as a perpetrator and the resulting criminal justice system involvement, fears of homelessness, issues of child protection involvement, and lack of access to culturally sensitive services (Langton, 2020: 15, 28–30). Although inquiry into First Nations young women's experience of intimate partner violence in remote Australia has been undertaken, First Nations culture is not homogenous and involves complex systems of lores/laws (Blagg et al., 2020: 16), culture, social structures, language groups and communities, and findings must also be considered in a wider context of colonisation. A compelling body of research and decades of activism continue to highlight and galvanise the argument for First Nations' self-determination in addressing family violence (Langton, 2020: 40) and the movement to a more deeply embedded intersectionality, including First Nations ways of knowing, being, and doing, into what is a traditionally a deeply Anglicised national discourse.

The intersections of youth, rurality, gender, and relationships

Theoretical inquiry into intersectional constructions of rurality and family violence seek to resist urges to 'other' rurality itself due to the risks of further marginalising victim-survivors (Sandberg, 2013: 351). Increasingly an intersectional lens is being applied to analyses involving rurality and violence (Sandberg, 2013: 351) in ways that identify the spatiality of violence and the recognition that 'violence sits in places' (Springer, 2011, cited in Little, 2017:

473). Social geographers are increasingly conceptualising rural violence as being 'unfolding processes', inherently connected to power discourses in unique locales (Little, 2017: 477). This raises questions of how issues of family violence in rural social geographies interact with youth social geographies, including those that relate to intimate relationships. Compared to adults and children, the social geographies of young people are largely overlooked in research (Valentine, 2008). Adolescence requires distinct sociocultural knowledge systems, skills, interactions, and developmental processes (Harms, 2010: 280–294), as young people undertake processes such as meaning-making about the world, risk-taking, identity exploration, and the establishment of initial intimate, sexual, and romantic relationships (Harms, 2010: 280–294). Adolescence not only involves experiences of connection and 'being', but also simultaneous hopes, dreams, and anticipated notions of 'becoming' (Aitken, 2001: 57).

The notion of rurally located young women's subjectivities of 'being' and 'becoming', as they are tied to locale, was explored in qualitative research undertaken by Senior and Chenhall (2012: 371) with First Nations young women aged between 13–23, in the Northern Territory. Reflecting the importance of the social geographies of place and community, this research considered First Nations' culture, systems, and subjectivities in the construction of the self. The young women described the importance of their role in cultural community maintenance and in enjoying activities such as basketball, which was a core community social activity, as well as their experiences of peer-organised 'walking about at night', which was riskier and allowed them time with young men without adult supervision (Senior and Chenhall, 2012: 376–377). The role of intimate relationships in these young women's sense of becoming included the perceptions that having children and getting married were inevitable, which the young women expressed led to risks of becoming invisible and of experiencing family violence (Senior and Chenhall, 2012: 379–380).

Qualitative research undertaken by Senior et al. (2017 204–216) with a sample of 88 young Australian First Nations people in remote, rural, and regional Northern Territory, Western Australia, and South Australia explored understandings of sexual violence, culture, gender, and relationships. Employing individual interviews, group work, and visual methodologies, this study explored the high level of emotional investment that young women placed in their romantic relationships and how this resulted in proactive behaviours to maintain relationships, as well as toleration of some forms of violence (Senior et al., 2017: 208–209). Young people's tolerance and acceptance of violence in relationships, and experiences of jealousy and gendered scripts of male dominance are observed in non-First Nations contexts (Senior et al., 2017: 215). This study also considered the dual issues regarding region and cultural group-specific explanations of sanctioned violence demonstrated through public fighting alongside that of private violence and the tensions that young women experienced in navigating both (Senior et al., 2017: 215–217). The young women detailed complexities in navigating their intimate relationships, sexual health, contraception, pregnancy risks, coerced consent, and sexual pressure, which aligned with broader gendered scripts positioning men in dominant roles creating relational power imbalances (Senior et al., 2017: 210–215). In both studies, the intersections of age, gender, rurality, and cultural context highlight the diversity of youth experiences and the need for age-appropriate, culturally and developmentally sensitive responses. These studies also highlight the importance of ensuring that diverse youth voices representing different Australian ruralities are present in criminology and family violence inquiry.

Implications for seeking support and justice

As family violence has become increasingly positioned as a key social and policy issue nationally, legal and justice responses have evolved to prioritise a victim-survivor-focused paradigm. This has included a shift in policing responses from the approach apparent in the 1980s of treating the issue as one for 'social work' to respond to, rather than a 'policing' issue (Ragusa, 2012: 689). The shift to a dominant legal and policing response in family violence has raised concerns about the positioning of police as 'critical first responders' to family violence incidents, who then subsequently enable gateways to legal support and justice processes (Ragusa, 2012: 689). Further, key reforms and inquiries have taken place, with attempts to impact the design of both state and national family violence systems. Of particular significance was the 2015 Victorian Royal Commission into Family Violence (RCFV), which was the first inquiry of its kind in Australian history, and the largest in national breadth and scope. The RCFV's (State of Victoria, 2016) 227 recommendations were adopted by the Victorian government, with the aim of transforming the state's responses to family violence. This included the establishment of common risk assessment frameworks that brought a more intersectional lens across sectors, the embedding of family violence and gender equality education curricula within state schools under the Respectful Relationships program, the establishment of safety and service hubs, mandatory qualifications for specialist family violence practitioners, and changes to the legal system to ensure victim-survivors have access to safety and justice (State of Victoria, 2016).

A wide range of policing and legal responses to family violence have also been enhanced under these reform actions, including the establishment of specialist family violence positions, the positioning of family violence as core police business, the establishment of specialist family violence courts, and multiple measures to enhance investigations and legal responses such as family violence intervention orders (State of Victoria, 2016). The implementation of such legal, educational, and social policing and justice measures under these reforms is important for victim-survivor safety and perpetrator accountability. Such responses, however, also require developmentally sensitive reflexivity and adaptability to ensure that young people have access to intervention and diversion – a key need highlighted by the RCFV (2015). In terms of rural young women's vulnerabilities to family violence, the RCFV also raised issues of geographical isolation, shortages of infrastructure (including public transport, education, employment, and social activities), and a severe lack of housing as compounding risks and adversely impacting the presence of other protective factors (State of Victoria, 2016: 524–526). From this perspective, adolescent development raises important complexities and understandings about the intersections between fields of youth-focused criminological inquiry and family violence, both conceptually and practically. For young women who experience intimate partner and family violence, the risks and vulnerabilities resulting from the intersections of adolescent development and gender are seriously impacted by residence in rural, remote, and regional areas.

The RCFV identified that young people generally were frequently 'falling through the gaps' in the family violence service system and were less likely than any other age group to seek support due to limited accessible information, their confusion, and the lack of available youth-orientated family violence policies and services (State of Victoria, 2016). A recent review undertaken by the Family Violence Reform Implementation Monitor (2020) explored the Victoria Police's Family Violence Intervention Orders and youth justice data and found that violence *within* adolescent relationships was the fastest growing form of adolescent family violence. However, despite the increasing visibility of adolescent intimate partner violence in statistics, currently most policy and scholarly discussion focuses on family violence enacted by adolescents in the home, in relation to parents, caregivers, and siblings (ANROWS, 2020: 7–8). Although a key outcome of the RCFV (State of Victoria, 2016) involved the implementation of primary prevention-focused Respectful Relationships' material in Victorian public schools (Victorian Government, 2020), the increased recognition, reporting, and rising rates of adolescent intimate partner violence raises concerns as to the availability of developmentally appropriate youth-orientated early intervention and response supports available to young people. This is significant given that the intersection of developmental age can create and compound complexities for young people's experience in accessing family and intimate partner violence supports (Whitman, 2007).

Complexities experienced by young people can result in barriers to safety and their access to justice due to fear of punishment from adults and/or authorities; concerns that confidentiality may not be maintained; fear of retaliation from perpetrators to self or others such as siblings; negative stereotyping and stigma; reliance on public transport to access supports; lack of signalling that supports are youth friendly; distrust towards adults; or shame, embarrassment, and a sense that their experiences won't be believed or taken seriously (Whitman, 2007: 11–12). These barriers can result in young people feeling a need to 'handle it on their own' (Whitman, 2007: 11–12) and can enable situations where young people rely on informal peer networks as a form of family and intimate partner violence support (State of Victoria, 2016: 136). For young women, such barriers alongside other issues, including a lack of access to emergency accommodation, can create climates conducive for the use of survival sex, homelessness, exploitation, and further intimate partner violence experiences (Watson, 2011: 267–268). The implications resulting from issues including homelessness and lack of social or support infrastructure and youth-specific supports for rural young women who experience intimate partner violence are recognised as a cause for concern by the RCFV (State of Victoria, 2016: 524), however remain largely underexplored in Australian family violence inquiry. Issues regarding public and social perceptions as a barrier to support-seeking (Senior et al., 2017) and lack of access to culturally contextualised formal sexual education services (Senior et al., 2020) have been raised through studies undertaken with First Nations young women in remote Australian communities. Accommodation and abortion access, particularly in the context of reproductive coercion, that are experienced by young rural and remote women were also identified by Hooker et al. (2019) as areas in need of further Australian inquiry from an adolescent intimate partner violence context.

The experiences of adult women in rural and remote areas may provide some insight into how young women in these locations experience justice and support-seeking for family and intimate partner violence. Internationally, rural areas have been described as at risk of becoming 'justice deserts' (Newman, 2016: 595) due to issues of systematic and spatial exclusion to justice resulting from austerity measures. Austerity results in the underfunding of justice services and mobility-related exclusion for people in rural locations because of limited transport options and lack of local contextualisation of legal services to local knowledge and needs (Newman, 2016: 593–604). Similar issues have been identified in an Australian context, as a result of the 'tyranny of distance' (Owen and Carrington, 2015: 230), in which access to service provision for both emergency and ongoing counselling supports was impacted by vast geographical distances, delaying response times and availability (Owen and Carrington, 2015).

Isolation can enable further power and control discourses, including lack of access to vehicles (Murray et al., 2019), experiences of stalking, restriction of movements, and blocking opportunities to escape (Ragusa, 2017). Financial control resulting from economic resources being tied to farm properties and lack of local employment options (Ragusa, 2017) influence rural and remote women's abilities to obtain and maintain independence, whilst the lack of access to emergency refuge and ongoing accommodation has been linked to risks of women returning to abusive relationships (Ragusa, 2017). The localised nature of small communities, concerns of shame and recognition, and a lack of cultural appropriateness of services have been identified as creating barriers when accessing support (Owen and Carrington, 2015; Murray et al., 2019).

The need for youth-specific approaches

International research into the primary prevention needs of young people in rural areas identifies the importance of ensuring that public health messaging about family violence targets areas including education and awareness to challenge violence-enabling community norms such as rigid gender stereotyping (Edwards et al., 2016: 441). Such programmes require implementation alongside actions to increase the social capital available to young people in rural areas, such as job creation and bystander activation training (Edwards et al., 2016: 442). Presently in Australia, the standardised Respectful Relationships' curriculum is not nationally mandated for all schools (ANROWS, 2020), although current research is being undertaken to identify curriculum needs (ANROWS, 2020). The importance of prevention activities such as teaching of the Respectful Relationships' curriculum for both metropolitan and rural youth as a form of violence prevention was also highlighted in the Victorian RCFV (State of Victoria, 2016: 46).

The current lack of youth-specific rural inquiry in Australia into young women and lack of widespread service and systemic responses can lead to the continuance of established patterns (Baker, 2003: 30), where young women feel pressures to self-navigate and self-manage not only their experiences of intimate partner violence, but processes to maintain their own safety. Such issues of young women self-managing their experiences and safety in response to intimate partner violence, have been identified in subsequent Australian studies alongside First Nations young women undertaken by Senior et al. (2020; 211) and in qualitative research undertaken into young metropolitan women in South Australia by Chung (2007: 1291–1292) and homeless young urban women in Melbourne (Watson, 2011: 257–260). The ways in which young women are required to individually manage structural issues as a result of limited service and policy responses can be further compounded in situations of intimate partner violence. Issues relating to homelessness, culturally and developmentally appropriate rural sexual health and reproductive services (Senior et al., 2020), and abortion access (Doran and Hornibrook, 2015: 4–8) further emphasises how youth intimate partner violence can have wide-reaching impacts on the current lives and futures of young women. The continued existence of this issue across national research without contradiction raises concern about the prolonged invisibility of young women in policy and the design and provision of safety and support services. Criminological inquiry into the intersections between youth, rurality, and family violence therefore has an important role to play in enhancing the understandings of developmentally sensitive policing, and legal, support, and social responses that challenge marginalisation and enhance young women's safety, dignity, and access to justice. The recognition of young women in Australian family violence discourses and the expansion of this conceptualisation to recognise the complex intersections of youth rurality on their safety and justice needs and experiences calls for both deeper understanding and action to challenge this marginalisation.

An increasing body of national family violence research continues to highlight how the complexities resulting from geography and gender create significant risks and particular barriers for adult women in accessing justice, safety, and support. The Anglocentric and androcentric nature of Australian rurality and rural identities create unique contexts and situations that impact not only experiences of intimate partner violence, but those of justice-seeking and justice-receiving for adult women. How the complexities of age, geography, and gender intersect to create and compound family and intimate partner violence barriers for young women is relatively unknown due to their submersion within adult family violence discourse (Johnston et al., 2022) and general lack of academic inquiry into rural young women's experiences of intimate partner violence (Hooker et al., 2019). Consequently, rural and remote young women are a hidden cohort amongst the broader family violence discourses in Australia. As this chapter has outlined, young women urgently require responsive and informed policy and access to services that recognise and respond to their unique needs resulting from the intersection of age, geography, and gender. Furthermore, within rural and remote Australia, young women require justice responses that firstly see them, and secondly ensure action and accountability for their safety from intimate partner violence.

References

Aitken, S.(2002)Putting young people in their place. In Aitken, S.(ed.) *Geographies of Young People*. London:Routledge, pp. 1–26.

Alston, M. (2012) Rural male suicide in Australia, *Social Science and Medicine*. Vol. 74, No. 4, pp.515–522. doi:10.1016/j.socscimed.2010.04.036.

Australian Bureau of Statistics (2016) Defining remote areas, *Australian Statistical Geography Standard (ASGS)*. Vol. 5, Remoteness Structure Available at: https://www.abs.gov.au/ausstats/abs@.nsf/Latestproducts/1270.0.55.005Main%20Features15July%202016?opendocument&tabname=Summary&prodno=1270.0.55.005&issue=July%202016&num=&view=.

Australian Bureau of Statistics (2023) National, state and territory population. Australian Government. Available at: https://www.abs.gov.au/statistics/people/population/national-state-and-territory-population/mar-2023.

Australian Institute of Health and Welfare (AIHW) (2019) Family, domestic and sexual violence in Australia: continuing the national story, *Australian Government*, Cat. No. FDV 3 Canberra Australia. Available at: https://www.aihw.gov.au/getmedia/b0037b2d-a651-4abf-9f7b-00a85e3de528/aihw-fdv3-FDSV-in-Australia-2019.pdf.aspx?inline=true.

Australia's National Research Organisation for Women's Safety (ANROWS) (2020) Australia's National Research Agenda to Reduce Violence against Women and their Children: ANRA 2020–2022. Available at: https://www.anrows.org.au/about/national-research-agenda-to-reduce-violence-against-women-and-their-children/.

Baker, J. (2003) Don't believe the hype: young women's experiences of male violence in the 'girl power' era, *Women Against Violence*. Vol. 14, pp.27–34.

Banyard, V.L. and Cross, C. (2008) Consequences of teen dating violence: understanding intervening variables in ecological context violence against women, *Violence Against Women*. Vol. 14, No, 9, pp.998–1013. doi:10.1177/1077801208322058.

Blagg, H., Tulich, T., Hovane, V., Raye, D., Worrigal, T., and May, S. (2020). Understanding the role of law and culture in Aboriginal and/or Torres Strait Islander communities in responding to and preventing family violence, Ngarluma/Jaru/Gooniyandi (Hovane), Kimberley and Pilbara region, WA, Jabirr Jabirr/Bardi (Raye), Dampier

Peninsula and Kimberley region, WA, Gooniyandi/Gija (Worrigal), Kimberley region, WA (Research report, 19/2020). Sydney: ANROWS.

Burgess-Proctor, A. (2006) Intersections of race, class, gender and crime: future directions for feminist criminology, *Feminist Criminology*. Vol. 1, No. 1, pp.27–47. doi:10.1177/1557085105282899.

Burton, C., Halpern-Felsher, B., Rehm, R., Rankin, S., and Humphreys, J. (2013) 'It was pretty scary': the theme of fear in young adult women's descriptions of a history of adolescent dating abuse. *Issues in Mental Health Nursing*. Vol. 34, No. 11, pp.803–813. doi:10.3109/01612840.2013.827286.

Carrington, K. and Scott, J. (2008) Masculinity, rurality and violence, *The British Journal of Criminology*. Vol. 48, No. 5, pp.641–666.

Chung, D. (2007) Meaning making of relationships: young women's experiences and understandings of dating violence. *Violence Against Women* Vol. 13, No. 12, pp.1274–1295. doi:10.1177/1077801207310433.

Connolly, J. and Josephson, W. (2007) Aggression in adolescent dating relationships: predictor and prevention, *The Prevention Researcher*. Vol. 14, No. 5, pp.3–5.

DeKeseredy, W. (2015) New directions in feminist understandings of rural crime, *Journal of Rural Sciences*. Vol. 39, pp.180–187. doi:10.1016/j.jrurstud.2014.11.002.

Dillon, G., Hussain, R., and Loxton, D. (2015) Intimate partner violence in the young cohort of the Australian longitudinal study on women's health: urban/rural comparison and demographic associations, *Advances in Mental Health*. Vol. 13, No. 1, pp.18–29. doi:10.1080/18374905.2015.1039752.

Dixson, M. (1999) *The Real Matilda: Women and Identity in Australia 1788 to the Present*, 4th edition. Sydney: UNSW Press.

Doran, F. and Hornibrook, J. (2015) Barriers around access to abortion experienced by rural women in New South Wales, Australia, *Rural and Remote Health*. Vol. 16, No. 1. doi:10.1111/ajr.12096.

Dymitrow, M. and Brauer, R. (2017) Performing rurality. But who?, *Bulletin of Geography: Socio-economic Series*. Vol. 28, pp.27–45. doi:10.1515/bog-2017-0032.

Dyrenfurth, N. (2007) John Howard's hegemony of values: the politics of 'mateship', *Howard Decade Australian Journal of Political Science*. Vol. 42, No. 2, pp. 211–230. doi:10.1080/10361140701319994.

Edwards, K. (2015) Intimate partner violence and the rural-urban-suburban divide: myth or reality? Critical review of the literature, *Trauma, Violence and Abuse*. Vol. 16, No. 3, pp.359–373. doi:10.1177/15248380114557289.

Edwards, K., Banyard, V., Moschella, E., and Seavey, K. (2016) Rural young adults lay theories of intimate partner violence: A qualitative examination, *American Journal of Community Psychology*. Vol. 458, No. 3, pp. 434–445. doi:10.1002/ajcp.12095.

Edwards, P.van de Mortel, T., and Stevens, J. (2019) Perceptions of anger and aggression in rural adolescent Australian males, *International Journal of Mental Health Nursing*. Vol. 28, pp.162–170. doi:10.1111/inm.12513.

Family Violence Reform Implementation Monitor (2020) Fourth report to Parliament (as at 1 November 2020) – tabled May 2021. Available at: https://www.fvrim.vic.gov.au/fourth-report-parliament-1-november-2020-tabled-may-2021.

Farrugia, D., Smyth, J., and Harrison, T. (2015) Affective topologies of rural youth embodiment, *Sociologia Ruralis*. Vol. 56, No. 1, pp.116–132. doi:10.1111/soru.12077.

Gervais, S. and Davidson, M. (2013) Objectification among college women in the context of intimate partner violence. *Violence and Victims*. Vol. 28, pp.36–49. doi:10.1891/0886-6708.28.1.36.

Gibbs, L., Block, K., Harms, L.MacDougall, C.Baker, E.Ireton, G.Forbes, D.Richardson, J., and Waters, E. (2014) Children and young people's wellbeing post-disaster: safety and stability are critical, *International Journal of Disaster Risk Reduction*. Vol. 14, No. 2, pp.195–201. doi:10.1016/j.ijdrr.2015.06.006.

Hage, G. (1998) *White Nation: Fantasies of Supremacy in a Multicultural Society.* Sydney: Pluto Press.

Harms, L. (2010) *Understanding Human Development: A Multidimensional Approach*, 2nd ed. South Melbourne, Victoria: Oxford University Press.

Hird, M.J. and Jackson, S. (2001) Where 'angels' and 'wusses' fear to tread: sexual coercion in adolescent dating relationships, *Journal of Sociology*. Vol. 37, No. 1, pp.27–43. doi:10.1177/144078301128756184.

Hooker, L., Theobald, J., Anderson, K., Billet, P., and Barons, P. (2019) Violence against young women in non-urban areas of Australia: a scoping review, *Trauma, Violence and Abuse*. Vol. 20, No. 4, pp.534–549. doi:10.1177/1524838017725752.

Horne, D. (1964) *The Lucky Country*. Sydney: Penguin Books Australia.

Hornibrook, D. (2015) Barriers around access to abortion experienced by rural women in New South Wales, Australia, *Rural and Remote Health*. Vol. 16, No. 1, p.3538. https://doi.org/10.22605/RRH3538.

Johnston, B., Flynn, C., and Gordon, F. (2022) Australia – a land for young women? Exploring young women's positioning in contemporary Australian family violence discourses, *Affilia: Journal of Women and Social Work*. pp.1–16. doi:10.1177/08861099221108381.

Kirkby, D. (2003) 'Beer, glorious beer': gender politics and Australian popular culture, *Journal of Popular Culture*. Vol. 37, No. 2, p.244.

Langton, M. (2020) Improving family violence legal and support services for Aboriginal and Torres Strait Islander Women (research report). ANROWS.

Little, J. (2017) Understanding domestic violence in rural spaces: a research agenda, *Progress in Human Geography*. Vol 41, No. 4, pp.472–488. doi:10.1177/0309132516645960.

Lombard, N. (2013) Young people's temporal and spatial accounts of gendered violence, *Sociology*. Vol. 47, No. 6, pp.1136–1151. doi:10.1177/0038038512458734.

Magnus A.M. and Donohue F.A. (2022) Reimagining access to justice through the eyes of rural domestic violence survivors, *Theoretical Criminology*. Vol. 26, no. 3, pp.434–455. doi:10.1177/13624806211035103.

Maurer, K. (2019) Distinctions in adolescent dating violence: An exploration of etiology, scope and prevention strategies of intimate partner violence in adolescence. In Bates, E. and Taylor, J. (eds.) *Intimate Partner Violence: New Perspectives in Research and Practice*. Abingdon, Oxford: Routledge.

Miolin, L. (2022) Two thirds of female workers in rural areas have been harassed, researcher says, amid mining sector scrutiny, *ABC News*. Available at: https://www.abc.net.au/news/2022-08-18/rural-women-vulnerable-to-workplace-harassment-researcher-says/101343908.

Moreton-Robinson, A. (2000) *Talkin' up to the White Women: Indigenous Women and Feminism*. Queensland: University of Queensland Press.

Munro, E. (2013) Feminism: a fourth wave?, *Political Insight*. Vol. 4, No. 2, pp.22–25. doi:10.1111/2041-9066.120.

Murdolo, A. (2015) Submission to the Royal Commission into Family Violence (Victoria) Multicultural Centre for Women's Health. Collingwood, Victoria. Available at: https://humanrights.gov.au/sites/default/files/53.%20Multicultural%20Centre%20for%20Women%27s%20Health.pdf.

Murray, S. and Powell, A. (2009) 'What's the problem?' Australian public policy constructions of domestic and family violence, *Violence Against Women*. Vol. 15, No. 5, pp.532–552. doi:10.1177/1077801209331408.

Murray, L., Warr, D., Chen, J., Block, K., Murdolo, A., Quiazon, R., Davis, E., and Vaughan, C. (2019) Between 'here' and 'there': family violence against immigrant and refugee women in urban and rural Southern Australia, *Gender, Place and Culture*. Vol. 26, No. 1, pp.91–110. doi:10.1080/0966369X.2018/1553862.

Newman, D. (2016) Attitudes to justice in a rural community. *Legal Studies*. Vol. 36, No. 4, pp.591–612. doi:10.1111/lest.12127.

Our Watch, Australia's National Research Organisation for Women's Safety (ANROWS), and Victoria Health (2015) Change the story: A shared framework for the primary prevention of violence against women and their children in Australia. Melbourne: Our Watch. Available at: https://media-cdn.ourwatch.org.au/wp-content/uploads/sites/2/2019/05/21025429/Change-the-story-framework-prevent-violence-women-children-AA-new.pdf.

Owen, S. and Carrington, K. (2015) Domestic violence (DV) service provision and the architecture of rural life: an Australian case study. *Journal of Rural Studies*. Vol. 39, pp.229–238.

Parkinson, D. (2019) Investigating the increase in domestic violence post disaster: an Australian case study, *Journal of Interpersonal Violence*. Vol. 34, No. 11, pp.2333–2362. doi:10.1177/0886260517696876.

Piper, A. and Stevenson, A. (2019) The long history of gender violence in Australia, and why it matters today, *The Conversation*. Available at: https://theconversation.com/the-long-history-of-gender-violence-in-australia-and-why-it-matters-today-119927.

Pini, B., Mayes, R., and Boyer, K. (2013) 'Scary' heterosexualities in a rural Australian mining town, *Journal of Rural Studies*. Vol.32, pp.168–176. doi:10.1016/j.jrurstud.2013.06.002.

Ragusa, A. (2012) Rural Australian women's legal help seeking for intimate partner violence: women intimate partner violence victim survivor's perceptions of criminal justice support services . *Journal of Interpersonal Violence*. Vol. 28, No. 4, pp.685–717 doi:10.1177/0886260512455864.

Ragusa, A. (2017) Rurality's influence on women's intimate partner violence experiences and support needed for escape and healing in Australia, *Journal of Social Service Research*. Vol. 43, No. 2. doi:10.1080/01488376.2016.124867.

Ragusa, A. and Ward, O. (2017) Unveiling the male corset, *Men and Masculinities*. Vol 20, No. 1, pp. 71–97. doi:10.1177/1097184X15613830.

Sandberg, L. (2013) Backward, dumb and violent hillbillies? Rural geographies and intersectional studies on intimate partner violence . *Affilia: Journal of Women and Social Work*. Vol. 28, No. 4. doi:10.1177/088610991354153.

Saunders, K. (1984) The study of domestic violence in colonial Queensland: sources and problems, *Historical Studies*. Vol. 21, No. 82, pp.68–84. doi:10.1080/10314618408595693.

Saunders, S. and Easteal, P. (2013) The nature, pervasiveness and manifestations of sexual harassment in rural Australia: does 'masculinity' of workplace make a difference?, *Women's Studies International Forum*. Vol. 40, pp.121–131.

Senior, K. and Chenhall, R. (2012) Boyfriends, babies and basketball: present lives and future aspirations of young women in a remote Australian Aboriginal community, *Journal of Youth Studies*. Vol. 15, No. 3, pp.369–388. doi:10.1080/13676261.2012.663890.

Senior, K., Chenhall, R., and Helmer, J. (2020) 'Boys mostly just want to have sex': young Indigenous people talk about relationships and sexual intimacy in remote, rural and regional Australia. *Sexualities*. Vol. 23, No. 8, pp.1457–1479. doi:10.1177/1363460720902018.

Senior, K., Helmer, J., and Chenhall, R. (2017) 'As long as he's coming home to me': vulnerability, jealousy and violence in young people's relationships in remote, rural and regional Australia, *Health Sociology Review*. Vol. 26, No. 2, pp.204–218. doi:10.1080/14461242.2016.1157697.

State of Victoria (2016) Royal Commission into Family Violence: Summary and recommendations, Parl Paper No 132 (2014–16). Available at: https://www.rcfv.com.au/MediaLibraries/RCFamilyViolence/Reports/Final/RCFV-Summary.pdf.

Summers, A. (1981) Hidden from history: women victims of crime. In Mukherjee, S.K. and Scutt, J.A. (eds.) (2015) *Women and Crime*. Abingdon, Oxford: Routledge, pp.22–30.

Summers, A (2016) *Damned Whores and God's Police*. First Published 1975. Sydney: NewSouth Publishing.

Tarzia, L., Douglas, H., and Sheeran, N. (2021) Reproductive coercion and the abuse against women from minority ethnic backgrounds: views of service providers in Australia. *Culture, Health and Sexuality: An International Journal for Research, Intervention and Care*. Vol. 24, No. 4, pp. 466–481. doi:10.1080/13691058.2020.1859617.

Taylor, K. and Sullivan, T. (2017) Bidirectional relationships between dating violence victimisation and substance use in a diverse sample of early adolescents, *Journal of Interpersonal Violence*. Vol. 36, No. 1–2, pp.862–891.doi:10.1177/0886260517731312.

Valentine, G. (2008) The ties that bind: towards geographies of intimacy, *Geography Compass*. Vol. 2, No. 6, pp.2097–2110. doi:10.1111/j.1749-8198.2008.00158.x.

Vaughan, C., Block, K. Sullivan, C., Hourani, J., Khaw, S., Jarallah, Y., Zannettino, L., Gregoric, C., Murray, L., Suha, M., Chen, J., Murdolo, A., and Sandhu, M. (2020) Multicultural and Settlement services supporting women experiencing violence: The MuSeS project. *ANROWS*. Vol. 11.

Victorian Government (2020) Family violence in Victoria: findings from the Victorian Population Health Survey 2017. Victoria, Australia. Available at: https://vahi.vic.gov.au/sites/default/files/2021-12/Family-violence-in-Victoria%20-%20November%202020.pdf.

Watson, J. (2011) Understanding survival sex: young women, homelessness and intimate relationships, *Journal of Youth Studies*. Vol. 14, No. 6. doi:10.1080/13676261.2011.588945.

Websdale, N. (1995) Rural woman abuse: The voices of Kentucky women. *Violence against Women*. Vol 1. (4) pp.309–338. doi:10.1177/107780129500100400.

Wendt, S. and Hornosty, J. (2010) Understanding contexts of family violence in rural, farming communities: implications for rural women's health. *Rural Society*, No. 20, No. 1, pp.51–63. doi:10.5172/rsj.20.1.51.

Whitman, J. (2007) Understanding and responding to teen victims: a developmental framework. *The Prevention Researcher*. Vol. 14, No. 1, pp.10–13.

Women's Services Network (WESNET) (2000) Domestic violence in regional Australia: a literature review. A report for the Commonwealth Department of Transport and Regional Services. Commonwealth of Australia.

World Health Organization (2021) Violence against women. Available at: https://www.who.int/health-topics/violence-against-women#tab=tab_1.

6

IRISH TRAVELLER MEN

Structural and Cultural Barriers, and Reoffending

Megan Coghlan

Introduction

Travellers are an Indigenous population in Ireland despite the Irish government only officially recognising the ethnic status of Travellers in 2017 (European Social Policy Network (ESPN), 2017; Raidió Teilifís Éireann (RTE), 2017). This chapter contributes to knowledge on the reoffending experiences of Irish Traveller men in the criminal justice system (CJS). The most recent Irish Census reveals a rapidly changing multicultural society with increasing numbers identifying as Irish Traveller (30,987 individuals, a 5.1% increase), Muslim (29.8% increase), and Orthodox Christian (37.5% increase) (Central Statistics Office (CSO), 2017). However, data on ethnicity of the prison population is not yet available (Doyle et al., 2022) In addition, although there are some recent exceptions such as the research from Brandon and O'Connell (2018) that investigated sentencing disparities between Irish and non-Irish nationals in the CJS, Bracken (2014) highlights a lack of research examining racism and discriminatory practices in a specific Irish criminal justice context. Thus, data on Travellers within the Irish CJS is difficult to find (Brandon and O'Connell, 2018). Indications from the Irish Penal Reform Trust (2014) reveal that Traveller men are between 5 and 11 times more likely to be imprisoned compared to non-Traveller Irish men, and Traveller women are 18–22 times more likely to be imprisoned compared to non-Traveller Irish women.

More generally, criminology has been criticised for a lack of meaningful exploration of the experiences of people from the global majority (Potter, 2015) or for not being founded in appropriate cultural and historical contexts (Moosavi, 2019). Criminology has therefore arguably legitimised the marginalisation of Indigenous populations through maintaining a western focus on research (Carrington et al., 2016). Limited research on Travellers comes at a time when criminology in Ireland has recently experienced significant growth and the role of history and politics are increasingly recognised as important in understanding people's experiences (Lynch et al., 2020). This chapter seeks to place the reoffending of Irish Traveller men into a structural and cultural context to understand reoffending experiences. This is important as there is a general lack of criminological focus on people of the global majority and more specifically there is a lack of knowledge about Travellers and reoffending in Ireland which links to a general paucity of research about Travellers' experiences of the CJS (Mulcahy, 2012).

As a lot of existing research on recidivism and criminal careers is quantitative in nature, theoretical knowledge of reoffending is somewhat underdeveloped. This chapter will use a conceptual framework developed from analysing desistance theories. Desistance is best described as a gradual process of change towards a crime-free life rather than an abrupt event (Maruna, 2019) and desistance research often focuses on reoffending, comparing people who reoffend and people who desist together to understand different offending journeys. Desistance theories focus on either one or a combination of social factors, subjective factors, structural factors, and more recently cultural factors to understand desistance (Farrall, 2019, 2021; Weaver, 2019). This chapter places a particular emphasis on structural and cultural factors to understand Irish Traveller men's experiences of reoffending. This approach is justified as the onset of offending, reoffending, and desistance are three separate stages in one overall offending process (Barry, 2007; Farrington, 2015) and therefore, the same categories of factors in different contexts can be used to understand reoffending and desistance.

Reoffending is a broad term that refers to a 'person's future criminal involvement…to refer to all criminal acts committed by a person' (Nagin et al., 2009: 120). Thus, reoffending is neither stable nor continuous but is a constantly changing state of officially detected and undetected behaviour influenced by a variety of factors. Recognising the fluidity of reoffending allows for the exploration of gender and ethnic identity alongside wider structural and cultural processes to develop a contextualised understanding of reoffending amongst Irish Travellers. This is imperative as contextual factors can influence people's behaviour and choices in processes of change (Segev, 2020). Structural factors stem from wider social, economic, cultural, or political processes (Farrall, 2019). Thus, culture, socio-culture properties, economic change, and contextual factors can determine people's values and behaviour. A Traveller label already results in experiences of discrimination and prejudice (Irish Traveller Movement, 2019), and the addition of structural factors may adversely affect members of the Traveller community compared to wider Irish society and explain experiences of reoffending. Zamble and Quinsey (1997) theorised that issues coping with the reality of release could result in reoffending and thus structural processes combined with a Traveller identity may exacerbate barriers to coping with a move away from crime and explain subsequent reoffending.

Farrall and Bowling (1999) used structuration theory to emphasise the need for addressing both individual choices, wider social forces, and structural factors to fully explain offending behaviour. It is therefore necessary to pay attention to the interaction between subjective factors such as a person's ethnic and gender identity and the wider social, economic, cultural, and political processes that impact an individual's life to understand choices and behaviour in a contextualised way (Farrall et al., 2011; King, 2013; Lindegaard and Jacques, 2013).

In examining Irish Travellers, the context of structural and cultural factors may shed light on barriers that could potentially restrict and constrain an individual's identity and behaviour and in this sense perhaps people who reoffend are not condemned to deviance (Maruna, 2001) but restricted by wider structural processes that intersect with identity. This chapter will now explore the Irish Traveller identity, masculine identity, structural barriers, and cultural barriers. Data from three case studies will then be presented and analysed in a wider structural and cultural context.

Irish Traveller identity and structural barriers

Being part of the Irish Traveller community shapes people's interactions with political, economic, cultural, and social processes. Travellers as a social group are named as such due to their nomadic lifestyle and may have a strained relationship with the settled population of Ireland as Irish people are often vehemently opposed to providing sites for Travellers close to their communities (Mulcahy, 2012). Exclusion and prejudice may thus inform Travellers' understandings of their identity. An individual's identity is comprised of an individual's perspective on life, the behaviour of an individual and the individual's way of life (Côté, 2006), and Traveller identities in particular are complex and fluid (Forster et al., 2022). Identities are thus negotiated based on social ties and structural barriers as wider cultural and political processes support the discrimination of the Traveller identity and influence Travellers' perception of that discrimination in Irish society (Donnelly-Drummond, 2016).

Culturally, the Traveller term emerged due to the nomadic identity of the Travelling community, and although many Irish Travellers are now settled, the nomadic lifestyle is still a large part of their identity and culture (Joyce, 2018). Discrimination against Travellers can be traced back to the 1500s where the nomadic lifestyle was first criminalised in Britain (Joyce, 2018). Irish Travellers are culturally distinct to the settled Irish population and this is linked to experiences of discrimination at the hands of the settled population (Bracken, 2014; Joyce, 2018; Mulcahy, 2012; Van Hout, 2010). For example, Travellers may perceive a clash between their culture and success at school, as being successful academically can mark an individual as different and may result in experiences of stigma from within the Traveller community itself (Forster et al., 2022). Many Irish Travellers leave school early which increases the risk of Travellers engaging in offending behaviour (Gavin, 2019).

Politically, Irish Travellers have been criminalised by the Irish state since 1963 through legislation (Irish Traveller Movement, 2019). Legislation can emphasise social marginalisation and criminalisation for the Traveller way of life – for example, the Housing (Miscellaneous Provisions) Act 2002 means that Travellers living on the side of the road can be prosecuted and have their property confiscated (Bracken, 2014; Joyce et al., 2017; Mulcahy, 2012). Despite this, criminology has yet to fully engage meaningfully in understanding the experiences of different ethnicities in the criminal justice system (Parmar, 2016). Travellers are now a protected group in Irish equality legislation and are included in anti-discriminatory initiatives (ESPN, 2017). However, Travellers are regularly stereotyped in society as criminals and as dishonest and immoral, emphasising the stigma associated with a Traveller identity (Joyce et al., 2017). In this case, the Traveller identity and intersecting structural factors may explain reoffending as a reaction to living in a community with few opportunities to advance in conventional society.

Altogether social stereotypes and economic inequality combined with political and public intolerance towards Travellers in Ireland are evident in Traveller living conditions, experiences of poverty, and access to healthcare (Joyce et al., 2017). Structural and cultural factors alongside a criminal record can result in double discrimination – discrimination due to ethnicity alongside discrimination due to a criminal record. This may partially explain why Irish Traveller men engage in reoffending. Taken together, the male Traveller identity combined with wider cultural and structural barriers may help to explain reoffending behaviour.

Cultural expectations, masculinity, and Irish Travellers

Masculinity alongside ethnicity is another important aspect of identity for Traveller men and the intersection of gender and ethnicity has not been commonly considered in relation to Traveller men (Hodgins and Fox, 2012). This is important as people's understandings of their own gender identity are influenced by cultural definitions of male and female (Wood and Eagly, 2015). Irish Traveller men persist with adhering to traditional characteristics of masculinity such as being the primary provider for the family and head of the family (Hodgins and Fox, 2012; Parker and McVeigh, 2013). This links to complex explanations of hegemonic masculinity which incorporate practical elements such as providing an ideal portrayal of men and emphasising how men should form relationships with women (Connell and Messerschmidt, 2005). Hegemonic masculinity also links to gender roles and identity that represents dominance over women and in some cases other men (Connell and Messerschmidt, 2005). Hegemonic masculinity may thus be important for understanding Irish Traveller experiences of masculinity and reoffending.

To fully understand hegemonic masculinity, there needs to be recognition of context, especially of patriarchy and the relationship between hegemonic masculinity, various subordinate masculinities, and women (Messerschmidt, 2019). Outside of this relationship and outside of understanding that the legitimisation of this relationship sustains unequal gender relations, hegemonic masculinity cannot be properly comprehended. As Messerschmidt (2019: 90) explains, 'gender hegemony functions to obscure unequal gender relations while effectively permeating public and private life, encouraging all to endorse, unite around, and embody such unequal gender relations.' Irish Traveller culture is linked to patriarchy with an emphasis on traditional gender relations whereby Traveller men are meant to protect the reputation of their family and community (Bracken, 2014; Hodgins and Fox, 2012). This cultural expectation legitimises the portrayal of hegemonic masculinity, thus Irish Traveller culture sustains individual and traditional understandings of what it means to be a man (Messerschmidt, 2019).

The combination and enactment of a hegemonic masculine and Traveller identity is relevant to reoffending as Travellers are overrepresented in the criminal justice system (Brandon and O'Connell, 2018) which may be related to cultural perceptions of Irish Traveller men as dominant or aggressive. This perception is sustained by the intersecting identities of class and gender whereby subordinate groups such as Travellers are subject to the authority of the dominant settled community (Sloan, 2016). This links to Cohen's (2002) characterisation of 'folk devils' whereby Travellers as a group are stigmatised by society and pressure is put on the authorities to do something about the group. Media coverage of Travellers contributes to a folk devil label by portraying misconceptions that Traveller men are aggressive which leads to further exclusion of Travellers from society (James, 2007). Status and providing for the family are important to Traveller men and difficult to achieve given misconceptions about the Traveller way of life resulting in marginalisation in society. In this gender and cultural context of exclusion, reoffending may provide a way to provide for family.

The Irish Traveller way of life is unique so it corresponds that Irish Traveller experiences of reoffending may also be unique. In examining subjective factors such as a Traveller and male identity in a context of structural and cultural barriers, new light can be shed on Irish Traveller men's reoffending.

Research design

Three cases will be discussed in this chapter, which are drawn from qualitative research intended to understand people's experiences of reoffending, with 28 people (10 women and 18 men) in Ireland. Given that the focus of this chapter is on Irish Traveller experiences of reoffending, the three particular cases are chosen as the participants all identified as Irish Travellers. These cases include Gerry, who had multiple charges for shoplifting and public order offences connected to alcohol; Pauliea, who also had multiple public order charges linked to alcohol and engaged in theft and driving offences; and Tommo, who had theft and robbery charges linked to drug and alcohol use. It is important to note that the names listed above are pseudonyms and that the research had ethical approval.

Semi-structured interviews were conducted, and each participant agreed to audio recording which was transcribed verbatim by the author. The interviews consisted of four main sections asking questions about background and growing up, early offending, intentions, and hopes for the future to develop a contextualised understanding of reoffending experiences. The interviews were retrospective so there may be some inaccuracies in memories and perspectives as it is possible that participants' perspectives on their past were influenced by their circumstances at the time of the interview (Kazemian and Farrington, 2005). However, this research was not primarily concerned with capturing detailed information such as age of onset and was more focused on understanding people's reasons for reoffending. In this sense, retrospective interviews are useful for exploring subjective and structural factors as they provide a platform for individuals to talk about their past experiences, but also demonstrate the changing nature of their identity and circumstances (Lundgren, 2011).

Semi-structured interviews were chosen for their flexibility so that follow-up questions and interactions were permitted throughout the interviews (Blee and Taylor, 2002). This was particularly important in the case of Gerry, Pauliea, and Tommo as the interview was not designed to specifically ask about ethnicity. Ethnicity emerged within the conversation itself, where all three participants spoke about their Traveller identity and linked that to their broader life and offending experiences. The advantage of the semi-structured format meant that the researcher could ask follow-up questions to explore ethnicity and reoffending in further detail.

Analysis

Thematic analysis was chosen given the in-depth nature of the interviews, and guidelines laid out by Braun and Clarke (2006) were followed. Thematic analysis helps to develop a richer understanding of participants' experiences, feelings, and thoughts (Dillon et al., 2019) which is particularly useful for understanding the impact of identity and structural barriers on reoffending. A software called MAXQDA facilitated the identification of initial codes across transcripts which were collated into themes. The basic themes were grouped into organising themes and the organising themes were arranged into two global themes: reoffending as a coping mechanism, and reoffending and advantage.

Understanding Irish Traveller experiences of reoffending

The global themes of reoffending as a coping mechanism, and reoffending and advantage shed light on the reoffending experiences of Irish Traveller men. The subsequent organising themes linked to each global theme are listed in Figure 6.1. Through these themes the chapter will demonstrate the interaction between identity, and cultural and structural factors to help explain reoffending.

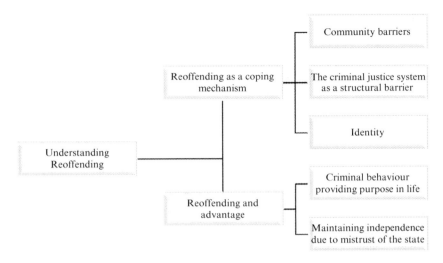

FIGURE 6.1 Understanding Reoffending: Global and Organising Themes

Reoffending as a coping mechanism

The first global theme identified that reoffending served as a coping mechanism in the face of barriers stemming from wider structural and cultural processes. This is especially significant for Gerry, Pauliea, and Tommo as Traveller men because they are more likely to experience marginalisation in relation to these processes compared to the non-Traveller Irish population. Reoffending behaviour therefore provided a mechanism for individuals to cope with discrimination and prejudice.

Community barriers

Growing up in a Traveller community introduced people to structural barriers stemming from economic and social processes. Economically, Travellers are exposed to poverty or what some scholars have called a culture of poverty (Mac Gréil, 2010, as cited in Costello, 2014).

> And em yeah just it was rough where I used to live and it was all the time stolen cars stuff like that so you kinda mix up with people you wouldn't mix up with today like at that time ya know. And em I got into a lot of trouble up there
>
> *[Pauliea].*

Thus, early offending became a means to escape from poverty linked to living within a Traveller community. The concept of 'anomie' explains crime as stemming from a gap between conventional societal goals and people's means of achieving those goals (Merton, 1938). It may be that goals in an Irish Travelling culture are different to conventional goals and traditional criminological theories do not necessarily apply to marginalised populations. In fact, research shows that Travelling culture is linked to leaving school early (Gavin, 2019) which does not align with a conventional sense of success. Instead, Irish Traveller men may prioritise status and providing financially for their family which may be underpinned by a masculine identity and this will be discussed in more detail later in the chapter.

Culturally and socially, growing up in a Traveller community was linked to adopting a tough persona to align with the hegemonic masculinity culture in the community.

> But yeah, a bit challenging, it's not like where you hear them communities where they're over in Dalkey [upper class Dublin] and you go over to Dun Laoghaire [upper class Dublin] it's not like where I've been from those kinds of areas so it is a bit tougher yeah. You have to be tough to be here
> *[Gerry].*

Despite the Irish state not recognising Travellers as an ethnic minority until 2017, the Traveller community through their culture and way of life have long been distinguished from settled communities and subject to discrimination (Gavin, 2019). This chapter shows that early experiences of discrimination encouraged individuals to adopt a masculine 'tough' exterior from a young age and, therefore, a masculine Traveller identity combined with cultural and structural barriers influenced people from childhood. Merton's (1938) idea of strain may apply in terms of experiences of exclusion potentially causing frustration, and early childhood experiences of exclusion may also help to normalise offending behaviour leading to the onset of offending (Webster et al., 2006).

Criminal justice system as a structural barrier

Having started offending, reoffending can be understood as a coping mechanism in the face of different structural barriers which can be aggravated by dual identities of Traveller and criminal. Link and Phelan (2001: 365) define stigma as 'when elements of labelling, stereotyping, separation, status loss, and discrimination co-occur in a power situation that allows the components of stigma to unfold'. Irish Travellers involved in reoffending thus experience stigma in two ways: stigma linked to identifying as a Traveller and stigma linked to a criminal record. In addition, a limited Spent Convictions and Certain Disclosures Act 2016 in Ireland is restricted in removing stigma as only certain minor offences become spent after 7 years. Thus, politically and socially, Ireland has not made it easy for individuals to reject the stigma and discrimination associated with the dual offender and Traveller label. Difficulties coping are linked to reoffending (Zamble and Quinsey, 1997) and in this context the inability to escape and cope with dual stigma can explain why reoffending continues for Irish Traveller men.

Socially, the criminal justice system can act as a barrier to reintegration for Travellers. Pauliea spoke about stigma from within the Travelling community itself in relation to trying to reintegrate into the community following a prison sentence.

> But em it's a bit hard to blend back in because you kind of get used to them [prison population] how they live and you're used to your own thing for so long on your own ya know. And they kind of don't understand that either ya know what I mean. Not where I come from anyway cause I'm a member of the Travelling community like ya know
>
> *[Pauliea].*

In a slightly different way, Gerry reflected on trying to hide his Traveller and offender identity from friends until interaction with the Gardaí (Irish police) revealed his dual identities and past involvement with the criminal justice system

> They'd [friend group] never think I'm a Traveller and then as soon as they [Gardaí] get to me, they ask 'what is your name and where are you from? Right can you step out of the car?' Oh fucking hell I would be the one caught with a warrant or something like that
>
> *[Gerry].*

The reality of being confronted with a dual identity of Traveller and offender can result in individuals anticipating rejection within conventional society (Moore et al., 2013). This can create pressure on individuals to disclose their identity to avoid stigma or decide to hide their identity (Forster et al., 2022). Gerry's attempts at hiding his identity were rendered moot after an interaction with the Gardaí, and reoffending can therefore act as a mechanism for coping with or rebelling against rejection.

Tommo emphasises the impact of this rejection in relation to his own behaviour, reflecting on his treatment by Gardaí because of his Traveller and offender identity. This perception of unfair treatment is not unique as Travellers have noticed disproportionate police responses, where the police tend to side with the settled population when disputes arise (Mulcahy, 2012). More recently, a report by Doyle et al. (2022) emphasised the over-policing of ethnic communities which can result in conflict, suspicion, and distrust between police and Travellers.

> Guards have a bad attitude to Travellers, they're biased. I'd rebel against the Guards. They intrude on you and abuse you. If you neglect a puppy, it'll bite you so what about a human?
>
> *[Tommo].*

This emphasises the idea that reoffending continues for Traveller men to cope with treatment by others because of the interaction between identity and wider social and political processes (Meek, 2007). Masculinity is also important, as Tommo alluded to, because violence and fighting can be considered a cultural practice in Traveller life (Bracken, 2014; Hodgins and Fox, 2012). Tommo spoke about 'traditional fighting in the Traveller community, and I'd be competitive so I used to watch that'. Therefore, reacting aggressively to perceived abuse by the police may be understood in the context of Traveller life and hegemonic masculinity whereby reoffending becomes a form of rebellion and empowerment. Thus, different forms of Traveller, masculine, and offender identity intersect, resulting in triple disadvantage that can encourage Traveller men to reoffend.

Economically, masculinity is also important to consider in relation to employment barriers, as Traveller men often perceive themselves as the provider for the family (Mac Gabhann, 2011; Parker and McVeigh, 2013). Therefore, persistent failure to secure employment can explain why men reoffend to restore their masculine image and position as provider for the family (Egleton et al., 2016). This is emphasised by Tommo who acknowledged that 'maybe getting a job would've helped [with desistance]' but this is difficult in the face of stigma linked to a criminal record and Traveller identity. Pauliea spoke about the shame linked to divulging information about past convictions and gaps in work experience that corresponded to time spent in prison, indicating that people may feel pressure to hide their identity (Forster et al., 2022).

> Sometimes it's kind of embarrassing when you go into a place like some places and they ask you where were you all this time do you know what I mean? And it's probably someone there and you say I'm in prison and they kind of look at you ya know
>
> *[Pauliea].*

There is a lack of literacy and lack of engagement with education within the Traveller community which already means that access to conventional employment is limited (Costello, 2014; Gavin, 2019; Forster at al., 2019). Poor education and difficulty in obtaining employment combined with a Traveller identity and criminal record demonstrates the interaction between identity and wider structural factors that explain reoffending to cope with shame or embarrassment.

For Gerry, overcoming educational barriers alone still did not result in employment as his criminal record restricted his ability to work.

> I couldn't get a job cause of me previous convictions so I was a bit pissed off then. So, like fuck that. So that brought me down an awful lot I was like do you know what no matter what you do in life, this is about two year ago I had that set point, I had this set of mind no matter what you do, like there's me

after going to college for fucking two year now, no matter what you do it's no good, fuck that or whatever you know?

[Gerry].

A tripartite masculine, Traveller, and offender identity can result in enhanced exclusion from conventional employment and, coupled with the effect of stigma, reoffending can be understood as a means to cope with exclusion and discrimination and restore masculinity by providing an alternative source of income. Tommo's analogy of a neglected dog biting to defend itself is quite powerful in this regard as it suggests that reoffending continues to cope with and guard against discrimination. Altogether, an individual's understanding of their own identity in the context of structural and cultural barriers can explain decisions to continue with crime as a form of coping with and overcoming barriers.

Reoffending and advantage

Along with reoffending serving as a coping mechanism, reoffending continued to be linked to the idea of advantage. Firstly, Irish Traveller men constrained by structural barriers are limited in obtaining conventional advantage, and advantages could thus be gained from criminal behaviour. Travellers tend to be isolated from society and feel distrust towards authorities (Forster et al., 2019). Secondly, reoffending provided advantage as a mechanism to maintain independence linked to mistrust of the criminal justice system or wider state support.

Advantage through criminal behaviour

Gains through criminal behaviour were spoken about in relation to masculinity. In particular, Tommo spoke about the 'buzz and the gains' from criminal behaviour. Mercan (2020) identified that enjoyment of crime is important to understanding reoffending and this links to research by Carlsson (2013) who found that reoffending behaviour is linked to age-specific meanings of masculinity. Therefore, reoffending may continue due to an immature rationality whereby the gains from offending are prioritised over the longer-term consequences. This is emphasised by Gerry who said 'I wasn't thinking of time to come. I was only living for the moment.' Therefore, reoffending may continue as men already marginalised from society may express masculinity and obtain enjoyment from risk-taking behaviour and rebelling against conventional methods of social control, while recognising that there can be financial rewards from reoffending (Carlsson, 2013; Mercan, 2020; Messerschmidt and Tomsen, 2018).

As discussed earlier in the chapter, financial reward is important due to exclusion from obtaining success in a conventional way with a dual Traveller and criminal identity. Crime therefore became an important alternative source of advantage in the lives of those depicted in these case studies.

> Yeah [there is a benefit to theft] you're like if you've no money like you're well capable of getting that for nothing so why when you have money do you actually have to spend it so fast like?
>
> *[Gerry].*

Similarly, Tommo reflected on offending when money was low and not fully caring about the potential consequences of that action.

> Money was low and I was with a friend... Only [consider consequences] of getting caught but then I'd just have to run faster
>
> *[Tommo].*

Given the economic barriers and exclusion from employment that respondents faced, it was common for reoffending to be perceived in positive terms as it represented a behaviour that was familiar, purposeful, and sometimes associated with rewards (Mercan, 2020). In sum, given bounded circumstances of poverty and exclusion, reoffending allowed men to express masculinity, gain financially, and enjoy the 'buzz' associated with reoffending.

Maintaining independence due to mistrust of the state

There was potential advantage linked to state-provided support for people involved in the criminal justice system, yet respondents were suspicious of state support (Forster et al., 2019). Specifically, Travellers can be distrustful of state organisations such as the police (Mulcahy, 2012) and this distrust may serve as a further barrier to accepting help or support from the criminal justice system, explaining why reoffending continues.

> I never really liked it [Probation] at all I thought oh Jesus Christ all these people want is you to sit down with a paper and pen all day
>
> *[Gerry].*

Gerry was forced to engage with the Probation Service early due to shoplifting offences. His fear of prison after being held on remand for a week encouraged Gerry to engage with Probation which was perceived as the lesser evil. Tommo also had a perception of support as unhelpful and spoke about never wanting to engage with support following periods of incarceration – 'I probably never wanted Probation before.' Lastly, Pauliea demonstrated very similar ideas in relation to criminal justice or wider welfare support.

> Well I won't lie now right of all the times I've been locked up in prison, I've never went to anybody like Probation em, social welfare people, I've never went to any of them
>
> *[Pauliea].*

Culturally, therefore, and linked to experiences of discrimination and marginalisation Travellers are distrustful of state services and people outside of their community which is known as cultural resistance (Costello, 2014) meaning that there are barriers when it comes to Travellers accepting support. Additionally, accepting support may challenge hegemonic masculinity characteristics such as strength and independence (Barken and Sims-Gould, 2020) resulting in reluctance to engage with welfare support. Linked to a marginalised position in Irish society and negative interactions with criminal justice, this research finds Travellers perceived support as unhelpful and potentially undermining the role of a Traveller man as provider for the family. This perception can result in a denial of criminal justice and wider state assistance which may encourage reoffending to continue over time as people can maintain their independence through offending. In a Traveller context, state support could go further in being culturally and historically constituted to ensure tailored support which corresponds with Southern criminology critiques of wider criminological research (Moosavi, 2019). Ultimately, by reoffending, individuals found a way to overcome structural barriers and identity constraints that they had very little control over, meaning that there was a perception that reoffending was something they could gain from while state support was distrusted.

This section thus explains continued reoffending through the idea of reoffending offering advantage and reoffending allowing independence due to mistrust of the state. Combining the two global themes together, reoffending can be understood as a coping mechanism and as a form of advantage. For Irish Traveller men, reoffending continues as their tripartite identity as Travellers, as men, and as men with a criminal record interact with wider structural and cultural factors which allows for a contextualised understanding of reoffending behaviour amongst Irish Traveller men to emerge. Wider barriers highlighted in these three case studies were: limited spent conviction legislation, exclusion from wider society, exclusion from conventional employment, poverty, differing cultural goals in terms of education, experiences of discrimination, and distrust. This context is crucial for developing an in-depth understanding of reoffending experiences amongst Irish Traveller men who are already likely to experience marginalisation from a young age due to their Traveller identity.

Conclusion

Exploring structural and cultural barriers alongside identity in this chapter allowed for an in-depth contextualised picture of Irish Traveller men's reoffending to emerge which is important as in-depth understandings of reoffending in Ireland are rare. This corresponds with a lack of wider criminological research about the experiences of people of the global majority. Irish Traveller men's reoffending experiences are marked by marginalisation, prejudice, and distrust. Thus, it is necessary to understand experiences of discrimination to make sense of Irish Travellers' reoffending behaviour. Placing Traveller experiences of reoffending in a structural and cultural context allowed for constraint and obstacles to emerge that developed a contextualised picture of reoffending.

Specifically, two understandings for Irish Traveller men's reoffending emerged. Firstly, reoffending behaviour can be understood as a coping mechanism in the face of constrained circumstances. Secondly, reoffending can be understood as a means of gaining advantage in constrained circumstances. Context is thus crucial for understanding reoffending amongst Irish Traveller men given the interaction that has been demonstrated in this chapter between a person's gender, ethnic, and criminal identity, and wider economic, political, cultural, and social processes. This interaction highlights how Traveller men are often excluded from engaging in conventional processes and how reoffending can serve to help cope with and overcome barriers. In overcoming barriers through reoffending, Irish Traveller men can gain a sense of masculinity, enjoyment, and income from reoffending while fulfilling their role as breadwinner in Traveller culture. Thus, structural processes combined with a Traveller identity can exacerbate barriers to moving away from crime and explain subsequent reoffending.

Ultimately Irish Travellers involved in the CJS are subject to tripartite disadvantage which delays desistance. Culturally and socially, Irish Travellers are labelled as dishonest or immoral, and the addition of a legal offender label serves to reinforce stigma about Travellers and cumulatively disadvantage reintegration into society. This chapter has drawn from only three cases to illustrate the reoffending experiences of Irish Traveller men, so it is inappropriate to make general conclusions. However, the idea of tripartite disadvantage illustrates a significant barrier to desistance that may be applied more widely to people of the global majority to understand their experiences within the criminal justice system. In increasingly multicultural societies, the lack of criminological research focusing on people from the global majority may contribute to the disadvantage different ethnicities face as their experiences of criminal justice are poorly understood. Further research is thus needed to develop contextualised knowledge of the experiences of people from the global majority within the criminal justice system in Ireland and abroad.

It is positive to note that ethnic identifier data is now being collected in the Irish CJS although research has noted a need for further improvement of data collection (Doyle et al., 2022). Data could be enhanced by further criminological research, that is mindful of culture and history, augmenting traditional understandings of criminality with contextualised knowledge from people of the global majority. While developing a contextualised understanding is important, the experiences of Traveller men in this chapter also highlight a need to investigate ongoing experiences of discrimination within the criminal justice system and over-policing of certain ethnicities.

References

Albertson, K., Phillips, J., and Fowler, A. 2020. 'Who Owns Desistance? A Triad of Agency Enabling Social Structures in the Desistance Process.' *Theoretical Criminology* 26, no. 1: 1–20. doi:10.1177/1362480620968084.

Barken, R. and Sims-Gould, J. 2020. 'Home Support Workers and Older Men: The Implications of Masculinity for Later Life Care.' *Men and Masculinities* 23, no. 3–4: 618–635. doi:10.1177/1097184X18804308.

Barry, M. 2007. 'Youth Offending and Youth Transitions: The Power of Capital in Influencing Change.' *Critical Criminology* 15, no. 2: 185–198. doi:10.1007/s10612-007-9024-6.

Blee, K.M and Taylor, V. 2002. 'Semi-Structured Interviewing in Social Movement Research.' In *Methods of Social Movement Research*, edited by B. Klandermans and S. Staggenborg, 92–117. Minnesota: University of Minnesota Press.

Blumstein, A., Cohen, J., and Farrington, D.P. 1988. 'Criminal Career Research: Its Value for Criminology.' *Criminology* 26, no. 1: 1–35. doi:10.1111/j.1745-9125.1988.tb00829.x.

Bosick, S.J., Bersani, B.E., and Farrington, D.P. 2015. 'Relating Clusters of Adolescent Problems to Adult Criminal Trajectories: A Person-Centered, Prospective Approach.' *Journal of Developmental and Life-Course Criminology* 1, no. 2: 169–188.

Bracken, D.C. 2014. 'Probation Practice with Non-Irish National Offenders in the Republic of Ireland.' *Irish Probation Journal* 12: 95–113.

Brandon, A.M. and O'Connell, M. 2018. 'Same Crime: Different Punishment? Investigating Sentencing Disparities Between Irish and Non-Irish Nationals in the Irish Criminal Justice System.' *The British Journal of Criminology* 58, no. 5: 1127–1146. doi:10.1093/bjc/azx080.

Braun, V. and Clarke, V. 2006. 'Using Thematic Analysis in Psychology.' *Qualitative Research in Psychology* 3, no. 2: 77–101. doi:10.1191/1478088706qp063oa.

Carlsson, C. 2013. 'Masculinities, Persistence and Desistance.' *Criminology* 51, no. 3: 661–693. doi:10.1111/1745-9125.12016.

Carrington, K., Hogg, R., and Sozzo, M. 2016 'Southern Criminology.' *British Journal of Criminology* 56, no. 1: 1–20. doi:10.1093/bjc/azv083.

Central Statistics Office (CSO). 2017. 'Census of Population 2016: Profile 7 Migration and Diversity.' https://www.cso.ie/en/releasesandpublications/ep/p-cp7md/p7md/ (25 November 2021).

Cohen, S. 2002. *Folk Devils and Moral Panics: The Creation of the Mods and Rockers.* London: Routledge.

Connell, R.W. and Messerschmidt, J.W. 2005. 'Hegemonic Masculinity: Rethinking the Concept.' *Gender and Society* 19, no. 6: 829–859.

Costello, L. 2014. 'Travellers in the Irish Prison System: A Qualitative Study.' *Irish Penal Reform Trust*. https://www.drugsandalcohol.ie/21915/ (6 December 2021).

Côté, J.E. 2006. 'Identity Studies: How Close are we to Developing a Social Science of Identity? An Appraisal of the Field.' *Identity* 6, no. 1: 3–25. https://doi.org/10.1207/s1532706xid0601_2.

Donnelly-Drummond, A. 2016. 'Deserving of Penalty and Public Outrage? The "Gypsy" within the Punitive City.' *Irish Probation Journal* 13: 208–224.

Doyle, D.M., Brandon, A., Garrihy, J., Adanan, A., Bracken, D., and Irish Penal Reform Trust. 2022. '"Sometimes I'm Missing the Words": The Rights, Needs and Experiences of Foreign National and Minority Ethnic Groups in the Irish Penal System.' *Irish Penal Reform Trust, Dublin.* https://iprt.ie/site/assets/files/7076/iprt_the_rights-_needs_and_experiences_of_foreign_national_and_minority_ethnic_groups.pdf (5 October 2023).

Dillon, G., Vinter, L.P., Winder, B., and Finch, L. 2019. '"The Guy Might Not Even to Be Able to Remember Why He's Here and What He's in Here for and Why He's Locked In": Residents and Prison Staff Experiences of Living and Working Alongside People with Dementia who are Serving Prison Sentences for a Sexual Offence.' *Psychology, Crime & Law* 25, no. 5: 440–457. doi:10.1080/1068316X.2018.1535063.

Egleton, M.C., Banigo, D.M., McLeod, B.A., and Vakalahi, H.F.O. 2016. 'Homelessness Among Formerly Incarcerated African American Men: Contributors and Consequences.' *Contemporary Social Science* 11 no. 4: 403–413. doi:10.1080/21582041.2016.1258590.
European Social Policy Network (ESPN). 2017. 'Ireland Grants Ethnic Minority Recognition for Irish Travellers.' https://ec.europa.eu/info/index_en (25 November 2021).
Farrall, S. 2019. 'The Architecture of Desistance: Exploring the Structural Sources of Desistance and Rehabilitation.' In *The Architecture of Desistance* edited by S. Farrall, 3–38. Abingdon, Oxon: Routledge.
Farrall, S. 2021. 'Politics, Research Design, and the "Architecture" of Criminal Careers Studies.' *British Journal of Criminology* 61, no. 6: 1575–1591. doi:10.1093/bjc/azab033.
Farrall, S. and Bowling, B. 1999. 'Structuration, Human Development and Desistance from Crime.' *British Journal of Criminology* 39 no. 2: 253–268. doi:10.1093/bjc/39.2.253.
Farrall, S., Gray, E., and Jones, P.M. 2020. 'Politics, Social and Economic Change, and Crime: Exploring the Impact of Contextual Effects on Offending Trajectories.' *Politics & Society* 48, no. 3: 357–388. doi:10.1177/0032329220942395.
Farrall, S., Sharpe, G., Hunter, B., and Calverley, A. 2011. 'Theorizing Structural and Individual-Level Processes in Desistance and Persistence: Outlining an Integrated Perspective.' *Australian & New Zealand Journal of Criminology* 44, no. 2: 218–234. doi:10.1177/0004865811405136.
Farrington, D.P. 2015. 'Cross-National Comparative Research on Criminal Careers, Risk Factors, Crime and Punishment.' *European Journal of Criminology* 12, no. 4: 386–399. doi:10.1177/1477370815584262.
Forster, N., Gallagher, M., and Cooper, C. 2022. 'Representations of Gypsy, Traveller, Roma, Showmen and Boater Communities in Higher Education Widening Participation Discourse: A Critical Review and Agenda for Future Research.' *Society for Research into Higher Education*. https://srhe.ac.uk/wp-content/uploads/2022/06/FORSTERfinalreport.pdf (12 October 2023).
Forster, N., Hodgson, P., and Bailey, C. 2019. 'Energy Advice for Traveller Communities in the context of Ethnic and Spatial Premiums: "Paying the Price" for Other People's Choices.' *Journal of Poverty and Social Justice* 27, no 1: 61–78. doi:10.1332/175982718X15451316707778.
Gavin, P. 2019. '"Prison is the Worst Place a Traveller Could Be": The Experiences of Irish Travellers in Prison in England and Wales.' *Irish Probation Journal*, 16: 135–152.
Government UK. 2018. 'Population of England and Wales.' https://www.ethnicity-facts-figures.service.gov.uk/uk-population-by-ethnicity/national-and-regional-populations/population-of-england-and-wales/latest (accessed 25 November 2021)
Healy, D. 2012. 'Advise, Assist and Befriend: Can Probation Supervision Support Desistance?' *Social Policy and Administration* 46, no. 4: 377–394. doi:10.1111/j.1467-9515.2012.00839.x.
Hodgins, M. and Fox, F. 2012. '"Causes of Causes": Ethnicity and Social Position as Determinants of Health Inequality in Irish Traveller Men.' *Health Promotion International* 29, no. 2: 223–234. doi:10.1093/heapro/das066.
Irish Department of Health. 2010. 'All-Ireland Traveller Health Study.' https://www.gov.ie/en/publication/b9c48a-all-ireland-traveller-health-study/ (accessed 20 November 2021).
Irish Penal Reform Trust. 2014. 'Travellers in the Irish Prison System: A Qualitative Study.' https://www.iprt.ie/iprt-publications/travellers-in-the-irish-prison-system-a-qualitative-study/ (accessed 25 November 2021).
Irish Traveller Movement. 2019. 'We are the Irish Traveller Movement'. https://itmtrav.ie/what-is-itm/ (accessed 24 June 2022).

James, Z. 2007. 'Policing Marginal Spaces: Controlling Gypsies and Travellers.' *Criminology and Criminal Justice* 7, no. 4: 367–389. doi:10.1177/1748895807082062.

Joyce, S. 2018. 'Mincéirs Siúladh: An Ethnographic Study of Young Travellers' Experiences of Racism in an Irish City.' *Research Repository*. https://researchrepository.ul.ie/articles/thesis/Minc_irs_Si_ladh_an_ethnographic_study_of_young_Travellers_experiences_of_racism_in_an_Irish_city/19833733/1/files/35255134.pdf (Accessed 12 October 2023).

Joyce, S., Kennedy, M., and Haynes, A. 2017. 'Travellers and Roma in Ireland: Understanding Hate Crime Data Through the Lens of Structural Inequality.' In *Critical Perspectives on Hate Crime*, edited by A. Haynes, J. Schweppe, and S. Taylor, 325–354. London: Palgrave Macmillan.

Kazemian, L. and Farrington, D.P. 2005. 'Comparing the Validity of Prospective, Retrospective, and Official Onset for Different Offending Categories.' *Journal of Quantitative Criminology* 21, no. 2: 127–147. doi:10.1007/s10940-10005-2489-0.

King, S. 2013. 'Transformative Agency and Desistance from Crime.' *Criminology and Criminal Justice* 13, no. 3: 317–335. doi:10.1177/1748895812452282.

Lewis, D.M. 2018. 'Living on the Edge: Young Offenders and Emotive Offending.' *Deviant Behavior* 39, no. 1: 111–125. doi:10.1080/01639625.2016.1263074.

Lindegaard, M.R. and Jacques, S. 2013. 'Agency as a Cause of Crime.' *Deviant Behavior* 35, no. 2: 85–100. doi:10.1080/01639625.2013.822205.

Link, B.G. and Phelan, J.C. 2001. 'Conceptualizing Stigma.' *Annual Review of Sociology* 27, no. 1: 363–385. doi:10.1146/annurev.soc.27.1.363.

Lundgren, A.S. 2011. '"I Was Struck Dumb": Identity Production in Swedish Class Grandparent Narratives.' *Pedagogy, Culture & Society* 19, no. 3: 403–417. doi:10.1080/14681366.2011.607926.

Lynch, O., Ahmed, J., Russell, H., and Hosford, K. 2020. *Reflections on Irish Criminology: Conversations with Criminologists*. London: Palgrave Macmillan.

Mac Gabhann, C. 2011. 'Voices Unheard: A Study of Irish Travellers in Prison.' *Irish Penal Reform Trust*. https://www.iprt.ie/international-news/uk-voices-unheard-a-study-of-irish-travellers-in-prison/ (accessed 15 November 2021).

Maruna, S. 2001. *Making Good: How Ex-Convicts Reform and Rebuild Their Lives*. London: American Psychological Association.

Maruna, S. 2019. 'Desistance.' In *The Sage Handbook of Criminology*, edited by E. McLaughlin and J. Muncie, 155–158. London: Sage.

Meek, R. 2007. 'The Experiences of a Young Gypsy-Traveller in the Transition from Custody to Community: An Interpretative Phenomenological Analysis.' *Legal and Criminological Psychology* 12, no. 1: 133–147. doi:10.1348/135532506X107165.

Mercan, B.A. 2020. 'Persistence and Career Criminality: Enjoying Crime!' *Crime, Media, Culture* 16, no. 2: 165–184. doi:10.1177/1741659019843153.

Merton, R.K. 1938. 'Social Structure and Anomie.' *American Sociological Review* 3, no. 5: 672–682. doi:10.2307/2084686.

Messerschmidt, J.W. 2019. 'The Salience of "Hegemonic Masculinity".' *Men and Masculinities* 22, no. 1: 85–91. doi:10.1177/1097184X18805555.

Messerschmidt, J.W. and Tomsen, S. 2018. 'Masculinities and Crime.' In *Routledge Handbook of Critical Criminology*, edited by W.S. DeKeseredy and M. Dragiewicz, 83–95. New York: Routledge. doi:10.4324/9781315622040.

Moore, K., Stuewig, J., and Tangney, J. 2013. 'Jail Inmates' Perceived and Anticipated Stigma: Implications for Post-Release Functioning.' *Self and Identity* 12, no. 5: 527–547. doi:10.1080/15298868.2012.702425.

Moosavi, L. 2019 'A Friendly Critique Of "Asian Criminology" and "Southern Criminology".' *British Journal of Criminology* 59, no. 2: 257–275. doi:10.1093/bjc/azy045.

Mulcahy, A. 2012. '"Alright in Their Own Place": Policing and the Spatial Regulation of Irish Travellers.' *Criminology and Criminal Justice* 12, no. 3: 307–327. doi:10.1177/1748895811431849.
Nagin, D.S., Cullen, F.T., and Jonson, C.L. 2009. 'Imprisonment and Reoffending.' *Crime and Justice* 38, no. 1: 115–200. doi:10.1086/599202.
Parker, G. and McVeigh, C. 2013. 'Do Not Cut the Grass: Expression of British Gypsy-Traveller Identity on Cemetery Memorials.' *Mortality* 18, no. 3: 290–213. doi:10.1080/13576275.2013.820178.
Parmar, A. 2016. 'Intersectionality, British Criminology and Race: Are We There Yet?' *Theoretical Criminology*, 21, no. 1: 35–45. doi:10.1177/1362480616677496.
Potter, H. 2015. *Intersectionality and Criminology: Disrupting and Revolutionizing Studies of Crime*. Abingdon, Oxon: Routledge.
Raidió Teilifís Éireann (RTE). 2017. 'Taoiseach: Travellers "A People Within Our People" as Ethnicity Recognised.' https://www.rte.ie/news/2017/0301/856293-travellers-etnic-status/ (Accessed 25 November 2022).
Segev, D. 2020. *Desistance and Societies in Comparative Perspective*. Abingdon, Oxon: Routledge.
Sloan, J. 2016. 'Men, Prison and Aspirational Masculinities.' In *Moving on From Crime and Substance Use: Transforming Identities*, edited by A. Robinson and P. Hamilton, 43–65. Bristol: Policy Press
Van Hout, M.C. 2010. 'The Irish Traveller Community: Social Capital and Drug Use.' *Journal of Ethnicity in Substance Abuse* 9: 186–205. doi:10.1080/15332640.2010.500583.
Weaver, B. 2019. 'Understanding Desistance: A Critical Review of Theories of Desistance.' *Psychology, Crime & Law* 25, no. 6: 641–658. doi:10.1080/1068316X.2018.1560444.
Webster, C., MacDonald, R., and Simpson, M. 2006. 'Predicting Criminality? Risk Factors, Neighbourhood Influence and Desistance.' *Youth Justice* 6, no. 1: 7–22. doi:10.1177/1473225406063449.
Wood, W. and Eagly, A.H. 2015. 'Two Traditions of Research on Gender Identity.' *Sex Roles* 73: 461–473. doi:10.1007/s11199-015-0480-2.
Zamble, E. and Quinsey, V.L. 1997. *The Criminal Recidivism Process*. Cambridge: Cambridge University Press.
Zara, G. and Farrington, D.P. 2016. *Criminal Recidivism: Explanation, Prediction and Prevention*. Abingdon, Oxon: Routledge.

7

RUSSIAN CRIMINOLOGY
A Silenced Voice?

Yulia Chistyakova

Introduction

It has long been broadly recognised that criminological knowledge has historically developed as ethnocentric and western-centric (Bosworth and Hoyle, 2011; Slade and Light, 2015; Moosavi, 2019) and has often supported colonialism and authoritarianism (van Swaaningen, 2021). The discipline of criminology tends to ignore non-western knowledge or see it as inferior, while at the same time asserting its own superiority and the universal validity and applicability of western knowledge (Moosavi, 2019; van Swaaningen, 2021). A number of scholars have called for a decolonisation of criminology (Cunneen, 1999; Agozino, 2003, 2004) and a move towards a postcolonial (Agozino, 2003; 2004) or decolonial (Blagg and Anthony, 2019; Dimou, 2021) criminology. Like other non-western criminologists, Russian scholars have struggled to have their voice heard. Western-centrism of criminology has been just one factor behind this. The voice of Russian criminology was silenced for decades during Stalin's rule when all social sciences were banned in the USSR. The revival and development of criminological knowledge post Stalin was crippled by the regime's expectation that criminology must be policy-oriented and firmly embedded within the Marxist-Leninist methodological and theoretical paradigm, leaving it no choice but to be an administrative branch of the state's crime control policy-making. Any theorising not consistent with Marxism-Leninism was ideologically wrong and therefore any theoretical efforts became redundant. In the post-Soviet years, Russian criminology began to develop links with foreign colleagues and institutions, while trying to make sense of the new realities of crime and crime control 'at home'. It was a low and slow start as epistemological and theoretical paradigms inherited from the Soviet period, the reluctance to part with Marxist approaches, and insufficient English language skills continued to hold

DOI: 10.4324/9781003260967-9

Russian scholars back in their attempts to make their voices heard. Russian scholars continue to be divided with regard to western scholarship, with some considering their own ideas and theories superior while others feeling they were far behind, which itself reflects the 'catching up' logic defining the 'less successful' empires (Tlostanova, 2022). All things considered, criminological knowledge in Russia remains stagnant and at best marginal in the global processes of criminological knowledge production dominated by Anglophone criminology.

What is interesting about Russian criminology and what is missing from the North/South debate is the unevenness and ambiguities of criminological thought making it hard to fit it neatly in the Global North/South or the West/the Rest dichotomies. A positivist, modernist project inspired and influenced by Western European ideas in the 19th century, it has continued on the modernist path in a Soviet incarnation of Marxism in the 20th century, was partially liberalised in the 1990s, with some critical voices emerging within it, and became increasingly conservative in the 21st century, questioning and critiquing western capitalist global domination, while at the same time embracing patriarchal, conservative ideas of a strong Russian state with a unique civilising mission. What we see today in Russian universities is a criminology firmly embedded in western criminological thought, but also shaped by a unique mix of Marxist, statist, patriarchal, orthodox and Slavophil ideas, and defining itself, at least in part, in opposition to the west.

This chapter will explore the issues and dilemmas of Russian criminology. Why is Russian criminology almost totally unknown outside Russia and Russian-speaking post-Soviet and Eastern European states, and can Russian criminologists escape the choice between isolation and dependency on western criminological knowledge and find their own voice? Can they engage with globally relevant criminological concerns while developing their own unique empirical, theoretical, and political insights? Before answering these questions, the Soviet and post-Soviet periods in the development of the discipline in Russia will be considered.

A history of Russian criminology

This section will look at the key stages in the development of the discipline in Russia from the 19th century to the present. These include the pre-Soviet period (19th century to 1917), the early Soviet period (1917–1920), the break in the development of criminology between the late 1930s to the 1950s, the revival of criminological scholarship in the 1950s–1980s, the post-Soviet development between 1991 and the early 2000s, and the recent years of stagnation.

19th century – the emergence of Russian criminology

The origins of Russian criminology can be traced back to the beginning of the 19th century. It generally followed the European path of development of criminological thought and scholarship (Gurinskaya, 2017), being initially inspired by the idea of using statistical data to explore patterns of crime (Radischev, 1952, cited in Shestakov, 2006: 52; Herman, 1832; Orlov and Khvostov, 1860), and by the end of the century to the early 20th century evolving into a discipline focusing on anthropological and sociological theories of crime. Social order came to be seen as the main cause of crime. Poor political and economic organisation and poor public morality were seen as the main reasons for criminal behaviour (Dukhovskoy, 1872, cited in Shestakov, 2006: 53), The classical ideas of 'free will' were challenged by some legal scholars who argued that social conditions of crime had to be explored (Dukhovskoy, 1872, cited in Shestakov, 2006: 53). The anthropological branch of Russian criminology developed in the 1880s. It was influenced by Lombroso's ideas and argued that crime was the result of pathological depravity and could be cured (Dril, n.d., cited in Shestakov, 2006: 54).

1917–1920s – the early years of Soviet criminology

In the early years of the Soviet regime, Soviet criminologists studied offender personality and their physical and biological traits, as well as social conditions, focusing primarily on disadvantaged and deprived social groups (Shelley, 1979a; 1979b). They examined the impact of rapid social, economic, and political change on patterns of criminality using statistical research; explored prison experiences; victims; and the effects of films on crime (Shelley, 1979a; 1979b). They also developed alternatives to punishment, rehabilitative programmes and crime prevention programmes (Shelley, 1979a; 1979b). Gilinskiy (2017) argues that criminology in that period mainly focused on the personality of the offender because Marxist ideology postulated that there couldn't possibly be any 'social' causes of crime in a socialist society. However, Shelley (1979a) points out that criminological scholarship of the time enjoyed relative freedom from ideological censorship and developed a range of theoretical perspectives on crime. Marxism was the official ideology to follow, but in practice only Moscow criminologists (working in view of the authorities) used Marxist methodologies, while peripheral scholars considered a wide variety of explanations of crime and used social-scientific and biomedical approaches within their research, directly challenging the Marxist view that crime would disappear in a socialist society. According to Shelley (1979a; 1979b), between 1917 and 1936 Soviet criminological scholarship advanced intellectually at least to the level of their western counterparts, if not further. Shestakov (2006), however, argues that from the first years of the Soviet regime, criminology was subject to ideological pressure by the party; all crimes had to be seen as the result of class struggle; the other idea developed by Lenin was the disappearance of crime with the removal of exploitation of the masses. Anything not fitting that explanation was subject to harsh critique.

1930s–1953 – politicisation of criminology and cessation of criminological research

Criminology became politicised and towards the end of the decade ceased to exist (Shelley, 1979a; 1979b; Solomon, 1974). The party ideologists launched a campaign against criminologists accusing them of 'neo-Lombrosianism and positivism' and a lack of commitment to Marxism (Solomon, 1974); they were criticised for being inconsistent with Marxist historicism and social determinism (Gurinskaya, 2017). Ideologists of the regime ordered criminologists to stop theorising and commit themselves to practical tasks such as organising criminal statistics. According to the leading communist ideologists of the time, since both crime and legal institutions were supposed to disappear in the near future there would no longer be a need to study crime (Solomon, 1974). The remaining criminologists were given the task of promoting the Soviet legal institutions (Solomon, 1974). Criminological work became a propaganda tool that provided justification for the repression of any potential opposition; groups such as wealthy farmers, 'speculators', and Central Asian and Caucasian cultures and religion became the targets (Shelley, 1979a), but criminologists themselves were not safe from the repressive hand of Stalin's regime (Gilinskiy, 2017). After 1938, criminological scholarship was no longer possible as studying crime would run the risk of exposing mass repression (Solomon, 1974).

1953–1980s – the revival of criminological scholarship

After Stalin's death, criminology started its comeback within law research institutes and departments, police academies, and some universities. The Institute for Research of Crime Causes and Crime Prevention was founded in Moscow in 1963 (Gilinskiy, 2017). As Solomon (1974: 135) describes, to legitimate themselves, criminologists had to demonstrate their 'ideological acceptability' and 'practical utility'. To be ideologically acceptable, criminology had to be Marxist and reject the so-called 'bourgeois' criminology which included any biological and psychiatric study of criminals. Instead, 'historical and dialectical materialism' was the only acceptable methodological foundation for criminological research (Gurinskaya, 2017). It also had to assume that all causes of crime were 'remnants of the past'. Moreover, criminologists were expected to play an ideological role in helping the regime demonstrate the advantages and achievements of the Soviet system. Ways to be practically useful were to conduct empirical research and provide criminal justice policy and crime prevention advice to local and central authorities, prepare crime statistics for practical use, and participate in law-making work (Solomon, 1974). All this meant that criminology re-emerged as an 'administrative' criminology of the Communist party (Gurinskaya, 2017). The party leaders saw it as a useful tool for the identification and elimination of any disorderly behaviours and groups that were inconsistent with their idea of the Soviet public order. Solomon

(1974) notes that some scholars were unhappy with criminology being part of and subservient to the legal and law enforcement institutions and argued for a separate 'social science' criminology. However, criminology remained part of legal scholarship because its legitimacy depended on it being the party tool for population control. Unsurprisingly, criminology of the time was empirically oriented (Gilinskiy, 2017).

While the majority of criminologists continued to work under the Marxist assumptions that crime was the 'remnant' of the capitalist system or the result of foreign capitalist influences, a few started to examine the social, economic, and political factors of crime in ways not dissimilar to those of western criminologists. It is not clear whether these ideas (rational choice, situational, sociopsychological, and self-control theories) were developed mostly independently or were to some extent informed and influenced by western criminology (Gurinskaya, 2022). As noted by Gurinskaya (2017), very few publications by Russian criminologists at the time made it to English language academic journals, but the journals these articles were published in were 'Soviet studies' not criminology journals, so most western criminologists would not be aware of this work (unless, of course, they were particularly interested in crime and justice in the USSR). It is also interesting that western radical and Marxist scholars were not aware of the Soviet interpretation of Marxism (Gurinskaya, 2017). However, there was more dialogue and exchange of ideas within the USSR and the Eastern Bloc (Gurinskaya, 2017).

'Bourgeois' criminology was accused of serving the interests of the capitalist class and seen as a purely ideological tool in its hands, helping protect the capitalist order. The work of radical/neo-Marxist and critical western criminologists was seen as progressive and theoretically and methodologically advanced but was criticised for not being radical enough as it advocated reforms instead of revolutionary violence (Gurinskaya, 2017). Gurinskaya (2017) also notes that access to western criminological scholarship in the USSR was limited and strictly controlled, and Soviet criminologists were not free to engage with these ideas; a total rejection of western theories of crime was the only possible position to take.

While operating in almost complete isolation from outside academic scholarship, Soviet criminology scholars nonetheless came up with explanations broadly similar to their western counterparts' 19th and early 20th century theories and ideas, such as the classical theories of free will and rational choice, and psychological and sociological positivism. However, Soviet criminologists were in some ways 'ahead' of western scholars: crime prevention and control of high-risk offenders (which only became a preoccupation of post-welfare western democracies in the 1990s–2000s) became the central focus and principal task of Soviet criminology from the 1960s (Gurinskaya, 2017). Crime prevention was of principal importance to the Soviet state, which wanted to anticipate and eliminate any crime, but more importantly any sign of opposition, 'nipping it in the bud' before it developed into a serious threat. It became clear by the 1960s that crime had not 'withered away' as Lenin predicted it would, so something had to be done to eliminate the remaining 'causes' of crime in society (Korobeinikov, 1985). In addition to the various crime prevention measures, from improving education and living standards to public patrols and comrades' courts, criminological study of different groups' motivations for law-breaking was prioritised. Different branches of criminological theory were developed looking at underage crime, female crime, violent crime, economic crime, and victimology (Zinnurov, 2019).

The 1980s saw a gradual relaxation of ideological controls and Russian criminologists started to engage with western scholarship (Gurinskaya, 2017). Joint conferences bringing together scholars from around the USSR as well as foreign colleagues began to take place (Gilinskiy, 2017). This period, the late 1980s in particular, and the times of Gorbachev's *perestroika*, was characterised by growing freedom from the official ideology and expanding space for scholarly debate and exchange.

1991–early 2000s – post-Soviet development of criminological thought

The decade immediately after the collapse of the USSR was the time when Russian criminologists experienced the most freedom (compared to the periods before and after) to travel, teach, do research, publish, and develop links with foreign colleagues. Since the 1990s, Russian criminologists have taken part in international conferences and the World Congresses of Criminology in Seoul (1998), Rio de Janeiro (2003), Barcelona (2008), Kobe (2011); annual conferences of the European Society of Criminology (since 2001); and other meetings (Gilinskiy, 2017). Connections were developed not only through purely academic knowledge exchange, but also via applied research 'projects' in policing and criminal justice reforms such as community policing projects aimed at improving the police's relationship with the public using western (mainly US and British) 'models' (e.g., Robertson, 2005; Brogden and Nijhar 2005). The 1990s saw an eastward flow of western ideas, institutional blueprints, discourses, and knowledge to post-Soviet states (Lendvai and Stubbs 2007). The various applied projects with western partners mushroomed throughout Eastern Europe and the former USSR during the decade. Typically, these projects were a 'one way' flow of knowledge where the western partners positioned themselves as experts and knowledge donors.

Inspired by the intellectual opening and exchange, there emerged an interest in sociological examination of crime and criminal justice, and academics and teams in Russia started researching these topics. Criminology started to move away from the Marxist understanding of crime as driven by social contradictions; crime came to be understood as an 'innate characteristic of society' (Shestakov, 1999, cited in Gurinskaya, 2022). However, the changes were mostly evident in the Russian periphery, not in Moscow (Gurinskaya, 2022). Some institutional developments were also evident. The Russian Criminological Association was established in 1991. In 1995, the Union of Forensic Scientists and Criminologists (a voluntary organisation bringing together scholars and practitioners working on social and criminal law policies) was created; it stopped its activities in 2002 but was revived in 2010 (Zinnurov, 2019). A number of other professional organisations emerged; among them are the St. Petersburg International Criminological Club and the Russian Criminological Association. According to Gurinskaya (2017: 130) there are also 'four state-funded federal research institutes that have criminology divisions. Three periodical specialised criminology journals and a number of law journals provide venue for publications'.

An important development in criminological thinking in the post-Soviet years was the recognition and acceptance by some scholars of social constructivist ideas and the ways in which the state plays a role in defining crime as well as the role of social and economic inequality in producing crime (Gilinskiy, 2017). Advances made by Russian criminologists in the post-Soviet years in empirical research include comparative cross-regional studies of crime rates, studies of violent crime based on interviews with prisoners, research on drug abuse and alcoholism, surveys of public attitudes towards the police, and research on torture in police custody.

2000s to present – stagnation of criminological scholarship

Since the early 2000s, the gradual consolidation of the authoritarian regime in Russia has led to the stifling of intellectual and academic freedoms (Gerber and Chapman, 2022; Voronkov, 2018). The contemporary state of criminology in Russia is often characterised as 'stagnant' (Matskevitch, 2011; Zhigarev, 2012; Nagornaja and Pogosova, 2011, cited in Gurinskaya, 2017: 130). Criminological work does not advance far beyond descriptive accounts of survey or statistical patterns and trends in crime (Kondakov, 2021). Empirical studies are fairly well developed and include a variety of topics such as organised crime, violence, corruption, hate crimes, economic crime, drug trafficking, and human trafficking (Gilinskiy, 2017). On the other hand, those who write PhDs in criminology are still driven by the ambition, in the best Soviet tradition, to develop a 'grand theory' or an all-explanatory world view of crime (Radaev, 2000, cited in Gurinskaya, 2022). There does not appear to be much critical discussion and debate. Many criminologists in Russia continue to reject constructivist ideas and look for objective 'causes' of crime. Criminology continues to be seen as a 'science' in the service of certain policy and practice needs. For example, a criminology textbook published in 2019 states that 'deviantology, addictology, administrative delictology, juridical statistics and judicial psychiatry are very important for the development of domestic criminology' (Zinnurov, 2019: 64). It is also stated that criminology is a 'sociological-legal science'.

Russian and western criminology: similarities and differences

The brief history of the development of Russian criminology in the Soviet and post-Soviet years shows some similarities and dissimilarities with western criminology. Theoretically, Russian criminology followed a strikingly similar path to the West even though it saw itself as 'lagging behind' western scholarship by several decades. There was the persistent perception of Western European knowledge being superior and progressive, with Europe leading the way and Russia following in its footsteps (although this seems to have begun to change recently, with calls for the development of 'Slavic' criminology).

Soviet criminologists enjoyed immeasurably less academic freedom compared to their western counterparts. Soviet criminology can be characterised as administrative, positivist, quantitative, and oriented towards reducing crime as defined by the state, so in this sense it fits neatly into the description of 'Asian' criminology provided by Moosavi and others (Moosavi, 2019; Fraser et al., 2017: 131; Lee and Laidler, 2013; and Suzuki et al., 2017: 6, cited in Moosavi, 2019: 266). While until the 1930s Russian and western criminologies developed along fairly similar paths, Stalin's regime marked the departure of Soviet criminology from this path, when biological determinism and positivism were declared a dangerous bourgeois science to be rejected and Lombrosian ideas came to be seen as reactionary and fascist. Furthermore, between the 1930s and 1960s when interactionism, social reaction, and labelling perspectives were on the rise in the West, in the USSR, criminology ceased to exist altogether. From the 1960s and until the dissolution of the USSR in 1991, when western radical and critical criminologists were actively challenging positivist and classical criminological thought, in the USSR, criminology re-emerged within very strict and narrow ideological frames of Marxism and dialectical materialism, with no space for critical discussion and reflection. While Marxism was also an inspiration for radical western criminologists, in the USSR it was imposed on social sciences dogmatically; every single piece of research and writing had to be built on Marxist (historical materialist) epistemological and methodological foundations. Crime was expected to 'wither away' but where it was found it was explained by social contradictions. Classical rational choice, situational, socio-psychological, and self-control theories, while broadly similar to western theories, may not have been borrowed entirely, as access to western criminological scholarship was limited. Finally, one area where the USSR appeared to be 'ahead' of the game was risk management and crime prevention, which Soviet criminology had been occupied with since the 1960s and which came to be seen as 'actuarial justice' in western criminology in the 1990s. Despite the differences, I agree with Moosavi (2019) that in many respects (culturally, religiously, politically) Russia may have more in common with the Global North than often assumed and this raises the question of Russian criminologists' identity, which we will come back to later on in this chapter.

The factors of continued marginalisation of Russian criminology

Given the peculiar path and characteristics of Russian criminology, what are the main factors contributing to its exclusion and marginalisation? The following sections will look at several reasons for this, such as the continued identification of criminology as a legal discipline, the country's subordinate position in criminological knowledge production, an identity crisis, continued adherence to Marxism and to serving the interests of the state, suspicious state and institutional barriers, and the lack of organised dissent and collective voice.

Criminology within law, subservient to state

Criminology continues to be taught within criminal law departments. There is still little recognition in Russia of criminology as a sociological discipline; it continues to be seen as a legal discipline in academic institutions, even in large universities that have international links, such as the Moscow School of Economics. Criminal justice policy continues to be an area mainly studied by jurists, not by sociologists, criminologists, or political scientists (Smorgunova, 2006). This stifles any attempts to move beyond the 'black letter law' approach and look at crime and its control from broader 'social harm', human rights, feminist, abolitionist, postcolonial, or other critical perspectives. There are few attempts to question, critically evaluate, and look beyond the existing, outdated frameworks of criminological thought, and to develop a new lens through which Russian society's understanding and responses to crime in the past and present can be critically re-examined (e.g., Shestakov, 2006; Kabanov, 2012).

Some Russian scholars continue to see criminology as a scientific discipline mainly focused on implementing crime prevention policies and supporting the government's responses to crime (e.g., Burlakov, 1998, cited in Shestakov, 2006). Some criminologists argue in favour of austere prison conditions and exposing serious offenders to psychological and physical pains as part of their punishment. Some support long-term imprisonment as an effective preventive mechanism (Shestakov et al., 2018) and others are supportive of the retention of the death penalty (Burlakov, cited in Shestakov, 2006) and repressive policies, arguing that they prioritise the interests of law-abiding citizens (Milyukov, cited in Shestakov, 2006). This suggests that, despite their anti-western stance, the conservative Russian criminologists have not really come up with anything new or radically different in regards to how to address crimes and harms and deliver justice in society. The conservative criminologists are concerned about the morality of the population and the potentially criminalising effects of 'global ideological networks' and 'oligarchic structures' leading to the moral decay of society; these scholars argue for the introduction of censorship in order to prohibit programmes showing violence and 'perversion' (Danilov, 2017, 2020). There are a minority of liberal-minded criminologists supporting liberal-democratic values and ideals and arguing for the need to humanise punishment, emphasising the value of human life and liberties and arguing against violence (Gilinskiy, cited in Shestakov, 2006).

Subordinate position within western-dominated international criminological debate

With greater access to western criminological scholarship via academic publications and conferences, Russian criminologists started to engage in criminological debates, albeit in a relatively weaker, subordinate position, and began to write in English and adopt western theories. Joint publications with western scholars empirically test or draw upon established western, often micro-level theories, arguments, or analyses (e.g., Mahesh and Gurinskaya, 2022; Lysova and Shchitov, 2015; Light and Slonimerov, 2020; Wheelock et al., 2011).

While there are examples of international collaboration and engagement, these are few and far between. Gurinskaya (2017: 132) argues that 'Western theoretical approaches and practices of crime control were brought to the attention of scholars by a number of criminologists and sociologists ... but were never fully integrated into the mainstream criminology textbooks'. As noted by Smorgunova (2006: 52), western critical criminological scholarship and research, such as studies of corporate and state crime, are not reflected in the work of Russian criminologists. The reason for this may not be solely the lack of English language skills or unwillingness to engage, but also limited applicability of western theories to post-Soviet realities. For example, the unique combination of capitalist relations with the patriarchal, feudal 'clan' structure of authority supporting the state (Kosals, 2006), and the continued dominance of informal relations in Russia playing a more important role than the law (Ledeneva, 2006), may require different epistemological frameworks. As Slade and Light (2015: 152) rightly point out: 'while the key concepts that dominate western criminology may indeed be useful ..., care should be taken with the wholesale adoption of concepts and theories'.

Identity crisis and ambivalence towards western criminology

After the collapse of the USSR, criminologists in the post-Soviet states and Russia had to find a way to speak about, conceptualise, and research the new realities and processes unfolding before their eyes, but the old Soviet criminological vocabulary did not necessarily provide the means for them to do so. Contemporary criminological work in Russia often continues to draw upon the Soviet adaptation of the Marxist dialectical materialist idea of 'social/dialectic contradictions' as an overarching explanation, or grand theory, of social inequalities, conflict, and injustices (e.g., Avanesov, 2012; Kudrjavtsev and Eminov, 2016; Kuznetsova and Luneev, 2005; Luneev, 2011; Milyukov, 2005; and Shestakov, 2006, cited in Gurinskaya, 2017, 2022).

Russian criminologists struggle to define their position in relation to western criminology. While western criminological theories are often unable to offer insights into Russian realities, alternative understandings of crime and justice that would reflect both the uniqueness of the post-Soviet space and commonalities of criminological issues and concerns with the rest of the world are yet to be developed. Perceived limitations and ideological biases of western knowledge led, in the 2000s, to a 'conservative turn' in social sciences in Russia leading to 'self-exclusion and intellectual revanchism' (Gurinskaya, 2022; Tlostanova, 2015, cited in Gurinskaya, 2022). Some social scientists turned to the ideas of Russia's unique path and the importance of challenging western ideologies; in criminology, some scholars called for the development of an Indigenous, Slavic criminology (Shestakov, 2015, cited in Gurinskaya, 2022). Supporters of a 'strong state' as a guarantor of law and order (which is the Global North's social science assumption, see Philippi, 2021; Carrington and Hogg, 2017) felt that Russia was disadvantaged in the global order, seeing European values as simply a smokescreen often covering up anti-Russian interests and politics. There is a danger here that Russian criminologists need to be aware of, paraphrasing Moosavi (2019), of becoming 'occidentalists' and reproducing the imperialist attitude they are trying to challenge. Yet others felt that the Soviet approaches and adaptations of Marxist ideas were outdated, and that Russian criminology was stagnant or in crisis (Gurinskaya, 2017).

State suspicion and institutional barriers

The Soviet elites have always looked at criminology with great suspicion, seeing it as a threat to the dominant communist ideology and to their own position, and at best as something of low value to the state and society. The contemporary Russian state no longer sees criminology as a useful ideological tool and the discipline suffers from underfunding, bureaucratisation and over-regulation of educational institutions, overall stagnation, and neglect. The contemporary state's attitude towards criminology is illustrated by the fact that the new State Educational Standards introduced in 2010 do not even mention criminology as a required part of the law curriculum (Gurinskaya, 2017: 131). Until recently, the state encouraged criminologists to publish in international journals to achieve higher positions in global rankings, a call which was met with resistance as Russian criminologists did not feel they had adequate knowledge and resources to do so. Again, perhaps ironically, this continued dependency on the state keeps the discipline firmly embedded within the modernist western paradigm. Criminology is not understood as a branch of sociology and is not taught at universities as an independent subject. Gilinskiy (2017) notes that there is no funding for empirical research and conferences, and only a few foreign publications are translated into Russian. Furthermore, the quality of official statistics of crime appears to be poor compared to other countries.

Perhaps most importantly, the consolidation of an increasingly authoritarian and far-reaching state over the past 20 years, preoccupied with its historical 'mission' and role as a great power at the centre of the 'Russian world' in opposition to the West (see e.g., Zevelev, 2016), has made open and critical discussion of crime, justice, and law and order nearly impossible. Social and political sciences are now evidently considered potentially threatening and harmful to society. In 2022, the Ministry of Education made the decision to remove the teaching of sociology, cultural studies, and political science from the programmes of all pedagogical universities of the country (Tarasov, 2022). Taken together, all these factors have made it challenging for Russian criminologists to survive as academics and continue advancing their discipline.

The lack of organised dissent and independent collective voice

Unfortunately, both the Soviet legacies and contemporary political system in Russia have made it difficult for the development of an independent collective voice within criminology powerful and confident enough to challenge the subservient position of the discipline within the state and its subordinate position within the global criminological discourse. It is as if social scientists in Russia continue to work in the shadow of its totalitarian past. There are teams conducting empirical research and holding regular meetings – for example, meetings of the St. Petersburg International Criminological Club – discussing various criminological topics, but theoretical, methodological, and empirical work remains fragmented (Kvashis and Puchkov, 2020). There is a difference between Moscow and its peripheries, with more freedom of discussion and perceptiveness to change in peripheral centres and teams, but this may begin to change as the 'dangers of theoretical diversity' were mentioned in the 2021 meeting of the Russian Society of Criminology (Gurinskaya, 2022).

Overall, there is no concerted effort to develop novel, non-orthodox, independent conceptual approaches or political positions; ideologically, criminologists in their majority, unsurprisingly, remain conformist. Some criminologists adhere to the ideology of the state and its epistemology. For example, a group of criminologists developing political criminology in Russia focus on threats to Russian sovereignty and security in the new geopolitical context; the main threat is identified as the 'global oligarchic power' led by the USA. Coloured revolutions in the former Soviet states and dissent and protest movements in Russia are understood as threats to Russia's sovereignty, organised and managed by the western oligarchic powers (Merkuriev, 2021; Smirnov, 2021; Shestakov, 2022; Pishikina, 2014). Looking at Russia and its foreign policy from a postcolonial perspective, Morozov (2013) describes it as a 'subaltern empire'. This characterisation of Russian foreign policy can be applied to the 'patriotic-statist' branch of Russian criminology too, which can be described as projecting a 'Russian subaltern empire' voice, opposing the West, yet using western language to criticise it, and articulating its own imperial ambitions in relation to the post-Soviet space (re-unification of the former Soviet states). However, the vision of Russia as a subaltern empire can be questioned as a denial of domination over and 'internal colonisation' of peoples living in Russia whose voices we do not hear (Koplatadze, 2019).

Critical voices within Russian criminology?

There is growing interest in Russia in developing criminology as an independent and critical discipline autonomous from law and legal scholarship. There are critical accounts of changes and transformations in law, policing, and criminal justice institutions in Russia and other post-Soviet states (Shestakov et al., 2011). In the early 1990s, Russian criminologists recognised the criminal acts of the Soviet leaders, giving criminological evaluation to Leninist and Stalinist terror and to other dictatorships and totalitarian regimes, as well as other political crimes such as predatory wars (Kabanov, 2012). Some scholars called for a criminological and legal evaluation of the 'communist terror' in Russia and of the errors of the Marxist-Leninist ideas of the 'birthmarks of capitalism' and of exploitation and impoverishment of the masses being seen as the root cause of crime. (Shestakov, 2006). They also offered criminological analyses of wars of aggression, corruption in the police and higher echelons of power, and political crimes (Shestakov, 2011, 2013; Kosals and Maximova, 2015; Danilov, 2011; Bachurin, 2017; Zorin, 2018). Unique insights into the operation of informal practices in Russia's courts are provided by Ledeneva's research on 'telephone justice', informal influence, and pressure on the judiciary (Ledeneva, 2006; 2008); the role of violent entrepreneurship in the making of Russian capitalism is explored by Volkov (2006). Nevertheless, some topics clearly remain taboo and critical analyses of contemporary policies and politics of the Russian state appear to be absent from the debates. Undoubtedly, critical voices in Russian criminology, theories and paradigms used, and perspectives, attitudes and issues that are and are not being discussed need to be understood in their historical and geopolitical context.

When considering marginalisation of Russian criminology, it is important to note that 'Russian criminology' is an ambiguous concept. The same can be said about many non-western criminologies; for example, Moosavi (2019: 261) with regard to Asian criminology, notes: 'one could still reasonably ask if Asian criminology is that which is produced by Asians, or informed by Asian culture, or about Asia or all three?' In a narrow sense, 'Russian criminology' refers to criminologists and criminological communities living and working in Russia. But what about Russian-speaking criminologists living abroad and writing and doing research about Russia? This would include Russian criminologists living in one of the former Soviet states or elsewhere in the world. It is not uncommon for Russian-born academics affiliated with and/or educated in western universities to research and publish on crime and justice in Russia (e.g., Tittle and Botchkovar, 2005; Botchkovar et al., 2018; Lysova, 2020). They have a 'native' knowledge and understanding of Russia, but it is debatable to what extent they can be identified (or indeed identify themselves) as 'Russian criminologists'. The latter group are more integrated into western criminology but their ability to articulate their own concerns in their own language and advance their own research agendas is limited. Finally, there is a large body of criminological research and literature about Russia produced by western scholars. For those identifying themselves as Russian criminologists, it is important to reflect, not only within their own Russian-speaking academic communities, but internationally, on their own position and role in producing and disseminating criminological knowledge, and whether and how their isolation and marginalisation can be overcome.

The war in Ukraine and Russian criminology

When considering Russian criminology, its voice today, and its future, it is impossible not to mention that at the time of writing, Russia is conducting a 'special military operation' in Ukraine (the Russian government's official term for the military action it started in Ukraine on 24 February 2022). It is a moment of existential shock, confusion, and disorientation for many in Russia, not least its social scientists – a moment of 'what is going on?' and 'how can we talk about this?'

I agree with Yusupova (2022:15) that to make sense of the events 'you have to look beyond President Putin and other prominent individuals …, beyond the geopolitical and economic factors in play'; instead, it is important to rethink Russia's colonial history. Russian criminology can begin to take steps towards engaging with decolonial and postcolonial critiques of criminology. One must remain cautious and sceptical, however, not ignoring western self-interest in promoting this discourse and distorting it 'away from its original emancipatory meaning' (Oskanian, 2022). On the other hand, one must be cautious of not asserting a new hegemony in the process of speaking against another. Neo-imperial ambitions can be explained and justified in ways similar to left decolonial critiques of the West's colonial expansion and calls for decolonisation and independence of nations. However, when combined with anti-liberalism and the emphasis on Russia's messianic role in the new world order, this becomes a call to replace one type of hegemony with another.

The agenda of a radical rejection of the Global North's epistemologies and knowledge systems (Blagg and Anthony, 2019) is persuasive and yet almost unimaginable in a country where this knowledge is so deeply embedded in society's identity and psyche. The process of critical reflection is impossible without self-reflection, which would involve looking into the foundations of Russian criminological knowledge and the processes of its production, and acknowledging its complicity in the practices it seeks to critique. It is also about questioning and dismantling the myths of Soviet Russia as a 'good empire' (Marat, 2022), 'anti-empire' (Oskanian, 2022) and a liberating force (Kassymbekova, 2022), or a state that 'colonised itself', (Etkind, 2015), recognising the inequalities, hierarchies of power, and harms of the colonial past and present (Tlostanova, 2022; Amelina, 2022; Schorkowitz, 2019; Morrison, 2016; Saveliev, 2021). There is a potential for Russian criminology to contribute to 'making visible what it facilitated to make invisible' (Dimou, 2021: 447) and making the voices of the silenced heard. However, this would require a radical rethinking of Russian criminology's epistemological and ontological foundations and of its role and position in relation to the state.

From this vantage point, Russian criminology can begin to oppose the northern criminology's claims to universalism (Philippi, 2021) without falling into the trap of combining an 'anti-imperialist critique' with an imperialist ambition (Morozov, 2013: 17). It is also important to remember that calls for decolonisation must come from the colonised people themselves. Van Swaaningen's (2021: 15) advice for criminology is a bottom-up approach, starting 'from the concrete, lived reality of the people and social movements in the countries we research'. Perhaps the peripheries of Russia are the places where these processes can begin to take place.

Conclusion

The future for criminology in Russia today looks uncertain, both domestically and internationally. Travelling, doing research abroad, collaboration with colleagues in joint projects, meetings in conferences and symposia, and participation in other scholarly exchanges have become difficult if not impossible. Russian scholars are likely to face increasing isolation and the freezing of international links, funding, and programmes. A likely scenario for Russian criminology under these circumstances (and certainly for those who continue to live and work in Russia) is localisation and/or a return to its purely administrative role (similar to the role it played in the Soviet period).

A more optimistic scenario is that some degree of academic freedom remains possible. Questions Russian criminologists cannot avoid are questions about the nature of state violence in its historical and geopolitical context, and how states can be called to account for the harms they perpetrate. Considering the pros and cons of the criminology of crimes of states, Friedrichs (2015: 111) argues that they are 'by any reasonable measure the most consequential of all crimes – the "crime of crimes" – and it is inherently absurd for the field of criminology to fail to attend to such crimes'. Admittedly, it is a very complex and tricky matter to discuss, and yet it seems impossible for criminologists to avoid engaging with these questions.

The realities and legacies of the post-Soviet space still await a criminological analysis; there are myths, silences, and gaps in knowledge about the Soviet and post-Soviet social and political order, including its colonial dimensions, that have not yet been openly discussed. Whether this becomes possible, and whether this reflection and debate will lead to any new criminological insights or paradigms, remains to be seen. The marginal status of mainstream criminology in Russia today is perhaps more evident than ever, yet there is a long and challenging way ahead towards the de-marginalisation of Russian criminology.

References

Agozino B (2003). *Counter-Colonial Criminology: A Critique of Imperialist Reason*. London: Pluto Press.

Agozino, B. (2004). Imperialism, crime and criminology: Towards the decolonisation of criminology, *Crime, Law & Social Change* 41: 343–358.

Amelina, A. (2022). Occupied Ukraine between colonialities of war and the migranticisation of dispossession, *National Center of Competence in Research*, available at: https://nccr-onthemove.ch/blog/occupied-ukraine-between-colonialities-of-war-and-the-migranticisation-of-dispossession/ (accessed 30 November 2022).

Bachurin, D.G. (2017). Kriminologicheskaya otsenka razmerov nomenklaturno-korruptsionnogo vneekonomicheskogo raspredeleniya v Rossiyskoy Federatsii. *Rossiskii Kriminologitcheskii Zhurnal*, 11 (3): 503–519.

Blagg, H. and Anthony, T. (2019). Introduction: Turning the Criminology Upside Down, in: Blagg, H. and Anthony, T. (eds.), *Decolonising Criminology: Imagining Justice in the Postcolonial World*. London: Palgrave Macmillan.

Bosworth, M. and Hoyle, C. (eds.) (2011). *What Is Criminology?* New York: Oxford University Press.

Botchkovar, E.V., Antonaccio, O., and Hughes, L.A. (2018). Neighbourhood disorder, collective sentiments and personal strain: Bringing neighbourhood context into general strain theory. *British Journal of Criminology*, 58: 455–477.

Brogden, M. and Nijhar, P. (2005). *Community Policing National and International Models and Approaches*. Portland, OR: Willan Publishing.

Carrington, K. and Hogg, R. (2017). Deconstructing criminology's origin stories, *Asian Criminology*, 12: 181–197.

Cunneen, C. (1999). Criminology, genocide and the forced removal of Indigenous children from their families. *The Australian and New Zealand Journal of Criminology*, 32 (2): 124–138.

Danilov, A.P. (2011). Kriminologitcheskii analiz agressii protiv Livii. *Kriminologiya: vchera, segodnya, zavtra*, 4 (23): 16–21.

Danilov, A.P. (2017). Criminal management of society through education is the subject of criminology of the spheres of science and education. *Kriminologiya: vchera, segodnya, zavtra*, 4 (47): 41–48.

Danilov, A.P. (2020). Globally organised government as a source of criminogenic legislation. *Kriminologiya: vchera, segodnya, zavtra*, 1 (56): 49–52.

Dimou, E. (2021). Decolonizing southern criminology: what can the "decolonial option" tell us about challenging the modern/colonial foundations of criminology? *Critical Criminology*, 29: 431–450.

Etkind, A. (2015). How Russia 'colonized itself': Internal colonization in classical Russian historiography. *International Journal for History, Culture and Modernity*, 3 (2): 159–172.

Friedrichs, D.O. (2015). Rethinking the criminology of crimes of states: monumental, mundane, mislabeled and miscalculated crimes. *Crime and Justice Journal*, 4 (4): 106–119.

Gerber, T. and Chapman, H. (2022). The destruction of academic freedom and social science in Russia. *PONARS Eurasia Policy Memo* No. 766.

Gilinskiy, Y. (2017). Soviet and post-Soviet Russian criminology – an insider's reflections. *International Journal of Comparative and Applied Criminal Justice*, 41 (3): 113–122.

Gurinskaya, A. (2017). Russian criminology as 'Terra Incognita': legacies of the past and challenges of the present. *International Journal of Comparative and Applied Criminal Justice*, 41 (3): 123–143.

Gurinskaya, A. (2022). Russian criminology, paper presented at the Oxford Law Faculty, 12 May 2022, available at: https://www.youtube.com/watch?v=s9LdQABUTRQ (accessed 25 November 2022).

Herman, K. (1832). Recherches sur le nombre des suicides et homicedes commis en Russie pendant les annes 1819 et 1820. *Memoires de l'cademie Imperiale des Sciences de S. Petersbourg.* Ser. 6. T I.: 3–20.

Kabanov, P.A. (2012). Diskussionnye voprosy sovremennoi rossiskoi politicheskoi kriminologii. *Yuridicheskie Issledovaniya*, 4: 240–267.

Kassymbekova, B. (2022). Decolonizing Russia: a moral and strategic imperative, available at: https://www.youtube.com/watch?v=-iGtFXs9gvo (accessed 30 November 2022).

Kondakov, A. (2021). The influence of the 'gay-propaganda' law on violence against LGBTIQ people in Russia: Evidence from criminal court ruling. *European Journal of Criminology*, 18 (6): 940–959.

Koplatadze, T. (2019). Theorizing Russian postcolonial studies. *Postcolonial Studies*, 22 (4): 469–489.

Korobeinikov, B.V. (1985). Sociopolitical and legal principles of crime prevention in the U.S.S.R. *Crime and Social Justice, Socialism, Capitalism and the Reproduction of Crime*, 23: 29–50.

Kosals, L. (2006). Essays on clan capitalism in Russia. *Acta Oeconomica* 57 (1): 67–85.

Kosals, L. and Maximova, A. (2015). Informality, crime and corruption in Russia: A review of recent literature. *Theoretical Criminology*, 19 (2): 278–288.

Kvashis, V.Y. and Puchkov, D.V. (2020). Criminology in modern Russia: its place in the system of science and role in life of society. *Advances in Social Science, Education and Humanities Research*, 420: 80–84.

Ledeneva, A. (2006). *How Russia Really Works: The Informal Practices That Shaped Post-Soviet Politics and Business*. Ithaca, NY: Cornell University Press.

Ledeneva, A. (2008). Telephone justice in Russia. *Post-Soviet Affairs*, 24 (4): 324–350.

Lendvai, N. and Stubbs, P. (2007). Policies as translation: situating trans-national social policies, in: Hodgson, S.M. and Irving Z. (eds.), *Policy Reconsidered: Meanings, Politics and Practices*, Bristol: Policy Press.

Light, M. and Slonimerov, E. (2020). How gun control policies evolve: gun culture, 'gunscapes' and political contingency in post-Soviet Georgia. *Theoretical Criminology*, 24 (4): 590–611.

Lysova, A. (2020). Challenges to the veracity and the international comparability of Russian homicide statistics. *European Journal of Criminology*, 17 (4): 399–419.

Lysova, A. and Shchitov, N. (2015). What is Russia's real homicide rate? Statistical reconstruction and the 'decivilizing process'. *Theoretical Criminology*, 19 (2): 257–277.

Mahesh, K.N. and Gurinskaya, A. (2022). Police legitimacy or risk avoidance: what makes people feel safe? *Journal of Crime and Justice*, 45 (1): 1–20.

Marat, E. (2022). Decolonizing Russia: A moral and strategic imperative, available at: https://www.youtube.com/watch?v=-iGtFXs9gvo (accessed 30 November 2022).

Merkuriev, V.V. (2021). Poisk modeli razvitiya kriminologii v xxi veke v usloviyakh novoi cholodnoi voiny, in: *Vektor Razvitiya Kriminologii v XXI Veke: tezisy dokladov vserossiskoi nauchno prakticheskoi konferentsii*, Vladimir: VlGU, 49–56.

Moosavi, L. (2019). A friendly critique of 'Asian Criminology' and 'Southern Criminology'. *British Journal of Criminology*, 59: 257–275.

Morrison, A. (2016). Russia's colonial allergy. *Eurasianet*, available at: https://eurasianet.org/russias-colonial-allergy (accessed 30 November 2022).

Morozov, V. (2013). Subaltern empire? *Problems of Post-Communism*, 60 (6): 16–28.

Orlov, I. and Khvostov, A. (1860). Materialy dlya ugolovnoi statistiki Rossii. *Zhurnal Ministerstva Yustitsii*, 10: 58.
Oskanian, K. (2022). The fraught complexities of 'Decolonising Russia', *Riddle*, available at: https://ridl.io/the-fraught-complexities-of-decolonising-russia/ (accessed 20 April 2023).
Philippi, A.P.Z.D.M. (2021). The import of southern criminology: post-colonialism trumps the defiance of universalism, the global crime. *Justice and Security Journal*, 2: 37–54.
Pishikina (2014). On the events in Ukraine and the role of criminology. *Kriminologiya: vchera, segodnya, zavtra*, 4 (35): 66–68.
Robertson, A. (2005). Criminal justice policy transfer to post-Soviet states: two case studies of police reform in Russia and Ukraine. *European Journal on Criminal Policy and Research* 11 (1): 1–28.
Saveliev, D. (2021). The eternal empire: decolonising Russia, in: Luntumbue, V., Raab, S., and Waters, A. (eds.), *Places in the Sun: Post-Colonial Dialogues in Europe and Beyond*, Brussels: Institute for a Greater Europe, 97–107.
Schorkowitz, D. (2019). Was Russia a colonial empire?, in: Schorkowitz, D., Chavez, J. R., and Schroder, I.W. (eds.), *Shifting Forms of Continental Colonialism*. London: Palgrave Macmillan, 117–147.
Shelley, L. (1979a). Soviet criminology after the revolution. *The Journal of Criminal Law and Criminology*, 70 (3): 391–396.
Shelley, L. (1979b). Soviet criminology: its birth and demise, 1917–1936. *Slavic Review*, 38 (4): 614–628.
Shestakov, D.A. (2006). *Kriminologiya*. Yuriditcheskii Tcentr Press.
Shestakov, D.A. (2011). Aggression against sovereign Libya, outline of charges. *Kriminologiya: vchera, segodnya, zavtra*, 4 (23): 10–15.
Shestakov, D.A. (2013). *Prestupnost Politiki. Razmyshleniya Kriminologa*. Amsterdam: SPb.
Shestakov, D.A. (2015). Tolerant legal consciousness: prisons for the people and irresponsibility for oligarchs? *Kriminologiya: vchera, segodnya, zavtra*, 4 (39): 13–17.
Shestakov, D.A. (2022). Kratko o voennoi operatsii na Ukraine. St. Petersburg International Criminology Club, available at: https://www.criminologyclub.ru/home/obschie-kriminologicheskie-novosti/437-kratko-o-voennoj-operatsii-na-ukraine (Accessed 10 March 2022).
Shestakov D., Dikaev, S.U., and Danilov, A.P. (2018). The chronicle of the St. Petersburg International Criminology Club. The Year 2017, *Kriminologiya: vchera, segodnya, zavtra*, 1 (48): 72–116.
Shestakov D.A., Kury, H., and Danilov, A. (2011). Changes in criminal law and sentencing practices in modern Russia: an assessment of new elements of punitiveness, in: Kury, H. and Shea, E. (eds.), *Punitivity. International Developments*. Vol. 2: Insecurity and Punitiveness. Bochum: Universitätsverlag, 509–549.
Slade, G. and Light, M. (2015). Crime and criminal justice after communism: why study the post-Soviet region?, *Theoretical Criminology*, 19 (2): 147–158.
Smirnov, L.B. (2021). Problemy obespecheniya natsionalnoi bezopasnosi rossii. *Politicheskaya Kriminologiya. St. Petersburg International Criminology Club*, available at https://www.criminologyclub.ru/home/the-last-sessions/419-2021-03-15-14-13-58 (accessed 10 March 2022).
Smorgunova A.L. (2006). Politicheskaya prestupnost: kriticheskaya kriminologiya i mezhdisciplinarnyi podchod. *Politeks*, 2 (1): 51–61.
Solomon, P. (1974). Soviet criminology: its demise and rebirth, 1928–1963. *Soviet Union*, I (2): 122–144.

Tarasov, A. (2022). Vo vsekh pedagogitcheskikh vuzakh otmenyayut prepodavanie sotsialnykh nauk i mirovoi kultury. Buduschim uchitelyam vse eto nezatchem. *Novaya Gazeta*, available at: https://novayagazeta.ru/articles/2022/03/23/pri-v-v-putine-mne-ni-razu-ne-p rikhodilos-priatatsia-po-podvalam?utm_source=fb&utm_medium=novaya&utm_campa ign=pedagogicheskie-universitety-rossii-pere (accessed 30 November 2022).

Tittle, C.R. and Botchkovar, E.V. (2005). Self-Control, criminal motivation and deterrence: an investigation using Russian respondents. *Criminology*, 43 (2): 307–354.

Tlostanova, M. (2022). Discordant trajectories of the (post-)Soviet (post)colonial aesthetics. *Interventions*, 24 (7): 995–1010.

van Swaaningen, R. (2021). Cultural bias in international criminology, in: E. Erez and P. Ibarra (eds.), *Oxford Encyclopaedia of International Criminology*. New York: Oxford University Press.

Volkov, V. (2002). *Violent Entrepreneurs: The Use of Force in the Making of Russian Capitalism*Ithaca, NY: Cornell University Press.

Voronkov, V. (2018). Russia's independent sociology under pressure. *ZOiS Spotlight*, available at: https://www.zois-berlin.de/en/publications/zois-spotlight/archiv-2018/ russias-independent-sociology-under-pressure, (accessed 30 November 2022).

Wheelock, D., Semukhina, O., and Demidov, N.N. (2011). Perceived group threat and punitive attitudes in Russia and the United States. *The British Journal of Criminology*, 51: 937–959.

Yusupova, M. (2022). Coloniality of gender and knowledge: rethinking Russian masculinities in light of postcolonial and decolonial critiques. *Sociology*, 1–18.

Zevelev, I. (2016). *Russian National Identity and Foreign Policy*. Washington, D.C.: Centre for Strategic and International Studies.

Zinnurov, F.K. (ed.) (2019). *Kriminologiya: Obshchaya Chast*. Kazan: KYUI MVD Rossii.

Zorin, A.V. (2018). *Politicheskaya Prestupnost: Kriminologitcheskii Analiz*. St. Petersburg: Rossiiski Gosudarstvennyi Pedagogocheskii Universitet Imeni Gertsena.

PART III
Perpetuating Marginalisation

8

THE POWER OF LISTENING

An Ethical Responsibility to Understand, Participate, and Collaborate

Natalie Rutter

Introduction

Research exploring desistance from crime has drawn upon narrative and longitudinal approaches (Maruna, 2001) to enable us to consider how change occurs (McNeill, 2006; Maruna, 2010). There is, however, a general push within criminology for more quantitative research, which is argued to hold stronger validity when, for example, attempting to make generalisations. This push is argued to be influenced by broader neoliberal narratives that shape wider university objectives where methodological choices may be made to suit metrics and goals over quality theoretical research (Armstrong, 2020). Understanding criminal behaviour from the perspective of individuals involved, or previously involved, in criminality has gained increasing attention (Larsson, 2019) with narratives being integral to desistance-based research (Weaver and Weaver, 2013). In addition, desistance research is commonly based upon a longitudinal design (Farrall and Calverley, 2006) as it enables a recognition, and understanding, of change that may occur over time (Maruna, 2017; Plano Clark et al., 2015). This, when coupled with a prospective approach (Sarnecki and Carlsson, 2018), has the potential to enable individuals to look forward, with the scope for participatory and collaborative research design.

Critics argue that previous work in this area has echoed the male centrality of criminology, presuming mirrored experiences of desistance across gender (Harding, 2018; Barr, 2018; Hart, 2017) and additional intersectionalities. Whilst this chapter focuses on the marginalisation of women's voices by drawing upon feminist literature and methodology to recognise power dynamics, it is critical to acknowledge further exclusions when considering additional demographics – for instance, how contemporary feminism is criticised for failing to consider the intersectional identities of, for example, Black women or

DOI: 10.4324/9781003260967-11

individuals within the LGBTQ+ community (Crenshaw, 1991). The focus of this chapter is on gender specifically, however other intersectional identities should be considered by researchers to recognise the importance of understanding an individual's lived experience and how both personal and social circumstances can influence this. Ultimately, when we understand the importance of intersectionality, we have the potential to disrupt and revolutionise how both criminology and criminal justice service delivery is carried out (Potter, 2015).

The suppression of the female voice is not new in criminological research (Smart, 1977; Carlen, 1990; Rumgay, 2004; Heidensohn, 2004; Barr, 2019) where their voices are often ignored and unheard (Fitzgibbon and Stengel, 2018). When women have been subjects of criminological research it has traditionally been conducted on them, rather than with them (Grace et al., 2022), with quantifiable 'facts' privileged over subjective experiences of criminalisation (Harding, 2020).

Gendered presumptions within a male-centric criminology create marginalisation for criminalised women and what may then be influencing factors in their desistance from criminal behaviour. Criminalised women are likely to have experienced domestic and/or sexual abuse (Covington, 2016), are often intertwined with substance misuse (Annison et al., 2019), and are likely to have sustained adversity through their exposure to experiences such as poverty (Barr, 2019). Research evidence demonstrates that women face additional difficulties of negotiating their desistance from crime because of their position in an unequal world, perpetuated by the inequalities of patriarchy (Barr, 2017). Patriarchal structures also face limited critique when attempting to understand desistance, and it's important we understand them because they provide the context for the vulnerabilities, and victimisation, faced by women through the differing social and structural positions in wider society (Rutter and Barr, 2021).

To ensure critical reflection, this chapter will also highlight and discuss the responsibility of researchers to recognise a range of complex ethical challenges through three key areas of discussion. Firstly, vulnerability and the potential for re-traumatisation (Presser and Sandberg, 2015), especially when sharing narratives that evidence previous trauma, abuse, and harm, each of which are disproportionality prevalent for criminalised women. Secondly, discussion will draw focus to how narrative and longitudinal research can challenge and blur relational boundaries between researchers and participants (Presser and Sandberg, 2015) as it requires a degree of trust and confidence, and how longitudinal methodology can also be somewhat intrusive (Sharpe, 2017). Thirdly this chapter will discuss how, as researchers when offering a platform for marginalised voices through narrative and longitudinal research, it is important that we question the power dynamics at play – this includes a recognition of wider patriarchal structures, inequality, and oppression felt by those involved in research alongside our position as researchers – in order to raise the question of who in fact benefits. Here, discussions will draw focus to the underpinning philosophical approach of pragmatism whilst considering the importance of actively listening and our ethical responsibility in striving to actively understand, participate, and collaborate made possible through varying methodological approaches (Armstrong and Ludlow, 2020).

The chapter concludes by arguing the importance of taking a qualitative approach within the field of criminology that challenges the male centrality of research, argued above, whilst ensuring we understand our ethical responsibilities as researchers to avoid potential harm and intrusion. This calls for us to recognise, and challenge, the power dynamics at play. Ultimately, this chapter highlights the importance of developing increasingly participatory and collaborative approaches through which to limit exclusion and recognise the value of expanding choice when developing our understanding of those often marginalised within the criminal justice system (CJS).

Understanding desistance-based research

Desistance from crime has become a key theoretical concept when discussing criminality. Initial theories of desistance were developed through research which explored the experiences of young, white, working-class men (Glueck and Glueck, 1950; Gottfredson and Hirschi, 1990; Laub and Sampson, 2001; Maruna, 2001; Farrall and Calverley, 2006) Traditionally, any reference to women within research on criminality was focused on their influence in supporting men to move away from criminal behaviour, through the 'love of a good woman' (Laub and Sampson, 2001; Barr, 2019). Some useful explorations within the field of desistance research highlight desistance as a continuous process (Weaver, 2019) influenced by individualities, complexities, and fluidity, represented through temporary suspensions (Piquero, 2004), a decline in frequency, and/or a reduction in severity (Loeber et al., 2016; Blokland and De Schipper, 2016) of criminal behaviour over time. Defining features of the desistance literature focus around how change occurs (McNeill, 2006; Maruna, 2010). Considering an interactionist perspective of desistance recognises the role of both individual agency and wider social structures. Here, the relationships between internal factors that can encourage an individual's capacity to act or influence their circumstance is considered alongside their access to social capital through, for example, relationships, employment opportunities (Farrall, 2004), and wider social environmental factors (LeBel et al., 2008).

Albeit useful, a cautionary approach to the application of this evidence base should be considered when applying this knowledge to the experiences of women due to their absence within research (Österman, 2017; Gomm, 2016) and theoretical explorations. As noted, original work in this area has echoed the male centrality of criminology and presumed a mirrored experience of desistance across gender (Harding, 2018; Barr, 2018; Hart, 2017). This inevitably marginalises the voices of women, their experiences, and what may influence their desistance. As a consequence, it is unclear whether the same evidence applies for women (Gelsthorpe and Wright, 2015). Research within the field of desistance has failed to consider or uncover the experiences of different demographics and characteristics of 'women' given that this is not a homogentisic group with the same experiences.

What is important across gender, and differing intersectionalities, is the acknowledgement that desistance is an individualised process that recognises 'one person's reason for changing their life … might be another person's reason to escalate offending' (Maruna, 2001: 25). Therefore, the process is difficult to generalise as it encompasses a range of individualised personal and contextual elements which will differ between each individual (Priestley and Vanstone, 2019). However, for women there are additional challenges of negotiating their desistance from crime due to their structural position in an unequal world, perpetuated by the inequalities of patriarchy (Barr, 2017). Within the CJS, across England and Wales, we are also witnessing the domination of neoliberal ideals of responsibilisation and individualisation (Rutter and Barr, 2021; Hart, 2017) which removes the recognition of wider structural inequalities that are also often influencing factors.

Research within criminology and desistance needs to critically engage with how the CJS embodies, perpetuates, and transforms existing social inequalities such as gender (Paik, 2017). Although desistance research has begun to include, and listen to, women's perspectives (Hart, 2017; Österman, 2017; Barr, 2019), studies often focus on the individual desister, to the detriment of both relational and structural analysis (Hart, 2017; Gålnander, 2020). It is thus important that research into desistance from crime considers, and challenges, gender as a social institution. This will then ensure there is a recognition of how this can influence external change and how this shapes an individual's experiences and their narratives over time. Fundamentally, the knowledge produced by feminist research should work towards pushing back the intersectional relations of power, inequality, and oppression felt by those who are the focus of the research (Glucksmann, 1994).

The importance of understanding lived experiences and expertise

As the introduction has highlighted, to ensure desistance research moves our understanding past what influences the process to consider how change occurs (McNeill, 2006; Maruna, 2010), the voices and experiences of individuals involved in the CJS are integral (Weaver and Weaver, 2013). Narratives are central to an individual's experience (Presser and Sandberg, 2015) and knowledge of them enables valuable and in-depth understanding – and we all lead 'storied lives' (O'Neill et al., 2014). Narratives are revealing (Giordano, 2010), enabling us to identity ourselves (Presser, 2016) whilst examining cognitive mediators between an individual and their environment (Maruna, 2001). Through individual narratives, we can understand a person's experiences, their current aspirations, and their expected future outcomes (Bell, 2002), with an aim to understand and confront, rather than predict and control (Maruna, 2015). This builds upon a naturalistic philosophy where individuals 'are partners in the research enterprise rather than subjects to be tested or examined' (Rubin and Rubin, 2012: 11–12). To ensure flexibility, the importance of listening is key, as narratives are related to an individual's experience which constantly changes and evolves (Presser and Sandberg, 2015), based upon both past and present experiences, but also on future aspirations. As Jobe et al. (2022) note, the importance of subjective experiences captured through first-person narratives is that they are personal and provide details that are otherwise hard to gain, give insight into thoughts and feelings, and provide the opportunity to understand why.

An individual's narrative consists of stories people tell about their life episodes, or about their lives as a whole (Ioannou et al., 2017). Through conducting our lives as stories, we are able to connect experiences, actions, and aspirations (Presser and Sandberg, 2015) by how we recount, generate, structure, create and populate our narratives at multiple levels of social life (Presser and Sandberg, 2019). This demonstrates the links between our capacity to exercise agency and the structural influences that surround us as we develop an understanding of our experiences and actions in relation to our identity and wider society (Pemberton et al., 2019). Women are regarded as highly relational beings, with a primary motivation to develop connections with others (Bloom et al., 2005; Covington and Bloom, 2006). The work of Bove and Tryon (2018) on 'Stories of Change' highlights that by telling their own stories women had an opportunity to reconstruct who they are and who they may wish to be, beginning a process of destigmatisation which enabled both the listener and teller to strip away any labels. This aligns with the argument that storytelling is a powerful experience which can have a lasting effect on the teller, and can be conceived as a therapeutic intervention alongside a methodological approach (Bove and Tryon, 2018).

Wider feminist research provides a philosophical grounding for deciding how we see knowledge and how we can ensure both adequacy and legitimacy. Here, we need to recognise and challenge the wider role of patriarchal structures, especially as an individual's narrative can also be seen as something that manipulates, (Presser, 2018) hurts, and constrains (Presser and Sandberg, 2019). The chapter presents a call to action to encourage researchers to move past traditional forms of knowledge that reproduce power imbalances present within society, and emphasises the importance of developing an understanding of how participation in research spaces should respond to wider oppression (Harding, 2020) and provide space to challenge stigmatisation (Jobe et al., 2022). Fundamental to ethically responsible research is how discussions around vulnerability and re-traumatisation blur with relational boundaries and the important role of power dynamics, to which we will now turn.

Vulnerability and the potential for re-traumatisation

Vulnerability and the potential for re-traumatisation (Presser and Sandberg, 2015) is a likely consequence of sharing narratives that evidence previous trauma, abuse, and harm. These experiences are disproportionally prevalent for criminalised women, often providing the backdrop to their involvement in criminal behaviour (Corston, 2007). Such experiences need to be acknowledged (Bloom et al., 2005; Covington and Bloom, 2006) and understood in their wider structural sense, but also in their personal impact within research methodology, decisions, and activity.

Trauma can be defined as 'any event that overwhelms a person's capacity for positive coping' (Covington, 2016: 2) and therefore something that is traumatic for one person may not be traumatic for another. It is essential that we question how trauma is defined, who is defining it, and how it is then linked to wider systems of both power and oppression (Becker-Blease, 2017). Research evidence demonstrates the importance of gender-responsive and trauma-informed service provision (Covington 2007; Hopper et al., 2010) with the need to consider both experiences and behaviour within the context of trauma (Rutter and Eden-Barnard, 2023). Whilst parts of the CJS, and agencies working within it, may recognise and incorporate elements of trauma-informed practice, the lack of flexibility and controlling structures of the system often work in direct tension to these ideas (Annison et al., 2019).

Trauma-informed approaches are underpinned by relational theory (Petrillo et al., 2019); they are grounded in a strength-based framework to understand and respond to the impact of trauma and recognise the importance of physical, psychological, and emotional safety to support opportunities for control and empowerment (Hopper et al., 2010). They are designed in a way that avoids triggering or re-traumatising people through prioritising the development of coping strategies alongside attempting to model healthy and growth-fostering relationships (Covington, 2014). Importantly, a trauma-informed approach promotes an important shift in language and moves from asking 'what has she done?' to instead asking 'what has happened to her?' (Covington, 2007). Research also argues that trauma-informed approaches should take place within an environment which is safe and provides choice to create a sense of shared responsibility and empowerment (Covington, 2016), enabling women to overcome shame and stigmatisation (Rutter and Barr, 2021).

As researchers, then, it is important we consider our responsibility in recognising trauma but also increase our understanding of it to create empowering research spaces. We should work to the same goals and principles as trauma-informed practice, considering the language we use and the environment we are creating when undertaking narrative and longitudinal research with criminalised women. Without gaining an understanding of trauma, it is extremely easy, and likely, for us to cause continued and additional harm when undertaking research. With this in mind, we also need to consider the methodologies drawn upon within our research, with calls to expand our use of relational, participatory, and humanising approaches (Petrone and Stanton, 2021). In support of this, we can look to work within the principles of trauma-informed care which incorporates the overarching principles of safety, choice, collaboration, trust, and empowerment. This aligns with the importance of understanding women's lived experience within criminal justice and ensures we listen to their voices whilst taking greater ethical accountability and responsibility as researchers to avoid additional harm and re-traumatisation.

Blurring relational boundaries

Narrative and longitudinal research can challenge and blur relational boundaries between researchers and participants (Presser and Sandberg, 2015) as it requires a degree of trust and confidence (Stanley, 2018). Here, researchers should offer some consideration and thought to their displays of both surface and deep acting: with surface acting required to build the trust and confidence with those involved in research (Waters et al., 2020) and deep acting regarded as being emotionally open to ensure positive emotional displays which allow researchers to connect with participants on a personal level (Dickson-Swift et al., 2009).

Critical reflection here is key to ensuring ethically sound relational boundaries. Arguments identify how the performance of emotional labour may suggest that individuals involved in research are a commodity (Waters et al., 2020). In addition, attempts at empathy, equity and 'friendship' are argued to have the potential to increase participants' vulnerability to exploitation, and as a consequence affect how they may be regarded as sources of data (Stacey, 1988). There are also distinct possibilities for seemingly 'faking friendship' (Duncombe and Jessop, 2002) to create real ethical challenges with regards to the power dynamics between researchers and those involved in research.

In addition to these relational boundaries, the potential intrusion of longitudinal research presents a particular ethical dilemma when considering the surveillant position, and therefore unequal power dynamics, of the researcher (Sharpe, 2017). Sharpe (2017: 234) reflects on the 'fine line between "walking alongside" (former) lawbreakers in order to gain a deep understanding of how their lives and narratives develop over time and reproducing everyday modes of security and surveillance'. Her reflections highlight that this is rarely acknowledged or considered within the ethical discussions of longitudinal and narrative research to recognise the invasion of privacy and reproduction of everyday experiences of stigma that are known to permeate the lives of criminalised women (Rutter and Barr, 2021; Sharpe, 2017). This highlights that at its worst longitudinal research can be felt as a form of sociological stalking for those participating (Sharpe, 2017) and for those carrying out research when reflecting on the emotional labour of conducting research. Guilt was recognised as a strong emotion expressed by researchers when asking for stories as an acknowledgment of their invasion of privacy, and also surrounding the possibility of re-traumatising individuals as a result of research involvement (Waters et al., 2020).

As researchers, we should reflect and question our own role within research to ensure the voices of those involved remain at centre stage to support participant empowerment over research biases which can affect the creation of knowledge. Again, drawing upon the role of emotion, the ways in which researchers manage this during data collection will ultimately shape any generation of data (Phillips and Earle, 2010). For these reasons, as researchers we have an ethical responsibility to consider how the knowledge collected within research, and how it is then circulated in public forums, will represent the voices of those involved and their interests. We need to work hard to guarantee that we do not speak for them, nor that we document how we think they may have felt to ensure we are not performing the act of ventriloquism (Sharpe, 2017).

When reflecting on our ethical responsibilities as researchers, both trustworthiness and authenticity require our thought (Guba and Lincoln, 1994). We have a responsibility to ensure that the findings we present are credible to the experiences of those involved but also that there is wider credibility to them (Shannon and Hambacher, 2014). The role of fairness with authenticity also requires us to ensure we present and represent a balanced view (Schwandt, 2007) which can be achieved when individuals are empowered to have a voice (Guba, 1981). We need to be able to offer more than just a recognition of the insider and outsider position (Jewkes, 2014) and how this should be reflected and continually negotiated to support the ethical production of knowledge. This enables us as researchers to question *whose knowledge* is presented by questioning the role of power within research and holding true the point that our structural position does not give us access to ways of knowing (Skeggs, 2004) – experience does.

Questioning power dynamics

When offering a platform for marginalised voices through narrative and longitudinal research, as researchers it's important we question the power dynamics at play, and in fact who benefits. As noted, within both wider criminology and desistance scholarship feminist research is still very much a marginal perspective offering a distinctive approach to research that is multi-dimensional, and works towards ensuring action against power (Harding, 2020). Harding (2020) argues that traditional forms of knowledge production serve to reproduce the power imbalances present within society. It is paramount we understand how participation in research spaces responds to wider oppression, as patriarchal structures have faced limited critique when attempting to understand women's desistance through their narratives (Rutter and Barr, 2021). Feminist research, methodologies, and knowledge production highlight the importance of pushing back on the intersectional relations of power, inequality, and oppression felt by those who are the focus of research (Glucksmann, 1994), especially given that there is a limited understanding of 'what it feels like for criminalised individuals to activate their lived experiences' (Buck et al., 2022).

However, whilst feminist researchers have made explicit the exercise of power within the process of research through the ontological basis of knowledge production (Sharpe, 2017), there are critiques surrounding the essentialism of suggesting that women's voices are a unified category. This draws back to the importance of recognising intersectionality to disrupt and revolutionise how both criminology and criminal justice service delivery is carried out (Potter, 2015) and how experiences are understood. The underpinning philosophical approach of pragmatism can enable research to challenge traditional power dynamics. Taking a pragmatic approach enables flexibility when considering research design, as the core principles argue there is no single and best method that leads to knowledge, and that knowledge is the product of the cultural context in which it is produced (Denscombe, 2014). Pragmatism emphasises the importance of learning in a changing world, with the need for experimentation and reflection (Pedler and Burgoyne, 2008) whilst promoting the idea that knowledge is based on the reality of the world we experience and live in (Onwuegbuzie et al., 2009). Critically thinking, every individual's real world is different, and the role of bias here requires reflection from researchers as an individual's narrative is interpreted differently by them, the researcher, and the audience (Harding, 2020). There is a clear risk that the production of knowledge within research is a political act given that a researcher's own personhood is always, in some way, part of the research. Therefore, a recognition of our position and how this influences the reflexivity, objectivity, and validity of research needs to be considered as a point of reflection (Letherby, 2002). When we recognise multiple realities within research, we demonstrate that there is no single or correct ontological understanding of the social world and that there are in fact 'multiple ontologies or multiple understandings of reality and ... each has validity' (Heap and Waters, 2018: 117)

Research that questions its epistemic authority demonstrates consideration to whose knowledge is recognised and validated and whose is silenced, with a privileged position also adding a certain form of objectivity, and a level of authority, to any claims of knowledge (Naples and Gurr, 2014). What is fundamental when challenging the power dynamics within research is the importance of actively listening, and our ethical responsibility in striving to actively understand, participate, and collaborate through varying methodological approaches. Here, we can draw upon PAR (Participatory Action Research) as an approach to ensure that as researchers we recognise the potential for harm and re-traumatisation, alongside the blurring of relational boundaries and the role of power within research.

Approaches that draw upon Participatory Action Research

The principles of PAR support a collaborative ethos and provide a voice to individuals traditionally seen as participants to place them at the centre of research (Lewin, 1946) through the principles of full participation (Pettinger et al., 2018) and through the politics of inclusion and representation by facilitating recognition (O'Neill, 2010). DeLyser (2014) identifies the importance of a liberatory agenda within PAR which reverses exclusionary and/or discriminatory practices by seeking to empower individuals. This ethos is important within research that involves individuals or groups who have been othered, and consequently face active stigmatisation in society. This can be seen with regards to criminalised women through the location of both shame and stigma in the experiences of their criminalisation and victimisation (Rutter and Barr, 2021). A key contributor to the methodological approaches of PAR is found in feminist research which refuses to accept theory, research, and ethical perspectives that demonstrate any notion of gender blindness (McIntyre, 2008). But of course, gender is not the only intersectionality we need to acknowledge – we need to recognise the individual.

In addition, research which draws upon the philosophy of PAR can create a collaborative environment that provides a voice to those participating in research to validate and prioritise their knowledge (DeLyser, 2014). It also provides the space to reposition vulnerability and power to re-frame the overall purpose of research (Armstrong and Ludlow, 2020). This situates those involved in research as the experts in their own lives whilst also offering the opportunity for collaboration throughout, with the overall goal of pursuing social justice (Pain, 2009), ultimately to ensure 'fair play' within research (McIntyre, 2008). For women, developing mutual relationships is key to their sense of self-identity and self-worth (Bloom et al., 2005; Covington and Bloom, 2006). This can therefore be key in supporting the development of ethical research methodologies when considering the importance of establishing trust and confidence for those involved.

Through participation and collaboration, PAR offers researchers a methodological approach that grapples explicitly with critiques of power, purpose, positioning, and personhood to disrupt more traditional research power dynamics that pigeonhole, marginalise, or privilege particular perspectives (Armstrong and Ludlow, 2020; Harding, 2020). Crucially, participatory research offers a counter-hegemonic way of undertaking research that can place women's voices at centre stage, whilst at the same time challenging exclusionary research practices (Jobe et al., 2022). As researchers, we should take a step back to reflect on the passionate argument put forward by Harding (2020), who suggests that drawing upon feminist methodologies and elements of PAR presents, 'an opportunity to flatten power hierarchies often felt within traditional research, by offering the potential to resituate those residing in the margins, bringing them into the centre of knowledge produced about (by) them' (Harding, 2020: 1).

Important reflections remain for scholars regarding who truly benefits from participation and/or collaboration in research to consider if involvement can cause harm to individuals in some circumstances, and therefore put into question the ethical responsibility of research. It is consequently important for those conducting research to truly reflect on whether the research itself and the methods that are used are ever in fact neutral due to the idea that every act or omission bears a consequence within it (Armstrong and Ludlow, 2020). This is important not only for research but also when considering practice and policy development.

Conclusion

This chapter has presented a discussion on the ethical responsibilities that can arise when undertaking qualitative research which draws upon narrative and longitudinal approaches within the discipline of criminology. The chapter has highlighted the importance of qualitative research within the field of desistance from crime, looking to a pragmatic philosophy, and drawing upon feminist literature and methodological approaches through the example of PAR. This has enabled discussions of power to argue the importance of understanding women's lived experiences within criminal justice and ensuring that we listen to these voices within research, practice, and policy to support participation and collaboration.

The chapter focused on three key areas of discussion. Firstly, vulnerability and the potential for re-traumatisation, especially when sharing narratives that evidence previous trauma, abuse, and harm, each of which are disproportionately prevalent for criminalised women. With this in mind, the chapter argued that we need to recognise trauma but also increase our understanding of it. We should work to the same goals and principles as trauma-informed practice and trauma-informed care, bearing in mind the language we use and the environment we are creating when undertaking narrative and longitudinal research with criminalised women. When considering the ethical guidelines surrounding social research (for example, European Commission, 2021; SRA, 2021) there is a frame of reference provided that can promote responsible and informed decision-making through reflective practice. There are, however, some general responsibilities of best practice which could more specifically recognise trauma. As researchers, seeking appropriate experience or training to become more trauma-informed in our approaches enables us to improve our professional knowledge, skills, and attributes to minimise the potential harm of those involved in our research. The practice of research within criminology has the power to both address adversity and trauma, or in fact perpetuate it at an individual and societal level (Edelman, 2022). A lack of understanding of trauma, and the behaviours, and/or responses that are an attempt to cope with experiences, can lead to misunderstanding people, their actions, and their reactions (Smeaton, 2019). Therefore, trauma-informed approaches should be integrated across research topics and designs to improve inclusion and experience (Edelman, 2022)

Secondly, the chapter discussed how narrative and longitudinal research can challenge and blur relational boundaries between researchers and participants (Presser and Sandberg, 2015), as it requires a degree of trust and confidence, and how longitudinal research can also be somewhat intrusive (Sharpe, 2017). Sharpe states that at its worst longitudinal research is a form of sociological stalking (Sharpe, 2017), and as researchers we need to consider the ethical responsibilities this places on us and how any possible impacts could be mitigated. This could be through, for example, continually ensuring freely informed consent, being mindful of how frequently we invite participation, and carefully considering how many times we make contact with those involved in research to encourage their continued participation. These questions also require us to reflect on the methods we use and their appropriateness and/or suitability for the research we are undertaking.

Thirdly, this chapter has discussed that as researchers when we offer a platform for marginalised voices through narrative and longitudinal research, we question the power dynamics at play, and in fact who benefits. The chapter argues that what is fundamental when challenging the power dynamics within research is the importance of actively listening and our ethical responsibility in striving to actively understand, participate, and collaborate through varying methodological approaches. Here, we can draw upon elements and principles of PAR as an approach to ensure that as researchers we recognise the role of vulnerability and re-traumatisation, the blurring of relational boundaries, and the role of power within research. Research should aim to include the ideas surrounding meaningful participation to ensure that it becomes so much more than process management because:

> It is only by moving beyond typologies of participation, towards an understanding of how participation in the created research space responds to the group's wider oppression, in this case by overcoming trauma or demonstrating reform, that collaboration with holders of lived experience can uncover subjugated knowledge and facilitate transformative action.
>
> *(Harding, 2020: 1).*

Lived experience within service delivery and research is regarded as a means of promoting individual empowerment alongside increasing the responsiveness of provision (Lewis, 2014). Let us recognise the power dynamics at play to support an increasingly participatory and collaborative approach in which to limit exclusion and expand our understanding of those often marginalised within the CJS. Ultimately, we need to recognise that power dynamics do not, and will not, change without discomfort (Armstrong and Ludlow, 2020), but we need to change them all the same.

References

Annison, J., Byng, R., and Quinn, C.(2019). 'Women Offenders: Promoting a Holistic Approach and Continuity of Care across Criminal Justice and Health Interventions', *Criminology & Criminal Justice*, 19(4), pp. 385–403.

Armstrong, E. K. (2020). 'Political Ideology and Research: How Neoliberalism Can Explain the Paucity of Qualitative Criminological Research', *Alternatives: Global, Local, Political*, 45(1), pp. 20–32.

Armstrong, R. and Ludlow, A. (2020). 'What's So Good About Participation? Politics, Ethics and Love in Learning Together', *Methodological Innovations*, 13(2), pp. 1–10.

Barr, U. (2017). 'Are Neoliberal, Patriarchal Societies Compatible with Desistance? A Consideration of the Experiences of a Group of English Women Caught up in the Criminal Justice System', in: Fletcher, S. and White, H. (eds.), *Emerging Voices: Critical Social Research by European Group Postgraduate and Early Career Researchers*. London: EG Press Limited, pp. 15–26.

Barr, U. (2018). 'Gendered Assisted Desistance: A Decade from Corston', *Safer Communities*, 17(2), pp. 81–93.

Barr, U. (2019). *Desisting Sisters: Gender, Power and Desistance in The Criminal (In) Justice System*. London: Palgrave Macmillan.

Becker-Blease, K. (2017) 'As the World Becomes Trauma–Informed, Work to Do', *Journal of Trauma & Dissociation*, 18(2), pp. 131–138,

Bell, J. (2002) 'Narrative Inquiry: More Than Just Telling Stories', *TESOL Quarterly*, 36(2), pp. 207–213.

Blokland, A. and De Schipper, N. (2016). 'How Important Are Life-Course Transitions in Explaining Desistance? Examining The Extent to Which Marriage, Divorce and Parenthood Account for the Age-Crime Relationship in Former Juvenile Delinquents', in: Shapland, J., Farrall, S., and Bottoms, A. (eds.), *Global Perspectives on Desistance: Reviewing What We Know and Looking to the Future*. Abingdon, Oxon: Routledge, pp. 144–169.

Bloom, B., Owen, B., and Covington, S. (2005). 'Gender-Responsive Strategies for Women Offenders (A Summary of Research, Practice, and Guiding Principles for Women Offenders)'. Washington, D.C.: National Institute of Corrections, U.S. Department of Justice.

Bove, A. and Tryon, R. (2018). 'The Power of Storytelling: The Experiences of Incarcerated Women Sharing Their Stories', *International Journal of Offender Therapy and Comparative Criminology* 62(15), pp. 4814–4833.

Broidy, L. and Cauffman, E. (2017). 'The Glueck Women: Using the Past to Assess and Extend Contemporary Understandings of Women's Desistance from Crime', *Journal of Developmental and Life-Course Criminology*, 3(2), pp. 102–125.

Buck, G., Tomczak, P., and Quinn, K. (2022). 'This Is How It Feels: Activating Lived Experience in the Penal Voluntary Sector', *British Journal of Criminology* 62(4): pp. 822–839.

Carlen, P. (1990). *Alternatives to Women's Imprisonment*. Milton Keynes: Open University Press.

Corston, J. B. (2007). *The Corston Report: A Report by Baroness Jean Corston of a Review of Women with Particular Vulnerabilities in the Criminal Justice System: The Need for a Distinct, Radically Different, Visibly-Led, Strategic, Proportionate, Holistic, Woman-Centred, Integrated Approach*. London: Home Office.

Covington, S. (2007). 'The Relational Theory of Women's Psychological Development: Implications for the Criminal Justice System', in: Zaplin, R. (ed.), *Female Offenders: Critical Perspectives and Effective Interventions*, 2nd edition. Sudbury, MA: Jones and Bartlett Publishers.

Covington, S. (2014). 'Creating Gender-Responsive and Trauma-Informed Services for Women in The Justice System', *Magistrate*, 70(5), pp. 2–3.

Covington, S. (2016). 'Becoming Trauma Informed: Toolkit for Women's Community Service Providers', *Centre for Gender and Justice*. Available at: https://www.onesmallthing.org.uk/resources-item/bti-tool-kit-and-guides/ (accessed 20 April 2021).

Covington, S. and Bloom, B. (2006). 'Gender Responsive Treatment and Services in Correctional Settings', in: Leeder, E. (ed.), *Inside and Out: Women, Prison, and Therapy*. Philadelphia, PA: Haworth Press, pp. 9–33.

Crenshaw, K. (1991). 'Mapping the Margins: Intersectionality, Identity Politics and Violence against Women of Colour', *Stanford Law Review*, 43(6), pp. 1241–1299.

DeLyser, D. (2014). 'Towards a Participatory Historical Geography: Archival Interventions, Volunteer Service, and Public Outreach in Research on Early Women Pilots', *Journal of Historical Geography*, 46, pp. 93–98.

Denscombe, M. (2014). *The Good Research Guide: For Small-Scale Social Research Projects*. Maidenhead: McGraw-Hill Education.

Dickson-Swift V., James E.L., Kippen S, and Liamputtong, P. (2009). 'Researching Sensitive Topics: Qualitative Research as Emotion Work', *Qualitative Research*, 9(1), pp. 61–79.

Duncombe, J. and Jessop, J. (2002). '"Doing Rapport" and the Ethics of "Faking Friendship"', in: Miller, T., Mauthner, M., Birch, M., and Jessop, J. (eds.), *Ethics in Qualitative Research*. London: Sage, pp. 107–122.

Edelman, NL. (2022). 'Trauma and Resilience Informed Research Principles and Practice: A Framework to Improve the Inclusion and Experience of Disadvantaged Populations in Health and Social Care Research', *Journal of Health Services Research & Policy*, 28(1), pp. 66–75.

European Commission (2021). 'Ethics in Social Science and Humanities', European Commission. Available at: https://ec.europa.eu/info/funding-tenders/opportunities/docs/2021-2027/horizon/guidance/ethics-in-social-science-and-humanities_he_en.pdf.

Farrall, S. (2004). 'Social Capital and Offender Reintegration: Making Probation Desistance Focused', in: Maruna, S. and Immarigeon, R. (eds.), *After Crime and Punishment: Pathways to Offender Reintegration*. Abingdon, Oxon: Routledge, pp. 57–82.

Farrall, S. and Calverley, A. (2006). *Understanding Desistance from Crime*. Maidenhead: Open University Press.

Fitzgibbon, W. and Stengel, C.M. (2018). 'Women's Voices Made Visible: Photovoice in Visual Criminology', *Punishment and Society*, 20(4), pp. 411–431.

Gålnander, R. (2020). 'Desistance from Crime – to What? Exploring Future Aspirations and Their Implications for Processes of Desistance', *Feminist Criminology*, 15(3), pp. 255–277.

Gelsthorpe, L. and Wright, S. (2015). 'The Context: Women as Lawbreakers', in: Annison, J., Brayford, J., and Deering, J. (eds.), *Women and Criminal Justice: From the Corston Report to Transforming Rehabilitation*. Cullumpton: Willan Publishing, pp. 39–58.

Giordano, P. (2010) *Legacies of Crime: A Follow-Up of the Children of Highly Delinquent Girls and Boys*. Cambridge: Cambridge University Press.

Glucksmann, M (1994). 'Working through Gender: The Inter-Weaving of New Technology in Workplace and Home', *Work, Employment and Society*, 8(4), pp. 623–628.

Glueck, S. and Glueck, E. (1950). *Unravelling Juvenile Delinquency*. Boston: Harvard University Press.

Gomm, R. (2016). 'Women Making Meaning of Their Desistance from Offending: An Interpretative Phenomenological Analysis', Unpublished PhD thesis. Durham University. Available at: http://etheses.dur.ac.uk/11567/.

Gottfredson, M. and Hirschi, T. (1990). *A General Theory of Crime*. Stanford: Stanford University Press.

Grace, S. and O'Neill, M. (2022). *Criminal Women: Gender Matters*. Bristol: Bristol University Press.

Guba, E. (1981). 'Criteria for Assessing the Trustworthiness of Naturalistic Inquiries', *Educational Communication and Technology Journal*, 29 (2), pp. 75–91.

Guba, E. and Lincoln, Y. (1994). 'Competing Paradigms in Qualitative Research', in: Denzin, N. and Lincoln, Y. (eds.), *Handbook of Qualitative Research*. Thousand Oaks: Sage, pp. 105–117.

Harding, N. (2018). 'Places on Probation: An Auto-Ethnographic Account of Co-Produced Research with Women with Criminal Biographies', in Plows, A. (ed.), *Messy Ethnographies in Action*, Malaga: Vernon Press, pp. 91–100.

Harding, N. (2020). 'Co-Constructing Feminist Research: Ensuring Meaningful Participation Whilst Researching the Experiences of Criminalised Women', *Methodological Innovations*, 13(2), pp. 1–14.

Hart, E. (2017). 'Prisoners Post Release: The Need for a "Critical Desistance"', in: Hart, E. and Van Ginneken, E. (eds.), *New Perspectives on Desistance: Theoretical and Empirical Developments*. London: Palgrave Macmillan, pp. 267–288.

Heap, V. and Waters, J. (2018). 'Using Mixed Methods in Criminological Research', in: Davies, P. and Francis, P. (eds.) *Doing Criminological Research*, 3rd ed. London: Sage, pp. 113–136.

Heidensohn, F. (2004). 'Gender and Crime', in: Maguire, M., Morgan, R., and Reiner, R. (eds.), *The Oxford Handbook of Criminology*. Oxford: Oxford University Press.

Hopper, E., Bassuk, E., and Olivet, J. (2010). 'Shelter from the Storm: Trauma-Informed Care in Homelessness Services Settings', *The Open Health Services and Policy Journal*, 3(2), pp. 80–100.

Ioannou, M., Canter, D., and Youngs, D. (2017). 'Criminal Narrative Experience: Relating Emotions to Offence Narrative Roles During Crime Commission', *International Journal of Offender Therapy and Comparative Criminology*, 61(14), pp. 1531–1553.

Jewkes, Y. (2014). 'An Introduction to "Doing Prison Research Differently"', *Qualitative Inquiry*, 20(4), pp. 387–391.

Jobe, A., Stockdale, K., and O'Neill, M. (2022) 'Stigma and Service Provision for Women Selling Sex: Findings from Community-based Participatory Research', *Ethics and Social Welfare*, 16(2), pp. 112–128,

Larsson, B. (2019). 'Morality Tales: Young Women's Narratives on Offending, Self-Worth and Desistance', *Probation Journal*, 66(3), pp. 318–334.

Laub, J. and Sampson, R. (2001). 'Understanding Desistance from Crime', *Crime and Justice*, 28, pp. 1–69.

LeBel, T.P., Burnett, R., Maruna, S., and Bushway, S. (2008). 'The "Chicken and Egg" of Subjective and Social Factors in Desistance from Crime', *European Journal of Criminology*, 5(2), pp. 131–159.

Letherby, G. (2002). 'Claims And Disclaimers: Knowledge, Reflexivity and Representation in Feminist Research', *Sociological Research Online*, 6(4), pp. 81–93.

Lewin, K. (1946). 'Action Research and Minority Problems', *Journal of Social Issues*, 2 (4), pp. 34–46.

Lewis, L. (2014). 'User Involvement in Mental Health Services: A Case of Power Over Discourse', *Sociological Research*, 19(1): 6.

Loeber, R., Stouthamer-Loeber, M., and Ahonen, L. (2016). 'Key Behavioral Aspects of Desistance from Conduct Problems and Delinquency', in: Shapland, J., Farrall, S., and Bottoms, A. (eds.), *Global Perspectives On Desistance: Reviewing What We Know and Looking To The Future*. Abingdon, Oxon: Routledge, pp. 85–98.

Maruna, S. (2001). *Making Good: How Ex-Convicts Reform and Rebuild Their Lives*. London; Washington, D.C.: American Psychological Association.

Maruna, S. (2010). 'Mixed Method Research in Criminology: Why Not Go Both Ways?', in: Piquero, A. and Weisburd, D. (eds.), *Handbook of Quantitative Criminology*. London: Springer, pp. 123–140.

Maruna, S. (2015). 'Foreword: Narrative Criminology as the New Mainstream', in: Presser, L. and Sandberg, S. (eds.), *Narrative Criminology: Understanding Stories of Crime*. New York: New York University Press, pp. vii–x.

Maruna, S. (2017). 'Desistance as a Social Movement', *Irish Probation Journal*, 14, pp. 5–20.

McIntyre, A. (2008). *Participatory Action Research*. Vol. 52. London: Sage.

McNeill, F. (2006). 'A Desistance Paradigm for Offender Management', *Criminology & Criminal Justice*, 6(1) pp. 39–62.

Naples, N. and Gurr, B. (2014). 'Feminist Empiricism and Standpoint Theory: Approaches to Understanding the Social World', in: Hesse-Biber, S.N. (ed.), *Feminist Research Practice: A Primer*, 2nd ed. Thousand Oaks: Sage, pp. 14–41.

O'Neill, M. (2010). 'Cultural Criminology and Sex Work: Resisting Regulation through Radical Democracy and Participatory Action Research (PAR)', *Journal of Law and Society*, 37(1), pp. 210–232.

O'Neill, M., Roberts, B., and Sparkes, A.C. (eds.) (2014). *Advances in Biographical Methods: Creative Applications*. Abingdon, Oxon: Routledge.

Onwuegbuzie, A.J., Johnson, R.B., and Collins, K.M. (2009). 'Call for Mixed Analysis: A Philosophical Framework for Combining Qualitative and Quantitative Approaches', *International Journal of Multiple Research Approaches*, 3(2) pp. 114–139.

Österman, L. (2017). *Penal Cultures and Female Desistance*. Abingdon, Oxon: Routledge.

Paik, L. (2017). 'Critical Perspectives on Intersectionality and Criminology: Introduction', *Theoretical Criminology*, 21(1), pp. 4–10.

Pain, R. (2009). 'Introduction: Doing Social Geographies', in: Smith, S., Pain, R., and Marston, S. (eds.), *The Sage Handbook of Social Geographies*. London: Sage, pp. 507–515.

Pedler, M. and Burgoyne, J. (2008). 'Action Learning', in: Reason, P. and Bradbury, H. (eds.), *The Sage Handbook of Action Research: Participative Inquiry and Practice*. London: Sage, pp. 319–332.

Pemberton, A., Aarten, P.G.M., and Mulder, E. (2019). 'Stories as Property: Narrative Ownership as a Key Concept in Victims' Experiences with Criminal Justice', *Criminology & Criminal Justice*, 19(4), pp. 404–420.

Petrillo, M., Thomas, M., and Hanspal, S.E. (2019). 'Healing Trauma Evaluation Report', *One Small Thing*. Available at: https://onesmallthing.org.uk/news-1/2019/6/12/healing-trauma-research.

Petrone, R. and Stanton, C.R. (2021). 'From Producing to Reducing Trauma: A Call for "Trauma-Informed" Research(ers) to Interrogate How Schools Harm Students', *Educational Researcher*, 50(8), pp. 537–545.

Pettinger C., Letherby G., Parsons J.M., Withers, L., Cunningham, M., Whiteford, A., D'Aprano, G., Ayres, R., and Sutton, C. (2018). 'Employing Participatory Methods to Engage an Under-Researched Group: Opportunities and Challenges', *Methodological Innovations*, 11, pp. 1–13.

Piquero, A. (2004). 'Somewhere Between Persistence and Desistance: The Intermittency of Criminal Careers', in: Maruna, S. and Immarigeon, R. (eds.), *After Crime and Punishment: Pathways to Offender Reintegration*. Abingdon, Oxon: Routledge, pp. 102–125.

Plano Clark, V.L., Anderson, N., Wertz, J.A., Zhou, Y., Schumacher, K., and Miaskowski, C. (2015). 'Conceptualizing Longitudinal Mixed Methods Designs: A Methodological Review of Health Sciences Research', *Journal of Mixed Methods Research*, 9(4), pp. 297–319.

Phillips, C. and Earle, R. (2010) 'Reading Difference Differently? Identity, Epistemology and Prison Ethnography', *The British Journal of Criminology*, 50(2), pp. 360–378.

Potter, H. (2015) *Intersectionality and Criminology*. Abingdon, Oxon: Routledge.

Presser, L. (2016). 'Criminology and the Narrative Turn', *Crime, Media, Culture: An International Journal*, 12(2), pp. 137–151.
Presser, L. (2018) *Inside Story: How Narratives Drive Mass Harm*. California: University of California Press.
Presser, L. and Sandberg, S. (2015). *Narrative Criminology*. New York: New York University Press.
Presser, L. and Sandberg, S. (2019). 'Narrative Criminology as Critical Criminology', *Critical Criminology*, 27(1), pp. 131–143.
Priestley, P. and Vanstone, M. (2019). 'Restoring Probation: A Declaration of Independence', *Probation Journal* 66(3), pp. 335–347.
Rubin, H.J. and Rubin, I. (2012). *Qualitative Interviewing: The Art of Hearing Data*, 3rd ed. London: Sage.
Rumgay, J. (2004). 'Scripts for Safer Survival: Pathways Out of Female Crime', *The Howard Journal*, 43(4), pp. 405–419.
Rutter, N. and Barr, U. (2021). 'Being A "Good Woman": Stigma, Relationships and Desistance', *Probation Journal*, 68(2), pp. 166–185.
Rutter, N. and Eden-Barnard, J. (2023). '"It is Nice to Know That for Once Someone is Not Just Saying that They're Backing Your Corner, They Are Actually Fucking Backing Your Corner": The Significance of Relational Factors in Women's Experiences of Probation Intervention', in: Masson, I. and Booth, N. (eds.), *The Routledge Handbook of Women's Experiences of Criminal Justice*. Abingdon, Oxon: Routledge, pp. 439–451.
Sarnecki, J. and Carlsson, C. (2018). 'Doing Longitudinal and Life-Course Criminological Research', in: Davies, P. and Francis, P. (eds.), *Doing Criminological Research*. London: Sage, pp. 297–320.
Schwandt, T. (2007). *The Sage Dictionary of Qualitative Inquiry*, 3rd ed. London: Sage.
Shannon, P. and Hambacher, E. (2014). 'Authenticity in Constructivist Inquiry: Assessing an Elusive Construct', *The Qualitative Report*, 19(52), pp. 1–13.
Sharpe, G. (2017). 'Sociological Stalking? Methods, Ethics and Power in Longitudinal Criminological Research', *Criminology & Criminal Justice*, 17(3), pp. 233–247.
Skeggs, B. (2004). *Class, Self, Culture*. Abingdon, Oxon: Routledge.
Smart, C. (1977). *Women, Crime and Criminology: A Feminist Critique*. Abingdon, Oxon: Routledge.
Smeaton, E. (2019). 'Trauma and Trauma-Informed Researchers', Social Research Association. Available at: https://the-sra.org.uk/SRA/SRA/Blog/Trauma%20and%20trauma-informed%20researchers.aspx.
Social Research Association (SRA) (2021). 'Research Ethics Guidance', Social Research Association. Available at: https://the-sra.org.uk/common/Uploaded%20files/Resources/SRA%20Research%20Ethics%20guidance%202021.pdf.
Stacey, J.(1988). 'Can There be a Feminist Ethnography?', *Women's Studies International Forum*, 11(1), pp. 21–27.
Stanley, E. (2018). 'Using Interviews as Storytelling in Criminological Research', in: Davies, P. and Francis, P. (eds.), *Doing Criminological Research*. London: Sage, pp. 321–339.
Waters, J., Westaby, C., Fowler, A., and Phillips, J. (2020) 'The Emotional Labour of Doctoral Criminological Researchers', *Methodological Innovation*, pp. 1–12.
Weaver, A. and Weaver, B. (2013) 'Autobiography, Empirical Research and Critical Theory in Desistance: A View from the Inside Out', *Probation Journal*, 60(3), pp. 259–277.
Weaver, B. (2019). 'Understanding Desistance: A Critical Review of Theories of Desistance', *Psychology, Crime & Law*, 25 (6), pp. 641–658.

9

FEMALE RESEARCHER IDENTITIES IN MALE SPACES AND PLACES

Claudia Smith Cox, Kerry Ellis Devitt, and Lisa Sugiura

Introduction

Defined by Roulston (2010: 116) as 'the researcher's ability to be able to self-consciously refer to him or herself in relation to the production of knowledge about research topics', reflexivity is an ongoing process of critical self-reflection which supports an awareness of the impact of self on social interactions. Whilst Roulston applied this to a research setting, reflexivity is also prominent within professional and work-based environments in order to promote learning, development, and change (Edwards and Nicoll, 2006). Reflexivity has been increasingly recognised as an essential component of qualitative research in order to acknowledge '… the construction of knowledge and power as an inherently social process' (Riach, 2009: 357).

We, the authors, are three female academics working in a criminology department at a university in England at the time of writing. Each of us have independently written about or published work relating to the impact of our identities on our research findings in the fields of policing, 'incels', and young adult men with prison experience. However, this chapter seeks to align our collective experiences of conducting qualitative research as women in male-dominated spaces and reflects the ongoing process of reflexivity that we have engaged with since completing our fieldwork. Being women played a pivotal role in our respective research projects, especially given the gendered dynamics integral within the subject matters we studied. Like Gailey and Prohaska (2011), two female researchers who shared their experiences of interviewing men about degrading sexual practices, we found that gendered interview relationships can be challenging due to the interactions – as are other forms of interplay outside of the research setting, of course – being rooted in conventional expectations of communication. As such, our reflections involved evaluating and assessing the situations in which we felt vulnerable or unsafe. We do not claim, however, to be representing all women when relating our experiences, and appreciate the heterogeneity of what it means to be a woman. As white (although R2 (Researcher 2 – Sugiura) is mixed-race but benefits from being 'white-presenting'), cis, heterosexual, middle-class, able-bodied women, we are acutely aware that we experience privilege over other women who have intersecting identities involving axes of oppression, and that these other attributes we possess positively impact upon our research and roles within the academy. This understanding of our identities having such privileged facets has been considered throughout our analyses and reflections so as not to misrepresent us as persons marginalised within society, but to instead highlight how our gender influenced our interactions with our research participants.

Furthermore, it is important to deconstruct our use of the term gender so that it is not merely conflated with sex. Unger (1979) demarcated between sex and gender by explaining sex as referring to a person's biological maleness or femaleness and gender as the non-physiological cultural aspects of being female or male. In this instance, sex is purely anatomical, whilst gender relates to expectations regarding feminine and masculine roles. Neatly separating sex and gender, however, is unrealistic as socially constructed expectations for women and men (gender) are not distinct from observations about women and men's physical bodies (sex) (Lips, 2020), and assumptions are often made about gender roles and stereotypes based on an interpretation of an individual's aesthetics (whether made correctly or incorrectly). Moreover, describing gender in binary terms excludes and pathologises persons who do not identify or fit neatly into traditional categories of masculinity or femininity (Barr et al., 2016; Valcore et al., 2021), and treating sex as immutable denies the existence of trans persons. In this chapter, ours is an inclusive use of the term gender to consider differences and expectations about us as women, caused by combinations of environment and biology.

Focusing on the perceived need to build rapport with participants in order to elicit useful data whilst ensuring researcher safety, this chapter will reflect on the impact our identities had on both our research and our participants, particularly in relation to gender, ethnicity, age, and social class. This chapter begins with a discussion on the importance of self-reflection and consideration of positionality in social research given the influence researcher identity can have on the research process and outcomes. This is followed by an overview of the research projects we have each undertaken in male-dominated spaces and places. We will then draw upon experiences from the field to demonstrate how our identities intersected and interacted with those of our participants to influence the research experience.

Throughout this chapter we will maintain the position that qualitative researchers cannot be impartial conduits of the truth; drawing upon examples from our research, we will demonstrate how our identities intersected and interacted with those of our participants to influence the research experience.

We present this chapter as a call to action for criminologists; firstly, to routinely acknowledge the impact of researcher identity on research and embed this within methodological narratives, and secondly, for academic institutions and structures to actively support researchers, with particular attention given to supporting women and researchers from other minoritised backgrounds who are disproportionately more likely to experience the issues discussed within this chapter.

Reflexivity and positionality in qualitative research

As noted by Ellis Devitt (2020) in her doctoral thesis, the importance of a reflexive approach is very much tied up with its own definition, i.e., that the researcher acknowledges and responds to their own presence within the research. Specifically, reflexivity encourages their continuous, dynamic, and subjective self-awareness in the research process alongside an acknowledgement of the impact a researcher can have on research findings and outcomes (Finlay, 2002). Gilgun (2008) extends this definition to also reflecting upon how the research is impacting the researcher. Reflexivity challenges the notion of knowledge production as independent, both of the researcher producing it, *and* of the objectivity of the knowledge itself (Husserl, 1970). Therefore, qualitative researchers should not simply report their findings, but question how those findings were constructed (Mortari, 2005: 2). This understanding is essential when conducting research that seeks to make sense of people's lived experiences. In examining our own worldview, we exercise caution in drawing conclusions about the lives of others. Indeed, without casting a reflective gaze, data can be easily decontextualised, manipulated, and distorted.

Berger (2013) talks of reflexivity in terms of turning the lens back on oneself, bringing one's own positionality into focus; the researcher takes responsibility for their own situatedness within the research. Reflexivity is a prerequisite for identifying one's positionality as it involves reflecting upon your own worldview, identity, values, and beliefs in order to understand the position you will adopt within your research (Holmes, 2020). Positionality places particular emphasis on the position of the researcher in relation to the position of the researched individual and/or group. As a starting point, researchers can assess whether they will be undertaking the research with insider or outsider status depending on the extent to which they share attributes and characteristics with the participant group. The answer is unlikely to be one or the other, but instead sits somewhere in-between the two extremes as the boundaries between insiders and outsiders become increasingly blurred (Merriam et al., 2001). Reflecting upon the researcher's positionality in relation to insider-outsider frameworks permits an understanding of the researcher's status in the research context as perceived by the participants. Collins and McNulty (2020) identify that the status the researcher ascribes to themselves and the status the participant assumes the researcher has can conflict with one another, posing challenges for building rapport.

Focusing specifically on gender, existing literature has demonstrated the ways in which the gender of the researcher and participant can influence positionality. More specifically, masculinity is both displayed and under threat when male participants are researched by female colleagues (Schwalbe and Wolkomir, 2001), a phenomenon documented by female researchers conducting research in masculine spaces (see Cox, 2020; Pini, 2005; Presser, 2005). Within each of the cited examples, male participants emphasised their heterosexuality, positioned themselves as powerful experts, and in turn sought to position the researcher as stereotypically feminine and lacking in power or expertise. For Presser (2005), this manifested through mild coercion and threats, for Cox (2020) experiencing unwanted sexual advances. Pini (2005) noted that traits typically aligned to hegemonic masculinity were most visible when her participants felt that their masculine identity was being challenged by questions regarding the absence of women in leadership positions given the threat this posed to their identity as 'powerful'.

These examples demonstrate the principles of positionality in practice, with the identity of the participant influencing how they positioned the researcher, subsequently impacting the research process. However, as Lavorgna and Sugiura (2022) note, explicit discussions of reflexivity and positionality seldom feature in methodological narratives despite their recognised importance, particularly for qualitative researchers exploring lived experiences. This was quantified by Gringeri at al. (2013) who found only 16% of articles in their sample of social work publications contained reflexive accounts. This closely mirrored an earlier study by Barusch et al. (2011) in which only 14% of surveyed researchers included reflexive accounts in publications. May and Perry (2011: 37) identify institutional barriers to reflexivity, stating that '... an absence of reflexivity in research practice can be symptomatic of an internal politics that takes organic belonging as unproblematic and any questioning of those relations as an act that automatically debunks supposedly self-evident truths'. This is evidenced through Probst (2015) whose research explored the reasons for an absence of reflexivity within social research. Despite researchers understanding the benefits of reflexivity, barriers to integrating it included the emotional labour that reflexivity required, and the perceived absence of support for research and publications based upon reflexivity given the value placed upon quantitative and objective research within academic institutions. This perception is unsurprising given reflexivity is rooted in feminist methodologies which, alongside female-led research, continue to be underrepresented in mainstream academic journals (Bendels et al., 2018; Hart, 2006; Weiss, 2016).

The term 'emotional labour' refers to the process of managing and regulating emotions as a condition of employment (Hochschild, 1983). Criminologists are already expected to perform high levels of emotional labour due to their engagement with vulnerable groups and sensitive topics within a discipline rooted in positivist, masculine, and outsider approaches to conducting research (Waters et al., 2020). This would suggest that as women conducting qualitative criminological research, the barriers to fully engaging with reflexivity and positionality as part of the research process are more prominent. Throughout the rest of this chapter, we intend to draw upon our own experiences of conducting social research in three different criminological fields in order to demonstrate why the routine integration of reflexivity and positionality must be supported and enabled by academic institutions. Firstly, each author will begin by providing an overview of the research projects they conducted in male spaces and places. The chapter will then go on to explore what the process of reflexivity taught us about our research findings.

Research summaries

Case study 1: policing

Policing can be categorised as a male-dominated space both in relation to the demographics of the police workforce and the reported culture of the organisation. As of March 2021, 67.6% of police officers in England and Wales identified as male; whilst this number has been steadily decreasing, the number of female officers being promoted has reduced and the number leaving policing has increased (Home Office, 2021). A culture of masculinity within policing has repeatedly been cited as one of the root causes of an absence of female representation or integration within all areas of policing. Categorised by the value placed upon heteronormativity, physical strength, crime-fighting, stoicism, and a 'them vs us' attitude, this culture is pervasively quoted as having a negative impact both within policing organisations and on police interactions with the public (Cockcroft, 2012; Heidensohn, 1992; Loftus, 2010). Whilst this is recognised as being an overly simplistic assessment of police culture (see Silvestri, 2017), there remains an overwhelming body of literature which identifies policing as being an environment which fosters a culture of hegemonic masculinity (Connell and Messerschmidt, 2005) which is unwelcoming of typically feminine values and traits.

As a 21-year-old student, the R1 (Author – Smith Cox) undertook a year-long piece of qualitative research with one police service in England as part of a formal programme of study. This included observing police officers working in frontline and managerial roles and conducting interviews with ethnic minority police officers regarding opportunities for lateral development into specialist policing units. Five years later, R1 returned to the same organisation to undertake an ethnographic study of diversity and inclusion in frontline uniformed policing. The discussions contained within this chapter are centred on the findings of observations which were conducted as part of the ethnography, namely the observation of uniformed police constables working in neighbourhood or response policing roles. Neighbourhood officers work to address community issues and provide a policing presence within a particular community, whilst response officers respond to calls for assistance made to the police by the public and engage in proactive patrols of their policing area. These are the roles occupied by the vast majority of police constables when they enter the organisation, with officers typically required to apply to move to a different role, such as traffic or investigations. Therefore, the officers who were observed within the latter piece of research represented a cross-section of gender, age, ethnicity, and policing experience relative to the demographics of the organisation at the time. However, it is worth noting that the officers who volunteered themselves to 'host' R1 for the duration of the shift within both pieces of research were predominantly male.

Navigating research involving predominantly male participants working within a culture often defined by its masculinity was challenging as a female researcher and required continuous reflexivity. Furthermore, R1 transitioned from being a full-time student to a full-time academic in between the two pieces of research taking place. This shifted the researcher/participant power dynamics considerably and resulted in significant differences in how participants perceived and interacted with R1, requiring adaptations to the approach taken to building rapport in order to generate meaningful data.

Case study 2: incels

Male misogynist incels (involuntary celibates) have been the subject of increased public scrutiny given their links with several high-profile mass murders, predominantly in Canada, the US and more recently the UK (Baele et al., 2019; Collins, 2019; Scaptura and Boyle, 2019; Tomkinson et al., 2020). Although the etymology of incel was originally gender-inclusive (see Alanna Boltwood, 1993) representing a source of support for lonely individuals unlucky in love, the term has since been appropriated by mainly cis, heterosexual men aggrieved at being unable to find sexual and romantic female partners that they desire. Today, incel has come to represent a community crystallised in misogyny and fatalistic ideologies, populating online spaces notoriously hostile to women and those who support gender equality.

R2 (Author – Sugiura) spent three years immersed in those platforms and others part of the broader so-called 'manosphere', absorbing incel culture as part of her ethnographic study into the formation of the incel community (Sugiura, 2021). Many sites are easily accessible as they do not require membership to observe activity and discussions, and as such direct interaction with other users is unnecessary. The very nature of the content, largely involving the denigration of women, however, emphasises that these are meant to be 'men-only' locations. The male claim to incel and manosphere spaces is the actualisation of an early post on 4Chan, an anonymous online forum, which stated that 'there were no girls on internet' (Penny, 2013), where women are unwelcome and reminded of their second-class citizenship, or indeed where some incels are concerned, even subhuman.

Alongside the online observations, R2 also undertook semi-structured interviews with former and current self-identified incels to understand their journey to inceldom (and beyond for those claiming to have 'ascended' the community). Some participants were purposely selected from their contributions on incel Reddit forums and contacted via the private messaging function on Reddit to gauge their interest in taking part in the study. Other participants had contacted R2 of their own volition, wanting to talk to her about their experiences after seeing her quoted in a national newspaper speaking about incels, and then consented to take part in a formal research study. The interviews were all conducted online via the private messaging function on Reddit or email. Despite providing the option to use virtual conferencing or the telephone, textual-based interaction was favoured by participants. Not only was it deemed unfeasible to offer offline in-person interviews, as participants could be based anywhere in the world due to the global nature of the internet, but the security and safety of R2 would also have been put at risk. Nevertheless, it was still recognised that this was a precarious research terrain to navigate, requiring R2 to employ various reflexive strategies and precautions throughout the process.

Case study 3: young adult men with prison experience

Few would challenge the position that the Criminal Justice System (CJS) comprises a predominantly male experience. Men account for over 95% of all people in prison (MoJ, 2022a) and over 90% of all people subject to Probation Orders (MoJ, 2022b). However, it is not simply the statistical dominance of males in the CJS that is of significance here, as has been previously attested to, it is about what cultural implications this dominance of numbers has – in particular, the way this can (and does) enable, promote, and legitimise, sometimes extreme, performances of masculinity within prison culture. Indeed, as Sabo et al. (2001: 5) observe, prison is a key institution for the 'expression and reproduction of hegemonic masculinity', i.e., masculinity which privileges toughness, dominance, heterosexuality, physical aggression, and emotional fortitude (Crewe et al., 2014; De Viggiani, 2012; Jewkes, 2002, 2005; Sabo et al., 2001).

As part of her doctoral thesis, R3 (Author – Ellis Devitt, 2020), conducted narrative interviews with ten young adult men, aged 19–24, all of whom were in the CJS, with most (N=9) having left prison within the nine months prior to interview. The interviews took place in person and were conducted within the grounds of the relevant (criminal justice affiliated) service that each participant was recruited from. At the time of interview, the young men all had been involved with the CJS for either half or most of their lives. As with the previous entries, this last case study considers the impact of gender (and to a lesser extent, age) on the research relationship, but here with a particular consideration of the additional impact of the participants' long histories with a (predominantly male) CJS, and with most coming from an environment where 'maleness' was the norm and the performance of masculinity the expectation.

Examples from the field

The research summaries presented above have provided an overview of the research the authors have conducted with male participants in spaces and places which are characterised by their inherent masculinity, namely policing, 'incels' and young adult men with prison experience. The process of reflexivity to establish positionality reflects the opinion of the authors that qualitative researchers cannot be impartial conduits of the truth as outlined in the introduction to this chapter. We maintain that rather than seeking to remove any influence the researcher may have on the research process and findings, we must instead be aware of it, reflect upon it, and acknowledge it continuously throughout data collection and analysis, as well as when engaging with research conducted by others. Within this section, we intend to illustrate what our ongoing process of reflexivity taught us about our research process and findings. More specifically, we will illustrate how the misalignment between where we situated ourselves and how our participants perceived us presented challenges to building rapport, thus requiring a dynamic approach to reflexivity and positionality. Particular emphasis will be placed on mixed aspects of our positionality, namely gender, age, ethnicity, and social class.

R3 (young adult males with prison experience) experienced gendered encounters which centred around the research participants' perceptions of researcher identity. Like Presser (2005), R3 also felt positioned in certain ways – often into familial or therapeutic personas, as the young men sought to renegotiate R3 into roles that eschewed her arguably more threatening 'researcher' or 'authoritative other' identities. R1 (policing) also felt positioned, seemingly for the same purpose of counteracting the perception of researcher as an authoritative other. This was perhaps to be expected given the inherent power and authority handed to those occupying policing roles and the fact that the research was taking place in the field (i.e., whilst participants were on-duty and in uniform), thus creating a desire to maintain the perception of being in charge and in control synonymous with policing and police culture. In both research cases, stereotypically heteronormative behaviours, such as 'banter' and flirtation, were experienced by the researchers. In some instances, the researchers' bodies became 'up for discussion' as the male participants sought to change up power differentials through turning the research lens back on to the researcher in ways that highlighted their physicality, personality, and individual characteristics, thus seeking to reinforce the participant as the holder of power during these interactions.

In R2's (incels) experience, however, any amorous advances were notably absent, and given the very essence of incels – the belief that they are repugnant to women – this was perhaps unsurprising. In addition, the mode of interviewing, in being purely textual with no face-to face element, also removed opportunities for participants to engage in commentary about physical attributes (which are ordinarily of great concern to incels). Nevertheless, R2 also encountered behaviours that suggested participants' efforts to challenge her perceived status as the authoritative other. These involved the questioning of her worldview, knowledge, and scientific understanding in a bid to assert their (male) superior intellect and dominance over the situation. Here, R2 did conform to a gender stereotype in feigning a lack of awareness of topics presented to her to appease participants and enable them to feel in control. On the surface, this 'playing stupid' appears to be anti-feminist, yet it is habitual activity for women coping with gendered microaggressions (Nadal et al., 2013). This demonstrates how the conflict between our actual and perceived identities resulted in performative behaviours; whilst the process of conducting research is often compared to that of a performance, as will be discussed later in this chapter, this process of surface acting in order to manage power imbalances is exhausting and emotionally draining for researchers, ourselves included (Thwaites, 2017).

Furthermore, and reflecting Pini's (2005) observations, R3 (young adult males with prison experience) noted the abundance of demonstrably male, prison-centred narratives centring hegemonic masculinities, e.g., the hardships of being 'inside', histories of fighting and violence, and disciplined physical training. This was also reflected by the police officers participating in R1's research, who would often recount stories of what they described as 'proper policing' which embodied masculine traits such as high-speed pursuits and 'going hands on' with a suspect. Gender, age, and our obvious differences in backgrounds were highlighted through stories structured in ways which seemingly aimed to inform, and even educate, the researchers about matters we must clearly not understand or be aware of. Whilst neither R1 or R3 have personal lived experience of the environments which the participants were recounting, any knowledge of prison or policing environments obtained through other means was often overlooked by participants, thus reinforcing the outsider status of the researchers. Outsider status has historically been valued for the objectivity it brings to the research process, however it can leave participants unconvinced of the researcher's ability to fully understand and appreciate their experiences, thus limiting the trust and openness shared between the researcher and participant group (Dwyer and Buckle, 2009). This reinforced the participants as the holders of power during the interview process; as researchers, we demonstrated a willingness to learn from our participants in order to build the trust and emotional safety that was limited due to our outsider status (Mayorga-Gallo and Hordge-Freeman, 2017).

In response to assumptions about our identities, we played out our own gender, age, and background stereotypes where it was advantageous to do so. R3 assumed maternal/sisterly roles, encouraging storytelling from the young adult men who were detailing their prison experiences, and 'rewarding' them for their enthusiasm and candour with smiles, encouragement, and enthusiastic body language. R1 also emphasised their femininity when interacting with male police officers, providing an empathetic listening ear when stories of poor mental health, strained home life, and declining working conditions were shared. This often went hand in hand with the presentation of the researcher as a young and therefore naïve student who was there to listen and learn, not control or manage the policing environment in which they were an observer. Despite being familiar with the well-documented challenges facing policing in England and Wales, the positioning of the researcher as lacking knowledge of the environment they researched meant that genuine responses of shock, disappointment, and awe about their lived experiences were well received. In both cases, we quickly picked up on the participants' positive reactions to our empathetic tones and worked more into our interactions so as to encourage similar and further storytelling.

R2 also found herself providing empathetic responses to the stories of what led her participants to inceldom, realising that this was necessary to ensure the continuation of dialogue – particularly when provocations were presented such as 'what do you make of that?' – as a means of self-preservation, and even due to the response being warranted in some situations. Yet simultaneously, R2 remained cognisant of avoiding validating the blame levied at women, attempts to claim victimhood, and moreover what Kate Manne (2017) terms 'himpathy' – where men's feelings are centred regardless of them perpetrating violence or harm. Providing a platform to people engaging in discriminatory and hateful behaviour risks affirming such harmful rhetoric and amplifying the very narratives they are trying to promote. Although the inclusion of the voices of incels in research is essential to fully appreciate how the culture and formation of the community operate, this does not mean rebranding misogynist incels as lonely, misunderstood men and downplaying the very real violence and dehumanisation experienced by women as a result of incel ideology.

Promoting gender identity over other parts of our identities, namely our 'researcher' identities, also worked as a neutralising and protective strategy. For R3, some of the young men with prison experience were more challenging to interview. Gailey and Prohaska (2011: 367), in their research into power and gender negotiations during interviews with men (as women), reported relinquishing control during their interviews to ensure the men would talk with them. Such techniques were exhibited in our style of interviewing, demonstrated by our use of humour, self-deprecation, and the frequent returning to 'safe' topics. Echoing similar strategies identified by R2 earlier in this chapter, R3 often played up a lack of knowledge in certain areas to encourage the participants to fill in the gaps, e.g., in not understanding certain illicit drug terminologies or showing a lack of awareness of how a prisons ran. In some cases, we promoted our identity as 'girl' or 'woman' rather than 'researcher', suspecting that these participants responded more favourably to the former.

Each of the experiences detailed so far within this section centre around the supposed importance of building rapport with research participants – an almost certain feature of research method guides and textbooks which view rapport as a prerequisite to useful data and findings. Rapport is seen as a fine line the researcher must carefully but accurately tread – failure to develop rapport will mean limited engagement and openness from participants, but too much rapport and you risk having an unwanted impact on the research process and findings (Cargan, 2007). The pressure to achieve the perfect level of rapport to avoid the discrediting of your research findings can feel overwhelming and unachievable for researchers, inducing feelings of guilt where the 'ideal interview' standard has not been met and the deployed methods are at odds with a feminist approach or identity (Dunscombe and Jessop, 2002). Trying to build rapport whilst controlling the extent to which relationships are formed is yet another example of the emotional labour experienced by qualitative researchers in that it requires you to be emotionally intelligent, set boundaries, and carefully manage the formation of relationships, often with people with whom you have no shared values or characteristics. Here, we must question whether the focus on rapport as an essential component of qualitative research is intrinsically harmful to researchers, for example, why must R2 be expected to build rapport with participants whose identity is centred around hostility towards women, and why must each of us be expected to endure gendered microaggressions in the name of securing rapport and eliciting useful data?

This discussion has highlighted the gap that can exist between a researcher's actual and assumed identity, and how this is informed by the interactions we have with our participants. As has been demonstrated through the given examples, our gender identity and how this was perceived by our male participants in stereotypically masculine environments was a significant contributory factor when adopting a researcher identity which would enable us to build rapport with participants in order to elicit useful data whilst ensuring researcher safety. Doing so required careful consideration, ongoing reflexivity, and at times had a notable impact on our wellbeing due to the emotionally demanding nature of performative research. It is for this reason that we seek to challenge the importance of rapport and query whether the seemingly unquestioned importance of it highlights a disregard for the wellbeing of qualitative researchers. The consequences of pursuing rapport with our participants by adopting a researcher identity which is underpinned by gendered assumptions and power imbalances will now be further explored.

The impact of 'performing' social research

Parallels have been drawn between conducting social research and theatrical performances, particularly where the research is conducted face to face. Rather than simply undertaking the research, qualitative social research requires rehearsal, carefully choreographed interactions, is vulnerable to errors and mistakes, and results in a new reality formed by the interactions between the researcher and participants (Denzin, 1970; Hermanns, 2004). The researcher may also be juggling several different roles within the research performance depending on the participant, the research environment, and the research plan, thus exposing more opportunities for error (Mason-Bish, 2018). Engaging in this performance requires seemingly unwavering confidence and is demanding on both the researcher's time and energy yet is regarded as an essential component of qualitative social research.

Within the previous section of this chapter, the authors outlined the ways in which our gender identity – often intersecting with age and social status – resulted in the assumption of a researcher identity which emphasised, altered, or minimised parts of our actual identity in order to build rapport with participants, elicit useful data, and ensure researcher safety. Most commonly this manifested through an emphasis on or dismissal of femininity. However, much like a theatrical performance, this can be exhausting for the researcher, particularly when the adopted identity requires the display of behaviours which conflict with the morals, ethics, and reality of the researcher's actual identity. Herein lies a conflict; does one prioritise research quality even if that means losing a sense of self as a result of the required research performance?

For R2, disregarding her gender identity when researching incels was employed as a safeguarding measure to avoid potential external conflict, but caused internal tensions. In these interviews the researcher's identity as a woman was often neglected or at least not directly acknowledged by participants, which is at odds with the obsession with women generally propagated by the community, and this led to some uncomfortable interactions. As the 'researcher', R2 was subjected to derogatory comments about women, but had to remain detached and was unable to respond as a woman. Interview questions had been designed to elicit views and given the reputation of the incel community, negativity towards women was expected. However, R2 was placed in a position whereby the 'researcher' identity was required to supersede that of her being a woman, ignoring the fact that in othering women and not addressing the blatant tension in the situation, that such insults also applied to her. Naturally, this might have been a deliberate tactic by participants to cause R2 discomfort and put a woman in her place without calling specific attention to her gender. Chakraborti and Garland (2015) posit that hate crimes are not limited to suppressing individuals, rather they are about controlling the community to which the individual belongs. Hatred espoused against women inevitably means that any woman can be affected, including those researching such issues, as it is factitious to presume aspects of ourselves can be divorced from our researcher identity.

In addition to tensions regarding gender identity, R2 also had intersecting complexities to manage regarding her ethnicity as a white-Asian woman when researching incels. Asian women are routinely fetishised and stereotyped as subservient and docile, often presented in the media as contrasting tropes of the 'delicate virginal lotus' and the 'sexual femme fatale dragon lady' (Uchida, 1998). Within incel parlance, Asian women are referred to as 'noodlewhores', and within the interviews this term arose along with other comments both praising and denigrating the contradictory assumed submissiveness and eroticism of Asian women. Despite these discussions not being directly aimed at her personally and benefitting from privilege arising from hegemonic assumptions relating to her being 'white-presenting', the exposure to beliefs both misogynist and racist in nature did impact upon R2, requiring her to reconsider her own position and again perform the role of impervious researcher.

Experiences such as those outlined throughout this chapter can result in researchers using 'sign vehicles' – for example, our appearance and our choice of language – in a bid to manipulate how we are perceived in similar situations in the future (Goffman, 1956). For example, due to the face-to-face nature of the research, R1 would give careful consideration to how to dress when joining a police officer for an observation shift. These decisions would be somewhat based on practicality, but predominantly centre around how the choice of clothing may help to minimise perceived femininity, thus limiting opportunities for discussion regarding her physicality, or maximise perceived femininity in order to reinforce the view of researcher as naïve and subordinate. The language used by R1 would also be routinely self-policed with a conscious effort made to use language which was not overly complicated or academic in nature to avoid perceptions of class imbalances being highlighted by participants.

We present these examples to provide only a snapshot of the impact performing social research can have on researchers whereby one's sense of morals, ethics, and identity conflicts with the research process. Our own wellbeing often came second to the perceived need to elicit useful data through the carefully controlled and emotionally laborious process of building rapport. In the final section of this chapter, we conclude by presenting two recommendations for both individuals and criminological institutions based upon these experiences.

Recommendations and conclusion

Throughout this chapter we have presented a number of tales from the field in order to demonstrate the impact our identities had on both our research and our participants as female researchers conducting research in male spaces and places. Being women played a pivotal role in our respective research experiences and findings, especially where being women intersected with age, ethnicity, and social class. We also observed a gap between our actual and perceived identities, often having to downplay or emphasise particular assumptions about who we are in order to assist us in building rapport with our participants, eliciting useful data, and ensuring our own safety.

We conclude this chapter by presenting two key recommendations; firstly, for individuals to routinely acknowledge the impact of researcher identity on research and embed this within methodological narratives; and secondly, for academic institutions and structures to actively support researchers, with particular attention given to supporting women and researchers from other minoritised backgrounds. We will now discuss each of these recommendations in turn.

Whilst the requirement for the researcher to be credible when publishing findings is widely recognised within the research community, we argue that the need to be regarded as credible by participants in order to seek 'the truth', thus resulting in credible findings, is potentially harmful to researchers. This is further amplified when considering that discussions of emotion have typically been excluded from methodological narratives due to fears of losing legitimacy and credibility (Blackman, 2007). Seeking 'the truth' and positioning oneself accordingly would require knowledge of the environment in which the participant operates and a fixed positionality within that environment, which in turn would limit social research to insider research only. Instead, we advocate for a move away from seeking to obtain 'the truth' and instead allowing research to generate knowledge of the environment in which the participants and researchers position themselves. Through the routine integration of reflexivity into methodological processes and narratives, we can give greater attention to the stories being told in a range of different research contexts, extracting value from findings which may conflict with one another based on the researcher's identity.

Throughout this chapter, we have sought to illustrate how the process of conducting research can have a very real and emotive impact on our sense of self, our presentation of self, and our wellbeing. This may not be routinely understood by those not engaged in research of this nature. Whilst Hochschild (1983) identifies the ability to manage and suppress emotions as a positive and useful skill in certain contexts, and Bergman Blix and Wettergren (2014) highlight the management of emotions as an essential skill in social research, we suggest that this is not always achievable when the research performance challenges your identity. Whilst existing literature has recognised the emotional impact of researching inherently sensitive topics, less attention has been paid to the emotional impact of setting and maintaining emotional boundaries which can result in the physical and emotional symptoms of stress manifesting (Rager, 2005). This highlights the significant impact on researchers where individuals and institutions fail to acknowledge and respond to the emotional impact of conducting social research, particularly for women and researchers from other minoritised groups. We highlight the disproportionate impact on minoritised groups due to the emotional impact of also being required to suppress their identity in everyday life, not just in a research context (Cohen and Garcia, 2005).

Whilst individuals can seek to understand and mitigate against these impacts through a continuous process of reflexivity, we also call upon research institutions to recognise this as an ethical issue which the institution must assume responsibility for. Whilst ethical guidelines are typically underpinned by an assumption of participants as a vulnerable population who require protection from harm, there is comparatively limited consideration given to the multiple ways in which researchers can be subject to harm. Failure to embed issues relating to positionality, reflexivity, and identity within ethical review processes, training, and guidelines can be interpreted as institutional failures to understand or recognise the emotional impact of performing social research. This leaves researchers at risk of only learning of these issues in the field or at the point of engaging with reflexivity. Knowledge may be shared by more experienced researchers but given the suppression of emotion within research narratives, as discussed elsewhere within this chapter, and the individualised nature of the impact of performing social research, this may not be sufficient. Additionally, external sources of information regarding specific ethical issues relevant to the researcher's chosen field or methodology are unlikely to align to the researcher's institutional ethical review practices, thus placing a greater burden on the individual to mitigate against the risk of harm to themselves and actively seek the support they require to continue with their research (Kingdon and Mattheis, 2021). We therefore reiterate that the emphasis should be placed upon research institutions to provide the support, information, and structures required to ensure researchers are prepared to navigate social research and the harm it can pose to our sense of self, our presentation of self, and our wellbeing.

Indeed, parallels might be easily drawn with Becker (1967) in 'Whose Side Are We On?' where the conflict faced by social researchers as they come to identify with their research participants is examined in terms of its influence on the research outcomes and the question of whether social research can ever be *truly* impartial is posed. Yet 60 years on, and despite the long-standing attention these issues have received within academic publications, criminology has yet to fully grasp the complexities of social research. This leaves researchers at risk of harm and may directly impact the quantity and quality of social research being conducted, particularly if women and researchers from other minoritised groups feel unsafe, isolated, and unsupported in undertaking it. We therefore reiterate that this is a call to action for academics, research publications, academic institutions, and ethics committees to protect both social researchers and the discipline of criminology through the teaching and embedding of reflexivity into every stage of the research process.

References

Baele, S. J., Brace, L., and Coan, T. G. (2019). From "incel" to "saint": analyzing the violent worldview behind the 2018 Toronto attack. *Terrorism and Political Violence*, 33(8), 1667–1691.

Barr, S. M., Budge, S. L., and Adelson, J. L. (2016). Transgender community belongingness as a mediator between strength of transgender identity and well-being. *Journal of Counselling Psychology*, 63(1), 87.

Barusch, A., Gringeri, C., and George, M. (2011). Rigor in qualitative social work research: a review of strategies used in published articles. *Social Work Research*, 35, 11–19.

Becker, H. S. (1967). Whose side are we on? *Social Problems*, 14(3), 239–247.

Bendels, M. H. K., Wanke, E. M., Benik, S., Schehadat, M. S., Schöffel, N., Bauer, J., Gerber, A., Brüggmann, D., Oremek, G. M., and Groneberg, D. A. (2018). Der Gendergap in der medizinischen Spitzenforschung [The gender gap in highest quality medical research – A scientometric analysis of the representation of female authors in highest impact medical journals]. *Dtsch Med Wochenschr*, 143(10), e85–e94.

Berger, R. (2015). Now I see it, now I don't: researcher's position and reflexivity in qualitative research. *Qualitative Research*, 15(2), 219–234.

Bergman Blix, S. and Wettergren, Å. (2014). The emotional labour of gaining and maintaining access to the field. *Qualitative Research*, 15(6), 688–704.

Blackman, S. J. (2007). 'Hidden ethnography': crossing emotional borders in qualitative accounts of young people's lives. *Sociology*, 41(4), 699–716.

Cargan, L. (2007). *Doing Social Research*. Lanham: Rowman & Littlefield Publishers.

Chakraborti, N. and Garland, J. (eds.) (2015). *Responding to Hate Crime: The Case for Connecting Policy and Research*. Policy Press.

Cockcroft, T. (2012). *Police Culture: Themes and Concepts*, 1st ed. Routledge.

Cohen, G. L. and Garcia, J. (2005). "I am us": negative stereotypes as collective threats. *Journal of Personality and Social Psychology*, 89(4), 566–582.

Collins, H. and McNulty, Y. (2020). Insider status: (re)framing researcher positionality in international human resource management studies. *German Journal of Human Resource Management*, 34 (2), 202–227.

Collins, P. (2019). Incel: How an online subculture has led to violence against women. *Blue Line*.

Connell, R. W. and Messerschmidt, J. W. (2005). Hegemonic masculinity: Rethinking the concept. *Gender & Society*, 19(6), 829–859.

Cox, C. E. (2020). 'Are you crewed up with that bird from the uni?' The complexities of conducting ethnographic research in policing. *Journal of Organizational Ethnography*, 9(3), 365–377.

Crewe, B., Warr, J., Bennett P., and Smith, A. (2014). The emotional geography of prison life. *Theoretical Criminology* 18(1), 55–74.

Denzin, N. K. (1970). *The Research Act in Sociology*. Aldine.

De Viggiani, N. (2012). Trying to be something you are not: masculine performances within a prison setting. *Men and Masculinities* 15(3), 1–21.

Dunscombe, J. and Jessop, J. (2002). Doing rapport, and the ethics of 'faking friendship', in: T. Miller, M. Birch, M. Mauthner, and J. Jessop *(eds.), Ethics in Qualitative Research*. Sage, 108–121.

Dwyer, S. C. and Buckle, J. L. (2009). The space between: on being an insider-outsider in qualitative research. *International Journal of Qualitative Methods*, 8(1), 54–63.

Edwards, R. (1998). Flexibility, reflexivity and reflection in the contemporary workplace. *International Journal of Lifelong Education*, 17(6), 377–388.

Edwards, R. and Nicoll, K. (2006). Expertise, competence and reflection in the rhetoric of professional development. *British Educational Research Journal*, 32(1).

Ellis Devitt, K. (2020). The life-stories of young adult men in the criminal justice system: A critical narrative analysis. Doctoral thesis, University of Portsmouth. https://pure.port.ac.uk/ws/portalfiles/portal/20474707/Kerry_Ellis_Devitt_Thesis_March_2020.pdf.

Finlay, L. (2002). Negotiating the swamp: the opportunity and challenge of reflexivity in research practice. *Qualitative Research*, 2(2), 209–230.

Gailey, J. and Prohaska, A. (2011). Power and gender negotiations during interviews with men about sex and sexually degrading practices. *Qualitative Research*, 11, 365–380.

Gilgun J. F. (2008). Lived experience, reflexivity, and research on perpetrators of interpersonal violence, *Qualitative Social Work*, 7(2), 181–197.

Goffman, E. (1956). *The Presentation of Self in Everyday Life*. Edinburgh: University of Edinburgh Social Sciences Research Centre.

Gringeri C., Barusch A., and Cambron C. (2013). Epistemology in qualitative social work research: a review of published articles, 2008–2010. *Social Work Research*, 37, 55–63.

Hart, J. (2006). Women and feminism in higher education scholarship: an analysis of three core journals. *The Journal of Higher Education*, 77(1), 40–61.

Heidensohn, F. (1992). *Women in Control: The Role of Women in Law Enforcement*. Oxford University Press.

Hermanns, H. (2004) Interviewing as an activity, in: U. Flick, E. Von Kardoff, and I. Steinke (eds.), *The Museum in Transition: A Philosophical Perspective*. Sage, 209–213.

Hochschild, A-R. (1983). *The Managed Heart – Commercialization of Human Feeling*. University of California Press.

Holmes, A. G. D. (2020). Researcher positionality – a consideration of its influence and place in qualitative research – a new researcher guide. *International Journal of Education*, 8(4), 1–10.

Home Office (2021). Police workforce, England and Wales. https://www.gov.uk/government/statistics/police-workforce-england-and-wales-31-march-2021/police-workforce-england-and-wales-31-march-2021#headline-workforce-figures.

Husserl, E. (1970). *The Idea of Phenemenology*. The Hague, The Netherlands: Nijhoff.

Jewkes, Y. (2002). *Captive Audience: Media, Masculinity and Power in Prisons*. Willan.

Jewkes, Y. (2005). Men behind bars: 'doing' masculinity as an adaptation to imprisonment. *Men and Masculinities*, 8(1), 44–63.

Kingdon, A. and Mattheis, A. (2021). Does the institution have a plan for that? Researcher safety and the ethics of institutional responsibility, in: A. Lavorgna and T. J. Holt (eds.), *Researching Cybercrimes: Methodologies, Ethics, and Critical Approaches*. London: Palgrave Macmillan, 457–473.

Lavorgna, A. and Sugiura, L. (2022). Blurring boundaries: negotiating researchers' positionality and identities in digital qualitative research. *Italian Sociological Review*, 12, 709–727.

Lips, H. M. (2020). *Sex and Gender: An Introduction*. Waveland Press.

Loftus, B. (2010). Police occupational culture: classic themes, altered times. *Policing & Society*, 20(1), 1–20.

Manne, K. (2017). *Down Girl: The Logic of Misogyny*. Oxford University Press.

Mason-Bish, H. (2018). The elite delusion: reflexivity, identity and positionality in qualitative research. *Qualitative Research*, 19(3), 263–276.

May, T. and Perry, B. (2011). *Social Research and Reflexivity: Content, Consequences and Context*. Sage.

Mayorga-Gallo, S. and Hordge-Freeman, E. (2017). Between marginality and privilege: gaining access and navigating the field in multiethnic settings. *Qualitative Research*, 17(4), 377–394.

Merriam, S. B., Johnson-Bailey, J., Lee, M-Y, Kee, Y., Ntseane, G., and Muhamad, M. (2001). Power and positionality: negotiating insider/outsider status within and across cultures. *International Journal of Lifelong Education*, 20(5), 405–416.

Ministry of Justice (MoJ) (2021). HM Prison and Probation Service annual staff equalities report: 2020 to 2021.

Ministry of Justice (MoJ) (2022a). Diversity of the judiciary: Legal professions, new appointments and current post-holders – 2022 Statistics.

Ministry of Justice (MoJ) (2022b). Probation data – Justice data.

Ministry of Justice (MoJ) (2022c). Prison population figures: 2022.

Mortari, L. (2005). Narrative inquiry e fenomenologia. *Encyclopaideia*, 9(17), 11–22.

Nadal, K. L., Hamit, S., Lyons, O., Weinberg, A., and Corman, L. (2013). Gender microaggressions: perceptions, processes, and coping mechanisms of women. *Psychology for Business Success*, 1, 193–220.

Penny, L. (2013). *Cybersexism: Sex, Gender and Power on the Internet*. A&C Black.

Pini, B. (2005). Interviewing men: Gender and the collection and interpretation of qualitative data. *Journal of Sociology*, 41(2), 201–216.

Presser, L. (2005). Negotiating power and narrative in research: implications for feminist methodology, *Signs*, 30(4), 2067–2090.

Probst, B. (2015). The eye regards itself: benefits and challenges of reflexivity in qualitative social work research. *Social Work Research*, 39(1), 37–48.

Rager, K. B. (2005). Compassion stress and the qualitative researcher. *Qualitative Health Research*, 15(3), 423–430.

Riach, K. (2009). Exploring participant-centred reflexivity in the research interview. *Sociology*, 43(2), 356–370.

Roulston, K. (2010). *Reflective Interviewing: A Guide to Theory and Practice.* Sage.

Sabo, D., Kupers, T. A., and James, W. (2001). *Prison Masculinities.* Temple University Press.

Scaptura, M. N. and Boyle, K. M. (2019). Masculinity threat, "incel" traits, and violent fantasies among heterosexual men in the United States. *Feminist Criminology*, 1(21), 278–298.

Schwalbe, M. and Wolkomir, M. (2001). The masculine self as problem and resource in interview studies of men. *Men and Masculinities*, 4(1), 90–103.

Silvestri, M. (2017). Police culture and gender: revisiting the 'cult of masculinity', *Policing: A Journal of Policy and Practice*, 11(3), 289–300.

Sugiura, L. (2021). *The Incel Rebellion: The Rise of the Manosphere and the Virtual War Against Women.* Emerald Publishing.

Thwaites, R. (2017). (Re)examining the feminist interview: rapport, gender 'matching', and emotional labour. *Gender, Sex and Sexualities*, 2.

Tomkinson, S., Harper, T., and Attwell, K. (2020). Confronting incel: exploring possible policy responses to misogynistic violent extremism. *Australian Journal of Political Science*, 55(2), 152–169.

Uchida, A. (1998). The orientalization of Asian women in America. *Women's Studies International Forum*, 21(2), 161–174.

Unger, R. K. (1979). Toward a redefinition of sex and gender. *American Psychologist*, 34(11), 1085.

Valcore, J., Fradella, H. F., Guadalupe-Diaz, X., Ball, M. J., Dwyer, A., DeJong, C., and Worthen, M. G. (2021). Building an intersectional and trans-inclusive criminology: responding to the emergence of 'gender critical' perspectives in feminist criminology. *Critical Criminology*, 29(4), 687–706.

Waters, J., Westaby, C., Fowler, A., and Phillips, J. (2020). The emotional labour of doctoral criminological researchers. *Methodological Innovations*, 13(2).

Weiss, E. (2016). Female underrepresentation in psychology journals. Feminist Studies Association. https://the-fsa.co.uk/2016/07/08/female-underrepresentation-in-psychology-journals/.

10

WHO IS 'THE PUBLIC' WHEN WE TALK ABOUT CRIME?

Interpreting and Framing Public Voices in Criminology

Anna Matczak

Introduction

Ever since the completion of my PhD, which put the perspectives and attitudes of Polish lay people towards the criminal justice system at the forefront, I have been a watchful observer of how the role and value of public voices are discussed in criminology and criminal justice by my fellow colleagues in the United Kingdom, Poland and the Netherlands. Depending on the researcher's vantage point and inclination, it appears that the voice and role of the public in criminology and criminal justice tends to be narrated either as a 'malevolent public', which speaks for an unspecified entity of people who are most of the time misinformed, punitive and in need of expeditious education, or a 'benevolent public', representing a more inclusive, but also romanticised, vision of citizens in the public sphere.

Given the volumes of attitudinal research (see Roberts and Stalans, 1997; Roberts and Hough, 2005; Donsbach and Traugott 2008), it is remarkable that the concept of the public has been used most of the time in criminology, and elsewhere too, as a self-explanatory and homogeneous entity, with very limited attempts to clarify who is actually meant by this term. It is not only this lack of specification of who constitutes the public, but also the representations – or, in other words, the narratives – of the public's views that appear to be ambiguous and require continuous discussion. This chapter signals the need for criminologists to reflect on and question their standpoints on the public, which are affected by their research orientations, research method training and choices, geographical origins, and/or their abilities to reflect on the topic.

In order to challenge the universal oversimplification of the meaning of 'the public', this chapter draws its inspiration from the perspective on crime and punishment discussed by Althoff et al. (2020) as social constructs with competing

DOI: 10.4324/9781003260967-13

narratives. According to the authors, narratives are irrevocably linked to the production of meanings and the power relations expressed in this specific production. It will be argued in this chapter that narratives about public voices, just like the ones about crime and punishment, change according to the context in which they are told. Stories are therefore not told by chance; rather, their contents are determined by social norms and conventions, and this also applies to how and why stories are told (Althoff et al., 2020: 6).

Just as crime and punishment attract different narratives, the value and role of the public in criminology and criminal justice have been constructed and reconstructed over the decades, experiencing a number of discursive shifts across different subdisciplines in criminology. If one considers 'the public sphere as involving a field of discursive connections' (Calhoun, 1992: 37), the inconclusive phenomenon of 'the public' has attracted numerous narratives, including linguistic and cultural communicative patterns established and negotiated in social institutions and processes, to which there is a tendency to ascribe a value. It is unsurprising that this narrated voice of the public, enmeshed within power relations, is often followed by a certain course of action, policy, and the attribution of responsibilities.

The perspective presented in this chapter is bound by my positionality as a Polish female criminologist currently residing in the Netherlands. Although I originally come from rural Poland, most of my adult life I have lived in urban metropolitan areas (Warsaw, London, The Hague), with 15 years of living abroad in two culturally and linguistically different countries. My academic worldview has been continuously shaped through the lens of my gender, education, institutional affiliation, background and/or position as a migrant. This unique combination of traits, life circumstances and various 'statuses' in society has given me plenty of opportunities either to witness or to experience firsthand how public life is governed by dominant voices and how the concept of 'otherness' contributes to the marginalisation of certain groups in the public sphere. Therefore, the choice of my PhD subject matter was motivated by the desire to give a direct voice to lay people, whose voices are most of the time narrated in the public domain with a varying degree of lingering misconceptions.

Who is 'the public'?

To begin with, the term 'public' can be understood as a realm blending active, engaged and passive citizens, who act more as spectators in the public domain (Price, 2008). However, this perspective appears to be too simplistic, especially when we consider that we have always been part of social networks, and that over the past two decades these have been increasingly revolutionised due to the use of information and communication technologies (Castells and Cardoso, 2005). Therefore, if anything, 'the public' is most likely woven from multiple publics (Fraser, 1990) or networks which have different origins and characteristic features, and which function with varying degrees of longevity and access to the public sphere, and varying levels of civic participation. Carrigan and Fatsis (2021) propose reimagining the concept of the public as an ecosystem composed of a sense of self (identity) and a way of life (practice) that makes room (space) for citizenship in everyday life. With this definition in mind, it is not difficult to notice immediately how certain groups, such as migrant/ethnic groups, senior citizens, LGBTQ+ people, persons with disabilities, military veterans, victims of crime, or ex-offenders, can be seen as invisible communities whose 'otherness' can place their public voices at a heightened risk of marginalisation from the mainstream public discourse. The marginalisation of any group at risk of marginalisation can be further amplified by adding another characteristic, e.g., rural vs. urban area, female vs. male, educated vs. uneducated, peace time vs. war time. This observation strongly resonates with Foucault's argument on how societies reproduce themselves through different systems of exclusion (Foucault, 2006).

In criminology, with very few exceptions, little attention has been paid to the conceptualisation of the public in the public sphere and its meaning in crime-related matters. One of these exceptions is the scholarship of Martina Feilzer, who observed that over the years in criminology and criminal justice, the different voices of arguably rational actors – for example, journalists and the media, politicians, reform groups, police officers, or judges – have been competing to dominate 'crime talk' in the public sphere. Their views are gathered, explored and narrated at three different levels: (1) the individual level, in the form of short stories, anecdotes; (2) the professional level, in the form of short stories linked to institutional stories; and (3) big stories – when society's stories become cultural products and constitute shared memory (Feilzer, 2020: 64). The criminological scholarship on different narratives of crime and criminal justice is often restricted to one of the aforementioned levels and one set of publics. The choice of which voices to research and which level to focus on already reveals certain assumptions about whose voices carry most weight or whose narratives matter more (Feilzer, 2020). Lay people's voices about crime, punishment and justice can be found in a broad range of public discourses, however, they are almost exclusively narrated by those who are perceived as rational actors in a public debate. Subsequently, these narratives operate vertically and horizontally with varying degrees of importance and are usually included to serve a different, perceived-to-be-more-important, objective.

The concept of the public is intrinsically interwoven with the concept of the public sphere; both are social phenomena believed to be central to the modern notion of democracy. The public sphere can be defined as comprising of multiple institutional communicative channels (for example, media, blogosphere and deliberative panels) that facilitate public conversations and the development of public opinion. Although the media is still argued to be the most important and powerful institutional communicative infrastructure of the public sphere (Enjolras and Steen-Johnsen, 2017: 101), these media channels, among which some are mainstream and some are secondary, vary somewhat in terms of their political and social impact. In addition, it is now broadly documented how the construction of crime news is governed by its own newsworthy logic, prioritising stories that meet the profile of an 'ideal' victim, offender and storyline, and marginalising those who do not fit into this profile (Jewkes, 2015).

It is also impossible to discuss the functioning of different publics in the public sphere without acknowledging the scholarly contribution of Jürgen Habermas, who described the quality of the public sphere as depending upon both the quality of discourse and the quantity of participation (Calhoun, 1992). The origins of this particular depiction of a public sphere can be traced back to the bourgeois public, an entity between the state and society, which institutionalised a set of practices that were seen as enabling a rational-critical discourse on political matters (Calhoun, 1992). Although Habermas' historical analysis of 'the public' led to the renewed existence of 'the public' in the public sphere, it amplified the romantic expectation of a rational public in the public sphere governed by reason. Only more recently has this view been challenged by the proposition that public participation includes both the mind and the body. Therefore, the rational discourse in the public space has to give way to the realm of sense and emotions (Carrigan and Fatsis, 2021).

The idealised vision of the public in the public sphere is also put into question by the recent analysis of how public (mostly urban) spaces have become intensely commodified, securitised, surveilled environments to accommodate and enhance consumerist behaviours more than civic, participatory ones (Carrigan and Fatsis, 2021). The increased privatisation of the public space has influenced our ability to see ourselves as 'public' through the lens of whether or not we have access to physical environments where public (consumerist) life happens. The precondition for being (part of the) public is now largely determined by our purchasing power rather than our status as citizens enjoying public space (Davis, cited in Carrigan and Fatsis, 2021).

The discussion around 'the public' and its role and value in the public sphere is often interwoven with the concept of public opinion, another compound concept that came into use in Europe in the 18th century as a result of a number of important historical processes and turning points: the growth of literacy, the development of the merchant class, the Protestant Reformation and the wider access to literature enabled by the printing press (Price, 2008). Despite remaining another imprecise term in the social sciences, public opinion, as a product of a gradual transformation of the public sphere, has rapidly become a distinctive area of research in the social sciences. As long as the concept of public opinion was mainly associated with an elitist (rational) public sphere, the role of public opinion in the public sphere was more likely to be narrated along the political-normative tradition of a desired process of providing citizens with information through which they achieve rational and informed judgements for the greatest good of society (Donsbach and Traugott, 2008). The gradual broadening of the public sphere, carried out in the name of democracy, has not only allowed more participants but, in particular, participants from diverse backgrounds to appear in the public sphere. This phenomenon is often represented by the rational actors as a gradual degeneration in the quality of public discourse and divisions. Habermas long observed that such a transformation of the 'public' may also mean disintegration of this sphere, the manipulation of people's views, and lack of respect and trust in public opinion, discussing the concept of the public as an entity deprived of critical discourse and constantly contested (Calhoun, 1992).

Contrary to a popular and widely accepted state of affairs, the concept of 'the public' remains a misconceived ideal that is constantly deprived of its defining nuance and complexity. The public opinion should be seen as lay people's voices dispersed in multiple networks of varying degrees of importance and agency. If public voices are represented in a public domain, they are usually narrated by those who are perceived as rational actors in public life with the goal to use public opinion as an independent variable to serve a different agenda. In the highly competitive public sphere, rapidly transformed by digitalisation and commodification processes, the role of the publics and the value of public opinion has been further compromised by the dividing discourse of a unenlightened, distant, malevolent public vs. a humane, approachable, benevolent one.

The disinhibition of public voices in the digital public sphere

The third, least developed, perspective on the ways we interpret and frame public voices in criminology is connected with accelerated digitalisation processes. The online landscape is increasingly becoming a complex environment where people's lives are more and more deeply embedded. The publics as we knew them some decades ago, when the aforementioned attitudinal research was conducted, are now publics that function in both the online and offline public spheres simultaneously – the impact of which is yet to be captured in criminology.

The rise and rapid development of networked and computer-mediated modes of communication has extended the traditional public sphere by pluralising the range of information providers and revolutionising the ways in which information is produced, processed and received (Enjolras and Steen-Johnsen, 2017). The online environment has become a convenient stage not only to engage in criminal activity through cyber-enabled or cyber-dependent crimes, or where one can fall victim to crime in cyberspace, but also to share views about crime-related matters and penal policies. Although the extent of meaningful online engagement is still a subject of exploration, the expansion of this environment has provided new points of entry into the public sphere for so-called 'netizens'. The digitalisation of the public sphere has rapidly facilitated the formation of various publics.

These diversified publics, who are also everyday online users, might say and do things in cyberspace that they would not ordinarily say and do in the face-to-face world. Suler (2004) has long observed this phenomenon, defining it as the online disinhibition effect, which might manifest in a benign form with a salutary impact on people's behaviours, or as a toxic disinhibition effect when people's behaviour online generates harmful, or even criminal, results. A good example of a benign online disinhibition effect is the idea of crowdsourcing criminology, which examines the ways in which online communities of ordinary citizens are provided with opportunities to participate in crowdsourced investigations, including being provided with a framework to analyse a missing person case study and the subsequent development of a television documentary in British Columbia, Canada (Gray and Benning 2019). Despite the fact that Suler's model comes in handy to understand the making of the modern and digitalised public sphere, it is still at risk of amplifying the already harmful division between good/benevolent and bad/malevolent publics.

The 'malevolent' publics

There is a well-accepted statement that in general we live in punitive societies (Garland, 2001; Simon and Sparks, 2013) and most public opinion research in criminology and criminal justice has repetitiously concluded that lay people, when asked about crime, punishment or justice, are mostly ill-informed and also influenced by sensationalist media representations of crime, and that this is why, most of the time, they are in favour of harsh, punitive responses to crime (see Roberts and Stalans, 1997; Roberts and Hough, 2005; Pratt, 2007; Kesteren, 2009). There is a strong argument in the literature that a lack of extensive experience with the criminal justice system can make lay people a convenient audience for mass media news, which in consequence makes the media the primary source of people's understanding of crime, punishment and justice (Ericson, 1991; Roberts et al., 2003; Levi, 2006).

This widespread consensus that there is, first of all, one public, and secondly, that the public's views can be constantly depicted as an aggregated item, has made lay people an inseparable part of the penal punitive language or the crime-opinion-policy nexus problem. The demand, or the perceived demand, among citizens for harsher penal policies has come to be seen as an inevitable product of democratic politics and crime, used by office-seeking, or office-securing, politicians to pursue their self-serving manifestos or to adjust their stance on crime in order to gain people's support (Bottoms, 1995; Jennings et al., 2016). Keijser (2014) has said that lay people's opinions may prove to be a wolf in sheep's clothing, since turning to people who constantly 'get it wrong' could be considered a characteristic of penal populism.

In sum, the narrative about public punitive sentiments, opinions and attitudes has become a politicised phenomenon and one of the dominant 'malevolent public' narratives about the value of lay people's views in criminology and criminal justice. Although Bottoms (1995: 40) acknowledges that penal punitiveness is something more than public opinion, the politicisation of public views and its cursory, fragmented representation in policymaking has become an integral feature of how lay people's views are narrated in the public sphere.

The aforementioned literature is a good illustration though that, if one chooses to do so, there are enough sources out there to construct and continue operating with the 'malevolent public' narrative.

The operationalisation of public punitiveness has been applied through a number of indicators, among them attitudes towards the death penalty, youth delinquency/anti-social behaviour, or confidence in the police and/or the criminal justice system. Not only has there been continuity with the concept of 'the public' as an unchallenged and vague term, but punitiveness and leniency are also acknowledged as being poorly understood and an under-theorised social construct in criminology and criminal justice (Matthews 2005; King 2008; Maruna and King, 2008). The nature and dynamic of lay people's understanding of justice still lacks an in-depth examination that captures the complexity, the multi-dimensional aspects and the type of networks they operate within. Turner (2018) and Feilzer (2020) observed that there is a distorted understanding of what lay people think about crime thanks to the dominant survey approach in this field, which has led to what Turner (2018) has coined 'aggregative, general, atomised, and passive (AGAP)' approaches to discussing people's views on crime, punishment and criminal justice. As a result, not only do we not make any scientific progress in the field, but we continue to enact selection bias and perpetuate the marginalisation of those whose presence in overwhelmingly quantitative attitudinal studies is limited, e.g., persons with disabilities, the homeless, institutionalised populations, ethnic/migrant communities and refugees who do not speak the language of the host country, Indigenous populations, and people with poor IT skills and/or Internet access (for a critical overview, see Freedman, 2004; Rehm et al., 2020). Quite often the same groups are presented in the discussion on the role and value of public opinion as problematic, hard to reach to educate about crime and not an 'ideal' type of public sphere user. As a response to the notorious difficulty of surveying migrant populations, the sampling methodology called 'respondent-driven sampling' has recently gained recognition as a suitable approach to recruit rare and elusive networks (see Tyldum, 2021).

Thus, the other issue that needs to be interpreted carefully is the state of current knowledge about public perceptions of the justice system and the methodology through which this knowledge has been accumulated. Survey research has a long tradition; it originated in the 1930s (in the US) and was born with the belief that public opinion is an object of measurement of what the general population thinks about a given topic. In addition, Turner (2018) has argued that the notion of public confidence in the justice system is a social construct that has been invented as a pre-existing commodity for research, and is supposedly best captured through the application of quantitative research tools. Not only has this approach paved the way for a one-dimensional and passive overview of what lay people think about crime, punishment and the justice system, but it has also advocated education as a knee-jerk panacea for the alleged cognitive deficit of public opinion.

On some occasions, it has been suggested that the interpretation of public views requires a more comprehensive examination. Carvalho and Chamberlen (2018) suggested considering people's punitiveness as a source of 'pleasure of punishment' or 'hostile solidarity', which is directly linked to the specific kind of solidarity that punishment produces. According to these two scholars, seeking pleasure through harsh punishment can also be interpreted as a belief that punishment serves a bonding function in society that promotes civil order as well as a sense of belonging and that allows an emotional release of anxiety, insecurity, anger and frustration.

Furthermore, even the modern demand for public apology, rather than pursuing the envisaged healing and forgiveness, often turns into a forced statement of regret that mainly reflects a desire to punish. This has been argued by Ellwanger (2012: 309), who said that apologies in the public sphere should be discussed as ritualistic public punishment and humiliation. Ellwanger asserted that because of its conceptual relationship with reconciliation and forgiveness, public apology operates as a rhetorical wolf in sheep's clothing with covertly punitive goals. The call for an apology can only ensure that the dialogue will be defined by agonism and antipathy on both sides – conditions that make forgiveness and reconciliation all but impossible.

A conventional reading of public opinion (polls), which are rarely subject to advanced statistical analysis, has been challenged by a number of advanced studies that have shown the complexity of these views, which are characterised as contradictory, nuanced and fragile (Roberts and Hough, 2005; Hutton, 2005), and selectively punitive and merciful (Stalans, 2002). While people may 'talk tough' in response to opinion polls that ask whether sentencing is harsh enough, when considering specific criminal cases and individual circumstances, lay people can be quite pragmatic sentencers and show considerable support for mitigating punishments (Hough and Roberts, 2011). The research by Maruna and King (2008) incorporates some nuance into this view, as their study findings indicate that lay people's support for harsh punishment is not logically incompatible with a belief in redemption. Moreover, the dimensional character of lay people's sentencing preferences and the role of empathy have been demonstrated in an Australian study of punitiveness and leniency and the implications for penal moderation (Lovegrove, 2013). Also, Feilzer quotes Bamberg (Feilzer, 2020: 77) to demonstrate that individual conversations about crime include 'juggling several story lines simultaneously'. This was echoed in her research that demonstrated how in individual accounts of crime and justice-related matters, people will draw on shared stories to anchor their opinions and attitudes (Feilzer, 2020), as well as in my doctoral study on Polish lay people's understanding of punishment and justice (Matczak, 2018).

The 'benevolent' publics

There is yet another pool of scholarly depictions and representations of the public that offers a different narrative, more communitarian in spirit. In the 'benevolent public' domain, lay people are often referred to as civil society, community or stakeholders, which is more inclusive, but still maintains the expectation of a more active and engaged role for lay people in decision-making processes. In fact, public opinion might even occasionally be discussed as the wisdom of the crowds against excessive faith in the single individual decision-maker (see Surowiecki, 2005). Similarly, in the field of safety and security, with some instances of risk management, lay people's role in estimating harm, can be valued more than that of scientists' (Mythen, 2014).

In the criminological literature, the perception of the publics as stakeholders has been analysed, among others, by Loader (2000), who observed a gradual relocation of responsibilities for crime prevention in the hands of individual citizens, seen by neoliberal policymakers as self-calculating, risk-monitoring, rational consumers of safety and security (Loader, 2000). The phenomenon of plural policing, meaning the involvement of multiple public and private actors in carrying out policing activities, not only represents a shift that departs from the state-centred policing framework, but also sees lay people as stakeholders who should be encouraged to participate in activities such as neighbourhood watch schemes or local partnerships against crime (Loader, 2000; Van Eijk, 2018).

The narrative about a promising role for lay people in the public sphere can also be found in the work of Albert Dzur, who has argued that lay people's views are central to the financial aspect of punishment and justice, as the functioning of criminal justice institutions is funded by lay people and their engagement with criminal justice policymaking should be regarded through their rights, duties and membership as individuals in a nation state (Dzur, 2014). In the research carried out by Cohen et al. (2006) on public preferences with regard to criminal justice spending, lay people are seen as rational citizens who, if given a choice to decide on budget allocation, would spend it on crime prevention, drug treatment and police rather than more prisons.

Correspondingly, the identification of study participants as criminal justice taxpayers resonates with the growing popularity of the justice reinvestment agenda. The term 'justice reinvestment' was conceived in the United States in an attempt to address the growing prison population, the substantial costs associated with it and the failure of imprisonment to fulfil any rehabilitative potential successfully (Brown et al., 2016). Justice reinvestment redirects the focus of the criminal justice debate from incarceration to community sanctions and measures; it entails 'preventative financing through which policymakers shift funds away from dealing with problems "downstream" (policing, prisons) and towards tackling them "upstream" (family breakdown, poverty, mental illness, drug and alcohol dependency)' (Lanning et al., 2011: 4).

The benevolent depiction of the public is also distinct in the field of restorative justice, where it is assumed that people are inherently good (Kirkwood, 2021) and where the presence of lay people – for example, in restorative circles or conferences – is perceived to create an opportunity for collective local responses to crime. In restorative justice, the community is seen as a network of social relationships that is damaged by the offender's actions. The specific nature of this community remains undetermined as a different group of people is constructed as a community anew each time an offence is committed (McCold, 1996; Lemley, 2001). Lay involvement in restorative justice means that people are given back direct and hands-on control of justice decision-making, acknowledging citizens' value, responsibility and capacity in dealing with conflicts in their communities and promoting a participatory approach to conflict prevention, management and mitigation as a value in itself (Dzur, 2008; Vasilescu, 2021). In addition, Braithwaite (2002) suggests that people's engagement in restorative interventions that require taking responsibility for matters that have previously been the state's responsibility leads to community empowerment in the long term. With a few exceptions (see Crawford, 1999, 2002; Strang and Braithwaite, 2001), there has been very little evaluation and criticism of the actual involvement of lay people in restorative justice practices, which has made many scholars in the field take lay people's openness and tolerance for granted.

Contrary to the narrative of the punitive, malevolent public, an interesting development, which has encouraged the reconciliation of lay participation and knowledge with professional and scientific expertise, is the growth of so-called citizen science. The idea first originated with the publication of Alan Irwin's book *Citizen Science: A Study of People, Expertise, and Sustainable Development* in 1995, in which citizen science was introduced as a means to involve lay people more deeply in natural science research in order to face environmental challenges. Bonney and colleagues' (2015) review of citizen (natural) science projects suggests that the goal of bridging the gap between the public and science can be achieved through, for example, lay people's involvement in data collection, data processing, curriculum-based projects or community science projects. The extent of citizens' role and involvement when planning and executing a citizen science project can be assessed and classified while taking into account the following factors: coordination, participation, community building, evaluation, openness and accessibility, entrepreneurship and funding, and the location of the project (Prainsack, 2014).

In the social sciences particularly, in spite of the relative dearth of popularised examples, citizen science projects build on the tradition and legacy of participatory research methods and can be a powerful practice for both the inclusion of marginalised communities and the design of new evidence-based policies supported by the participation of citizens (Albert et al., 2021: 120). In addition to the general promise of citizen science, in the social sciences, where there is a heightened notion of responsibility towards researched communities and individuals, there is the additional benefit of co-producing with the public. This might increase the quality, relevance and impact of the research undertaking, as well as provide the opportunity to critically reflect on the issues at stake, to revisit how knowledge is generated and disseminated and how evaluation is enhanced (Albert et al., 2021: 120).

The noble rationale behind the idea of citizen science is to shift the perception about the public knowledge deficit and start a dialogue of public engagement, which aims to enhance lay people's understanding of science, empower them, and build trust between scientific institutions and the public. This approach is more inclusive and dialogical than in the 'malevolent publics' narrative, which advocates for more traditional education. While the growth and popularity of citizen science has been greatly facilitated by the development of the Internet, very little evaluation has been conducted of citizen science projects and there is limited evidence regarding whether these objectives are being met (Bonney et al., 2015).

My last example of where the benevolent public narrative is present is in the concept of public criminology, which came into existence along with the realisation that criminologists need to learn how to communicate with politicians, policymakers, criminal justice professionals and civil societies – the latter being naturally saturated with 'crime talk' (Chancer and McLaughlin, 2007: 157). The emergence of a public criminology agenda has brought renewed opportunities to find innovative methods to communicate criminological research and collaborate with diverse publics (Uggen and Inderbitzin, 2010). Loader and Sparks (2010) acknowledged that criminology has historically combined intellectual curiosity and the quest for rigorous research standards with reformist ambitions. However, the researchers warn that this should not mean accepting folk wisdom. On the contrary, the authors define the role of public criminology as one to restrain and/or challenge public opinion.

> To be a criminologist, to an important degree, is to have committed oneself already to the idea that crime problems can and should be subjected to reason, method, evidence, analysis, and knowledge and to have taken a stand against, or at least assumed some distance from, lay opinion and political judgment. It is thus often to have placed oneself on a collision course with social and political actors who advance their crime and justice projects in ignorance (wilful or otherwise) of criminology's hard-earned lessons
> *(Loader and Sparks, 2010: 776).*

In order to do public criminology reasonably well, one needs to understand the complex and constrained environment of policymaking, which is intensely political and not always welcoming and open towards scientific evidence (Rock, 2010: 751). The extent of the public presence and engagement within public criminology is questioned by Ruggiero (2012), who finds the application of public criminology very difficult and argues that in order to meet the objective of public criminology, criminologists have to move beyond the narrow focus on crime and return to its sociological roots that place crime as a conflict alongside the notion of social movement and social change.

In contrast to the 'malevolent public' narrative, the literature reviewed in this section suggests that there is an alternative pool of scholarly resources that give the public and their voices a chance. The aforementioned perspectives are more inclusive, dialogical and participatory. Nonetheless, with little evaluation and critical thinking, the 'benevolent public' discourse might at times represent as far-fetched and elusive an orientation as the one about the malevolent publics.

Conclusions

The objective for this chapter was to show how I have observed the concept of the 'public' being researched and narrated in criminology over the years in three different countries and how various narratives about the role and value of lay people can be classified to align with the preconceived perception of either the 'benevolent' or the 'malevolent' public agenda. This simplified dichotomy is used deliberately in this chapter to instigate some reflection amongst criminologists on what the 'public' means to us in our own research, teaching and advocacy work, and how much recognition we give to the diversity of groups in our societies.

In addition, despite the much-discussed constraints of public opinion polls, lay people's views are almost exclusively gathered through conventional public opinion surveys, and these narratives are often deprived of their historical, cultural, linguistic, socio-political and economic contexts (Matczak, 2018). The dominant application of quantitative methodologies to research public attitudes has silenced the magnitude of different and sometimes elusive communities, whose access to the public sphere and media representation is limited. As a consequence, the concept of the 'public' has forever become enmeshed in the language of penal punitiveness, amplified by continuous generalisation, which makes the concept of 'the public' constantly compromised and, as a result, subject to marginalisation. There is enough criminological research to state that public opinion about crime, punishment and justice occurs on a spectrum. Thus, there is a need not only to shift away from the dichotomous division between liberal vs. punitive public views, but also to address the heterogeneity of people's views vertically (individual, collective) and horizontally (in different networks/publics/target groups).

There is a necessity to popularise the investigation of lay people's views and opinions through (more inclusive) qualitative research methods that not only expose the multi-layered complexity and dependency of these views, but also assist in capturing the wider socio-political and economic context in which such views operate (see, for example, Taylor and Addison, 2011). How public narratives should be collated, identified and analysed is not yet fully developed (Feilzer, 2020); however, the dominance of public opinion polls is obvious, and the field would benefit from applying more discourse and content analysis, semi-structured interviews and biographical methods. The progress of attitudinal research in criminology and criminal justice can be advanced by applying, for example, a narrative criminology framework, which advocates the power of telling and sharing stories in constructing a narrative identity - a complex relationship between a story and 'reality' (Sandberg and Ugelvik, 2016). Only then will we be able to disaggregate the views of various fractions of society, contextualise their stories, and further explore people's punitive stance, its aetiology and dynamics.

The role of public views in a justice system, the value of public opinion in criminology and a degree of public confidence in criminal justice have come to be seen as essential for the system to be viewed as legitimate and well-functioning. However, many criminologists have conveniently accepted that the concept of 'the public' is researched as an amorphous entity that consumes crime news disseminated through the mass media, rather than an interconnected, deliberating body of diverse publics that can also discover their own views through conversation and deliberation.

Public opinion, which should be seen more as a sea inside which civil society swims, is 'the middle ground between the generalities of high-flow discourse and the ongoing, concrete events of everyday life' (Alexander, 2006: 4). Crime and punishment are social constructs that are experienced in different forms and to different degrees by different social groups/publics. Public narratives, just like crime and criminal justice narratives, are negotiated at different levels and to different degrees and are deeply culturally and temporally embedded (Feilzer, 2020).

There is still very little attention and realisation among criminologists regarding the variety of narratives about lay people. Also, we rarely make a conscious decision about how we choose to see lay people in our criminological research. This direction is most of the time predetermined or dictated by what and how our topic has been researched and discussed in our respective criminological domains so far. Reflecting on how we interpret and frame public voices might eventually assist us all to advance the debate on the role and value of different publics in criminology and criminal justice.

References

Albert, A., Balázs, B., Butkevičienė, E., Mayer, K., and Perelló, J. (2021). Citizen Social Science: New and Established Approaches to Participation in Social Research. In: Vohland K., Land-Zandstra, A., Ceccaroni, L., Lemmens, R., Perelló, J., Ponti, M., Samson, R., and Wagenknecht, K. (eds.), *The Science of Citizen Science*. Cham: Springer.

Alexander, J.C. (2006). *The Civil Sphere*. Oxford: Oxford University Press.

Althoff, M., Dollinger, B., and Schmidt, H. (2020). Fighting for the 'Right' Narrative: Introduction to Conflicting Narratives of Crime and Punishment. In: Althoff, M., Dollinger, B., and Schmidt, H. (eds.), *Conflicting Narratives of Crime and Punishment*. London: Palgrave Macmillan, pp. 1–22.

Bonney, R., Phillips, T.B., Ballard, H.L., and Enck, J.W. (2015). Can Citizen Science Enhance Public Understanding of Science? *Public Understanding of Science*, 25(1), 1–15.

Bottoms, A.E. (1995). The Philosophy and Politics of Punishment and Sentencing. In: Clarkson, C.M.V. and Morgan, R. (eds.), *The Politics of Sentencing Reform*. Oxford: Oxford University Press.

Braithwaite, J. (2002). *Restorative Justice and Responsive Regulation*. Oxford: Oxford University Press.
Brown, D., Cunneen, C., Schwartz, M., Stubbs, J., and Young, C. (2016). *Justice Reinvestment: Winding Back Imprisonment*. London: Palgrave Macmillan.
Calhoun, C. (1992). Introduction: Habermas and the Public Sphere. In: Calhoun, C. (ed.), *Habermas and the Public Sphere*. Cambridge: The MIT Press.
Carrigan, M. and Fatsis, L. (2021). *The Public and Their Platforms Public Sociology in an Era of Social Media*. Bristol: Bristol University Press.
Carvalho, H. and Chamberlen, A. (2018). Why Punishment Pleases: Punitive Feelings in a World of Hostile Solidarity. *Punishment & Society*, 20(2), 217–234.
Castells, M. and Cardoso, G. (2005). *The Network Society: From Knowledge to Policy*. Massachusetts: Center for Transatlantic Relations, Johns Hopkins.
Cohen, M.A., Rust, R.T., and Steen, S. (2006). Prevention, Crime Control or Cash? Public Preferences Towards Criminal Justice Spending Priorities. *Justice Quarterly*, 23(3), 317–335.
Cowell, A.J., Hinde, J.M., Broner, N., and Aldridge, A.P. (2013). The Impact on Taxpayer Costs of a Jail Diversion Program for People with Serious Mental Illness. *Evaluation and Program Planning*, 41, 31–37.
Chancer, L. and McLaughlin, E. (2007). Public Criminologies: Diverse Perspectives on Academia and Policy. *Theoretical Criminology*, 11, 155–173.
Crawford, A. (1999). Questioning Appeals to Community Within Crime Prevention and Control. *European Journal on Criminal Policy and Research*, 7(4), 509–530.
Crawford, A. (2002). The State, Community, and Restorative Justice: Heresy, Nostalgia, and Butterfly Collecting. In: Walgrave, L. (ed.), *Restorative Justice and the Law*. Devon: Willan Publishing.
Donsbach, W. and Traugott, M.W. (2008). Introduction. In: Donsbach, W. and Traugott, M.W. (eds.), *The Sage Handbook of Public Opinion Research*. London: Sage, pp.1–6.
Dzur, A. (2008). *Democratic Professionalism, Citizen Participation and the Reconstruction of Professional Ethics, Identity and Practice*. Pennsylvania: Pennsylvania State University Press.
Dzur, A. (2014). Repellent Institutions and the Absentee Public: Grounding Opinion in Responsibility for Punishment. In: Ryberg, J. and Roberts, J.V. (eds.), *Popular Punishment: On the Normative Significance of Public Opinion*. New York: Oxford University Press.
Ellwanger, A. (2012). Apology as Metanoic Performance: Punitive Rhetoric and Public Speech. *Rhetoric Society Quarterly*, 42(4), 307–329.
Enjolras, B. and Steen-Johnsen, K. (2017). The Digital Transformation of the Political Public Sphere: A Sociological Perspective. In: Steen-Johnsen, K., Engelstad, F., Larsen, H., Rogstad, J., Polkowska, D., Dauber-Griffin, A.S., and Leverton, A. (eds.), *Institutional Change in the Public Sphere: Views on the Nordic Model*. Berlin: De Gruyter, pp. 99–117.
Ericson, R.V. (1991). Mass Media, Crime, Law, and Justice. *British Journal of Criminology*, 31(3), 219–249.
Feilzer, M. (2020). Public Narratives of Crime and Criminal Justice: Connecting 'Small' and 'Big' Stories to Make Public Narratives Visible. In Althoff, M., Dollinger, B., and Schmidt, H. (eds.), *Conflicting Narratives of Crime and Punishment*. London: Palgrave Macmillan, pp. 63–86.
Foucault, M. (2006). *History of Madness*. Khalfa, J. (ed.). Abingdon: Routledge. (First published in French in 1961 as *Folie et Déraison: Histoire de la folie à l'âge classique*. Paris: Librarie Plon.)

Fraser, N. (1990). Rethinking the Public Sphere: A Contribution to the Critique of Actually Existing Democracy. *Social Text*, 25/26, 56–80.

Freedman, D.A. (2004). Sampling. In: Lewis-Beck, M.S., Bryman, A., and Liao, T. F. (eds.), *The Sage Encyclopaedia of Social Science Research Methods*. Thousand Oaks: Sage, pp. 986–989.

Garland, D. (2001). *The Culture of Control: Crime and Social Order in Contemporary Society*. Oxford: Oxford University Press.

Gray, G. and Benning, B. (2019). Crowdsourcing Criminology: Social Media and Citizen Policing in Missing Persons Cases. *SAGE Open*, 1–15.

Hough, M. and Roberts, J. (2011). Custody or Community? Exploring The Boundaries of Public Punitiveness in England and Wales. *Criminology and Criminal Justice*, 11(2), 181–197.

Hutton, N. (2005). Beyond Populist Punitiveness. *Punishment & Society*, 7, 243–258.

Irwin, A. (1995). *Citizen Science: A Study of People, Expertise and Sustainable Development*. Abingdon: Routledge.

Jennings, W., Farrall, S., Gray, E., and Hay, C. (2016). Penal Populism and the Public Thermostat: Crime, Public Punitiveness, and Public Policy. *Governance: An International Journal of Policy, Administration, and Institutions*, 30(3), 463–481.

Jewkes, I. (2015). *Media and Crime*. London: Sage.

Keijser, J.W. (2014). Penal Theory and Popular Opinion: The Deficiencies of Direct Engagement. In: Ryberg, J. and Roberts, J.V. (eds.), *Popular Punishment: On the Normative Significance of Public Opinion*. New York: Oxford University Press.

Kesteren, J. (2009). Public Attitudes and Sentencing Policies Across the World. *European Journal of Criminal Policy Research*, 15, 25–46.

King, A. (2008). Keeping a Safe Distance: Individualism and the Less Punitive Public. *British Journal of Criminology*, 48(2), 190–208.

Kirkwood, S. (2021). *A Practice Framework for Restorative Justice. Aggression and Violent Behaviour*, 63(3).

Lanning, T., Loader, I., and Muir, R. (2011). Redesigning Justice: Reducing Crime through Justice. Report, Institute for Public Policy Research, UK, December.

Lemley (2001) Designing Restorative Justice Policy: An Analytical Perspective. *Criminal Justice Policy Review*, 12(1), 43–65.

Levi, M. (2006). The Media Construction of Financial White-Collar Crimes. *British Journal of Criminology*, 46, 1037–1057.

Loader, I. (2000). Plural Policing and Democratic Governance. *Social and Legal Studies*, 9(3), 323–345.

Loader, I. and Sparks, R. (2010). What Is to Be Done with Public Criminology? *Criminology and Public Policy*, 9(4), 771–781.

Lovegrove, A. (2013). Sentencing and Public Opinion: An Empirical Study of Punitiveness and Lenience and Its Implications for Penal Moderation. *Australian and New Zealand Journal of Criminology*, 46(2), 200–220.

Maruna, S. and King, A. (2008). Selling the Public on Probation: Beyond the Bib. *Probation Journal*, 55(4), 337–351.

Matczak, A., (2018). Understandings of Punishment and Justice in the Narratives of Lay Polish People. PhD thesis, London School of Economics, London.

Matthews, R. (2005). The Myth of Punitiveness. *Theoretical Criminology*, 9(2), 175–201.

McCold P. (1996). Restorative Justice and the Role of Community. In: Galaway, B. and Hudson, J. (eds.), *Restorative Justice: International Perspectives*. New York: Criminal Justice Press.

Mythen, G. (2014). *Understanding the Risk Society: Crime, Security and Justice*. London: Springer.
O'Malley, P. (1992). Risk, Power and Crime Prevention. *Economy and Society*, 21(3), 252–275.
Prainsack, B. (2014). Understanding Participation: The 'Citizen Science' of Genetics. In: Prainsack, B., Werner-Felmayer, G., and Schicktanz, G. (eds.), *Genetics as Social Practice*. Farnham: Ashgate.
Pratt, J. (2007). *Penal Populism*. Abingdon: Routledge.
Price, V. (2008). The Public and Public Opinion in Political Theories. In: Donsbach, W. and Traugott, M.W. (eds.), *The Sage Handbook of Public Opinion Research*. London: Sage, pp. 11–24.
Rehm, J., Kilian, C., Rovira, P., Schield, K.D., and Manthey, J. (2020). The Elusiveness of Representativeness in General Population Surveys for Alcohol. *Drug and Alcohol Review*, 40(2), 161–165.
Roberts, J.V. and Hough, M. (2005). *Understanding Public Attitudes to Criminal Justice*. Maidenhead: Open University Press.
Roberts, J.V. and Stalans, L. (1997). *Public Opinion, Crime, and Criminal Justice*. Boulder: Westview Press.
Roberts, J.V., Stalans, L.J., Indermaur, D., and Hough, M. (2003). *Penal Populism and Public Opinions: Lessons from Five Countries*. New York: Oxford University Press.
Rock, P. (2010). Comment on 'Public Criminologies'. *Criminology and Public Policy*, 9(4), 751–767.
Ruggiero, V. (2012). How Public Is Public Criminology? *Crime, Media, Culture*, 8(2), 151–160.
Sandberg, S. and Ugelvik, T. (2016). The Past, Present, and Future of Narrative Criminology: A Review and an Invitation. *Crime, Media, Culture: An International Journal*, 12(2), 129–136.
Simon, J. and Sparks, R. (2013). Punishment and Society: The Emergence of an Academic Field. In: Simon, J. and Sparks, R. (eds.), *The Sage Handbook of Punishment and Society*. London: Sage, pp. 1–20.
Stalans, L. (2002). Measuring Attitudes to Sentencing. In: Roberts, J.V. and Hough, M. (eds.), *Changing Attitudes to Punishment: Public Opinion, Crime and Justice*. Cullompton: Willan.
Strang, H. and Braithwaite, J. (2001). *Restorative Justice and Civil Society*. Cambridge: Cambridge University Press.
Suler, J. (2004). The Online Disinhibition Effect. *Cyberpsychology & Behaviour*, 7, 321–326.
Surowiecki, J. (2005). *The Wisdom of Crowds*. New York: Anchor.
Turner, E.R. (2018). *Public Confidence in Criminal Justice*. London: Palgrave Macmillan.
Uggen, C. and Inderbitzin, M. (2010). Public Criminologies. *Criminology and Public Policy*, 9(4), 725–749.
Taylor, Y. and Addison, M. (2011). Placing Research: 'City Publics' and the 'Public Sociologist', *Sociological Research Online*, 16(4).
Tyldum, G. (2021). Surveying Migrant Populations with Respondent-Driven Sampling: Experiences from Surveys of East-West Migration in Europe. *International Journal of Social Research Methodology*, 24(3), 341–353.
Van Eijk, C. (2018). Helping Dutch Neighborhood Watch Schemes to Survive the Rainy Season: Studying Mutual Perceptions on Citizens' and Professionals' Engagement in the Co-Production of Community Safety. *Voluntas*, 29, 222–236.
Vasilescu, C. (2021). Security, Democracy and Cities Conference: Promoting Urban Security in Complex Societies and the Role of Restorative Justice. European Forum for Restorative Justice. https://www.euforumrj.org/en/security-democracy-and-cities-conference.

11

WHOSE CRIMINOLOGY?

Marginalised Perspectives and Populations Within Student Production at the Montreal School of Criminology

Alexis Marcoux Rouleau, Ismehen Melouka, and Maude Pérusse-Roy

Introduction

In 2020, global and local mobilisations re-emerged around anti-Black and anti-Indigenous racism in policing, and emptying or even abolishing prisons. Criminology's role in maintaining the status quo and in erasing marginalised populations came into focus within the socio-political landscape. This had echoes within university departments (Kitossa and Tanyildiz, 2022) including our own, the Montreal School of Criminology in Québec, Canada. As doctoral students, we addressed an open letter to professors and department leaders, calling for concrete commitments and changes within the School's criminological education and practice. We insisted on the importance of encouraging critical scholarship and of adapting curricula to tackle intersecting structural phenomena which affect system-impacted individuals. Although this letter was co-signed by many peers, department leaders dismissed us by invoking the all-encompassing need for objectivity within scientific pursuits such as criminology: taking a stance was declared unsuitable for academics. However, several professors, lecturers, and practitioners published an open letter echoing our stance. Professors and graduate students defended a range of positions regarding policing and racism, reform, and abolition within local news media.

We realised an epistemological cleavage was at the root of these debates: as multiply marginalised doctoral students who identify with those whom we study, taking a stance made sense as we did not see ourselves, nor our research, as inherently value neutral. Indeed, our respective positionalities inform how we experience academia and how we approach research. We detail these positionalities hereafter to contextualise the present study and because we believe transparency is key to rigorous quantitative research. Alexis is a non binary

DOI: 10.4324/9781003260967-14

trans and queer disabled white settler from a middle-class background, whose history of victimisation connects them to their research subjects. Their work draws on feminist, queer, and abolitionist criminology and victimology. As an immigrant Arab woman, Ismehen is also a financially privileged settler. Her work on reconciliation draws on zemiology, victimology, and peace-making criminology. Maude is a cis, white settler woman studying police repression of activist women through a feminist perspective. She is sensitive to class issues as a first-generation postsecondary student. The value and scientificity of our work have at times been called into question by peers and professors given our common emphasis on social justice, while two of us have struggled with feeling like hyper-visible 'Others' in this department consisting mainly of white, heteronormative, and abled individuals.

In summer 2020, we were advocating for social justice-oriented criminology recognising that science exists *in* rather than *outside* of society. This was incompatible with the premises guiding many of our professors' and peers' scholarship, which subscribe to dominant epistemologies and ontologies. We realised that, as uncomfortable as we were with our professors' and peers' disengagement from social issues, what we were asking challenged their core understanding of science and was uncomfortable to them as well. Facing this epistemological and ontological divide, we decided to embrace and engage with this collective discomfort as the starting point for empirical inquiry (Chadwick, 2021). Therefore, we developed a project attempting to gain insight into the criminological perspectives and underlying epistemological premises put forth by the Montreal School.

In the current chapter, we empirically investigate the prevalence of and relationship between marginalised populations and criminological perspectives based on two decades' worth of thesis and dissertation abstracts published by the Montreal School. Like Laidler and Lee (2016), we assume that departmental and disciplinary trends are reflected within student production. Indeed, criminological knowledges – including topics, theories, and methodologies – are produced and conditioned by various institutions which themselves exist within certain social, political, and economic contexts such as neoliberalism (Loader and Sparks, 2012; Koehler, 2015; Bertrand, 2008; Garland, 1992). These institutions and their actors exert a range of pressures on criminological knowledge production (Loader and Sparks, 2012; Koehler, 2015; Brantingham et al., 2018; F.-Dufour et al., 2018; Garland, 1992; Foucault, 1975). For instance, universities and departments have a say in who is admitted and hired, and which programmes and classes are offered. Research councils determine funding priorities based on pressing issues, as formulated by media, lobbyists, and governments. Agencies such as prisons, youth protection services, or private security firms mediate access to research participants, sites, and data; they may even veto the circulation of certain results. Publishers and professional associations affect which knowledges are disseminated and how (Loader and Sparks, 2012; Garland, 1992).

As early career researchers and practitioners, master's and doctoral students are subjected to these institutional and social pressures and may experience additional professional pressures. Given shifts in higher education and the job market, reproducing disciplinary and departmental tendencies could be an advantageous career move. Indeed, the commercialisation and commodification of higher education within the local and global neoliberal context has impacted students' views of their education (Stockdale and Sweeney, 2019; Stockdale et al., 2021; Barton et al., 2010). Whereas higher education was once understood as a space for intellectual or social fulfilment, it is now promoted as an investment towards future employment, whether as practitioners, researchers, or professors (Barton et al., 2010). Although 74% of American criminology doctoral graduates transitioned to tenure-track professorships in 2007 (Frost and Clear, 2007), recent anecdotal evidence suggests a decrease in the availability of such positions and an increase in competitiveness within the academic job market (Radatz and Slakoff, 2021). Academic job candidates are expected to gain significant experience in research, publishing, teaching, and service while completing their degrees (Sitren and Applegate, 2012; Radatz and Slakoff, 2021). Faced with these institutional, social, and professional pressures, graduate students may prefer to optimise their time by reproducing the disciplinary and departmental status quo.

What is this disciplinary and departmental status quo which may be magnified within student production? We begin with an overview of the Montreal School's history to situate criminological perspectives adopted by the department's master's and doctoral students. We then distinguish three major perspectives within criminology as a discipline, before delving into our methodology and results. We conclude with a discussion of these results.

The Montreal School of Criminology

As of 2022, the University of Montreal School of Criminology is the largest criminology department within the French-speaking world, housing over 1,000 students, 58 professors and permanent researchers, two research institutes, 130 classes, and 200 internships annually (École de Criminologie, n.d.). There are multiple undergraduate programmes pertaining to criminology, security, and policing studies, with options to focus on clinical intervention or on research. There are multiple master's degree options, programmes with graduate-level classes but no written work, and one PhD programme requiring a dissertation. Nearly 7,000 students have graduated from the Montreal School of Criminology since its establishment.

The University of Montreal's School of Criminology was founded in 1960, which coincides with the institutionalisation of the discipline through the creation of criminology programmes in the UK and North America (Brantingham et al., 2018; Bertrand, 2008; Koehler, 2015). These emerging programmes mark the inception of a new criminology, taught at the intersection of social sciences, law, psychology, and even medicine. Given its social science roots, criminology faces a crisis of legitimacy as a science; thus, the Montreal School is pressured into favouring applied social sciences committed to resolving concrete social issues (Bertrand, 2008). Through these social and political pressures, the School develops a strong inclination towards training professionals who work within the justice system, thereby legitimising its existence (Bertrand, 2008). Also contributing to the institutionalisation of criminology as a discipline is the 1968 inauguration of a peer-reviewed journal housed by the Montreal School. From 1975, this journal was entitled *Criminologie*, exclusively publishes in French, and focuses on empirical findings concerning crime and criminal justice in Québec (F.-Dufour et al., 2018; Brantingham et al., 2018).

To address concrete criminological problems, the Montreal School initially favours research on the aetiology of crime and on clinical practices attempting to reform delinquent behaviour, before concluding such interventions have a limited impact on crime statistics (Bertrand, 2008). In the 1970s and 1980s, some researchers at the School were influenced by sociological developments and grew interested in the effects of penal institutions on criminalised groups (Bertrand, 2008). Although social reaction theories gained traction at the School, until the 1990s these were only marginally influenced by critical perspectives compared to sister departments (Bertrand, 2008). Criminologists at the Montreal School and in Québec have largely shirked abolitionism yet appear to share a humanist, liberal, and minimalist approach to the criminal-legal system, favouring alternatives to incarceration for instance (Bertrand, 2008).

In 2015, the Québec Professional Order of Criminologists was established, consecrating professional and clinical interventions as developed within conventional criminology. Certain acts, such as evaluating criminogenic factors, are reserved for clinical criminologists trained at one of three criminology departments including the Montreal School. Practitioners' roles are thus designed to align with the criminal-legal system's objectives, meaning criminologists are bound to contribute to institutions' functioning (Quirion, 2018). This has implications for the criminological perspectives put forth at the Montreal School, which reflect three major perspectives existing within the discipline.

Criminological perspectives

Inspired by F.-Dufour et al. (2018) and Garland (1992), we distinguish three criminological perspectives which rest on different ontological and epistemological premises pertaining to the existence of *crime* and *criminal*. In the next pages, we explore these perspectives' main themes as well as their relationship to the status quo and marginalised populations. Table 11.1 summarises this section.

TABLE 11.1 Summary of criminological perspectives

Criminological perspective	Stance on crime	Stance on marginalised populations	Examples
Conventional *status quo*	Stems from a criminal personality. Should be objectively measured so as to be predicted, controlled, or treated. Emphasis on biopsychological and situational factors.	Ignores or glosses over socio-demographic characteristics.	Deterrence theory, situational crime prevention, actuarial tools, etc.
Social reaction *challenges the status quo*	Socially constructed and cannot be measured objectively. Emphasis on social norms and processes.	Critique of criminalisation, which targets marginalised populations.	Perceptions of justice-involved individuals or institutions, labelling, etc.
Zemiology and critical criminology *alternatives to the status quo*	De-emphasised. Focus is on social harms, radically reforming or even abolishing the criminal-legal system.	Centres marginalised populations and denounces injustices.	Restorative justice, prison abolition, decolonial criminology, etc.

Conventional criminology as the status quo

Conventional criminology has stood out as the dominant research stream since the beginning of the discipline's history and has oriented its development (Cartuyvels, 2007; F.-Dufour et al., 2018). Characterised by a positivist stance on crime, criminals, and crime control, this perspective posits that a *criminal nature* exists and that a *criminal personality* lies within every offender's biology or psychology. What differentiates criminals from non-criminals and what causes crime must thus be unearthed (Cartuyvels, 2007; DeKeseredy, 2010). This positivist stance implies that behaviours can and should be measured objectively. In criminology, the positivist thesis originates from Lombroso's work in the late 19th century, where physical characteristics and nature are indicative of a criminal personality. Although Lombroso's thesis was quickly discarded by the scientific community (Zedner, 1991), the underlying ontology and epistemology still impact criminological research: think of research into criminal genes or into antisocial personality disorder. Following conventional criminology's (neo)positivist imperative, objective measures are necessary to identify the causes of crime, to predict its occurrence, to treat criminals, and to control their behaviours. Conventional criminology also favours optimising the criminal-legal system through accurate and efficient actuarial tools which enable the identification and management of risky populations. This applied criminology then orients penal measures which are considered adapted to criminal individuals (Cartuyvels, 2007).

Social reaction and challenging the status quo

The first challenge to conventional criminology emerged at the end of the 19th and beginning of the 20th century, following Durkheim and the Chicago School whose works confront fundamental premises by asserting that a criminal essence does not exist (Cartuyvels, 2007). Instead of framing deviant or criminalised behaviour as the result of psychology or biology, proponents argue that social factors such as anomie or poverty contribute to crime. Social reaction reframes crime as a social construct defined through a normative framework such as law (Cartuyvels, 2007). The social reaction perspective argues it is impossible to study criminals and crimes objectively because these do not possess an ontological status; they do not exist thus can only be studied empirically through a constructivist stance (Cartuyvels, 2007).

Studies in the social reaction stream offer a critical reading of criminalisation, of the application of social and penal norms, and of these norms' effects on communities and individuals (Bertrand, 2008; Cartuyvels, 2007; DeKeseredy, 2010; F.-Dufour et al., 2018). Marginalisation processes affecting individuals and communities become the focus of these studies. Indeed, the status quo is no longer bearable to those who are consistently targeted by social and penal state interventions based on their race, class, citizenship, and more.

Critical criminologies and alternatives to the status quo

Critical criminology is a theoretical current characterised by the will to reform science and therefore includes several perspectives such as feminist criminology, Marxist criminology, green criminology, and cultural criminology (Renzetti, 2018; Pepinsky, 2006; White, 2013; Muzzatti and Smith, 2018). These perspectives do not limit themselves to state definitions of crime. They can include the search for alternatives to controlling crime and criminality, for example through penal abolitionism and restorative justice (F.-Dufour et al., 2018). To challenge the political, economic, or social status quo, critical criminologies focus on social justice by considering interactions between structures such as gender, race, and class. Unlike conventional criminology, critical criminology allows researchers to focus on traditionally overlooked crimes like white-collar crimes, sexual and gender-based violence, the abuse of state power, and crimes against humanity (DeKeseredy and Dragiewicz, 2018; Wemmers, 2017). Critical criminology also facilitates the consideration of victims and their needs while allowing the researcher a free political posture rather than a superficial neutrality; per this perspective, no study, methodology, data collection, or analysis can claim it is 'value free' (DeKeseredy and Dragiewicz, 2007: 877).

For instance, antiracist and decolonial approaches have emerged as responses to unequal balances of power in criminological research. Conventional criminology 'has tended to focus on the numerical incidence of race and disproportionality in criminal justice outcomes, defaulting to a positivist lens of quantification, rather than theorising race's complex material and symbolic manifestations in the intersection with crime, control and social order' (Phillips et al., 2020: 2). Further, foundational criminological work is overtly racist and eugenistic, while even critical perspectives have invested colour-blindness (Phillips et al., 2020). In Canada and the UK, criminologists have been more concerned with structural racism in the US rather than in our own backyards, occulting our collective colonial past and present (Maynard, 2017; Phillips et al., 2020). Indigenous populations in Canada are marginalised and targeted by the decision-making mechanisms in which conventional criminology uncritically participates, for example under youth protection services and the criminal-legal system (Clark, n.d.; Posca, 2018). Colonial past and present, systemic discrimination, and socio-economic precariousness exacerbate violence faced by Indigenous people, and particularly women (National Inquiry into Missing and Murdered Indigenous Women and Girls (Canada) et al., 2019).

Similarly, feminist criminologies point out conventional criminology's long-standing tradition of omitting women and girls. Building on social reaction and critical criminologies, feminist criminologies urge researchers to place marginalised women's voices at the heart of research and to develop gender-specific analyses and clinical practices (Balfour and Comack, 2014). Relatedly, queer criminology 'is a theoretical and practical approach that seeks to highlight and draw attention to the stigmatization, the criminalisation, and in many ways the rejection of the Queer community, which is to say the LGBTQ+ (lesbians, gay, bisexual, transgender, and queer) population, as both victims and offenders, by academe and the criminal legal system' (Buist and Lenning 2015: 20). Queer criminology rejects work rooted in homophobia or presenting queer individuals as perverse deviants, while drawing upon feminist and other critical criminologies as well as queer theory (Buist and Lenning, 2015).

Zemiology is the study of social harms (F.-Dufour et al., 2018; Ugwudike, 2015). Zemiologists consider crime as a social construct which should be redefined to include violations of fundamental human rights (Schwendinger and Schwendinger, 1970). Indeed, dependence on powerful institutions tends to legitimise the criminalisation of several social prejudices, like the institutionalisation of unhoused or mentally ill individuals as well as people who use drugs (Hillyard and Tombs, 2007). By selecting a handful of social harms and rendering these illegal, the criminal-legal system prioritises a limited category of harms which are then controlled and repressed (Reiman and Leighton, 2015). Thus, zemiologists are interested in all potential causes of suffering such as racism, transportation accidents, abuses of power, or violations of human rights by corporations (F.-Dufour et al., 2018; Hillyard and Tombs, 2007).

Although different from the above perspectives, victimology is worth mentioning due to its specific concern: preventing victims' suffering and favouring their healing (Wemmers, 2003). Indeed, victims' fates have been neglected by conventional criminologists both in research and practice (Wemmers, 2017). Through a human rights approach, victimologists stipulate that crime, as listed in the Criminal Code, is not what exclusively defines the status of victim – thus, today victimology covers a range of subjects such as intergenerational trauma, child soldiers, reconciliation processes, and psychological healing (Wemmers, 2017).

The above perspectives centre marginalised populations and argue in favour of developing knowledges specific to these populations while questioning the criminological status quo. This brings us to the current study, which investigates the prevalence of and relationship between marginalised populations and criminological perspectives at the Montreal School.

Methodology

In this chapter we analyse master's theses and doctoral dissertations[1] published in the Montreal School of Criminology's institutional repository (Papyrus, n.d.). Data collection involved manually extracting metadata for all available theses and dissertations. We deductively coded information contained in the abstract and metadata as all major elements should be included therein. Coding was separated equally between co-authors. We ensured inter-coder agreement by working side by side, by talking through any difficulties until we reached a consensus, and by clarifying the code book[2] as needed.

Our population consists of all theses and dissertations available online as of July 2020 (μ=408). These documents were submitted between 1998 and 2019 (Md=2011, Mo=2016); the repository notes that student production submitted prior to 2003 may not have been uploaded systematically. Most student production was completed at the master's level (n=341; 83.6%). There were 383 separate authors, indicating some students had completed two graduate degrees at the Montreal School. There were 77 (co-) advisors who on average had each supervised six theses or dissertations, although one professor had supervised 10% (n=41) of all student production.

Our dependant variable, *non-conventional perspectives*, as well as our independent variables pertaining to design, domain, and marginalised or otherwise vulnerable populations are described in Table 11.2

Analyses were conducted in SPSS version 23. We calculated frequencies and percentages for all measures. Due to the small number of cases, the non-heterosexual and migrant variables were excluded from bivariate and multivariate analysis. Given our dichotomous dependent variable, multivariate analysis consisted of conducting a series of binary logistic regressions. The following variables were never statistically significant predictors of the dependent variable: gender, victims, substance use and gambling, mental health and personality disorders. Excluding gender and victims never influenced the strength of the model, whereas removing the other two variables reduced Nagelkerke's R^2 by 0.5%. Despite this small effect, substance use and gambling as well as mental health and personality disorders were excluded from the final model as there were too many variables relative to the population size. The model presented in Table 11.3 is the one with the best predictive strength relative to the least number of variables (7, where dummy variables for domain count as 1).

TABLE 11.2 Variables and their dimensions per the coding guide

Variable	Dimensions and coding guide
Non-conventional perspectives (*Dependent variable*)	1=non-conventional. *Social reaction*: attempting to understand social norms and their effects; social construction and representations of crime or criminalised people; labelling. *Zemiology, critical, alternatives*: emphasis on social harms, critiques of and alternatives to the system such as those formulated within feminist or green criminology, transformative justice. (*Combined for multivariate analysis given lack of cases*). 0=conventional. Aetiology and treatment of criminalised or deviant behaviour, profiling, what works, criminal networks, management of populations, etc.
Explicit theoretical framework	1=yes. Includes explicit epistemology. 0=no.
Includes qualitative methods	1=yes. Qualitative or mixed methods. 0=no. Quantitative methods.
Doctoral dissertation	1=yes. 0=no. Master's thesis.
Domain	1=behaviour. Focus on people who commit or endure deviant or criminalised behaviours, or on clinical practices targeting behaviours. 2=event. Emphasis on crime as an event or act, space-time convergence, macroscopic trends in frequency of a given act, forensic trace (*reference group in multivariate analysis*). 3=sociological. *System*: focus on law or policy; public and private organisations responding to crime, for instance police, prisons, probation, and banks; and individuals' experiences living or working within such systems. *Society*: focus on society at large, media coverage, non-justice-involved individuals' perceptions of crime or of the criminal-legal system (excluding professionals working within the system). (*Combined for multivariate analysis due to scarcity of cases*).
Age	1=yes. Considers age or age-related vulnerability such as minors, elderly people, and focus on youth protection services. Includes parents of justice-involved minors since parents can be a proxy, especially for very young children who might not be capable of giving informed consent. 0=no. Includes studies centring those who abuse minors.
Gender	1=yes. Considers women, girls, trans individuals, or gender concepts such as toxic masculinity. 0=no. Includes studies focusing on men who assault women, without reference to a gendered framework.
Non-heterosexual	1=yes. Lesbian, gay, bisexual people were mentioned in the study. 0=no.
Race	1=yes. Considers Indigenous, Black, Arab, Latinx, Asian, or otherwise racialised groups or individuals, or social representations of racialisation. 0=no.

Variable	Dimensions and coding guide
Migrant	1=yes. Considers immigrants or refugees. 0=no.
Class	1=yes. Discusses poverty, houselessness, social capital, unemployment, education level, or white-collar crime. 0=no.
Substance use and gambling	1=yes. Mentions of substance use, abuse, addiction, or gambling. 0=no. Focus on illicit markets involving buying or selling substances.
Mental health and personality disorders	1=yes. Considers problems and illnesses tied to mental health such as suffering, anxiety, or experiencing psychological violence; neurodivergence and personality disorders; as well as psychopathy. 0=no.
Victims	1=yes. Study includes victims of criminalised or deviant acts. 0=no.

TABLE 11.3 Descriptive statistics (μ=408)

Variable	%	N
Criminological perspectives		
Conventional	71.6	292
Social reaction	21.8	89
Zemiology, critical, alternatives	6.6	27
Design		
Explicit theoretical framework	36.5	149
Qualitative or mixed methods	52.6	215
Doctoral dissertation	16.4	67
Domain		
Behaviour	53.9	220
Event	13.5	55
System	27.7	113
Society	4.9	20
Marginalised and vulnerable populations		
Age	31.6	129
Gender	21.3	87
Non-heterosexual	0.5	2
Race	9.8	40
Migrants	3.4	14
Class	12.5	51
Substance use and gambling	14.2	58
Mental health and personality disorders	20.1	82
Victims	17.9	73

Results

Descriptive results

Table 11.3 presents descriptive statistics for our population of 408 theses and dissertations from the Montreal School, completed between 1998 and 2019 and published online.

More than two in three studies rely on conventional *criminological perspectives*; one in five focus on social reaction; one in 15 rely on zemiology, critical criminology, or alternatives. In terms of *design*, only one in three abstracts explicitly mention a theoretical or epistemological framework; one in two studies deploy qualitative methods at least in part; one in six are doctoral dissertations. As for *domain*, more than half of student production focuses on criminal or deviant behaviour; a quarter centre systems, institutions, or organisations; one in eight consider crime as an event; one in 20 focus on citizens, media, or social representations of criminological subject matter. Nearly one third of student production focuses on groups facing age-related vulnerability; of these 129 studies, only three consider elderly populations. One in five studies consider gender and one in five consider mental illnesses or personality disorders. Although 35.8% of studies focus on types of crimes which implicate a human victim whose physical or psychological integrity is affected (n=146), only 17.9% of studies consider victims. One in seven studies consider substance use and gambling. One in eight studies consider class and, of these, one in five focus on houselessness (n=9). About one in ten studies consider race and, of these, one in five are specifically about Indigenous people (n=8). Of 408 studies, 14 consider migrants and refugees and only two explicitly consider non-heterosexual individuals.

Multivariate results

Table 11.4 presents results from a logistic regression predicting reliance on non-conventional perspectives within the Montreal School's student production, based on population and domain variables.

The model successfully predicts reliance on non-conventional perspectives which question the status quo (Chi^2=149.43, $p<0.001$). The model predicts outcomes in the dependant variable more accurately than having no model (Nagelkerke R^2=0.457, where 0 would mean the model is no better than having no model, and where 1 would indicate a perfect prediction).

Based on the odds ratios, studies considering race and those centring the sociological domain show the strongest likelihood of adopting a non-conventional criminological perspective. Indeed, studies considering race are over seven times more likely to question the status quo as opposed to those which do not specify race. Studies focusing on sociological aspects within criminology are over six times more likely to question the status quo than those which focus on

TABLE 11.4 Binary logistic regression predicting non-conventional perspectives within student production at the Montreal School based on design, population, and domain (μ=408)

Independent variables	Odds ratio		SE	95% CI Lower	Upper
Design					
Incl. qualitative methods	5.882	***	0.345	2.992	11.564
Theoretical framework	2.266	**	0.296	1.269	4.048
Doctoral dissertation	2.484	*	0.361	1.223	5.044
Populations					
Age	0.316	**	0.363	0.155	0.643
Class	4.179	**	0.424	1.821	9.588
Race	7.317	***	0.455	2.998	17.858
Domain					
Event	Ref.		Ref.	Ref.	Ref.
Sociological	6.482	***	0.511	2.380	17.655
Behavioural	1.557		0.504	0.580	4.179
Constant	0.023	***	0.553		
μ	408				
Nagelkerke R^2	0.457				
Cox & Snell R^2	0.318				
Chi^2	149.430	***			

Note: SE: standard error; CI: confidence interval. *: $p<0.05$. **: $p<0.01$. ***: $p<0.001$.

crime as an event. Studies relying at least in part on qualitative methods are nearly six times more likely to adopt a non-conventional perspective than exclusively quantitative studies. Studies mentioning indicators of social class are four times more likely to question the status quo than those which do not mention class. Studies considering minors or the elderly are over three times more likely to *take part* in the status quo. Doctoral dissertations are more than twice as likely to question the status quo than master's theses, as are studies mentioning a theoretical framework in the abstract as opposed to those which do not. Lastly, studies focusing on crime as a behaviour rather than as an event are not statistically significant predictors of questioning the status quo.

Discussion

In this chapter, we present results from a study attempting to gain insights into criminological perspectives and underlying epistemologies at the Montreal School of Criminology in Québec, Canada. We examine the prevalence of and relationship between marginalised populations and criminological perspectives based on 20 years and over 400 theses and dissertations published by the Montreal School, positing that student production magnifies departmental and disciplinary trends.

Unsurprisingly, the majority of student production at the Montreal School of Criminology relies on conventional perspectives such as the aetiology of crime, population management, the *what works* perspective, and clinical approaches to treating or reducing criminal behaviours. Most of the remaining studies fall into the social reaction category, meaning core concerns include understanding social norms and their effects, the social construction of crime and deviance, labelling, or the legitimacy of control. Only a handful of studies focus on social harms and critiques of, and alternatives to, current systems. These results tell us that the Montreal School of Criminology remains committed to conventional criminology, which we interpret as reflective of various institutional, social, and professional pressures on the production of criminological knowledges. Indeed, students are likely to choose topics aligning with their professors' areas of expertise, which in turn may be influenced by the department's heritage, local and international disciplinary trends, funding agencies' priorities, and the tendency to hire the School's own graduates (Brantingham et al., 2018; F.-Dufour et al., 2018). This aligns with prior research identifying a 'Montreal School effect' within the province's French-language criminological journal, meaning that scholars educated at or affiliated to this department tend to publish conventional criminological work (F.-Dufour et al., 2018). Further, given the commercialisation and commodification of higher education, the topics, theories, methodologies, and overall perspectives chosen by graduate students may favour expediency over in-depth, critical engagement.

A minority of student production falls within non-conventional criminological perspectives such as social reaction, critical criminology, zemiology, and reparative justice. Considering the Montreal School's historical attachment to conventional criminology, as well as other institutional, social, and professional pressures, graduate students may be less familiar with or less interested in non-conventional perspectives. Non-conventional criminology's lack of prevalence is also reflected within provincial publications (Bertrand, 2008; F.-Dufour et al., 2018).

As for domain, more than half of dissertations and theses focus on behavioural aspects of criminology, meaning these centre individuals who commit or are targeted by criminalised or deviant behaviours, or clinical interventions meant to reduce such behaviours. This makes sense since the department was founded as a professional School with a strong emphasis on applied social sciences and clinical intervention, while currently being closely linked to a professional order (Bertrand 2008; Quirion, 2018). This may also explain why only one third of theses and dissertations explicitly mention a theoretical or epistemological framework; students and their supervisors may feel less of a need to draw on theory to understand and orient real-world practices, although, of course, all scholars could benefit from in-depth engagement with these issues (e.g., Garland, 1992). It is also important to reiterate that we coded abstracts and metadata: theoretical frameworks may be explicit within the documents themselves.

Among the marginalised and vulnerable populations we screened for, age, gender, and mental health and personality disorders are most often considered within student production. One third of theses and dissertations consider groups who face age-related vulnerability – mostly minors – while one in five consider gender, and the same proportion include mental health and personality disorders. Although gender is accounted for in a minority of studies, one in five is a much higher prevalence than anticipated. Indeed, the tenets of feminist criminology underscore mainstream criminology's general lack of interest towards women and girls (Balfour and Comack, 2014). Overall, although one third of studies focus on crimes which affect human victims, only one in six studies include victims. This aligns with victimology's tenet that victims are often overlooked within criminology (Wemmers, 2017). From over 400 studies, only two explicitly consider non-heterosexual individuals, confirming queer criminology's tenet that academia neglects queer populations (Buist and Lenning, 2015).

Less than one in ten studies consider race and one in 50 consider Indigenous peoples. This reflects criminology's tendency to avoid discussing race and colonialism (Phillips et al., 2020; Maynard, 2017). While coding we got the impression that many studies intentionally avoid mentioning race and class even when it is implicit to the subject matter. We counted 27 studies where race or ethnicity are omitted despite thinly veiled assumptions pertaining to whom is involved in street gangs, terrorism, or extremism (6.6%). This could be indicative of white settler scholars' so-called colour-blindness and discomfort in identifying and addressing race due to white guilt, fear of being called racist, and denial of the colonial status quo (Regan, 2010). Slightly more studies consider class than the number of studies considering race, perhaps reflecting the wider trend of flattening race in favour of discussing class (Phillips et al., 2020).

Our results indicate that studies considering racialised populations, the sociological domain, social class, or relying on qualitative methods show the strongest likelihood of relying on non-conventional criminological perspectives. Doctoral dissertations and studies with explicit theoretical frameworks also increase this likelihood. In other words, the minority of criminologists who intentionally engage with race and poverty do so through critical, zemiological, and social reaction perspectives. This engagement may precede students' work or may have emerged through contact with these populations' own wariness towards the criminal-legal system (Maynard, 2017). Studies which include systemic or structural subject matter potentially allow critical engagement with power structures as opposed to behavioural criminological studies, which are perhaps more strongly tied to clinicians taught to work *within* the system rather than against it (Bertrand, 2008; Quirion, 2018). As for qualitative studies, those published by *Criminologie* invoke epistemological, ethical, and political justifications, such as denouncing inequities and the importance of centring social actors' own voices as found within standpoint feminism and cultural studies

(Poupart and Couvrette, 2018), whereas quantitative publications are intrinsically tied to conventional perspectives (F.-Dufour et al., 2018). It makes sense that dissertations and theses completed at the School housing this journal would show similar tendencies.

Doctoral dissertations may also be more likely to question the status quo given the much longer and deeper engagement with theory and data which is expected at this level. Similarly, theory-driven master's theses may afford more space to critical analysis than practice-driven work. We wish to be clear that we are not demeaning our peers, simply pointing out systemic issues regarding our department and discipline's inner workings. In our experience, our graduate student peers are critical thinkers and many view non-conventional criminologies quite positively. Some peers have told us they choose to adopt a conventional perspective in their work for various reasons, including: because they have never learned about other perspectives, due to pre-existing datasets, in order to graduate more quickly, through fear their supervisors would reject non-conventional approaches, through fear this would antagonise the institutions they study, and due to feelings of inadequacy when faced with the inaccessible language of theory-heavy work.

As for studies considering populations who are vulnerable given their age, these *decrease* the likelihood of relying on non-conventional perspectives, meaning these are heavily linked to conventional criminological perspectives. The overwhelming majority of these studies focus on minors, youth protection services, and clinical interventions aimed to prevent youths from offending. In other words, these studies tend to be more concerned with protecting children and avoiding future criminal careers than criticising systems which punish children and tear them away from their families (Maynard, 2017).

Overall, our results point to a co-constitutive relationship between conventional criminology and the Montreal School. Turning our gaze to criminology produced within the Global North may illuminate the widespread emphasis on conventional criminology in our department. Tracing citation networks within English-language criminology journals, Koehler's (2019) dissertation identifies core themes and theories which are consistently engaged with – pointing to a conventional criminology. Authors working within the periphery (what we refer to as non-conventional) also engage with these core themes, whereas the opposite cannot be said. This strengthens the difference between the core and the periphery (Koehler, 2019) or, in our words, between the status quo and its critiques or alternatives. Commenting on French, British, and American criminology, Mary (2020) similarly observes fashionable topics taking root while non-conventional perspectives have sharply declined since their heyday in the 1970s to 1990s. As we have discussed, conventional criminology tends to ignore certain marginalised populations. For instance, British criminology's neglect of marginalised populations can be understood as the extension of dominant manners of thinking embodied by those holding power within the wider context of neoliberalism (Loader and Sparks, 2012).

Our analysis also points to similarities between studies with conventional and non-conventional perspectives when considering certain other marginalised and vulnerable populations. Indeed, inclusion of victims, gender, mental health and personality disorders, substance use, and gambling never predict reliance on non-conventional perspectives. This means that although marginalised populations are considered in a minority of studies, those studies which do include such populations draw on a range of criminological perspectives. This is encouraging from a methodological standpoint. Indeed, one of our common goals as scientists is arguably to do 'good' science. But how good can our science be if it neglects the very populations who are criminalised, victimised, and present within the systems and institutions we study?

Conclusion

As described in our positionality statements, we are criminologists from marginalised backgrounds who work with marginalised populations and within non-conventional perspectives. As such, we have consistently felt stifled by the overwhelming emphasis on conventional criminology within the Montreal School. We cannot condone conventional criminology which embodies 'violence work' (Kitossa and Tanyildiz, 2022) and rests on 'paradigms of repression' (Bertrand, 2008). Yet we do not consider ourselves to have the moral nor academic high ground, nor do we presume we can tell colleagues what to do. We can simply urge criminologists in Montreal and beyond, focusing on all domains and working within all perspectives, to afford more importance to marginalised populations and to meaningfully account for race and class. As Phillips et al. (2020: 2) underscore, mere inclusion of race as a variable is insufficient but should reflect a 'substantive engagement with race's constitutive dynamism' and an explicit theorisation of race and racism. Criminologists would also benefit from engaging with criminological knowledges produced in the Global South and from engaging with abolitionist criminology (Loader and Sparks, 2012; Kitossa and Tanyildiz, 2022).

The inner workings of a department have the potential to influence criminology as a discipline, in addition to structuring research and intervention methods. According to Quirion (2018), criminological training must integrate critical perspectives so practitioners can work with humanist and reflexive perspectives, while separating themselves from institutions of social control. We argue this is equally important when training researchers, lest the knowledge we produce be used to strengthen repressive and violent institutions.

In closing, we encourage our colleagues to engage in disciplinary reflexivity (Phillips et al., 2020). To remain relevant, the Montreal School and our western peers need to renew and freshen our perspectives both in research and within clinical training. Since instigating this project in 2020, we have seen evidence of such changes through the Montreal School's interdisciplinary hires, new courses, and the creation of financial incentives for Indigenous students. We can only hope for more in the coming years.

Notes

1 Other types of student production such as internship reports are excluded as these are not subjected to the same requirements and do not place the same level of emphasis on research.
2 Our database and full codebook are available online in French (Marcoux Rouleau, Melouka, and Pérusse-Roy, 2022a, 2022b).

Acknowledgements

We thank professors Chloé Leclerc, Ashley T. Rubin, and Johann Koehler for their encouragements, as well as the Montreal School of Criminology and the International Centre for Comparative Criminology for their help in funding this research.

References

Balfour, Gillian, and Elizabeth Comack, eds. 2014. *Criminalizing Women: Gender and (in)Justice in Neo-Liberal Times.* Black Point, Nova Scotia: Fernwood Publishing.
Barton, Alana, Karen Corteen, Julie Davies, and Anita Hobson. 2010. 'Reading the Word and Reading the World: The Impact of a Critical Pedagogical Approach to the Teaching of Criminology in Higher Education.' *Journal of Criminal Justice Education* 21(1): 24–41.
Bertrand, Marie-Andrée. 2008. 'Nouveaux Courants en Criminologie: "Études sur la Justice" et "Zémiologie".' *Criminologie* 41(1): 177–200.
Brantingham, Paul, Patricia Brantingham, and Bryan Kinney. 2018. 'Criminology in Canada: The Context of Its Criminology.' In *The Handbook of the History and Philosophy of Criminology*, edited by Ruth Ann Triplett, pp. 360–376. Hoboken, NJ: John Wiley & Sons, Inc.
Buist, Carrie, and Emily Lenning. 2015. *Queer Criminology.* London: Routledge.
Cartuyvels, Yves. 2007. 'La Criminologie et ses Objets Paradoxaux: Retour sur un Débat Plus Actuel Que Jamais?' *Deviance et Societe* 31(4): 445–464.
Chadwick, Rachelle. 2021. 'On the Politics of Discomfort.' *Feminist Theory*, 22(4): 556–574.
Clark, Scott. n.d. 'Surreprésentation des Autochtones dans le Système de Justice Pénale Canadien: Causes et Réponses.' Division de la Recherche et de la Statistique (DRS) du Ministère de la Justice.
DeKeseredy, Walter S. 2010. *Contemporary Critical Criminology.* New York: Routledge.
DeKeseredy, Walter S., and Molly Dragiewicz. 2007. 'Understanding the Complexities of Feminist Perspectives on Woman Abuse: A Commentary on Donald G. Dutton's Rethinking Domestic Violence.' *Violence Against Women* 13(8): 874–884.
DeKeseredy, Walter S., and Molly Dragiewicz. 2018. *Routledge Handbook of Critical Criminology*, 2nd ed. London: Routledge.
École de criminologie. n.d. 'Présentation.' École de criminologie – Université de Montréal. https://crim.umontreal.ca/notre-ecole/presentation/ (last accessed 7 January 2022).
F.-Dufour, Isabelle, Marie-Pierre Villeneuve, and Joane Martel. 2018. 'Portrait de la Criminologie Québécoise des Dix Dernières Années Selon le Courant, la Méthodologie et l'appartenance Institutionnelle des Auteurs.' *Criminologie* 51(1): 143–167.
Foucault, Michel. 1975. *Surveiller et Punir: Naissance de la Prison.* Paris: Gallimard.
Frost, Natasha A., and Todd R. Clear. 2007. 'Doctoral Education in Criminology and Criminal Justice.' *Journal of Criminal Justice Education* 18(1): 35–52.

Garland, David. 1992. 'Criminological Knowledge and its Relation to Power – Foucault's Genealogy and Criminology Today British Criminology Conference 1991.' *British Journal of Criminology* 32(4): 403–422.
Giroux, Dalie. 2020. *L'œil du Maître: Figures de l'imaginaire Colonial Québécois*. Montréal, Québec: Mémoire d'encrier.
Hillyard, Paddy, and Steve Tombs. 2007. 'From "Crime" to Social Harm?' *Crime, Law and Social Change* 48(1): 9–25.
Kitossa, Tamari, and Gökbörü Sarp Tanyildiz. 2022. 'Anti-Blackness, Criminology and the University as Violence Work: Diversity as Ritual and the Professionalization of Repression in Canada.' In *Diversity in Criminology and Criminal Justice Studies*, edited by Derek M. D. Silva and Mathieu Deflem, pp. 39–61. Sociology of Crime, Law and Deviance. Bingley: Emerald Publishing Limited.
Koehler, Johann. 2015. 'Development and Fracture of a Discipline: Legacies of the School of Criminology at Berkeley.' *Criminology* 53(4): 513–544.
Koehler, Johann. 2019. 'Making Crime a Science: The Rise of Evidence-Based Criminal Justice Policy.' UC Berkeley. https://escholarship.org/uc/item/9zg905pr (last accessed 7 January 2022).
Laidler, Karen Joe, and Maggy Lee. 2016. 'Thirty Years of Criminology at HKU: Themes and Trends in Crime and Its Control.' *Social Transformations in Chinese Societies* 12(1): 21–36.
Loader, Ian, and Richard Sparks. 2012. 'Situating Criminology: On the Production and Consumption of Knowledge About Crime and Justice.' In *The Oxford Handbook of Criminology*, edited by Rodney Morgan, Robert Reiner, and Mike Maguire, 5th ed., pp. 3–38. New York: Oxford University Press.
Marcoux Rouleau, Alexis, Ismehen Melouka, and Maude Pérusse-Roy. 2022a. 'Base de Données des Mémoires et Thèses de l'École de Criminologie de l'Université de Montréal 1998–2020.' *ResearchGate*. 5 January 2022. doi:10.13140/RG.2.2.34175.48806.
Marcoux Rouleau, Alexis, Ismehen Melouka, and Maude Pérusse-Roy. 2022b. 'Livret de Codification.' *ResearchGate*. 12 May 2022. doi:10.13140/RG.2.2.25786.88002.
Mary, Philippe. 2020. 'Réflexions sur la Criminologie Critique.' In *Enjeux Criminologiques Contemporains: Au-Delà de l'insécurité et de l'exclusion*, edited by Carolyn Côté-Lussier, David Moffette, and Justin Piché, pp. 261–270. Ottawa: Les Presses de l'Université d'Ottawa.
Maynard, Robyn. 2017. *Policing Black Lives: State Violence in Canada from Slavery to the Present*. Black Point, Nova Scotia: Fernwood Publishing.
Muzzatti, Stephen L., and Emma M. Smith. 2018. 'Cultural Criminology.' In *Routledge Handbook of Critical Criminology*, edited by Walter S. DeKeseredy and Molly Dragiewicz, 2nd ed.London: Routledge.
National Inquiry into Missing and Murdered Indigenous Women and Girls (Canada), Marion Buller, Michèle Audette, Brian Eyolfson, and Qajaq Robinson. 2019. 'Reclaiming Power and Place: The Final Report of the National Inquiry into Missing and Murdered Indigenous Women and Girls.' https://www.mmiwg-ffada.ca/final-report/ (last accessed 7 January 2022).
Papyrus. n.d. 'Faculté des Arts et des Sciences – École de Criminologie – Thèses et Mémoires.' Université de Montréal Institutional Repository. https://papyrus.bib.umontreal.ca/xmlui/handle/1866/3002 (last accessed 7 January 2022).
Pepinsky, Harold E. 2006. *Peacemaking: Reflections of a Radical Criminologist*. Ottawa: University of Ottawa Press.
Phillips, Coretta, Rod Earle, Alpa Parmar, and Daniel Smith. 2020. 'Dear British Criminology: Where Has All the Race and Racism Gone?' *Theoretical Criminology* 24 (3): 427–446.

Posca, Julia. 2018. 'Portrait des Inégalités Socioéconomiques Touchant les Autochtones au Québec.' P-423. Institut de Recherche et d'informations Socioéconomiques.

Poupart, Jean, and Amélie Couvrette. 2018. 'Les Méthodes Qualitatives en "Terrain Criminologique": Mise en Perspective et Usage de ces Méthodes dans la revue Criminologie.' *Criminologie* 51(1): 201–229.

Quirion, Bastien. 2018. 'Un Demi-Siècle d'intervention en Criminologie. Approche Critique et Enjeux Actuels Autour de la Création de l'Ordre Professionnel des Criminologues du Québec.' *Criminologie* 51(1): 291–315.

Radatz, Dana L., and Danielle C. Slakoff. 2021. 'A Practical Guide to the Criminology and Criminal Justice Job Market for Doctoral Candidates: Pre-Market Preparation through Offers and Negotiations.' *Journal of Criminal Justice Education* 0(0): 1–20.

Regan, Paulette. 2010. *Unsettling the Settler Within: Indian Residential Schools, Truth Telling, and Reconciliation in Canada*. Vancouver: UBC Press.

Reiman, Jeffrey, and Paul Leighton. 2015. *The Rich Get Richer and the Poor Get Prison: A Reader*. New York: Routledge.

Renzetti, Claire M. 2018. 'Feminist Perspectives.' In *Routledge Handbook of Critical Criminology*, edited by Walter S. DeKeseredy and Molly Dragiewicz, 2nd ed. London: Routledge.

Schwendinger, Herman, and Julia Schwendinger. 1970. 'Defenders of Order or Guardians of Human Rights.' *Issues in Criminology* 5(2): 123–158.

Sitren, Alicia H., and Brandon K. Applegate. 2012. 'Hiring Criminology and Criminal Justice Academics: The Perceived Importance of Job Candidates' Attributes.' *Journal of Criminal Justice Education* 23(1): 23–40.

Stockdale, Kelly J., and Rowan Sweeney. 2019. 'Exploring the Criminology Curriculum.' In *Papers from the British Criminology Conference* 19: 84–105. London: British Society of Criminology.

Stockdale, Kelly J., Rowan Sweeney, and Clare McCluskey Dean. 2021. 'Exploring the Criminology Curriculum – Using the Intersectionality Matrix as a Pedagogical Tool to Develop Students' Critical Information Literacy Skills.' *Journal of Criminal Justice Education* 0(0): 1–19.

Ugwudike, Pamela. 2015. *An Introduction to Critical Criminology*. Bristol: Policy Press.

Wemmers, Jo-Anne M. 2003. *Introduction à la Victimologie*. Montréal, Québec: Presses de l'Université de Montréal.

Wemmers, Jo-Anne M. 2017. *Victimology: A Canadian Perspective*. Toronto: University of Toronto Press, Higher Education Division.

White, Rob. 2013. 'The Conceptual Contours of Green Criminology.' In *Emerging Issues in Green Criminology: Exploring Power, Justice and Harm*, edited by Reece Walters, Diane Solomon Westerhuis, and Tanya Wyatt, pp. 17–33. Critical Criminological Perspectives. London: Palgrave Macmillan.

Zedner, Lucia. 1991. 'Women, Crime, and Penal Responses: A Historical Account.' *Crime and Justice* 14: 307–362.

12

BRINGING PRISON ABOLITION FROM THE MARGINS TO THE CENTRE

Utilising Storywork to Decentre Carceral Logic in Supervision and Beyond

Latoya Aroha Rule and Michele Jarldorn

Introduction

This chapter critically presents an argument for abolishing the Prison Industrial Complex (PIC) and is located within the story of how our roles as teacher and learner overlap, becoming much more than the 'typical' student-supervisor role, and ultimately how we continue to develop our relationship toward solidarity as abolitionists. This is because, at its foundation, abolitionism requires an understanding of relationality. We employ the idea of research as resistance (Brown and Strega, 2005) from our position as being the 'type' of People who are usually 'researched on' through our membership in various marginalised groups. Drawing on our personal stories throughout this work speaks to more than who we are as individuals; instead, our stories reflect our 'worldview and value system' (Behrendt, 2019: 175) and consider how those views and values shape our work and our relationship. This approach in part follows a 'Decolonizing Indigenous Storywork' Methodology (Archibald et al., 2019), alongside Brown and Strega's suggestion that there is both a 'need and necessity for researchers to not only acknowledge but also examine their location and how that location permeates their inquiry at every level' (2005: 10). Hence, we begin by locating and positioning ourselves.

Latoya descends from Aboriginal – Wiradjuri, and Māori – Te Ātiawa peoples. They are a non-binary, Takatāpui (queer) person who grew up on Kaurna Land (Adelaide) and now resides on Gadigal Land (Sydney) where they work as a Research Associate and PhD candidate at Jumbunna Institute. Due to family violence and its negative effects, Latoya was an early high school leaver, entering university after completing a free, community-based education programme. As a creative process, Latoya utilises podcasting in their research work to open space and opportunities to publish with communities who have experienced the deaths of their loved ones in police custody, prisons, and through state-sanctioned violence.

DOI: 10.4324/9781003260967-15

Latoya's honours research, which Michele co-supervised, utilised Indigenous Standpoint Theory and Thematic Discourse Analysis to explore the 2014 death in custody of a young Aboriginal woman, Ms. Dhu, in Western Australia (Rule, 2019). As an abolitionist, Latoya advocates against state violence – particularly focusing on coronial inquests and other legal processes relating to deaths in custody, violent restraints, uses of force, and especially the use of spit hoods.

Michele is a white woman; a settler in a colonial state living on unceded Kaurna Land. She is a survivor of domestic violence, raised a child as a sole parent, and spent some of this time homeless. Like Latoya, she did not complete high school and entered university as a mature-aged student. Her doctoral research used Photovoice to learn about the experiences of prison and release of formerly incarcerated People, arguing that the project of abolition fits well within a radical social work framework (Jarldorn, 2018).

In positioning ourselves in this way, we are neither objective nor neutral but view our research, teaching, and activism as seeking emancipatory social change. Our lived experiences of racial, gendered, and class-based violence inform our academic work. We volunteer in the communities we research alongside as part of our contribution to prison abolition. Hence, we recognise the importance of utilising Standpoint Theory (Harding, 2004; Moreton-Robinson, 2015) throughout this chapter. We acknowledge and are grateful for the determination, activism, allyship, and intellectual contributions that abolitionists outside of universities have contributed to how we think, act, and write (see, for example, Warriors of the Aboriginal Resistance, Indigenous Peoples Movement, Sisters Inside, Critical Resistance).

Utilising Storywork as a decolonising methodology

Yarning or Storytelling in a decolonising sense is the foundation for building culturally safe relationships which are steeped in respect and awareness. Articulating their standpoint further, Rule (2019: 12–14) explains:

> I do not seek to, nor can I expect to, become a knower in certain aspects of my own world because I am not limited to a capitalist Western-scientific epistemology that constructs knowledge as exhaustive and absolute. Importantly, my Creator and Ancestors, and their inter-spatial transfer of knowledge, guide my understandings and thus, my choices and actions continue to be informed by them. This stands in contrast to a Western-scientific epistemology … Yarning (storytelling) is integral to decolonising research as it not only offers context through disrupting Western-scientific research paradigms but also provides a more nuanced comprehension of phenomena forming Indigenous knowledge production.

The space to share stories and voice is rarely afforded to First Nations Peoples. Indigenous knowledges have long been silenced by dominant colonising discourses. Linda Tuhiwai Smith (2012: 64) explains that 'imperialism and colonialism are the specific formations through which the west came to "see", to "name" and to "know" Indigenous communities', arguing that research practices positioning Aboriginal People and knowledge systems as inferior and uncivilised are both unethical and commonplace. Hence, the relationship fostered between student and supervisor in our circumstance was intentionally cognisant of promoting a decolonising framework, working to resist the continuation of the colonial legacy to subjugate Aboriginal knowledges through building a different type of practice within and between us, from within the institution.

Tanganekald and Meintangk woman, Professor Irene Watson (2016), argues that as a method, Storywork resists 'ongoing colonial ordering'. When Peoples' stories, those of the 'researched' and the researcher, are negated to the periphery this can be experienced and explained as acts of violence, violence that silences the truths of lived experience, thus privileging the perspectives of colonial power. Watson (2016: 33) defines colonial violence and power as a product of the continuing colonial project, arguing that:

> The colonial project is ultimately about justifying the occupation and exploitation of Indigenous Land and the maintenance of unequal relationships between non-native and native; it is of paramount importance that the colonised remain contained as objects of the colonial state. And for the Indigenous, the only trajectory is to become totally absorbed and assimilated into the state.

Using Storywork as a method (Archibald et al., 2019) values storytelling as a powerful mechanism for articulating thousands of years of knowledge existing well before colonial conquest (McQuire, 2019). For Aboriginal People, stories have been used to translate at least 80,000 years of history and intergenerational experiences orally, through art, drawings, paintings, and weaving, for navigation, sustainability, and survival. Storywork is also resistance work as this method does not normally fit into the neat, quick search for answers in research or teaching through western viewpoints. Instead, stories privilege subjugated narratives of survival over neoliberal, carceral strategies of restriction. Stories in this sense are respectful of perspectives and experiences, more so than the ordinary value provided to 'timeframes', 'timeliness', and 'timely submission', each of which, in the context of research, are constructs supporting the hegemonic narrative of western university systems. Providing space and time for stories contributes to healing from trauma (Behrendt, 2019). Time structures lived experiences; while in a capitalist world, time is a generous gift. For Behrendt (2019: 183) storytelling is an aspect of self-determination, arguing that storytelling 'takes our voices from the margins and puts them in the centre. That should be a guiding part of our practice'. Sharing, respecting, and developing our story has been the central theme upon which we have built our allyship and is the method we have used to create this chapter; hence, we begin by reflecting upon how we first met.

Our collaboration grew out of a meeting at a new student information session. As an eager PhD student trying to fit in at university, Michele volunteered to talk to new students about where their studies might take them, using that platform to talk about her role in working with people whose gambling had seen them become entangled in the criminal 'injustice' system. Latoya was drawn to Michele's story, sensing that Michele could see past the constraints of the institution in applying value to what Latoya articulates as 'the why behind the what' or the life behind the outcome. At that first meeting, we were 'seen' by each other, through recognition of our lived experiences of membership of marginalised groups. This was a refreshing alternative to being seen as 'lesser than' for what we lacked in formal preparation for university.

Since then, we have shared and learned a lot about ourselves. We both pursued formal study to practically support our families, financially, materially, and emotionally. For Latoya, while growing up in family violence impacted their adulthood, university enabled their development as an advocate for themselves, their family, and their community. Latoya often turned to Michele as a trusted support person in their journey, while it was Michele who introduced Latoya to abolitionist discourse to articulate their lived experience in the academy.

Michele openly shared her lived experience with Latoya, building trust, understanding, and rapport. Behrendt (2019: 176) articulates an Indigenous standpoint and worldview as opposite to western traditions of objectivity, stating that 'Indigenous approaches ... understand that where you are placed – your positioning or your standpoint – will fundamentally influence the way you see the world'. Little did we imagine that a decade later we would consider each other extended family, or be writing together as we are here to reflect upon how our commitment to change through scholarly activism shapes our work.

Our experiences of the PIC, especially as young people, were vastly different. Michele remembers that as a child her family would drive past Yatala Labour Prison (YLP) on their way into the city. Every time, her father would point to the prison to remind any kids mucking around in the back seat of the car, 'that's where you'll end up if you don't behave'. YLP is an imposing series of buildings, set back from the road on a hill, not far from Adelaide's CBD. The visible placement of prisons in this way is not accidental. Instead, it is a purposeful visual reminder, a not-so-subtle act of social control, and a threat to the community of the possibility of imprisonment – and death.

Michele did end up in YLP, and the neighbouring Adelaide Women's Prison, although as a newly graduated social worker. For 18 months Michele was a 'professional visitor' in her role as a gambling counsellor, specialising in working with women. The experience was transformative. It became obvious that prisons are incapable of being therapeutic spaces and that a significant majority of prisoners experienced interpersonal and structural violence and were members of oppressed and marginalised groups. Women eligible for early release options could not access this through the lack of housing. When they were released, most returned to the same social problems underpinning their criminalisation. Experiences of release were rarely smooth. It was not unusual for women to be turned out of the gates with no ID, no money, and a clear plastic bag of belongings, often into homelessness (Jarldorn et al., 2022). Some women's previous experiences of release were so traumatising, they chose not to seek the early release they were entitled to, while many came to fear an impending release date.

Latoya had been inside prisons as a visitor of family members since they were a young child – but they never imagined they would experience the grief of a loved one dying inside. In 2016, Latoya's brother, Wayne Fella Morrison, a 29-year-old father, fisherman, and artist died after being remanded in custody for six days in YLP. He was cuffed, with a spit hood forced over his head, and placed face down in the prone position in the back of a prison transport van with eight guards inside. He died three days later in the intensive care unit of the Royal Adelaide Hospital (for a detailed account, see Kurmelovs, 2018). Since the Royal Commission into Aboriginal Deaths in Custody (RCIADIC) (1991) report was released, every Aboriginal death in custody prompts a mandatory coronial inquest to investigate the underlying cause and the factors surrounding the death. There have been few cases where charges have been laid, and there have been zero convictions for any of these deaths.

Aboriginal deaths in custody

In 1987 the RCIADIC was formed to investigate why Aboriginal People were dying in custody in Australia. The RCIADIC concluded that young Aboriginal men and women were the targets of police surveillance, with police brutality and racism playing a significant part in the rate of deaths in custody. In her 'Dark Tourism' essay, Brook (2009: 266) reflects upon memories of visiting her brother when he was in Adelaide Gaol in order to critically analyse the findings of the RCIADIC, writing:

> Indigenous prisoners may have been no more likely to die in custody than any other prisoners but were far more likely – 29 times more likely – to be arrested and imprisoned than other Australians. The life circumstances of people going to prison, combined with the brutalising experience of incarceration itself, means that many prisoners die untimely deaths.

Successive state and federal governments in Australia have failed to implement most of the 339 RCIADIC recommendations. Thirty years after the tabling of RCIADIC, there have now been over 500 deaths of Aboriginal People in custody. We urge governments to enact the RCIADIC recommendations and to fulfil their obligations to acknowledge and respect the significant labour of the people and communities who painstakingly contributed their stories, experiences, and expertise to RCIADIC.

FIGURE 12.1 First Nations families and allies stop traffic on a busy city street, holding placards featuring Aboriginal People who have died in custody. Wurundjeri Land, Melbourne, Australia.
Source: Charandev Singh, December 2018.

Often the response to families and communities seeking justice for a death in custody is to hold a coronial inquiry. Yet coroners' proceedings rarely provide 'justice' to Aboriginal families, rather, in many ways they act as the 'mop and bucket' of the state, wiping away responsibility of the state and the state's actors, and imparting perpetual delay in the grief and justice process – the forever stain left for Aboriginal Land and people (Rule, 2021b). Often, families are faced with silence about the truths of what happened to their loved ones, and in some cases, they're told to remain silent during the coronial inquest to avoid the 'risk' of disrupting justice through the coronial inquest system – justice which is yet to be seen in any internal manner through such a court. One significant issue that remains within this system is the inability of coroners to make findings and recommendations that adequately respond to the wants and needs of families for accountability, despite families and allies' sustained efforts in making submissions and seeking systemic change. In the very rare instance when coroners have recommended further investigation and directed their findings to the Department for Public Prosecutions, no state authority has ever been convicted for the death in custody of an Aboriginal person in Australia (Whittaker, 2018). As Cunneen and Tauri (2019: 8) explain, 'the type of callous disregard for Indigenous well-being which was so extensively documented by the RCADIC remains a fundamental problem today'. Nothing changes if nothing changes.

The oppression many Aboriginal women experience in Australia is amplified as they are fed through a white, patriarchal criminal (in)justice system that has little understanding of the cultural and gendered complexities specific to Aboriginal women (Kina, 2005). Aboriginal women have the highest rate of re-incarceration of all cohorts of people in Australia (ABS, 2021). Imprisonment does nothing to improve their lives. Minimal attention has been paid to Aboriginal women's deaths in custody in Australia. While the RCIADIC remains the most significant document produced to date around the incarceration of Aboriginal People, 'gender' does not feature as a theme or frame of analysis throughout the entire report, despite 11 of the 99 deaths investigated in the RCIADIC involving Aboriginal women. Similarly, none of the 339 RCIADIC recommendations mention gender, advocate for a gendered lens or use an intersectional approach. While some recent national inquiries have made gestures towards correcting this omission (for example, The Royal Commission into the Protection and Detention of Children in the Northern Territory (NT Royal Commission, 2017); Pathways to Justice – Inquiry into the Incarceration Rate of Aboriginal and Torres Strait Islander Peoples (Australian Law Reform Commission, 2017)), discussion and recommendations made concerning Aboriginality and gender are minimal.

In their critique of the role of the state in Aboriginal deaths in custody, Baldry and Cunneen (2014) advocate for a review of colonial patriarchy in Aboriginal women's experiences in custody. Deploying discourse analysis, Rule (2019) explored themes used in the coroner's report and media articles relating to the death in custody of Ms. Dhu, a Yamatji woman who lived in Port Hedland, a mining town around 1,600 kilometres north of Perth in Western Australia. Ms. Dhu died in excruciating pain on the concrete floor of the Port Hedland police station cells from septicemia, untreated because of the racism underlying the (in) actions of the police and medical staff. Ms. Dhu was denied help and accused of 'faking' her symptoms. Rule (2019: 32) found that Ms. Dhu and other Aboriginal People are positioned in public discourse as being 'unworthy of being mourned' and blamed for their own deaths in custody, and argues that Aboriginal deaths in custody are operationalised through the criminal (in)justice system:

> In rendering Aboriginal People inherently responsible for their own oppression and consequent death, a wider discourse of the perceived necessity for the state to further regulate Aboriginal bodies through the carceral system is re/produced.

It is in the re/production of criminalising discourse upon Aboriginal People, before any application of arrest or sentencing, where criminology presents itself as most terrifying. The intergenerational implications of this system are far-reaching, especially as the Australian government continues to defend its decision to lock-up children from the age of ten, the majority of whom are Aboriginal and Torres Strait Islander (Allam, 2021).

Thinking critically about criminology

As the final chapter of this volume, we encourage readers to take a step back and rethink the purpose of criminology, 'prison research', and prison 'reforms' and to use this as the impetus for change. Despite significant evidence that prisons cause multiple harms to individuals and communities, much of the current research – often funded by correctional services – points out the problems *created* by the PIC while skirting around the solution, which, as agreed by many other scholars, is the abolition of prisons. As Yuin woman Vickie Roach (2022) argues, abolition has many benefits, none so important as preventing Aboriginal deaths in custody.

In the 2021 Annual John Barry Memorial Lecture in Criminology (Ironfield et al., 2021), Latoya joined with four other Aboriginal scholars and activists to discuss and critique the impact of criminology on Aboriginal People in Australia. During the lecture, Gomeroi scholar and poet Alison Whittaker raised the necessity of non-reformist reforms. She identified these as 'reforms to systems that denormalise and limit, rather than calibrate and expand, the reach of prisons and police …' As Amanda Porter (2016; Ironfield et al., 2021) – a Brinja Yuin academic activist – detailed, '… the issue with much criminology research is that it decentres the perspectives of policed communities in favour of those doing the policing'. In the face of families seeking justice for their loved ones and their own experiences of state-sanctioned violence, wielding the weapon of silence exacerbates the lack of accountability by those in positions of power.

Rather than seeking revolutionary transformation, much of criminology's current position upholds '*psychological terra nullius*' (Behrendt, 2002: 7), with respect to even the most critical schools of criminology. Amanda Porter (Ironfield et al., 2021) suggested that it is through the acts of hearing, understanding, and applying the knowledges of Indigenous People and those with lived carceral experience that the goals of decarceration, abolition, and decolonisation can be realised.

Futility of reform

In the face of so much evidence attesting to the systemic, intergenerational brutality and violence of the PIC, it can be tempting to think that perhaps reforming prisons might help. Yet, the problems of reforming prisons are 'wicked problems' (see Huey et al., 2022), simply because possible solutions lead to and create more complex problems. This is because prisons are not the only problem; the PIC is a tangled mess of connecting policies, institutions, and professional disciplines underpinned by the political leverage of the ideals of 'tough on crime' and 'public safety' which skillfully draw upon emotions such as fear and outrage (Jackson and Meiners, 2011). Historically, prison reform had little to do with creating an equal society but was more about resolving religious tensions and creating 'a sense of dependency and obligation between rich and poor' (Ignatieff, 1978: 153). Yet the idea of reform, by its very nature, serves to maintain the status quo (see, for example, Shaylor, 2009; Schenwar and Law, 2020). The argument made by Quinney 50 years ago still rings true, where 'reforms never go beyond the interests of the capitalist system itself; they merely update the existing institutions in order to assure the survival of the system' (1974: 169).

Audre Lorde spoke to the problems with seeking 'reform' when she wrote that 'the master's tools will never dismantle the master's house' (1984: 123). What Lorde meant was that liberation 'gifted' from oppressors includes caveats and clauses that prevent anything but slow, incremental, minimal 'change'. In her critique of prison reforms, Karlene Faith (2000: 164) argued:

> Every reform raises the question of whether, in Gramsci's terms, it is a revolutionary reform, one that has liberatory potential to challenge the status quo, or a reform reform, which may ease the problem temporarily or superficially, but reinforces the status quo by validating the system through the process of improving it.

Although the project of prison abolition and reforming prisons are not 'mutually exclusive strategies' (Baldry et al., 2015: 173), often reforms extend the reach of the prison by *improving* how the prison system *functions for the benefit of prison management*. For example, calls for women's prison reforms have centred on the misguided belief that if prison spaces were more feminine – for example, women guarding women, women holding management positions, and delivering 'women focused' programmes – the pains of imprisonment would be mitigated (Shaylor, 2009). Similar calls have been made for 'all women police stations', Indigenous prisons, drug treatment prisons, and so on (for a critique of these ideas, see Porter et al., 2021). The rise of 'carceral feminism', which seeks to use imprisonment to resolve social problems, such as coercive control, is misguided, based upon flawed assumptions using 'carceral logics' that prisons and their associated industries can resolve gendered violence (Watego et al., 2021; Davis et al., 2022). As Debbie Kilroy explains, 'focusing on reform is a distraction from the work that would genuinely build up and empower women and girls in prison' (Gregorie, 2021: para 16). Reformist approaches simultaneously fail the women they were intended to support and fuel the growth of the PIC (Schenwar and Law, 2020). This is compounded by the fact that reformists often ignore the voices of racialised, criminalised individuals, their families, and their communities.

Radical transformation, radical futures

Decolonising practice and thinking are necessary, especially when living in a settler-colonial state founded on racial violence. The white Australia familiar to us today was born from the British prison system. An early rendition of the PIC, Britain's invasion, theft, and colonisation of Aboriginal Land, served a dual purpose – resolving the rising public concerns of overflowing prisons and hulks in Britain's cities and harbours, and shoring up claim to strategic, resource-rich land (Hughes, 1987). Over 80 years, more than 160,000 people were sentenced to transportation (Hughes, 1987). Many died on the journey, few arrived in good health, and once they arrived, most were utilised for compulsory public work – exploited for their labour for settlers or made to work on government-sponsored colony-building projects.

Before colonisation, Aboriginal People cared for country and kin for over 80,000 years, sustaining highly contextual and organised societies (Pascoe, 2014) capable of responding collectively to social problems. For colonisers, refuting the existence of Indigenous ways of being and doing justified the theft of land and resources. The opportunity to create a prison-less future was lost to the genocidal project, through the imposition of laws, policies, and practices embedded within a colonial legal system that continues to devastate Aboriginal communities (Tatz, 1999). From the moment that colonisers staked their land claim, Aboriginal People have experienced the ongoing colonial violence of surveillance, policing, and imprisonment (Gilbert, 1978). The doctrine of 'terra nullius' or 'land belonging to no one' is implicit in the ongoing theft of First Nations Land globally. This view is grounded in violence, abuse, dispossession, and erasure. As Erin Marie Konsmo – a Métis (Alberta), genderqueer artist – states, 'Our bodies are not 'Terra Nullius ... From an Indigenous Feminist perspective, resistance to violent legal frameworks (such as terra nullius) can be taken up when we fight for the self-determination of our bodies as Indigenous Peoples' (Konsmo and Lilley, 2013: para 2)

Colonial borders and boundaries have systematically criminalised Aboriginal People. Whether that is certain boundary lines that Aboriginal People were prevented from crossing during a curfew because of segregation, or having to gain exemption certificates to leave state-sanctioned missions, some of which Aboriginal People continue to reside upon today (Edmonds, 2012). Forced transition, forced mobility, forced displacement, forced labour, and forced assimilation (Huggins, 1998) set the precedent and expectation that Aboriginal People are subjugated into regulated spaces through forced removal from society – all of which are enacted through official policy and colonial social structures. Thus, radical 'self-transformation' in this space is highly unlikely. The Australian Federal Government's National Agreement on Closing the Gap – which purports to reduce Aboriginal child imprisonment rates – set their expectation for a reduction in carceral settings by 15% by the year 2031 (Department of the Prime Minister and Cabinet, 2020). Even with the bar set so low, this target is unlikely to be met, especially while the Australian government refuses to raise the minimum age of criminal responsibility (Crofts, 2015)[1] thus committing another generation of children to prison. This systemic racism is reflected in the often-used term that as a group, Aboriginal People are 'disproportionately represented' or 'over-represented' in custodial settings across Australia. Such statements exemplify colonial carceral logic, where the presence of prisons shapes our thinking, in both obvious and more subtle ways.

Prison abolition

One of the unfounded assumptions about prison abolition is that it is a simplistic idea entailing the tearing down of prison walls. When Michele first raised the idea of framing her PhD research through an abolitionist framework, she was accused of 'Pollyanna thinking'. While this term is rooted in psychology, the term is often used to quash ideas that challenge existing social structures. Yet as Clear (2005: 183) argues, it is Pollyanna thinking to believe that incarceration and associated carceral logics will resolve social problems or ensure people feel safe in communities.

For First Nations Peoples, the presence of prisons is more than an image of social control – they are the outward-facing image of colonial settler violence (Tauri and Porou, 2014), and this colonial settler violence is enacted through policing. As Narungga woman Cheryl Axleby recently argued, 'Governments need to start addressing the underlying drivers of inequality and injustice in our communities instead of just throwing money at police to respond' (Brennan, 2022: 30). We agree, and this statement supports another abolitionist demand – defunding the police to invest in communities instead.

Abolition is a practice, a verb rather than a noun or an adjective. Abolition encompasses what we think, what we do, and how we do it rather than being just an abstract idea or theory (Kaba, 2021). Abolition requires a dismantling of institutional responses to social problems and begins with understanding the depth, breadth, and reach of the PIC. Although defunding and abolishing the police is a key aspect of the project of abolition (Purnell, 2021: 7), the deployment of carceral logics in education systems contributes to the growth of the PIC (Kaba and Meiners, 2014/2021). Similarly, social work delivered uncritically props up the PIC, where the innocent-sounding roles of 'helping' or 'doing good' are grounded in social control informed by carceral logic through regulating poor and racialised bodies (Leotti, 2021; Piven and Cloward, 1971).

Derecka Purnell (2021: 127) explains the practice of abolition well, writing:

> More than seeking a single solution to one kind of violence, abolition study and praxis requires activists and community residents with political will, imagination and commitment to experimentation, implementation, and evaluation.

Dismantling the PIC requires tackling the reformist push for the increased use of home detention, where the legacies of the prison creep into the home and responsibility for surveillance and control is extended to families and communities (Schenwar and Law, 2020). Using an abolitionist lens frames home detention, parole, and other 'non-prison' alternatives as 'open air prisons' (Lean, 2021).

Rarely does a person become a prison abolitionist overnight. Many abolitionists are former prisoners (see, for example, Kilroy and Lean, 2022; Roach, 2022; Lean, 2021; Olsson, 2005), while others take this position after working or researching within the criminal (in)justice system, where they shift from wanting to make a difference from within the system, to realising that this is impossible (Jarldorn, 2020). Some begin their abolitionist journey through involvement in protests against the injustices within the PIC, while others join as resistance to the cruel and degrading treatment experienced by their families (Kaba, 2021; Purnell, 2021; Rule, 2021a). Abolition requires working hard in, and with, communities to provide caring, safe spaces and ensuring equitable access to resources (Rule and Behrendt, 2021). Importantly, abolitionism is also about working on ourselves when carceral logic defines our thinking.

An exceptional quality of abolitionists is their capacity to combine knowledge of the criminal (in)justice system with advocacy, art, and activism. While over and over criminological research has been carried out *on* criminalised Aboriginal People, rarely does this go further than producing written work for publication and prestigious conference gigs. Rather than seeking radical change through scholarly activism, the evidence of the harms created by the PIC becomes diluted and shaped into calls for reforms. As we have discussed, reforms often result in the growth of the PIC, thus we seek to enact 'non-reformist reforms' (see, for example, Ben-Moshe, 2013; Sudbury, 2009; Gilmore, 2007; Schenwar and Law, 2020) to reduce the reach of the PIC.

Non-reformist reforms

An example of a non-reformist reform is the #BanSpitHoods campaign led by Latoya and their family following Wayne Fella Morrison's death. Through organising national protests, global collaborations, media engagements, artworks, creative actions, and petitioning, 'Fella's Bill', otherwise known as the South Australian Statutes Amendment (Spit Hoods Prohibition) Bill 2021, was passed by law, resulting in a ban on spit hoods in South Australia – the first state to ban these anywhere in Australia. The Act also amended five other acts.[2] While the Act carries a maximum penalty of two years' imprisonment, this relates to restricting the practice of those who hold power under the Act such as employees of the Department of Correctional Services. Spit hoods are now physically removed from the prison and other spaces in this state.

The organising strategy utilised throughout the #BanSpitHoods campaign was founded on abolitionist principles. This meant that rather than attempting to *reform* police and correctional officer behaviours through additional training or advocating for the implementation of new and costly personal protective equipment, the campaign team drafted legislation themselves, providing this to members of the South Australian Parliament. There is now a national and international call for banning spit hoods. Across Aotearoa (New Zealand), the campaign to ban spit hoods is underway, following a 20-fold increase in use

FIGURE 12.2 Latoya lays native flowers and a 30,000-strong petition on the steps of the Parliament of South Australia, calling for the legislated ban on spit hoods. Kaurna Land, Adelaide, South Australia.
Source: Sia Duff, May 2021.

over the previous decade (JustSpeak, 2022). Likewise, protests to ban spit hoods have occurred across the United States (Watkins, 2020). It is these types of non-reformist reforms developed and enacted by and within communities that demonstrate the intellectual and organising capacity of communities to devise and create abolitionist alternatives.

Disrupting colonial discourse through the lens of decolonisation and abolition thinking is critical (Rule, 2019; Jarldorn, 2020; Davies et al., 2021). Just as we have demanded that social workers must do better, we demand the same of criminologists – or rather, that they rethink the role of criminology altogether. Criminology functions to perpetually recycle criminal discourse, reaffirming its place as a necessity within the continuing colonial project – one working to dissect, dismember, and displace Indigenous Peoples and Lands.

As scholars discussed in the Annual John Barry Memorial Lecture in Criminology (Ironfield et al., 2021), questions have been posed as to whether – or if it is even possible – to abolish the discipline of criminology itself due to its foundations as a colonial legacy. As we often discuss, the constraints of working within any institution, including universities and prisons, require careful navigation in ways that facilitate abolitionist principles (for us) of working and being. However, much of our supervision relationship occurred outside of the university where we challenged expectations held of us by forming an allyship

FIGURE 12.3 Staged uniformed prison officers donning spit hoods, protesting outside the coronial court during the inquest into Wayne Fella Morrison's death. Kaurna Land, Adelaide, South Australia.
Source: Charandev Singh, May 2021.

and becoming extended family for each other. The expectations of distance, for example, of setting careful boundaries for personal 'safety', is comparable to how society, the social work discipline, and the carceral state conceptualise appropriate treatment of oppressed, raced, classed, and gendered communities. We also believe that a true ally relationship must centre respect for Indigenous Land and recognise that all land is Indigenous Land.

Ways forward

Davies et al. (2021) propose ways that research in the social sciences can be informed by the prison abolition movement through using methodological approaches which centre abolitionist frameworks and leveraging university resources for the benefit of communities. Abolition work can also be practised through research and writing. Activist scholarship can contribute to the engagement and learning of diverse and marginalised students at universities (Van Der Meer, 2018), while Russell (2015: 222), reflecting on their 'militant research', suggests that activism and the academy need not be separate activities or positions, but 'reimagin[ed] … as a machine for the production of other worlds'. While academic works are vital in theorising abolition, the voices of people with lived experience of prison inform their arguments, with nuance, context, and love as they develop practical community-led responses to harm.

As we end this chapter I (Michele) reflect upon our decade of allyship. I have watched as Latoya has taken risks, put the collective rights of Aboriginal peoples before any personal gains, spoken out in the media, critiqued existing practices, and challenged people in and with power to do better. I marvel at Latoya's determination and reflect upon how quickly our initial roles as teacher (Michele) and learner (Latoya) were reversed. The privilege of writing this chapter with Latoya has taught me enormously. My experience echoes that described by bell hooks (2003), of being an enlightened witness, watching, listening, and learning. Having the opportunity to be a small part of Latoya's story is a privilege. I can only imagine the radical changes they will bring to the world by combining their passionate practical and academic activism.

As emerging and early career researchers we are concerned with transformative justice and take seriously the idea proposed by Angela Davis that we must always act as if it were possible to radically transform the world. Throughout this chapter, we sought to explore the idea of relationship-based supervision, intertwining stories of our allyship, stories, and practices which refute the hierarchical and 'at arm's length' sense of 'mentor and mentee', in turn drawing upon the sometimes deeply personal experiences of lifting each other as we climb (Davis, 1990). We identify this relationship as one that works towards breaking down the traditional hierarchical relationships within universities which generate barriers to authentic knowledge creation – a decolonising approach (Smith, 2012).

Grasping Angela Davis's notion of radical transformation, I (Latoya) conceptualise the need for an opening-up of 'Blak space', where acts of decolonisation are both possible and tangible. '"Blak space" is where Aboriginal People exist, survive and thrive. It is itself counter-discourse of Aboriginal People as displaced; non-belonging; non-sovereign"' (Rule, 2019: 4). This concept is being developed further in my doctoral research, which focuses on the experiences of Aboriginal women surviving the coronial inquest process into their loved one's deaths. My research is for and about the mothers, sisters, and cousins of those who have died in custody who continue to lead resistance to state violence through advocating for justice. 'Blak space' is a concept where Aboriginal people have voice and power in being self-determining. Valuing the importance and power in breathing, by utilising the creative element of podcasting, this research provides space for our voices to be heard from beyond the academy in their humanising, most powerful form.

Prisons, and as an extension, prison research, can invisiblise and silence criminalised people. As researchers and educators, our work should seek to convince society of the futility of using prisons as a response to social problems. Ensuring that emerging scholars are not shoehorned into producing more of the same research on criminalised people is transformative for scholars and those they are researching for and with. The deliberations and solutions presented in this chapter reflect who we are in centring our lived experiences, histories, present struggles, and ongoing love for marginalised communities and for each other. Rather than observe and report, clamour for transformative change. Risk your prison-funded research grants and service provision funding with 'gag clauses' which prevent you speaking out against the violence of the carceral state (Kilroy and Quixley, 2021: 28–29) and ask yourself if your work is transformative, or will it contribute to the wicked problems of reform?

Notes

1 Allies and academics in Australia have been calling on the Australian government to raise the age of criminal responsibility for years. Currently, in Australia, children can be imprisoned in youth detention centres from the age of ten. Many activists go further, arguing that raising the age is not enough and that all youth detention should be abolished entirely.
2 The five Acts amended were: the Correctional Services Act 1982, the Mental Health Act 2009, the Sheriff's Act 1978, the Summary Offences Act 1953, and the Youth Justice Administration Act 2016.

References

ABS. 2021. Corrective Services, Australia. Australian Bureau of Statistics. November 25. Retrieved from: https://www.abs.gov.au/statistics/people/crime-and-justice/corrective-services-australia/sep-quarter-2021#key-statistics.

Allam, Lorena. 2021. Jailing of nearly 500 children aged 13 and under a 'failure' by Australia's top legal officers, advocates say. *The Guardian*. July 27. Retrieved from: https://www.theguardian.com/australia-news/2021/jul/27/jailing-of-nearly-500-children-under-13-a-failure-by-australias-top-legal-officers-advocates-say.

Archibald, Jo-Ann, Q'um Q'um Xiiem, Jenny Bol Jun Lee-Morgan, and Jason De Santolo. 2019. *Decolonizing research: Indigenous storywork as methodology*. London: Zed Books.

Australian Law Reform Commission. 2017. Pathways to Justice – Inquiry into the incarceration rate of Aboriginal and Torres Strait Islander Peoples, Final Report No 133. Retrieved from: https://www.alrc.gov.au/wp-content/uploads/2019/08/final_report_133_amended1.pdf.

Baldry, Eileen and Chris Cunneen. 2014. Imprisoned Indigenous women and the shadow of colonial patriarchy. *Australian & New Zealand Journal of Criminology*. 47(2): 276–298.

Baldry, Eileen, Bree Carlton, and Chris Cunneen. 2015. Abolitionism and the paradox of penal reform in Australia: colonialism, context, cultures and co-option. *Social Justice: A Journal of Crime, Conflict and World Order*. 41(3): 168–189.

Behrendt, Larissa. 2002. Mabo ten years on: a psychological terra nullius remains. *Impact*, June, 7–9. https://law.anu.edu.au/sites/all/files/behrendtjune02mabo.pdf.

Behrendt, Larissa. 2019. Indigenous storytelling: decolonizing institutions assertive self-determination: implications for legal practice. In *Decolonizing research: Indigenous storywork as methodology*, eds. Jo-ann Archibald, Q'um Q'um Xiiem, Jenny Bol Jun Lee-Morgan, and Jason De Santolo, pp.175–186. London: Zed Books.

Ben-Moshe, Liat. 2013. The tension between abolition and reform. In *The end of prisons: reflections from the decarceration movement*, eds. Mechandthild Nagel and Anthony Nocella, pp.83–92. Netherlands: Brill/Rodopi.

Brennan, Dechlan. 2022. Why Australia's Indigenous people fear the police. *The Diplomat*. March 22. Retrieved from: https://thediplomat.com/2022/03/why-australias-indigenous-people-fear-the-police/.

Brook, Heather. 2009. Dark tourism. *Law Text Culture*. 13(1): 260–272.
Brown, Leslie and Susan Strega. 2005. *Research as resistance: critical, Indigenous and anti-oppressive approaches*. Toronto: Canadian Scholar's Press.
Clear, Todd. 2005. Places not cases? Re-thinking the probation focus. *The Howard Journal*. 44(2): 172–184.
Crofts, Thomas. 2015. A brighter tomorrow: raise the age of criminal responsibility. *Current Issues in Criminal Justice*. 27(1): 123–131.
Cunneen, Chris and Juan Marcellus Tauri. 2019. Indigenous peoples, criminology and criminal justice. *Annual Review of Criminology*. 2: 359–381.
Davies, Elizabeth Jordie, Jenn Jackson, and Shae Streeter. 2021. Bringing abolition in: addressing carceral logics in social science research. *Social Science Quarterly*. 1–8.
Davis, Angela Y. 1990. *Women, culture and politics*. New York: Random House.
Davis, Angela Y, Gina Dent, Erica R. Meiners, and Beth E. Richie. 2022. *Abolition. Feminism. Now*. Chicago: Haymarket Books.
Department of the Prime Minister and Cabinet. 2020. National Agreement on Closing the Gap. Retrieved from: https://www.closingthegap.gov.au/sites/default/files/files/national-agreement-ctg.pdf.
Edmonds, Penelope. 2012. Unofficial apartheid, convention and country towns: reflections on Australian history and the New South Wales Freedom Rides of 1965. *Postcolonial Studies*. 15(2): 167–190.
Faith, Karlene. 2000. Reflections on inside/out organizing. *Social Justice*. 27(3): 158–167.
Gilbert, Kevin. 1978. *Living Black: Blacks talk to Kevin Gilbert*. Ringwood, Victoria: Penguin Books.
Gilmore, Ruth. 2007. *Golden gulag: prisons, surplus, crisis and opposition in globalizing California*. Berkeley, CA: University of California Press.
Gregorie, Paul. 2021. Imagining prison abolition is not difficult, says Sisters Inside's Debbie Kilroy. *Sydney Criminal Lawyers*. December 21. Retrieved from: https://www.sydneycriminallawyers.com.au/blog/imagining-prison-abolition-is-not-difficult-says-sisters-insides-debbie-kilroy/.
Harding, Sandra. 2004. *The feminist standpoint theory reader: intellectual and political controversies*. New York: Routledge.
Huey, Laura, Lorna Ferguson, and Jennifer L. Schulenberg. 2022. *The wicked problems of police reform in Canada*. London: Routledge.
hooks, bell. 2003. *Teaching community: a pedagogy of hope*. New York: Routledge.
Huggins, Jackie. (1998). *Sister girl*. St Lucia, Queensland: University of Queensland Press.
Hughes, Robert. 1987. *The fatal shore: A history of the transportation of convicts to Australia, 1787–1868*. London: Collins Harvill.
Ignatieff, Michael. 1978. *A just measure of pain: The penitentiary in the industrial revolution, 1750–1850*. London: Macmillan.
Ironfield, Natalie, Tabitha Lean, Alison Whitaker, Latoya Rule, and Amanda Porter. 2021. Abolition on Indigenous land: alternative futures and criminology's role. Annual John Barry Memorial Lecture in Criminology, University of Melbourne. March 18. Retrieved from: https://www.youtube.com/watch?v=peA6_WdIbtE.
Jackson, Jessie Lee and Erica Meiners. 2011. Fear and loathing: Public feelings in anti-prison work. *Women's Studies Quarterly*. 39(1–2): 270–290.
Jarldorn, Michele. 2018. Radically rethinking imprisonment: A Photovoice exploration of life in and after prison in South Australia. Doctoral Thesis, Flinders University.
Jarldorn, Michele. 2020. Radically rethinking social work in the criminal (in)justice system in Australia. *Affilia: Journal of Women and Social Work*. 35(3): 327–343.

Jarldorn, Michele, Bec Neill, and Linda Fisk. 2022. The complexities of accessing and keeping housing for formerly incarcerated women in South Australia. *Parity*. 35(1): 40–41.

JustSpeak. 2022. Retrieved from: https://www.justspeak.org.nz/.

Kaba, Mariame. 2021. *We do this 'til we free us: abolitionist organising and transforming justice*. Chicago, Illinois: Haymarket Books.

Kaba, Mariame and Erica Meiners. 2014/2021. Arresting the carceral state. In *We do this 'til we free us: abolitionist organising and transforming justice*, ed. Mariame Kaba, pp. 76–81. Chicago, Illinois: Haymarket Books.

Kilroy, Debbie, and Tabitha Lean. 2022. The not so easy, simple solution. *Journal of Prisoners on Prisons*. 30(2), 91–95.

Kilroy, Debbie and Suzi Quixley. 2021. A word waiting to happen. In *The Routledge International Handbook of Penal Abolition*, eds. Michael J. Coyle and David Scott, pp. 21–31. London: Routledge.

Kina, Robbie. 2005. Through the eyes of a strong Black woman survivor of domestic violence: an Australian story. In *Global lockdown: race, gender, and the prison-industrial complex*, ed. Julia Sudbury, pp. 67–72. Abingdon, Oxon: Routledge.

Konsmo, Erin Marie, and PJ Lilley. 2013. 'Art through a birch bark heart': an illustrated interview with Erin Marie Konsmo. *Radical Criminology*. 2: 69–102.

Kurmelovs, Royce. 2018. Three missing minutes, and more questions: Why did Wayne Fella Morrison die in custody? *NITV*. September 12. Retrieved from: https://www.sbs.com.au/nitv/feature/three-missing-minutes-and-more-questions-why-did-wayne-fella-morrison-die-custody-1.

Lean, Tabitha. 2021. Why I am an abolitionist. *The Overland*. June 8. Retrieved from: https://overland.org.au/2021/06/why-i-am-an-abolitionist/.

Leotti, Sandra. 2021. Social work with criminalised women: governance or resistance in the carceral state? *Affilia: Journal of Women and Social Work*. 36(3): 302–318.

Lorde, Audre. 1984. *Sister outsider: essays and speeches*. New York: Crossing Press.

McQuire, Amy. 2019. Black and white witness. *Meanjin Quarterly*. Retrieved from: https://meanjin.com.au/essays/black-and-white-witness/.

Moreton-Robinson, Aileen. 2015. *The white possessive: property, power and indigenous sovereignty*. Minnesota: University of Minnesota Press.

NT Royal Commission. 2017. The Royal Commission into the Protecting and Detention of Children in the Northern Territory. Retrieved from: https://www.royalcommission.gov.au/child-detention/final-report.

Olsson, Kris. 2005. *Kilroy was here*. Sydney: Bantam.

Pascoe, Bruce. 2014. *Dark emu: Aboriginal Australia and the birth of agriculture*. Broome, Western Australia: Magabala Books.

Piven, Frances Fox and Richard Cloward. 1971. *Regulating the poor: the functions of public welfare*. New York: Pantheon Books.

Porter, Amanda. 2016. Decolonizing policing: Indigenous patrols, counter-policing and safety. *Theoretical Criminology*. 20(4): 548–565.

Porter, Amanda, Ann Louise Deslandes, Crystal McKinnon, and Marlene Longbottom. 2021. Women's police stations in Australia: would they work for 'all' women? *The Conversation*. September 17. Retrieved from: https://theconversation.com/womens-police-stations-in-australia-would-they-work-for-all-women-165873.

Purnell, Derecka. 2021. *Becoming abolitionists: police, protests, and the pursuit of freedom*. London: Verso Books.

Quinney, Richard. 1974. *Critique of legal order: crime control in a capitalist society*. Boston: Little, Brown and Company.

Roach, Vickie. 2022. The system is not failing, it is working to harm First Nations people. *Journal of Prisoners on Prisons*. 30(2): 35–38.
Royal Commission into Aboriginal Deaths in Custody (RCIADIC). 1991. Final Report. Australian Government. Retrieved from: http://www.austlii.edu.au/au/other/IndigLRes/rciadic/.
Royal Commission into the Protection and Detention of Children in the Northern Territory. 2017. Final Report. Australian Government. Retrieved from: https://childdetentionnt.royalcommission.gov. au/Pages/Report.aspx.
Rule, Latoya. 2019. 'But don't you think that sometimes they bring it upon themselves?' Implicating the colonial project in the death of Ms Dhu. Unpublished Honours Thesis, Flinders University.
Rule, Latoya. 2021a. We need a national ban on spit hoods. *Rolling Stone*. April 16. Retrieved from: https://au.rollingstone.com/culture/culture-features/national-ban-spit-hoods-25190/.
Rule, Latoya. 2021b. Family: visions of a shared humanity. Exhibition at the AGNSW. Retrieved from: https://www.artgallery.nsw.gov.au/media-office/family/.
Rule, Latoya and Larissa Behrendt. 2021. The families of Indigenous people who die in custody need a say in what happens next. *The Conversation*. April 28. Retrieved from: https://theconversation.com/the-families-of-indigenous-people-who-die-in-custody-need-a-say-in-what-happens-next-159127.
Russell, Bertie. 2015. Beyond activism/academia: Militant research and the radical climate and climate justice movement(s). *Area* 47 (3): 222–229.
Schenwar, Maya and Victoria Law. 2020. *Prison by any other name: the harmful consequences of popular reforms*. New York: The New Press.
Shaylor, Cassandra. 2009. Neither kind nor gentle: the perils of gender responsive justice. In *The violence of incarceration*, eds. Phil Scraton and Jude McCulloch, pp. 145–163. New York: Routledge.
Smith, Linda Tuhiwai. 2012. *Decolonizing methodologies: research and indigenous peoples* (2nd ed.) London: Zed Books.
Sudbury, Julia. 2009. Maroon abolitionists: Black gender-oppressed activists in the anti-prison movement in the US and Canada. *Meridians*. 9(1): 1–29.
Tatz, Colin. 1999. Genocide in Australia. *Journal of Genocide Research*. 1(3): 315–352.
Tauri, Juan Marcellus and Ngati Porou. 2014. Criminal justice as a colonial project in settler-colonialism. *African Journal of Criminology and Justice Studies*. 8(1): 20–37.
Van Der Meer, Tony. 2018. Fighting to be different in the academy. *Workplace: A Journal for Academic Labor*. 30(1): 352–359.
Watego, Chelsea, Alissa Macoun, David Singh, and Elizabeth Strakosch. 2021. Carceral feminism and coercive control: when Indigenous women aren't seen as ideal victims, witnesses or women. *The Conversation*. May 25. Retrieved from: https://theconversation.com/carceral-feminism-and-coercive-control-when-indigenous-women-arent-seen-as-ideal-victims-witnesses-or-women-161091.
Watkins, Ali. 2020. What are spit hoods and why do police use them? *New York Times*. September 3. Retrieved from: https://www.nytimes.com/2020/09/03/nyregion/spit-hoods-police.html.
Watson, Irene. 2016. First Nations and the colonial project. *Inter Gentes*. 1(1): 30–39.
Whittaker, Alison. 2018. The unbearable witness, seeing: a case for Indigenous methodologies in Australian soft law. *Pandora's Box*. 25: 23–35.

13
FINAL REFLECTIONS

Kelly J. Stockdale and Michelle Addison

It is important to explicitly acknowledge in the conclusion of the book that we, as editors of the collection, do not have all the answers when it comes to addressing deep-seated issues relating to race, gender, class, dis/ability, sexuality, and other often intersecting inequalities generated and perpetuated within academia, society, or the criminal justice system. What we reflect on in our own practice and hope to encourage others to talk about, question, and challenge is how these inequalities are reproduced and perpetuated by the people who research, write about, and publish in relation to crime, criminology, and criminal justice, either consciously or not.

As part of doing this work, Michelle and I have often talked about how we locate our own voices within the book, alongside wider discussions on finding our own place within the academy - and even if the academy is a place we would want to be part of. The question of how to be part of a system that produces and reproduces inequalities, that thrives on individualism and one-upmanship, that values a certain type of academic/academic work/academic writing more than others is one we keep coming back to. We gave much thought to our role and position as editors of the collection and how to introduce and conclude the book in ways that do not unquestioningly conform to the manner the canon dictates things are written. Yet, as we reach the conclusion it is interesting to reflect on how, even with this mindset, this book still follows publisher guidelines and many traditional academic conventions. Part of finding our own voices is about navigating the politics of having your own voice in academia.

As part of finding and sharing our voice, it is important to reflect on our positionality - why we have produced this edited collection in the first place. The work Kelly has been doing on the criminology curriculum since 2019 was inspired by and actioned after a talk by Jason Arday and Heidi Mirza on

DOI: 10.4324/9781003260967-16

'Dismantling Race in Higher Education' (Durham University, 1st March 2019) where they called for collective responsibility – insisting that white academics needed to call for and create change and not expect those who are already marginalised, racialised, and oppressed within academia to take on this responsibility. At the time as a (white, working-class, first-generation scholar, queer but not 'out') early career lecturer and single parent, I was already drowning with a teaching workload four times that of my (white, middle-class, male, straight) peers. I came away from that talk – as I had other talks and other workshops - galvanised to do something different ... and then found myself straight back in the classroom teaching the same old 'criminology' in the same old way (see Stockdale and Sweeney, 2019, 2022; Stockdale et al., 2022) in modules that had been designed and written by others, and working on papers that I was already committed to write. I wished then for a book like this, one including a wide range of experiences and perspectives that I could read and absorb and learn from, one that speaks to the intersectional issues that rest at the heart of the discipline, and one that would influence my thinking, teaching, and research – which covers a wide range of areas but has criminology and criminal justice at its core.

Michelle's position comes from being a first-generation scholar and trying to understand what it means to be an 'imposter' in certain places and around certain people (see Addison et al., 2022). Unpicking how class, gender, and other aspects of identity are mobilised as part of 'playing the game' and 'getting ahead', and how this serves the interests of some and not others – particularly in higher education – has been a knotty problem I will never tire of and one which gave me passion for this project (see Addison, 2016). A recent re-reading of Gayatri Chakravorty Spivak's essay 'Can the Subaltern Speak?' - reminded me once more of the politics and epistemic violence surrounding the construction of marginalised and minoritised voices. Spivak reminds us of the 'ferocious standardising benevolence' that comes with trying to speak *for* those, and assimilate into the 'centre', those who are marginalised (1988: 91). Furthermore, this epistemic practice of taking up space (and simply widening the 'centre') actually serves as a 'double displacement' (see Spivak, 1988) of the subaltern - persons who wish to speak but who find themselves simultaneously assimilated into the centre whilst also being located as the colonial 'other', muted and spoken for by those who state they 'know' better. Spivak argues that within the prevailing western hegemonic epistemic apparatus the 'subaltern' are always represented and reconstituted in ways that act as a foil for the constitution of a 'good society' – reproducing imperialist ideas about knowledge and knowing. For Spivak, the subaltern cannot speak, at least not within hegemonic parameters of knowledge production:

> Yet the assumption and construction of a consciousness or subject sustains such work and will, in the long run, cohere with the work of imperialist subject-constitution, mingling epistemic violence with the advancement of learning and civilization. And the subaltern woman will be as mute as ever
> *(Spivak, 1988: 90)*.

This serves as a stark reminder to us all to question the mechanisms of knowledge production in criminology, and to reflect on Spivak's question – can the subaltern speak, or are these persons being spoken for? When we critically engage with crime, criminalisation, deviance, social harm, and criminal justice systems who is *knower* and who is *known*? Whose voices are we hearing, and whose interests are being served?

In conceptualising, editing, and writing this text, Michelle and I have constantly reflected on and acknowledged our own whiteness, our own privileges in that, while we have had many issues and challenges, we have both found permanent jobs (after much precarity and raising families) within the academy, and have had our work published. We have been conscious from the start of this project that there is a weight and privilege embedded within the editing process, and within our own individual decision-making too; it was our wording on the original call for chapters, our pre-existing networks and social media connections through which that call was made, it was our choice as to which chapters were included and excluded, and it was our communication and the way we approached working relations with the authors in the book that will get us to the finish line without losing anyone on the way. In our desire to be a driving force for change and to create space for marginalised voices, we also became gatekeepers to that space – what would Spivak have to say about this?

We are also mindful, as academics in the UK, of the pressures of the Research Excellence Framework (REF) by which our written work is judged and submitted (or not) as part of our department's REF strategy. Books, of which edited collections sit lower than monographs in the ranking, are seen as 'inferior' to journal articles (Macfarlane, 2017). What constitutes research 'excellence' is difficult to define, and the framework by which work is judged itself perpetuates existing inequalities across higher education; data from the most recent REF 2021, for instance recognises how Black, Asian, and Minority Ethnic research leaders were initially missing from nominations to sit on REF assessment panels (where research excellence is defined and awarded) – a reminder that 'being nominated for opportunities by peers is something that is often taken for granted by individuals from privileged groups, where obstacles to progression are seldom encountered' (Khan et al., 2022: n.p.). Discussing the fairness and openness of the REF system, Khan et al. (2022) remind us of the importance of allyship and supporting colleagues. They also point to the role of personal responsibility in challenging structural racism that impacts on academic research. As editors of this book, we hope it will be read widely by colleagues and students and will have impact on the discipline by drawing attention to the collective and also multiple ways in which diverse and intersecting experiences, people, and research have been marginalised, minimised, silenced, and excluded from criminology. Yet, offering this as a book, to you - the reader - to immerse yourself in, and not, for example, as a special edition in a journal, provides a 'lesser' REF 'output' to academics who have written it - academics who may already be experiencing marginalisation and discrimination in the academy. How do we challenge these structures whilst also being part of them? It can be noted that as editors our names are reverse-ordered on the introduction and this final concluding chapter - so we are both able to 'claim' a submission, and institutional recognition, for the labour involved in editing the collection. We are finding our place in the academy, we are part of the system and playing the game, while also questioning what that place means, and how to create change from our position within it.

In addition to these personal reflections, a wider, global change was occurring; the concept for the book was discussed in September 2019, and our initial drafts ended up lying dormant as the pandemic spread and national lockdowns in England meant we were home and home-schooling our young families whilst juggling academic pressure (and processing loss, grief ... in fact, too long a list of emotions to cover here). Our initial call for papers was circulated exactly three years ago in June 2020 when in England we were 'coming out' of the initial COVID-19 pandemic lockdowns. We met and walked together along a north-east beach, having socially distanced discussions whilst also feeling the enormity of being 'back' in the world, in a social situation, in an academic situation, but with a huge weight of loss and fear and questioning. Should we try and do this? A book that we both very much believed in but like many things had shrunk in importance. 'How can we be expected to continue "as normal"? Things aren't normal!' being a well-used line in our work conversations at the time. We had set a deadline with the publisher with a built in a six-month contingency, precisely because how could we expect people to write, never mind write at 'normal' - for the academy - relatively fast-paced speeds? We wanted to build in time, to create something that was not borne from the stress and pressure that so often forms part of the publication process. Yet even with the extra time we have still pushed the deadline back further; the last 18 months in UK higher education has been tumultuous, as our union, UCU, called for action in relation to pay, pensions, inequality, and working conditions. Structured around the 'four fights' campaign, it explicitly calls for university bosses to close the gender and ethnicity pay gaps present within UK universities and higher education establishments. We have stood shoulder to shoulder with our colleagues on picket lines with our children, dogs, banners, and hot water bottles (it is the north-east of England after all!). We stood for, fought for, and hoped for change. We are writing this concluding chapter while our employers deduct up to 100% of our pay for taking part in the UCU marking and assessment boycott. Creating change often comes at a cost. It may mean for some (many?) authors in this book that their words were written outside of their paid and workloaded hours. For some authors, outside of the academy or without a permanent academic contract, there has been no pay or renumeration for their writing within these covers. We would ask you to pause and consider the implications of a publication model and an academic workload model that relies on people working without pay or renumeration: how these structures enable some to be heard – while silencing and excluding others.

We hope this book disrupts 'traditional' criminological narratives. We hope it prompts you, the reader, to consider ideas and experiences of people and places that you have not previously considered as you have engaged with criminological theory, ideas, and research. Thinking about the conclusion of the book, we want to think about the purpose of the text and the chapters that comprise it in the following ways:

1. If you are a student studying criminology (at an undergraduate or postgraduate level) we want you to reflect on many of the chapters in this book and consider what they mean for you in your studies. We want you to think about whose perspectives you have been exploring the issues of crime and criminal justice from, and why those perspectives dominate. We encourage you to look at your reading lists and explore the examples that you are given in the material that you're being taught. How are they framed? *Why* are they framed that way?

2. We want you to question and challenge who is included and who is excluded, whose voices have been prioritised and whose voices have been marginalised within the work you have been set? Hear Spivak's words – 'can the subaltern speak?' If there are parts, pieces, and chapters here you have never considered previously then we want you to start to consider them. We want you to reconsider, we want you to rethink, we want you to reframe, and we want you to reorganise your work and your thoughts. You are the practitioners of the future who can make a difference in the 'real' world. You are the future academics whose voices we hope to read, and we want to learn from. We want you to think of going beyond what you were being taught.

3. We would signpost you one last time to Alexis Marcoux Rouleau, Ismehen Melouka, and Maude Pérusse-Roy's work in Chapter 11 - see how dominant thoughts and ideas prevail across academia - when you are considering writing a dissertation or thesis give thought and reflection as to whose ideas you are being asked to incorporate and whose ideas are not considered. Consider the issues raised by Natalie Rutter in Chapter 8 and what your ethical responsibilities are as a researcher. Pause and consider each and every stage: from the research topic to the research methods, the theory you choose, and the way in which you draw your conclusions and incorporate reflective practice throughout. If you are engaged in literature-based research, give consideration to the all-encompassing but infrequently delineated *'they'* in your discussions; Consider Chapter 10 as Anna Matczak questions around *who* is the 'voice of the public', and what assumptions are made of them.

4. If you are an academic and you are looking at teaching material, we want you to reconsider what you are teaching, how it is framed, and which scholars are cited. Often, we may want to make our reading broader, and we may want to include perspectives from elsewhere whilst also acknowledging we are in a cycle of knowledge production – what we were taught

as undergraduates influences what we believe a degree must contain. Give thought to Chapter 2 and Stephen J. Macdonald and Donna Peacock's argument that demonstrates how theorising in other fields has failed to intersect with criminology. Reflect on Chapter 3 and read further the work of the Indigenous scholars cited by Stephen D. Ashe and Debbie Bargallie. We encourage you to consider the colonial history behind much criminological theorising as discussed by Esmorie Miller in Chapter 4. Change can be difficult and introducing new content may not seem important when there are other competing demands on our time. This book has been purposeful in that it is not a book that is 'just' about race and crime or gender and crime – it is a book that you can pick up and read to reflect on epistemic apparatus.

5. If you are an academic and you are doing research, think about how your research is framed: who is included, who is excluded. Explore other examples that you could be drawing on. We hope this book helps to prompt thinking; you may consider and reconsider the methods that you are using; think about how certain methods fit with certain work and your own privileges and barriers faced when conducting research. Appraise how the research process may be different for others – particularly important if you are working on a project as a team, or if you have a position of line-management or responsibility for hiring and promoting. Contemplate the issues raised by Claudia Smith Cox, Kerry Ellis-Devitt, and Lisa Sugiura within Chapter 9, and Latoya Aroha Rule and Michele Jarldorn in Chapter 12 and the additional emotional labour and toll many criminological projects have on academics who are connected to or impacted themselves personally by the research they do, and who cannot, or who refuse to be 'impartial' and 'neutral'.

6. If you are interested in thinking about a broader range of perspectives than are traditionally discussed within criminology, then we would draw your attention to the middle section of the book. Bianca Johnston, Faith Gordon, and Catherine Flynn discuss their research in Chapter 5 highlighting how different factors intersect, and how policy and practice can ignore those in need when they fail to consider experiences of people at these intersections. Likewise, Megan Coghlan in Chapter 6 encourages us to be mindful of less visible structural and cultural barriers that exist for those who are justice-involved. Our criminological imagination is stretched further by Yulia Chistyakova in Chapter 7, and we consider the political landscape that can shape and influence the discipline, and how it presents itself across different areas, temporalities, and regimes.

Concluding chapters traditionally are supposed to summarise the preceding content and draw out key tenets for you, the reader, to digest – especially if you're in a hurry and the pressures of the academic machinery mean you have turned to this chapter first. We go against this grain and take you on a detour instead (sorry – *not sorry?*).

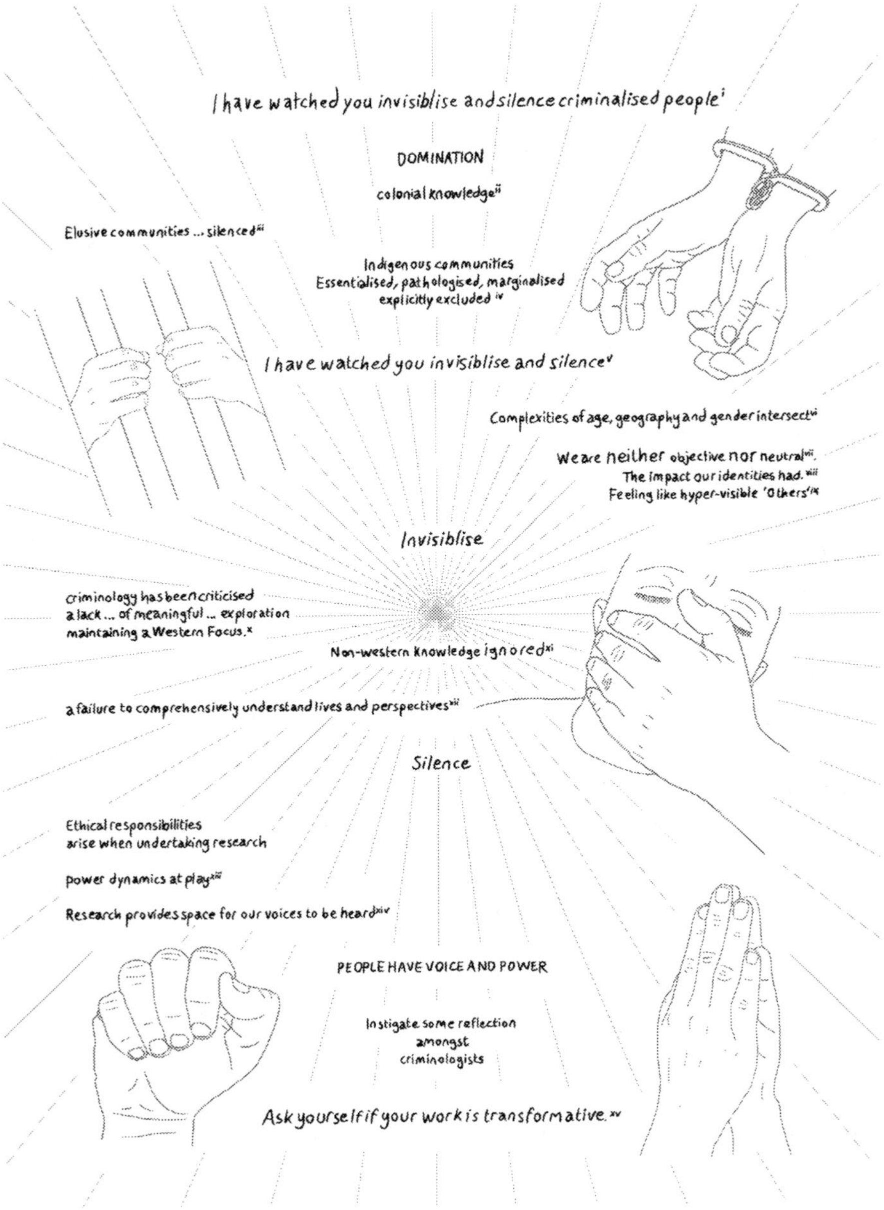

FIGURE 13.1 'Marginalised Voices in Criminology', by Kelly J. Stockdale and Michelle Addison

Notes: Quotes take from this volume as follows: i, v, xii, xv Rule and Jarldorn; ii Miller; iv Ashe and Bargallie; v Smith Cox, Ellis-Devitt, and Sugiura; vii Rouleau, Melouka, and Pérusse-Roy; ix Johnston, Gordon, and Flynn; x Rutter; xi Coghlan; xii Chistyakova; xiv Macdonald and Peacock.

Source: Design and illustration by Stephens-Griffin.

From our discussion above, and because of how we view our role as editors of this collection, it seemed wrong in many ways for the book to end on our words. We have spent a lot of time also considering how to write or create something that encapsulates the book as a whole and the multiple and diverse ideas and experiences that it covers. Reading through each of the enclosed chapters we saw many of the same themes emerge. From this we have selected and joined together specific words and phrases from each of the chapters around those themes to create a poem (based on the concept of using I-poem (n.d.) in qualitative research and decentring the researcher – or in this case editors - and crafting something that makes scholarship more accessible/something different from 'traditional' ways in which these collections are formed and produced).

We encourage you to pause for reflection and consider the wise words of our contributors assembled here for you, the reader, to start to make sense of the invisible threads that run across the different stories and experiences of those who have been marginalised and excluded in criminology.

References

Addison, M. (2016). *Social Games and Identity in the Higher Education Workplace: Playing with Gender, Class and Emotion.* Basingstoke: Palgrave Macmillan.

Addison, M., Breeze, M., and Taylor, Y. (eds.) (2022). *Imposter Syndrome in Higher Education Handbook.* Basingstoke: Palgrave Macmillan.

I-poem project (n.d.). https://i-poemproject.wixsite.com/udel (4th July 2023).

Khan, R., Ross, F., and Parkes, T. (2022). All voices matter – what REF 2021 can tell us about the involvement of people from Black, Asian and Minority Ethnic communities in research assessment. *About the REF – Blogs.* https://www.ref.ac.uk/about-the-ref/blogs/all-voices-matter-what-ref-2021-can-tell-us-about-the-involvement-of-people-from-black-asian-and-minority-ethnic-communities-in-research-assessment/ (11th July 2023).

Macfarlane, B. (2017). The REF is wrong: Books are not inferior to papers. *Times Higher Education.* https://www.timeshighereducation.com/opinion/ref-wrong-books-are-not-inferior-papers (11th July 2023).

Spivak, G. C. (1988). Can the subaltern speak? In C. Nelson, and L. Grossberg (eds.), *Marxism and the Interpretation of Culture.* Basingstoke: Macmillan Education, pp. 271–313.

Stockdale, K. J. and Sweeney, R. (2019). Exploring the criminology curriculum. *Papers from the British Criminology Conference: An Online Journal by the British Society of Criminology* Vol. 19: 84.

Stockdale, K. J. and Sweeney, R. (2022). Whose voices are prioritised in criminology, and why does it matter? *Special Issue of Race and Justice: Anti-racism & Intersectionality in Feminist Criminology & Academia: Where Do We Go from Here?* Vol 12, no. 3: 481–504. doi:10.1177/215336872211026.

Stockdale, K. J., Sweeney, R., McCluskey-Dean, C., Brown, J., and Azam, I. (2022). Exploring the criminology curriculum – reflections on developing and embedding critical information literacy. In S. Young and K. Strudwick (eds.), *Challenges of Teaching Criminology and Criminal Justice.* London: Palgrave Macmillan.

SUBJECT INDEX

Aboriginal
    activism 41, 202; Black space 215; climate justice 47; culture 35, 40, 41, 42, 45, 48, 203; land 203; law 36–38, 39, 46–47; overrepresentation in criminal justice systems 34, 39, 44, 44–45, 202, 205, 207; prison/behaviour change programmes 41, 45, 46; researchers 25, 202–203
activism 2, 20, 22, 41, 42, 48, 81, 183, 202–204, 208, 212, 214, 215
alternatives to criminal justice 7, 40, 41, 43, 112, 185, 186, 187–189, 190, 191, 192, 194, 196, 211, 213,
Australia 5, 6, 32–53, 61, 63, 75–91, 173, 201–219

British Columbia 171

Canada 37, 153, 171, 182–200
child removal: 42–43, 61, 81, 196
colonialism 2, 38, 41, 42, 54–71, 123, 124, 203, 210, 221, 225;
    colonial gaze 41, 43; colonial violence *see* violence; colonisation – impact of 37, 45, 55, 66 203, 207, 210, 153; colonisation – legacies of 34, 48, colonialism and criminology 35, 36, 61, 62, 64, 110, 123, 188, 195, 213; decolonial 54–71, 110, 186, 187, 213; settler-colonialism 34, 36, 37, 39, 44, 45, 46–47, 48, 203, 209.

criminological theory
    Asian criminology 117, 122; biological positivism 14–15, 16, 17, 18, 19, 25, 26, 28, 59, 112, 113, 117; conventional criminology 7, 185, 186–187, 188, 194, 196, 197; critical criminology 19–22, 27, 186, 187–188, 192, 194, 208; cultural criminology 24–27, 187; decolonising criminology 56, 213; dis/ableist criminology 5, 3–28; European criminology 32, 36, 62, 111, 117; green criminology 47, 187, 190; Indigenous contributions to 48–49; mainstream criminology 37, 43, 208, 187; public criminology 176; queer criminology 188, 195; realism 21–24, 25, 27, 28; Russian criminology 110–128; Southern criminology 104, 124; soviet criminology 114, 117; American criminology 32, 36, 184, 196; Slavic criminology 117; Western criminology 39, 114, 116–117, 119–120, 122, 196; *see also* Marxism
culture/cultures 23, 24–26, 26, 28, 33, 47, 61, 71, 80, 81, 82, 93, 94, 96, 98, 113, 122, 152, 153, 154, 157; *see also* masculinity culture 99; Police culture 152–154, 155; prison culture 154

decolonial, 6, 34, 54–74, 110, 123, 186, 187, 215
decolonising 2–3, 7, 33, 38, 43, 202–203, 209 213

Subject Index 229

desistance, 6, 92–109, 131–147
drugs, alcohol and substance use 41, 96, 116, 157, 174, 185, 189, 191, 192, 197, 209

epistemic (in)justice 5, 32–53, 54–71, 139, 221, 225
equality, diversity, and inclusion (EDI) 2,
ethics 5, 6, 34, 159, 160, 162,

feminism 3, 22, 41, 48, 59, 62–64, 66, 68, 75, 76, 118, 131, 134, 135, 138, 140, 141, 151, 158, 183, 187, 188, 190, 195, 209, 210

gender 4, 5, 6, 7, 14, 17, 26, 35, 45, 54–71, 207
Global North 111, 117, 120, 123, 196
Global South 26, 111, 197

identity 2, 4, 25, 35, 36, 46, 48, 75–90, 91–109, 117–124, 131–132, 134, 135, 140, 148–165, 168, 177, 221
Indigenous
  knowledge 33, 34, 35, 38, 42, 43, 45, 48, 49, 61, 202; Indigenous families, 61; Indigenous land 203, 210, 213, 214; Indigenous scholarship 39, 47; Indigenous voices 32, 33, 36, 38, 40, 41, 42, 43, 45, 47
injustice 2, 39, 48, 119, 186, 204, 211, 212
intersectionality 5, 19, 22, 25, 26, 39, 56, 59, 75, 76, 81–83, 131, 132, 134, 138, 139, 140, 207, 221,

justice
  'Black justice' 42; social justice 39, 42, 46, 49, 140, 183, 187,

knowledge production 3, 15, 42, 43, 44, 49, 62, 111, 117, 118, 138, 150, 183, 202–203, 221–223, 224

LGBTQ+ 1, 3, 40, 75, 132, 188. *see also* sexuality

marginalisation 1, 4–8, 60, 64, 66, 75, 86, 92, 95, 98, 104, 117–123, 131, 132, 167, 168, 172, 177, 187, 222
marginalised populations 99, 182, 183, 185, 186, 189, 194, 196, 197,
Marxism 19, 20, 22, 27, 28, 110–128, 187,
media 24, 25, 26, 41, 44, 159, 168, 171, 177, 178, 182, 183, 190, 192, 207, 212, 215,

mental health 13, 15, 17, 18, 20, 21, 26, 27, 41, 77, 157, 189, 191, 195, 197, 216,

neoliberal 2, 3, 21, 24, 25, 27, 131, 134, 174, 184, 203,
New Zealand/Aotearoa 32, 33, 35, 37, 61, 63, 212
non-reformist reforms 208, 212–214

police 34, 39, 40, 43–44, 61, 77, 83, 84, 100, 101, 103, 113, 115, 116, 122, 152–153, 155, 156, 160, 168, 172, 174, 182, 183, 190, 201, 205–208, 209, 210, 211, 212;
police culture 152, 155; over policing 100, 105; racist policing 44, 48
positionality 7, 149, 150–152, 155, 161, 167, 197, 220
poverty 21, 22, 23, 26, 58, 95, 98, 103, 104, 132, 174, 187, 191, 195,
power 2, 3, 4, 25, 33, 36, 38, 45, 47, 48, 57, 59, 60, 66, 77, 80, 82, 83, 85, 99, 120, 121, 122, 129–147, 148, 151, 153, 155–158, 169, 177, 187, 188, 195, 196, 203, 208, 215;

disempower 19, 32, 36, 46, 48, 61, 101; police power 43, *see also* police; power relations 38, 47, 167; systems of power 25, 28, 45, 59, 123, 136, xii, 3, 5

prison 15, 16, 17, 44–46, 92, 100, 101, 103, 112, 116, 118, 148, 154–158, 174, 182, 183, 186, 190, 201–219;
  abolition of 46, 208, 211–12; deaths in custody 44, 202; 205 hyper-incarceration; 44–45 reform 209, 212; prison research 215–216; *see also* Aboriginal
privilege 8, 36, 132, 139, 140, 149, 154, 160, 183, 203, 222, 225
public opinion 168–178

racism 34, 39, 41, 43, 44, 92, 160, 182, 195, 197, 205, 207, 210;
  antiracism 34, 59, 182, 187; institutional racism 48; structural racism 182, 188, 222; systemic racism 81, 210
research methods 7, 34, 157, 166, 175, 177, 214, 224;
  attitudinal research 166, 170, 177; participatory action research 155; qualitative research 82, 86, 96, 141, 148–152, 155, 158, 177; reflexivity 139, 148, 150–152, 153, 155, 158, 161,

162, 197; research access 114, 119, 183; research ethics 5, 6, 34, 159, 160, 162; research supervision 213, 215
rurality 75–91

sexuality 7, 26, 45, 79, 80, 151, 154, 195, 220, *see also* LGBTQ+,
social class 7, 14, 18, 22, 23, 45, 149, 155, 160, 193, 195;
  middle class 35; working class 1, 14, 21, 22, 27, 58, 60, 61, 65, 67, 80, 133; upper class 99
social control 4, 36, 37, 45, 102, 197, 204, 211,
social harm 28, 118, 186, 188, 190, 194, 222
social structures 81, 133, 210, 211
stigma 23, 26, 54–71, 80, 84, 94, 95, 95, 99, 100, 101, 102, 121, 135, 136, 137, 140, 188.
stolen land 33, 36, 45
story telling/storywork/yarning 7, 42, 46, 66, 135, 156, 157, 201, 202–205
structural barriers 22, 80, 94–95, 97, 98, 99, 102, 104

Torres Strait Islands/islander people 34, 39, 40, 41, 42, 45, 46, 47, 48, 49, 78, 207

United Kingdom 14, 24, 56, 153, 166, 184, 188, 222, 223
United States/North America 32, 37, 44, 59, 153, 174, 184, 213, 153

urban 6, 60, 77, 78, 86, 167, 168, 169

violence
  child abuse 12, 40; colonial violence 203; 209–210, 211; deaths in custody 44, 205–206; domestic violence 40–41, 76, 202; family violence 6, 40–44, 75–87, 203, 204; intimate partner violence 75–78, 81, 84–87; police violence 43, 44, 210; sexual violence 40–41, 47, 76–78, 82, 132, 187

youth 82, 172, 196, 216;
  Black youth 57, 58; imprisonment 204, 207, 210, 216; indigenous youth 39, 43, 44, 61, 65, 188, 207, 210; youth penal reform 54–75; working class youth 58, 67; young men 80, 82, 154, 155–158; young women 61, 77–78, 80, 81–83, 85–87

INDEX OF NAMES

Ahmed, S. 3,
Arday, J. 3

Bacevic, J. 1, 3, 33–35, 39
Behrendt, L 34–37, 42–43, 201–204, 208, 212
Bhopal, K. 3–4
Braithwaite, J. 175
Braun, V. 97
Breeze, M. 3

Chakraborti, N. 159
Connell, R. 1, 95–96, 152,
Crawford, A. 175
Crenshaw, K. 59, 61, 63–63, 132

Davis, A. 215,
Davis, M. J. 47
Derrida, J. 25
Donzelot, J. 60
Dzur, A. 174–175

Fanon, F. 56, 66
Feilzer, M. 168, 173, 177–178
Foucault 25, 60, 168, 183
Fraser, N. 117, 167
Fricker, M. 33–35

Gilbert, K. 210
Goffman, E. 160

Hills-Collins, P. 59, 62,
hooks, bell 215

Jewkes, Y. 138, 154, 169

Loader, J. 174, 176, 183, 196–197
Lorde, A. 209

Marchetti, E. 46
Marx, K. 2, 19–20, 27–28, 110–115, 117–120, 122, 187
Messerschmidt, J. W. 95–96, 102, 152

Porter, A 32, 35, 38–40, 43–44, 209

Reiman, J. xi, 188,

Spivak, G. 221–222, 224

Whittaker, A. 44
Wacquant, L. 45
Walby, S. 59

Printed in the United States
by Baker & Taylor Publisher Services